Lecture Notes in Computer Science   10486

Commenced Publication in 1973
Founding and Former Series Editors:
Gerhard Goos, Juris Hartmanis, and Jan van Leeuwen

Editorial Board

More information about this series at http://www.springer.com/series/7409

Muhammad Younas · Irfan Awan
Irena Holubova (Eds.)

Mobile Web and Intelligent Information Systems

14th International Conference, MobiWIS 2017
Prague, Czech Republic, August 21–23, 2017
Proceedings

Springer

Editors
Muhammad Younas
Oxford Brookes University
Oxford
UK

Irfan Awan
Department of Informatics
University of Bradford
Bradford
UK

Irena Holubova
Department of Software Engineering
Charles University
Praha 1
Czech Republic

ISSN 0302-9743   ISSN 1611-3349   (electronic)
Lecture Notes in Computer Science
ISBN 978-3-319-65514-7   ISBN 978-3-319-65515-4   (eBook)
DOI 10.1007/978-3-319-65515-4

Library of Congress Control Number: 2017948178

LNCS Sublibrary: SL3 – Information Systems and Applications, incl. Internet/Web, and HCI

Printed on acid-free paper

This Springer imprint is published by Springer Nature
The registered company is Springer International Publishing AG
The registered company address is: Gewerbestrasse 11, 6330 Cham, Switzerland

Preface

This volume contains research articles that were presented at the 14th International Conference on Mobile Web and Intelligent Information Systems (MobiWis 2017). MobiWis was held in Prague, Czech Republic, during August 21–23, 2017.

Mobile Web usage is continuously increasing with the increase in mobile devices such as smart phones and tablets. According to Statcounter[1], more people are now accessing Web/Internet content through mobile devices than through desktop computers. Statcounter's statistics show that more than 50% of the 2.5 million websites were accessed through mobile devices in October 2016. The success of the mobile Web comes from significant developments in various technologies such as high-speed wireless networks, powerful mobile/smart phones and devices, and the state-of-the-art software systems and tools.

The International Conference on Mobile Web and Intelligent Information Systems (MobiWis) aims to advance research on and practical applications of mobile Web, intelligent information systems, and related mobile technologies. It provides a forum for researchers, developers, and practitioners from academia, industry, and the public sector, in order to share research ideas, knowledge, and experiences in the areas of mobile Web and information systems. The call for papers for MobiWis 2017 included new and emerging areas such as: mobile Web systems, recommender systems, security and authentication, context-awareness, mobile Web and advanced applications, cloud and IoT, mobility management, mobile and wireless networks, and mobile Web practice and experience.

MobiWis 2017 attracted a good number of submissions from different countries across the globe. This year the number of submissions was 77. All the papers were reviewed by multiple members of the Program Committee. Based on the reviews, 27 papers were accepted for the conference — with 23 full and four short papers, leading to an acceptance rate of 35%. The accepted papers covered a range of topics related to the theme of the conference. The technical program of MobiWis 2017 also included invited talks from two large international corporations. These were delivered by Dr. Markus Aleksy (ABB Corporate Research) and Dr. Mazin Yousif (T-Systems, International). The invited talks were delivered in conjunction with the co-located conferences of the IEEE 5th International Conference on Future Internet of Things and Cloud (FiCloud 2017) and the Third International Conference on Big Data Innovations and Applications (Innovate-Data 2017), IEEE-TCI.

We would like to thank the invited speakers for delivering interesting and thought-provoking talks. We also thank all the Program Committee members who provided valuable and constructive feedback to the authors and to the Program Chairs.

---

[1] "Mobile and tablet internet usage exceeds desktop for first time worldwide" by Statcounter Global Stats, http://gs.statcounter.com/press/mobile-and-tablet-internet-usage-exceeds-desktop-for-first-time-worldwide.

We also thank Prof. Albert Zomaya (general chair), Dr. Barbara Masucci (workshop coordinator), (publicity chair), Dr. George Ghinea (international liaison chair), and Dr. Ondrej Krejcar (publicity chair). We would like to thank the local organizing team of the Charles University, Prague, for their great help and support.

Our sincere thanks also go to the Springer LNCS team, Alfred Hofmann, Anna Kramer, and Abier El-Saeidi, for their valuable support in the approval and production of the conference proceedings.

August 2017   Muhammad Younas
                                                                              Irfan Awan
                                                                           Irena Holubova

Organization

General Chair

Albert Zomaya   The University of Sydney, Australia

Program Chair

Irfan Awan   University of Bradford, UK

Local Organizing Chair

Irena Holubova   Charles University, Prague, Czech Republic

Publication Chair

Muhammad Younas   Oxford Brookes University, UK

Workshop Coordinator

Barbara Masucci   University of Salerno, Italy

International Liaison Chair

George Ghinea   Brunel University, UK

Publicity Chair

Ondrej Krejcar   University of Hradec Kralove, Czech Republic

Program Committee

Abdel Lisser	University of Paris Sud, France
Agnis Stibe	Massachusetts Institute of Technology (MIT), USA
Andrea Omicini	University of Bologna, Italy
Aneta Poniszewska-Maranda	Lodz University of Technology, Poland
Anis Ouali	EBTIC, UAE
Apostolos Papadopoulos	Aristotle University of Thessaloniki, Greece
Artur Niewiadomski	Siedlce University, Poland
Bryan A. Knowles	Western Kentucky University, USA
Carlos Calafate	Technical University of Valencia, Spain
Chi (Harold) Liu	Beijing Institute of Technology, China

Christophe Feltus	Luxembourg Institute of Science and Technology, Luxembourg
Ciprian Dobre	Politehnica University of Bucharest, Romania
Costas Mourlas	University of Athens, Greece
Dan Johansson	Umea University, Sweden
DO van Thuan	Linus AS, Norway
Dragan Stojanovic	University of Nis, Serbia
Fatma Abdennadher	National School of Engineering of Sfax, Tunisia
Florence Sedes	Paul Sabatier University, France
Grace Lewis	Canegie Mellon University, USA
Hadi Otrok	Khalifa University, UAE
Ivan Demydov	Lviv Polytechnic National University, Ukraine
Jeng-Wei Lin	TungHai University, Japan
Jingwei Li	The Chinese University of Hong Kong, Hong Kong, SAR China
John Lindström	Luleå University of Technology, Sweden
Jorge Sa Silva	University of Coimbra, Portugal
Jozef Juhar	Technical University of Košice, Slovakia
Jung-Chun Liu	TungHai University, Japan
Nor Shahniza Kamal Bashah	Universiti Teknologi MARA, Malaysia
Karl Andersson	Luleå University of Technology, Sweden
Katty Rohoden	Jaramillo Universidad Técnica Particular de Loja, Ecuador
Koralia Pappi	Aristotle University of Thessaloniki, Greece
Lalit Garg	University of Malta, Malta
Lidia Ogiela	AGH University of Science and Technology, Poland
Lulwah AlSuwaidan	King Saud University, Saudi Arabia
Maher Ben Jemaa	ReDCAD-ENIS, Tunisia
Marek R. Ogiela	AGH University of Science and Technology, Poland
Maria Luisa Damiani	Università degli Studi di Milano, Italy
Masahiro Sasabe	Osaka University, Japan
Michal Gregus	Comenius University in Bratislava, Slovakia
Mohamed Ben Aouicha	Sfax University, Tunisia
Novia Admodisastro	Universiti Putra Malaysia, Malaysia
Ondrej Krejcar	University of Hradec Kralove, Czech Republic
Pablo Adasme	University of Santiago de Chile, Chile
Paolo Nesi	University of Florence, Italy
Perin Unal	METU, Turkey
Philippe Roose	IUT de Bayonne, France
Pınar KIRCI	Istanbul University, Turkey
Rafidah Noor	University of Malaya, Malaysia
Renata Galante	Universidade Federal do Rio Grande do Sul, Brazil
Riccardo Martoglia	University of Modena and Reggio Emilia, Italy
Sergio Ilarri	University of Zaragoza, Spain
Shakeel Mahate	ABB Corporate Research, USA

Engineering Augmented Reality
Applications in Industrial Settings
(Abstract Invited Talk)

Markus Aleksy

ABB Corporate Research, Wallstadter Str. 59, 68526 Ladenburg, Germany
markus.aleksy@de.abb.com

Abstract. The engineering of augmented reality applications utilized in industrial settings can be a complex and difficult task. On one hand, 'smart' and 'context-sensitive' mobile applications can provide excellent user experience, if they are nonintrusive and have user-centric interfaces, On the other hand, they are hard to design, test, maintain, and integrate. Additionally, the development of such applications requires the utilization of appropriate hardware devices, augmented reality frameworks, as well as improved interaction techniques to consider the limitations and opportunities provided by current mobile & wearable devices. In this talk, we will share our experiences gained during the last years focusing on the development of augmented reality application. The addressed topics will cover existing devices, framework support, use cases, requirements, and interaction styles. Moreover, we will present the results of several case studies carried out in the domain of industrial field service and describe the obtained results.

Acknowledgments

This research was partially supported by the German Federal Ministry of Education and Research (BMBF) under grant number 16KIS0244. The responsibility for this publication lies with the authors.

References

1. Aleksy, M., Brönmark, J., Mahate, S.: Microinteractions in mobile and wearable computing. In: 30th IEEE International Conference on Advanced Information Networking and Applications (AINA 2016), Crans-Montana, Switzerland, 23–26 March 2016, pp. 495–500. IEEE (2016)
2. Aleksy, M., Rissanen, M.J.: Utilizing wearable computing in industrial service applications. J. Ambient Intell. Hum. Comput. **5**(4), 443–454 (2014)

3. Aleksy, M., Vartiainen, E., Domova, V., Naedele, M.: Augmented reality for improved service delivery. In: 28th IEEE International Conference on Advanced Information Networking and Applications (AINA 2014), Victoria, BC, Canada, 13–16 May, 2014, pp. 382–389. IEEE (2014)
4. Aleksy, M., Vartiainen, E.: Visualization approaches in augmented reality applications. In: Younas, M., Awan, I., Mecella, M. (eds.) MobiWIS 2015. LNCS, vol. 9228, pp. 84–90. Springer, Cham (2015)

Contents

Security and Mobile Network Systems

Mobile and Wireless Networking

Web, Cloud and Distributed Systems

Advanced Web and Mobile Systems

Route Recommendations to Business Travelers Exploiting Crowd-Sourced Data

Thomas Collerton, Andrea Marrella, Massimo Mecella$^{(\boxtimes)}$, and Tiziana Catarci

Sapienza Università di Roma, Rome, Italy
{collerton,marrella,mecella,catarci}@diag.uniroma1.it

Abstract. Business travellers are those people who attend work-related meetings and in their few hours of spare time would like to see the best that the host city can offer in terms of cultural activities and sightseeings. In this work we present a complex architecture, consisting of mobile applications and back-end server components, which supports business travelers in recommending possible routes matching their preferences within their timing constraints. The three main contributions are (i) a set of machine learning algorithms that can be used to detect a queuing state of a user with a high degree of accuracy, (ii) how to determine user's positioning, and (iii) how to practically realize a planner providing a reasonably good enough route plan within a handful of seconds. Preliminary tests demonstrate that the single components of the proposed architecture are feasible and provide good results.

1 Introduction

In recent years, a category of tourism has gained popularity, known as "business tourism", i.e., people who attend work-related meetings away from their hometown and in their few hours of spare time would like to see the best that the host city can offer in terms of cultural activities and sightseeings, such as monuments and museums [16]. This kind of tourism has been also fueled by the presence of emerging forms of social and technological developments that rely on sensors, big data and new ways of connectivity and exchange of information (e.g., IoT, RFID, social networks, etc.), which allow to supply business travelers with better mobility, location-based interactive services and, consequently, faster decision support [7].

The data and information intensity of business tourism has led many researchers to investigate intelligent ways to exploit ICT technologies for unlocking the power of data in order to provide more enjoyable and customized tourism experiences [6,24,25]. As a matter of fact, today's personal devices such as smartphones and tablets are almost ubiquitous, and provide arrays of sensors and antennas which can be exploited to determine various information about the user, such as her/his position and whether s/he is moving or standing still, like in a queue.

So far, ICT research in business tourism mainly provides ad-hoc case studies of existing initiatives [18,21,23] and is mostly concerned with the development of

© Springer International Publishing AG 2017
M. Younas et al. (Eds.): MobiWIS 2017, LNCS 10486, pp. 3–17, 2017.
DOI: 10.1007/978-3-319-65515-4_1

location-based technologies for tracking users' position within the cultural area (e.g., iBeacon sensors) and of mobile applications enabling travelers to share their personal experiences on social networks to help other travelers in their decision making process [7].

In this paper, we aim at presenting a general-purpose software framework called NEPTIS PLANNER, which is part of the much broader NEPTIS project [14] that focuses on developing ICT-based solutions for augmented fruition and intelligent exploration of cultural heritage. NEPTIS PLANNER offers business travelers with personalized and automatically generated routes to efficiently visit a cultural area. It is able to manage the interconnection, synchronization and concerted use of different IoT technologies for extracting crowd-sourced data from fellow tourists (e.g., to identify the waiting time to visit a specific attraction). NEPTIS PLANNER leverages on automated planning techniques [5] to reason over such data and on the traveler's preferences (e.g., the maximum available time to visit a cultural area) in order to generate on-the-fly a personalized route within the cultural area that respects the traveler's needs.

The rest of the paper is organized as follows. In Sect. 2 we provide an overview of the approach and architecture of the proposed system, whereas Sects. 3 and 4 present the main contributions of this work, i.e., how it is possible to detect queuing and visiting times with minimal user intervention, and how to solve a planning problem allowing the computation of a recommended route for a small and medium sized museum in a reasonable time frame, which is vital given the mobile context. Section 5 concludes the paper by discussing possible future extension of the work.

2   System Overview

NEPTIS PLANNER realizes an architecture whose purpose is to provide a business traveler with a route to a set of cultural areas (e.g., museums, churches, monuments, etc.) in her/his surroundings given her/his current position and other inputs, such as a time constraint, that is how much time s/he is willing to spend for a cultural tour of the area s/he is currently in, or a list of attractions s/he would like to visit.

The system is thought for being used by two main actors:

- the *curator*, which is the user responsible for the insertion, update and deletion of information about cultural areas. For example, in the case of "open air" monuments, relevant information is their names and coordinate locations, while for "closed" museums it is relevant to know their topology (i.e., how rooms are connected between each others) and their available attractions;
- the *tourist*, which is the user/traveler who can request the compilation of a route plan within the cultural area through an application installed on her/his smartphone.

The client side of the system is provided by the tourist's mobile application (currently realized in Android), while the curator interacts with the system

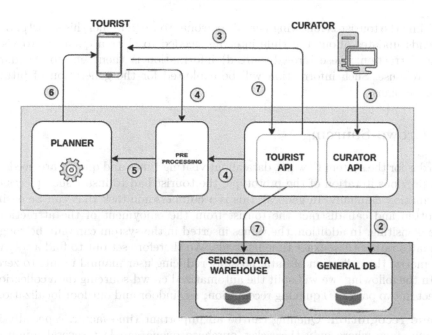

Fig. 1. NEPTIS PLANNER workflow diagram

through a Web application. The back-end is a Node.JS server, responsible for handling requests from the clients via two sets of APIs, one for each actor. Alongside the server there is the planner component responsible for the creation of route plans, preceded by a pre-processing module which translates raw data into input files for the planner. The persistence layer has a relational database holding data inserted by the curator, as well as users' and curators' login credentials, and a data warehouse containing time intervals data coming from the tourists' smartphones. Figure 1 shows the basic workflow of the system:

1. The curator inserts or updates information about the cultural area s/he is responsible for. For example, this includes the list of rooms and the attractions within their premises in the case of a closed museum, or the list of monuments and their coordinates in the case of an open air museum;
2. Data are stored into a relational database;
3. The tourist mobile application exploits these data in order to help the tourist in the compilation of the request for a personalized route plan;
4. When the tourist finally completes the above step, the system feeds the needed data (both from the data warehouse and the user input) to the pre-processing module, which encodes the request for the subsequent stage;
5. The resulting files are then fed to a planning system (i.e., the planner) which will compute a cultural route plan that satisfies the constraints inserted by the tourist;
6. The output of the planning system is then sent back to the tourist, who will then start her/his own tour;

7. While the tourist is following her/his personal route plan, her/his smartphone sends updates about the time intervals needed to clear a queue or to visit an attraction; these (crowd-sourced) information is then sent to the data warehouse. Such information will be exploited for the generation of future route plans.

3   Crowd-Sourcing

In order for the system to work, data about visiting times and queues are needed. In a previous iteration of the prototype, the tourist had to insert such pieces of information manually. In general, this is a cumbersome task that can be easily forgotten and can distract the tourist from the enjoyment of the attractions s/he is visiting. In addition, the values inserted in the system can only be rough estimates rather than exact time intervals. We therefore set out to find a way to automatize the collection of data, possibly reducing user manual inputs to zero.

In the following, we will split the automatized crowd-sourcing data collection aspect in two parts: *(i)* queuing recognition; *(ii)* indoor and outdoor localization.

Queue recognition. Queuing can be an important time factor, especially in big museums where only the ticket purchase queue can last several minutes, if not hours. Although not common, some attractions can also have a lengthy waiting time before they can be fully experienced by the tourist, such as the Mona Lisa painting in the Louvre in Paris or the Sistine Chapel in the Vatican Museums in Rome. We define a user to be in a "queuing state" when s/he is either standing still or having brief bursts of movement lasting a few seconds. We take into account actions such as taking the smartphone out of the pocket or purse, taking pictures of the surroundings and similar small movements as part of the queuing state. For testing purposes, the GPS sensor included in the smartphone has been used as control and tests have been run in open fields, away from potential sources of disruption for the satellite signal. Given a certain time window Δt and a chosen threshold value of walking speed v_t, we say that a user has walked during Δt if has moved more than $v_t \cdot \Delta t$ meters.

The research literature on movement recognition is gaining a lot of momentum in the past few years, mainly due to the ever growing presence of devices such as smartphones and tablets, which pack several hardware sensors such as accelerometers, gyroscopes, magnetic compasses, etc. However, despite their popularity, the Android platform does not provide a good library for such a task; the only interface that comes close to our target is the Android Activity Recognition API[1], which is supposedly capable of guessing whether the user is walking, running or is in a car, with the help from sensors and usage data collected by Google. However, for now, tests returned lackluster results.

Therefore we chose to implement and test the approach given by Ravi in [15]: given the signals of all the three axis of the accelerometer, we sample them

---

[1] cf.   developers.google.com/android/reference/com/google/android/gms/location/ActivityRecognitionApi.

with a sampling frequency of 50 Hz (or 1 sample every 20 ms), and store the samples in a sliding window of size 256, which gives us a time interval of 5.12 s. For each of these windows, we compute their average, their standard deviation and their energy, defined as $\frac{1}{|w|}\sum |f|^2$, where $|w|$ is the window size and f is a frequency value of the Fourier-transformed signal, obtained via the Fast Fourier Transform algorithm implemented in the Apache Commons Math Java library[2]. The extracted data are then used by a machine learning classifier included in the Weka data mining tool[3]. Table 1 shows the chosen algorithms and their respective degrees of accuracy with regards to the GPS signal control.

We tested some of the algorithms described in [15], both on their own and combined with others. Tests have been executed on a Google Nexus 5X and a Huawei Honor 7. Generally speaking, tests proved that this approach is effective and yields very good levels of accuracy for all used algorithms. However classifiers such as k-NN, decision tree and decision tables on their own had issues at detecting actions such taking the smartphone out of the pocket while standing, misclassifying it as a walking movement, which brings their accuracy rate between 75 and 81%. An odd combination of them, such as the one shown in the table, alongside a majority voting decision mechanism, manages to improve the detection rate up to 90%, while the neural network, implemented by the MultiLayerPerceptron class in Weka, achieved the best accuracy levels. In any case, in order to minimize the rate of false positives and negatives, we do not take into account the single sample window, but rather we pick a dynamic queue of five consecutive windows and determine the final outcome by choosing the classification decided by the majority.

Table 1. Used classifiers and their accuracy degree

Algorithm	Accuracy (%)
Neural network	96
k-NN (15 neighbours)	80
k-NN (20 neighbours)	78
Decision tree (C4.5)	81
Decision tables	77
SVM	75
k-NN (15) Decision tree (C4.5) Decision tables	90

Localization. Queuing is not the only time consuming activity to take into account, but also the time needed to move between the available monuments

---

[2] cf. http://commons.apache.org/proper/commons-math/.
[3] cf. http://www.cs.waikato.ac.nz/ml/weka/.

as well as to visit them completely, or their single attractions. We describe two different scenarios, which involve outdoor and indoor localization respectively.

Let's assume a user is visiting an outdoor area, such as Piazza di Spagna in Rome. The area contains attractions such as the Barcaccia fountain, the staircase and the facade of Trinità dei Monti. We say that the user has begun her/his visit when s/he gets near the monument and that s/he is over when s/he moves away from it. To achieve this target, we implemented a geofencing algorithm which uses the Android localization service via the GPS sensor. Each monument is associated with a latitude-longitude coordinate and a radius value, therefore the user is considered to be in the visiting state when her/his distance from given coordinates is lower than the radius and vice versa.

Now let's assume that the user is in a closed environment such as a museum, where the satellite signal can be barely reached, if at all, since it requires a line-of-sight connection. The analyzed literature on the subject of indoor tracking and localization focuses on three methods:

- image recognition, where the position of the device can be guessed from its camera. A detailed study can be found in [1] and a basic implementation in the context of cultural heritage is described in [17], however the proposed method requires the user to have more or less the smartphone in her/his hands and potentially on the upright position, which can get rather uncomfortable;
- analysis of sensors' data such as accelerometers and magnetic compass [10]. We tested very briefly this method, however the sensors in the tested smartphones were not precise enough and users' actions can be random enough to generate some noise to make the readings even less precise;
- RSS (Radio Signal Strength) of multiple WiFi signals from various access points, which allows a classification based upon the triangulation of these signals [8]. This requires a training set of all the interested areas.

We approached the latter case, because it requires the least amount of input from the user and, provided that the location has some WiFi access points, can provide interesting results. We tested this approach with FIND[4], an open-source software which implements a server that stores RSS fingerprints and classifies incoming beacons with a Naive Bayes or SVM algorithm. We used the ground floor of our department as a test bed, treating the area in front of the seven available rooms as a wall with exposed paintings, both in a crowded and almost empty corridor. The device used for this test is a Google Nexus 5X. Table 2 shows the detection accuracy for each of the rooms. All the tested rooms have been detected with an accuracy exceeding 95% with the exception of room A2, which is slightly lower due to it being very close to room A1, which was our target threshold, and therefore we can consider FIND a suitable tool for our target.

---

[4] cf. http://www.internalpositioning.com/.

Table 2. The rooms and their detected accuracy

Room	Accuracy (%)
A1	96,67
A2	94,55
A3	96,96
A4	96,00
A5	97,14
A6	96,29
A7	97,14

4 On the Synthesis of Route Plans

Given the time intervals data received from the smartphones of the users visiting a cultural area C, the target is to provide a business traveler that wants to visit C with a route plan R that can be completed in the *minimum time required to maximize the traveler's needs and preferences.*

The problem can be represented through a directed graph $G(V, E)$, which holds information about the topology of C. We call such a graph a *topology graph*. Each node $v \in V$ represents a single distinguishable *zone* of C (e.g., if C is a museum, zones correspond to museum's rooms), i.e., a cluster of *attractions* belonging to v. There is a special "dummy" node labeled as "Entry/Exit" that defines the entry/exit point of C.

Edges of G are of two kinds, E_{conn} and E_{att}, with $E_{conn} \cup E_{att} = E$ and $E_{conn} \cap E_{att} = \emptyset$. Each edge $e_x \in E_{conn}$ is used to represent a *physical connection* (be it a corridor, a door, a staircase) between two different nodes $v_i, v_j \in V$, and is labeled with the estimated time t_{conn_x} required to move between them. On the other hand, any edge $e_y \in E_{att}$ that insists on the same node $v \in V$ (i.e., a *loop* edge) represents the *visit* of a single attraction located in v. Loop edges e_y are labeled with a certain *score* w_y, which is calculated taking into consideration the average rating rt_y given by the users to the attraction and the time needed to visit it (i.e. $t_{queue_y} + t_{visit_y}$).

The rating of an attraction can assume values in the $\{1, 5, 10\}$ domain, while the times are expressed in minutes. We assume that if an attraction has a long queue or visit time, then its visit is considered more important than some other which has perhaps the same rating. Consequently, we calculate w_y such that $w_y = rt_y \cdot (\frac{1}{t_{queue_y} + t_{visit_y}} \cdot 100)$. In this way, it follows that the smaller the value of w_y, the more relevant is the visit of the attraction labeled with w_y.

As a running example, Fig. 2 shows the floor plan of the local civic museum of Bracciano, a town north of Rome which has been used for some tests of this work, and the left-hand part of Fig. 3 shows its graph representation. Notice that in the

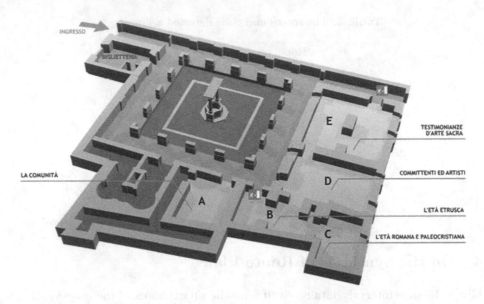

Fig. 2. A sketch of the floor plan of the local civic museum of Bracciano.

running example each node has one loop edge, each representing an attraction in that zone (labelled for simplicity as $a0, a1, a2, a3, a4$).

Given the above model, the problem can be defined as *finding a path in the topology graph that minimizes the total score of visited attractions and the time for moving between different zones*. This allows — consequently — to minimize the overall time required to a business tourist for a satisfactory visit of C. This problem is known in literature as the ORIENTEERING PROBLEM, a variant of the Traveling Salesman Problem (TSP) where the objective function is to maximize or minimize the total value associated to each node of the graph.

The problem is known to be NP-hard, as well as APX-hard, and some heuristic and approximation algorithms, described in [4, 20, 22] have been studied, even if no efficient implementations, to the best of our knowledge, are available.

In order to tackle this issue and generate quality route plans in a reasonable time, we decided to adopt techniques coming from the *automated planning* field, which is a branch of Artificial Intelligence (AI) that aims to the realization of automated systems for the synthesis of organized sequences of real-world activities [5]. To this aim, in the following sections we first show some preliminaries on automated planning necessary to understand the rest of the paper, and then we present our solution to encode the problem of synthesizing a route plan as a planning problem in AI, which can be solved by state-of-the-art planners. Finally, we discuss some experiments performed through two state-of-the-art planners that demonstrate the versatility of our approach and its feasibility in realistic settings.

Basics of Automated Planning. Automated planning operates on explicit representations of states and actions. The Planning Domain Definition Language (PDDL) is a de-facto standard to formulate a *planning problem* $\mathcal{P} = \langle I, GL, \mathcal{P_D} \rangle$, where I is the initial state of the world, GL is the desired goal state, and $\mathcal{P_D}$ is the planning domain.

A planning domain $\mathcal{P_D}$ is built from a set of *propositions* describing the state of the world and a set of *actions* Ω that can be executed in the domain. An *action schema* $a \in \Omega$ is of the form $a = \langle Par_a, Pre_a, Eff_a \rangle$, where Par_a is the list of *input parameters* for a, Pre_a defines the *preconditions* under which a can be executed, and Eff_a specifies the *effects* of a on the state of the world. Both preconditions and effects are stated in terms of the *propositions* in $\mathcal{P_D}$. Propositions can be represented through boolean predicates and fluents. In the remainder of the paper, we remain consistent with PDDL terminology [3]: a *predicate* is a boolean property of the world and *fluents* are used to express numeric properties, such as the actions' cost. Both the values of predicates and fluents can change as result of the execution of actions. PDDL includes also the ability of *typing* the parameters that appear in actions and *constraining* the types of arguments to predicates and fluents.

There exist several forms of planning in the AI literature. In this paper, we focus on planning techniques characterized by *fully observable, static* and *deterministic* domains, i.e., we rely on the classical planning assumption of a "perfect world description" [26]. Concretely, this implies that: *(i)* any planning action only provides deterministic and observable effects; *(ii)* a complete knowledge of the initial state I is available.

A solution to a planning problem is a sequence of actions—a *plan*—whose execution brings from initial state I to some state that satisfy goal GL. The plan is said to be *optimal* if it minimizes the sum of action costs. Automated planning has made huge advances in the last twenty years, leading to solvers able to create plans with thousands of actions for problems described by hundreds of propositions (see, for example, [2,11–13]). In this work, we represent planning domains and problems making use of the STRIPS fragment of PDDL 2.1 [3], enhanced with the numeric features provided by the "level 2" of the same language. Such features are used to keep track of the costs of planning actions and to synthesize plans satisfying pre-specified metrics.

Encoding as a Planning Problem. In order to encode the problem of synthesizing a route plan as a planning problem in PDDL, in addition to the topology graph we made use of a second graph containing as many nodes as are the number of attractions that the traveler would like to visit (cf. the right-hand part of Fig. 3). We call such a graph a *visit graph*, and its use is devoted to avoid the generation of route plans containing empty lists of attractions.

In the planning domain $\mathcal{P_D}$, we provide two abstract types called `attraction` and `node`. The first captures the attractions involved in the loop edges of the topology graph. The second is used to identify the nodes of the topology graph (through the sub-type `topology_node`) and of the visit graph (through the sub-

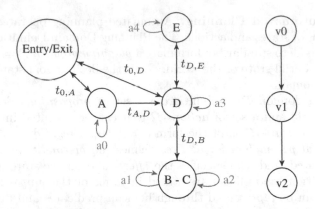

Fig. 3. The museum's floor plan graph remodeled for the planning problem.

type `visit_node`). To capture the structure of the topology/visit graph and to monitor their evolution, we defined four *domain propositions* as boolean predicates in $\mathcal{P}_\mathcal{D}$[5]:

- `(cur_node ?n - node)` holds if n is the current node of a topology/visit graph.
- `(edge ?n1 - node ?n2 - node)` holds if there exists an edge from two different nodes n1 to n2 of a topology/visit graph.
- `(visited ?a - attraction)` holds if the attraction a is visited.
- `(at ?a - attraction ?n - topology_node)` indicates that the attraction a is located in a zone represented by the node n.

Furthermore, we define three *numeric fluents* in $\mathcal{P}_\mathcal{D}$: *(i)* `(move-cost ?n1 - topology_node ?n2 - topology_node)` records the time required to move from n1 to n2; *(ii)* `(visit-cost ?a - attraction)` reflects the score associated to the visit of the attraction a; *(iii)* `(total-cost)` keeps track of the overall cost of the route plan under construction.

In the planning problem $\mathcal{P}$, we first define a finite set of constants required to properly ground all the domain propositions defined in $\mathcal{P}_\mathcal{D}$. In our case, constants will correspond to the nodes and attractions instances involved in the topology/visit graph. Secondly, we define the *initial state* of $\mathcal{P}$ to capture the exact structure of the topology/visit graph. This includes the specification of the current nodes of the graphs (in I, the current nodes of the topology and of the visit graph are "Entry/Exit" and $v0$, resp.) and of all the existing edges that connect two different nodes of the graphs. Furthermore, in I the exact location of any attraction is specified, while it is assumed that no attraction has been yet visited. Thirdly, we define the goal condition GL as the conjunction of the *final nodes* of the two graphs. The final node of the topology graph is (again) "Entry/Exit", while the final node of the visit graph depends by the number of

---

[5] Variables are distinguished by a "?" character at front, and the dash "-" is used to assign types to the variables.

attractions that the traveler aims to visit; in our running example, it is $v2$ (cf. Fig. 3).

The plan to reach GL from I is constituted by a sequence of planning actions that allow to perform movements between nodes in the two graphs and to eventually reach the final nodes. Specifically, in $\mathcal{P}_D$ we provide two planning actions that allow: (i) to move between two nodes of the topology graph, or (ii) to visit an attraction (not yet visited) of the topology graph; the latter allows also to move forward in the visit graph.

```
(:action move
 :parameters(?n1 - topology_node ?n2 - topology_node)
 :precondition (and (cur_node ?n1) (edge ?n1 ?n2))
 :effect (and (not (cur_node ?n1)) (cur_node ?n2)
           (increase (total-cost) (move-cost ?n1 ?n2))))

(:action visit
 :parameters(?a1 - attraction ?s1 - topology_node
          ?v1 - visit_node ?v2 - visit_node)
 :precondition (and (cur_node ?n1) (at ?a1 ?n1) (not (visited ?a1))
              (cur_node ?v1) (edge ?v1 ?v2))
 :effect (and (not (cur_node ?v1)) (cur_node ?v2) (visited ?a1)
           (increase (total-cost) (visit-cost ?a1))))
```

Readers should finally notice that the execution of the move (or visit) action makes total cost of the route plan increases of a value equal to (move-cost) (or (visit-cost)). Since our purpose is to minimize the total cost of the generated route plan, the planning problem also contains the following specification: (:metric minimize (total-cost)).

Preliminary Validation. The approach has been positively assessed using automatically generated PDDL files that describe problems of growing complexity. We performed our experiments with a machine equipped with an Intel Core i7-4770S CPU 3.10 GHz Quad Core and 16 GB RAM. The ideal target was to compute *optimal routes*, i.e., route plans that allow a traveler to minimize the time required for a visit by maximizing its quality (in terms of the ratings of the visited attractions).

To this aim, we performed experiments by making use of the SymBA*-2 [19] planning system (winner of the sequential optimizing track at the 2014 International Planning Competition), which performs a bidirectional A* search to find optimal plans.

However, since automated planning is known to be PSPACE-complete and optimal algorithms can take a major toll on computation time [5], we decided to run further experiments using a sub-optimal heuristic based on FF (that is, forward chaining heuristic, see http://www.fast-downward.org/Doc/Heuristic) running on the Fast Downward planning system [9], in order to return near-optimal solutions (i.e., solutions with less quality than optimal ones) in a shorter time.

Table 3. Execution times for some of the performed tests

Rooms	Attractions	Visit	Time (seconds)
15	75	25	1,08
20	140	25	2,27
20	220	15	3,40
30	150	25	2,33
30	330	25	7,28

To have a sense of the scalability with respect to the size of the problem, we generated PDDL files representing topology graphs of growing complexity. Specifically, topology graphs used for the experiments have the following properties:

– a number of nodes varying from 10 to 30;
– each node can host from 1 to 15 attractions;
– each node can be connected just to another node (like in a single link chain), or it has 50%–30% chance of being connected to two-three other nodes.

In addition, we customized the number of attractions to be visited in the visit graph and those that must be necessarily included in the route, as follows: *(i)* from 5 to 50 attractions; *(ii)* from 0 to 5 randomly chosen "must visit" attractions[6].

Figure 4 shows the computation time comparison between the two planning algorithms on four selected problems, specifically those which describe a graph with 10 nodes, 5 to 25 selected visits and a variable number of attractions that have been selected as a "must visit". For each problem, we wanted to monitor the performances of the planning systems given the number of attractions (on the x axis) and the complexity of the modeled area (that is, the number of connections for each node, one plot for each kind of connection; therefore each algorithm has three plots associated with it).

Tests show that FF manages to maintain a stable performance and stay below 3 s, while SymBA*-2 has a more random pattern and can take 100 times longer than FF. SymBA*-2 tends to have an exponential growth as the number of attractions and nodes increase. Even in the case of larger domains, such as the ones shown in Table 3, FF can come up with a solution in less than 30 s, which is the target maximum wait time which we would like to achieve.

Figure 5 shows the total score of the selected attractions for the same problems; while SymBA*-2, which is based upon an optimal A* algorithm, always returns the best result, FF is never far off from it, managing to even get the exact same value. Therefore we can say that, between FF and SymBA*-2, the earlier is the more appealing solution.

---

[6] Must visit attractions are specific attractions that a user explicitly asks to visit and that must appear in the generated route plan.

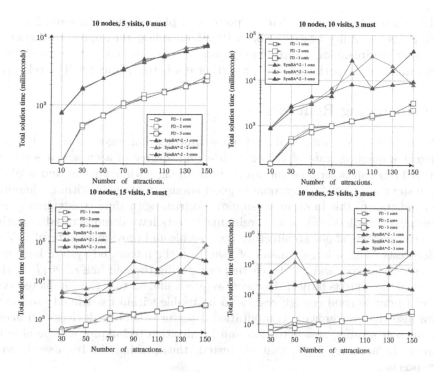

Fig. 4. Comparison of computation times between FF and SymBA*-2

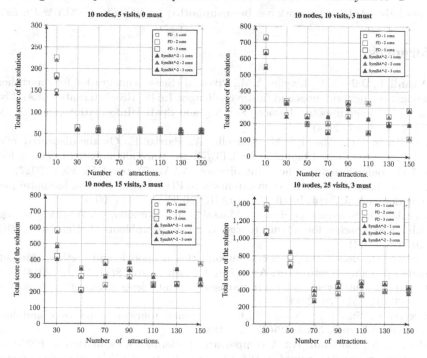

Fig. 5. Comparison of the quality of the solutions obtained by FF and SymBA*-2

The reader should notice that the power of a planning-based approach is also linked to its versatility. Starting from a PDDL encoding, the approach allows one to plug in new planning algorithms/systems at basically no cost. In the future we can improve the performance even further if a better planner will be released.

5   Concluding Remarks

In this work we have shown that a set of machine learning algorithms can be used to detect a queuing state of a user with a high degree of accuracy, a software such as FIND can determine the user's positioning within a room and a planning system can provide a reasonably good enough route plan within a handful of seconds, all of this in order to support tourists with time constraints (such as business travellers). Thus far, preliminary tests have demonstrated that the single components of our architecture are feasible and provide good results. Validation tests (with a large number of users) on the integrated system have not yet been performed, and will be carried out during the 2nd half of 2017, in the context of the NEPTIS project. However we are confident that the completed system will provide good enough results to be usable within its defined use cases. Given also the ever growing computational power of mobile devices and accuracy of their sensors, new detection and localization techniques will be able to improve the accuracy levels that we tested, thus making the framework even more precise.

Acknowledgments. This work has been supported by *NEPTIS – PON03_PE_0214*.

References

1. Aicardi, I., Dabove, P., Lingua, A.M., Piras, M.: Sensors integration for smartphone navigation: performances and future challenges. In: ISPRS - International Archives of the Photogrammetry, Remote Sensing and Spatial Information Sciences, vol. XL-3, pp. 9–16 (2014)
2. De Giacomo, G., Maggi, F.M., Marrella, A., Patrizi, F.: On the disruptive effectiveness of automated planning for LTLf-based trace alignment. In: Thirty-First AAAI Conference on Artificial Intelligence (AAAI-17), pp. 3555–3561 (2017)
3. Fox, M., Long, D.: PDDL2.1: an extension to PDDL for expressing temporal planning domains. J. Artif. Intell. Res. (JAIR) 20(1), 61–124 (2003)
4. Gavalas, D., Konstantopoulos, C., Mastakas, K., Pantziou, G.: A survey on algorithmic approaches for solving tourist trip design problems. J. Heuristics 20(3), 291–328 (2014)
5. Geffner, H., Bonet, B.: A concise introduction to models and methods for automated planning. Synth. Lect. Artif. Intell. Mach. Learn. 8(1), 1–141 (2013)
6. Gretzel, U.: Intelligent systems in tourism: a social science perspective. Ann. Tour. Res. 38(3), 757–779 (2011)
7. Gretzel, U., Sigala, M., Xiang, Z., Koo, C.: Smart tourism: foundations and developments. Electron. Mark. 25(3), 179–188 (2015)
8. Hatami, A., Pahlavan, K.: A comparative performance evaluation of RSS-based positioning algorithms used in WLAN networks. In: IEEE Wireless Communications and Networking Conference, vol. 4, March 2005

9. Helmert, M.: The fast downward planning system. J. Artif. Intell. Res. (JAIR) **26**, 191–246 (2006)
10. Jin, Y., Toh, H.S., Soh, W.S., Wong, W.C.: A robust dead-reckoning pedestrian tracking system with low cost sensors. In: 2011 IEEE International Conference on Pervasive Computing and Communications (PerCom), pp. 222–230, March 2011
11. de Leoni, M., Marrella, A.: Aligning real process executions and prescriptive process through automated planning. Expert Syst. Appl. **82**, 162–183 (2017)
12. Marrella, A., Lespérance, Y.: Synthesizing a library of process templates through partial-order planning algorithms. In: Nurcan, S., Proper, H.A., Soffer, P., Krogstie, J., Schmidt, R., Halpin, T., Bider, I. (eds.) BPMDS/EMMSAD-2013. LNBIP, vol. 147, pp. 277–291. Springer, Heidelberg (2013). doi:10.1007/978-3-642-38484-4_20
13. Marrella, A., Mecella, M., Sardiña, S.: Intelligent process adaptation in the SmartPM system. ACM TIST **8**(2), 25:1–25:43 (2017)
14. di Palermo, U.: Neptis. Soluzioni ICT per la fruizione e l'esplorazione "aumentata" di beni culturali (2015)
15. Ravi, N., Dandekar, N., Mysore, P., Littman, M.L.: Activity recognition from accelerometer data. In: 17th Conference on Innovative Applications of Artificial Intelligence, IAAI 2005, vol. 3, pp. 1541–1546. AAAI Press (2005)
16. Robinson, P.: Tourism: The Key Concepts. Routledge, Oxford (2012)
17. Rubino, I., Barberis, C., Xhembulla, J., Malnati, G.: Integrating a location-based mobile game in the museum visit: evaluating visitors behaviour and learning. J. Comput. Cult. Herit. **8**(3), 15:1–15:18 (2015)
18. Sigala, M., Chalkiti, K.: Investigating the exploitation of web 2.0 for knowledge management in the Greek tourism industry: an utilisation-importance analysis. Comput. Hum. Behav. **30**, 800–812 (2014)
19. Torralba, A., Alcazar, V., Borrajo, D., Kissmann, P., Edelkamp, S.: Symba: a symbolic bidirectional planner. In: International Planning Competition, pp. 105–108 (2014)
20. Toth, P., Vigo, D.: Vehicle Routing: Problems, Methods, and Applications. SIAM, Philadelphia (2014)
21. Tu, Q., Liu, A.: Framework of smart tourism research and related progress in China. In: International Conference on Management and Engineering (CME 2014), pp. 140–146 (2014)
22. Vansteenwegen, P., Souffriau, W., Oudheusden, D.V.: The orienteering problem: a survey. Eur. J. Oper. Res. **209**(1), 1–10 (2011)
23. Venturini, A., Ricci, F.: Applying Trip@dvice recommendation technology to www.visiteurope.com. Front. Artif. Intell. Appl. **141**, 607 (2006)
24. Werthner, H.: Intelligent systems in travel and tourism. In: 18th International Joint Conference on Artificial Intelligence (IJCAI 2003) (2002)
25. Werthner, H., Alzua-Sorzabal, A., Cantoni, L., Dickinger, A., Gretzel, U., Jannach, D., Neidhardt, J., Pröll, B., Ricci, F., Scaglione, M., et al.: Future research issues in it and tourism. Inf. Technol. Tour. **15**(1), 1–15 (2015)
26. Wilkins, D.E.: Practical Planning: Extending the Classical AI Planning Paradigm. Morgan Kaufmann, San Francisco (1988)

Audio Story and AR Platform for Youth Engagement

Kari Salo[1(✉)], Merja Bauters[1], and Tommi Mikkonen[2]

[1] Helsinki Metropolia University of Applied Sciences, Helsinki, Finland
{kari.salo,merja.bauters}@metropolia.fi
[2] University of Helsinki, Helsinki, Finland
tommi.mikkonen@helsinki.fi

Abstract. We have developed an audio story sharing and audio augmented reality platform for cultural institutions. Using the platform, cultural institutions can develop creative extracurricular activities. Our platform contains backend service for audio content management and three separate Android applications to support audio story sharing and augmenting reality with soundscapes. This paper introduces the results from two workshops, suitable as extracurricular activities for students that have utilized the platform. To assess how students experience workshops and the platform we have developed an instrument to measure engagement. Our instrument is based on student engagement research. With this instrument we are able to analyze not just the engagement as a whole but also the behavioral, emotional and cognitive engagement components. Workshops create holistic experiences; thus, we need to take into account the platform and context when measuring user engagement.

Keywords: Student engagement · Soundscape · Audio story · Android · Audio augmented reality · Extracurricular activity

1 Introduction

Participation in extracurricular activities is connected to adolescents' positive development. Several studies have linked these activities to positive psychological and academic outcomes [1]. Adolescents who participate in the extracurricular activities during high school have higher self-esteem and lower rates of depression. They have higher grades, test scores, school engagement and educational aspirations. Thus schools are willingly co-operating with parties who can offer extracurricular activities. To this end, cultural institutions, like museums, art galleries and libraries organize extracurricular activities for youth. These extracurricular activities are one approach to attract more visitors. At the same time they develop new activities, such as context-aware audio guides, augmented reality and 3D modeling based applications, and interactive digital storytelling [2–4] to provide interactive experiences for an audience familiar with of digital interaction.

To support extracurricular activities, we have developed audio story sharing and audio augmented reality platform for cultural institutions. Our platform consists of an audio digital asset management system (ADAM), a management application, and three mobile applications. The platform is modular so that a user, for instance a cultural

© Springer International Publishing AG 2017
M. Younas et al. (Eds.): MobiWIS 2017, LNCS 10486, pp. 18–32, 2017.
DOI: 10.1007/978-3-319-65515-4_2

institute, is able to pick up only those mobile applications that they need. In all cases a back-end system is needed. ADAM contains functionalities to manage the assets, and an interface for the management application and a mobile application over the Internet. The management application is an administration console for managing the assets and users. The mobile applications are Story Sharing, NFC Writer and Soundscape Mixer, which enable creating stories and soundscapes [5, 6].

This paper introduces two workshops that have utilized our platform. Both workshops are suitable as extracurricular activities for students. As a part of the workshop concept we have defined pedagogical objectives for learning purposes. In the workshop chapter we will describe pedagogical objectives in a more detailed level. To assess how interesting and useful a workshop and platform are we need a measurement instrument, which is capable of describing the workshop engagement. We have based our measurement instrument on the three–dimensional student engagement construct [7] as most engagement scholars agree on that definition [8, Epilogue]. We will also describe the developed measurement instrument and how we have assessed the two different workshops.

2   Audio and Extracurricular Activity

Museums, art galleries and other cultural institutions have for long cooperated with educational institutes to provide another aspect into the studied subjects. We have developed a platform for sharing audio stories and augmenting audio reality by using soundscapes. The stories are often curated and to some extent they are interactive like Holocaust Survivor's interactive storytelling [9]. To provide advanced interaction, the interactive digital storytelling research is looking for ways to provide a platform, which combines a game engine and an interactive curated narrative environment [10]. These examples rely on visual and audio elements. In recent years tangible narratives have emerged which use tangible user interfaces. One example in museum context is smart replicas [11]. When a replica is placed into a case that contains a NFC tag, a curated story will be triggered. Some projects, like Object stories and 100 toys, have invited visitors to participate by telling their own story [12]. Our platform concentrates on audio presentation. It supports also curated audio stories, but we differentiate from the other digital storytelling systems by allowing the visitors to indicate emotions onto the visitor stories. There is also a possibility for combining soundscapes and audio stories as visitor enriched audio stories. In addition, the modularity allows cultural institutions to select the appropriate elements they deem suitable for their aims, which is important for easy appropriation by the cultural institutions. They need to have a choice on how and what to use for tying the exhibitions to the pedagogical aims of nearby educational institutions.

In augmented reality, we have focused on the acoustic environments. A soundscape is created out of multiple, time-varying sound sources [13]. When a user creates a soundscape, which describes the acoustic environment of some location, we can say that soundscape forms audio augmented reality. Location aware soundscapes combine typically location-based mobile applications and audio. Tactical Sound Garden platform enables users to leave location-based sounds and other users to listen to them in that particular position [14]. Klang.Reise is an installation of video and audio recordings inside a closed spherical space [15]. The goal is to demonstrate different sounds of a selected place and how these sounds change over the time. The Sound Design Accelerator (SoDA) project provides software for soundscape generation. SoDA is targeted to sound designers [16]. Our approach is somewhere in between these, the target audience being museum visitors, such as students, as was in Klang. Reise project. Just like in Tactical Sound Garden, we are asking visitors to share soundscapes. The difference is that we expect users to create the soundscapes from simple sound components (audio files) available in the backend system. We do not expect visitors to be familiar with reverberation, resonance, or other acoustic terms, which makes it easier to appropriate the use of the application smoothly. Thus, our application is in well-established genre, but we have enhanced the way it can be used based on the previous projects experiences. We have also created an implementation for cultural institutes which is easier to execute [17]. Next we will explain our framework and engagement measuring instrument for the extracurricular activities.

3   Developing the Measurement Instrument

Engagement as a term and structure has several definitions. Some researchers define engagement as a synonym for motivation [18, 19], relying on motivational theories, such as flow theory, interest theory and self-determination theory. In recent years there has been increased research on engagement, where engagement and motivation have been defined as separate constructs. Today, most motivation and engagement researchers agree that motivation is the precursor of engagement, where motivation is intent and engagement is action [8, Epilogue]. As our context is extracurricular activities we will rely on the student engagement definition: multidimensional structure consisting of behavioral, emotional and cognitive engagement [7, 8, Epilogue].

In a study [18] the extracurricular activity experiences were measured and compared among middle school students. This research covered activities from sports and arts to socializing, academic enrichment and sit-down games. This was a one-year study with two one-week data sampling periods using Experience Sampling Method (ESM). Students were positively engaged and exhibited high intrinsic interest and concentrated effort during sports and arts. Positive emotion was highest in sit-down games, arts and academic enrichment activities. Concentrated effort was lowest when socializing. Importance was lowest when socializing and during sit-down games [18]. These results point out how differently students experience the extracurricular activities depending on the type of activity. For us the results give a good example of the importance creative activities have for broader success in students' studies.

The engagement research has emphasized the understanding of contextual factors. In situ instrument is one that aims to capture students' real situation – specific experiences of engagement that could not be assessed with traditional questionnaires. It emphasizes the importance of investigating situation-specific variations in engagement [8, 20]. The findings support the idea that moment-to-moment experiences of engagement may congeal to long-term engagement trajectories [8]. In the in situ instrument, factors of behavioral and cognitive engagement become mixed and hard to distinguish from each other. As behavioral and cognitive aspects are closely related, also we are paying attention to them in our research. Although, the in situ instrument and related research have provided understanding of the factors that influence student experience, there is limited information on how physical learning spaces affect student engagement. Previous research has shown that an institution's physical environment has significant implications on teaching and learning processes as well as social practices [8, 21, 22]. Bennet has argued that physical spaces and tools influence learning behavior, as different spatial designs determine activities in which students can and cannot engage [23]. The impact of physical spaces becomes more prominent when pedagogical practices move away from the traditional, teacher-centered approach towards a more flexible, student-centered approach and non-school environments such as museums. From a social constructivist viewpoint, this interaction is a vital component in the creation and development of knowledge [24, 25]. In our framework, we cannot separate the tools used and context where the actions occur.

The measurement instruments of student engagement vary a lot. This is due to the fact that student engagement structure has been defined with different number of subcomponents and even if researchers are using the most typical three component structure then there has been variations in the content of items describing subcomponents. We are using the definitions from Fredricks, Blumenfeld and Paris [7]. Behavioral engagement is most commonly defined in three ways: positive conduct, such as following the rules, involvement in learning and academic tasks including behaviors, like effort, persistence, concentration and attention, and participation in school-related activities. Emotional engagement refers to students' affective reactions, like interest, boredom, happiness, sadness, and anxiety. Cognitive engagement refers to attention to task, task mastery, a willingness to go beyond what is required and a preference for challenging tasks. The types of engagement are interrelated, but there is no clear evidence how different types of engagement interact. For example, it is likely that emotional engagement leads to increases in behavioral and cognitive engagement [7].

On methods how to gather the data, the most common for studying engagement include student self-report surveys, experience sampling, interviews and observations. In Handbook of research on student engagement, a comparative analysis of various methods and 11 self-report instruments has been described [26]. Another study contains 21 instruments: 12 student self-reports, 3 teacher reports, and 4 observational measures. Out of the 12 student self-reports only 5 include subscales that address all three dimensions of engagement [27]. Our target is to use observations and self-report questionnaires. As described in [8, pp. 765–768] self-report methods are useful for assessing emotional and cognitive engagement, which are not directly observable. Behavioral engagement is observable. Thus we use observational methods to assess behavioral engagement. In addition, we will use also a self-report questionnaire, as observations do not provide information on participant's thinking or quality of effort or feelings during activities. The self-report questionnaire is relying on three-part typology of student engagement [7]. Questions are adapted and modified from School Engagement Scale [28], Student Engagement in Schools Questionnaire (SESQ) [29] and School Engagement Survey (SES) [30]. All three questionnaires are targeted to school and classroom environment. They contain questions for behavioral, emotional and cognitive engagement. School Engagement Scale is developed by Fredricks, Blumenfeld and Paris. This questionnaire provides a good starting point including the Likert scale. SESQ divides emotional engagement questions into liking for learning and liking for school. Liking for school in our case is not relevant. In SESQ behavioral engagement takes into account extracurricular activities as a general concept. Both SESQ and SES have several relevant questions in all three engagement areas. When filtering out direct classroom and school related questions we have been able to pick up six questions for each engagement areas. As our context is two different extracurricular activities we have modified questions addressing these activities.

Qualitative methods (self-report questionnaires and observations) were used to understand the quantitative data gathered [31]. Using a qualitative paradigm illuminates the people behind the numbers and helps to understand what is observed, it provides richer understanding that mere statistics [32]. The qualitative methods also support the three measurement components: observation allows studying of behavioral aspect especially when mixed with self-reporting questions related to behavior and cognitive aspects. The questionnaires allow us to understand the emotional aspects of the users that cannot be seen from behavior. Our workshops require intense work and thus are not huge in participant numbers which makes is hard to generalize the findings. The studies are case studies, mixing quantitative and qualitative data.

4   The Gdańsk City Gallery Workshops and Results

Two workshops were organized in the Gdańsk City Gallery, Poland. Workshops aimed at studying student engagement in activities organized in the City Gallery using our platform. The focus of the first workshop was the level of engagement during the workshop where students share their own audio stories. In addition, we studied how easy/difficult the interaction with the Audio Sharing application is. The second workshop concentrated on soundscapes. We aimed at understanding the level of engagement during the workshop and verify if the interaction with the Soundscape Mixer application was experienced as easy as it was in the Finnish museum context [17].

Both workshops had a pedagogical plan. Pedagogical objectives for the audio story workshops were to understand that: sharing a memory or story about yourself could open a new angle to one's personality or strengthen the existing view of one's personality; sharing ideas is an important part of learning; emotions are dependent on context and person; and if a story is related to some artifact, then the user should understand that different stories demonstrate how an artifact can be described from many different angles. Pedagogical objectives for the soundscape workshop were to understand that: a soundscape is a composition of several audio components; urbanization and technology have changed the city soundscape and that a soundscape is a subjective experience.

The framework used was the student engagement structure with three components [7] consisting of questions relating to emotions, behavior and cognitive aspect of engagement. There were six questions per component. As part of behavioral engagement we asked how much and how long student was concentrating, putting effort, and paying attention to workshop or was her/his focus somewhere else. Emotion wise we asked how much interest, boredom, happiness, excitement and enjoyment students had. In order to understand cognitive engagement we asked about level of challenge, attention to task, task mastery, and a willingness to go beyond what is required. Questions from different components were mixed in a questionnaire. Three questions were reverse scored to prevent individuals from adopting a rapid response pattern with the Likert scale ratings without reading the question. In addition to engagement related questions, we checked also how familiar students were with the smart phones and how easy/difficult the interaction with the mobile application was (Fig. 1). Audio Story and Soundscape Questionnaire had almost the same questions. Only questions 12 and 16 of engagement part and last two questions of application interaction part were modified to be more related to workshop and application context.

Audio Story Query

Your mobile phone

	iPhone	Android phone	Windows phone	Other	I don't have a phone
What kind of mobile phone do you use?	○	○	○	○	○

think about the workshop from start to end (from introduction to discussion) when you answer the questions below

	Never	On Occasion	Some of the Time	Most of the Time	All of the Time
I tried my best in the workshop	○	○	○	○	○
I felt happy in the workshop	○	○	○	○	○
During the workshop I discussed with other students to make sure I understood what was expected from us	○	○	○	○	○
I paid attention during the introduction	○	○	○	○	○
I felt bored in the workshop	○	○	○	○	○
When I listened to the introduction, I tried to understand information better by relating it to things I already know	○	○	○	○	○
During the workshop I just pretended I am working	○	○	○	○	○
I felt excited by the work in the workshop	○	○	○	○	○
When I listened to the introduction, I tried to figure out how the information would be useful in real world	○	○	○	○	○
I just did enough to get by	○	○	○	○	○
I was interested in the tasks done during the workshop	○	○	○	○	○
When I was recording and listening stories I tried to figure out how this would be useful in real world	○	○	○	○	○
During the workshop my mind wandered	○	○	○	○	○
I enjoyed learning new thing in the workshop	○	○	○	○	○
Tasks done during the workshop were challenging	○	○	○	○	○
I tried hard to do my part during the recording, listening and discussion	○	○	○	○	○
I enjoyed working with other students in the workshop	○	○	○	○	○
I tried to see similarities and differences between things I learned in the workshop and things I already know	○	○	○	○	○

How would you grade the Audio Story application?

	Strongly Agree	Agree	Undecided	Disagree	Strongly Disagree
Pleasant to use	○	○	○	○	○
Worked well	○	○	○	○	○
Was fitting to the task	○	○	○	○	○

	Yes	No
Have you used similar applications before?	○ Yes	○ No
Would you use the app elsewhere than in this workshop?	○ Yes	○ No
Did you know what the icons meant?	○ Yes	○ No
Did you succeed in recording your story?	○ Yes	○ No
Did you succeed in listening stories?	○ Yes	○ No

Fig. 1. Audio story workshop questionnaire

For studying both workshops we used mixed methods with the selection of methods – observation and self-reporting questionnaires were used – and with the analysis. Three researchers were present at the place where the observations were made. Data was gathered by observation notes, and notes from discussion between the researchers on the place. The notes were rewritten to clear them up. The self-reporting questionnaires in paper format were collected at the end of workshop. For analysis we used the data gathered from the workshops. We executed simple statistical measurements from the self-reporting questionnaires. These were combined with the observation and discussion notes data. We also used the researchers' impression and experiences from the workshops. However, while we had three researchers in the workshops executing the observation, we had two researchers analyzing the data. One of the researchers analyzing the data was not present in the workshops. Thus, allowing a different view into the data while the other researcher had the self-experience also available for analyzing the data. Therefore, we can say that we used triangulation with the data gathering and analysis [33]. Both studies were conforming to the ethical guidelines, and consent forms were signed by all students taking part in to the workshops.

4.1 Audio Story Workshop

The Gdańsk City Gallery was selected to be the workshop place for two reasons: they have good connections and experience in working with local secondary schools, and we wanted to test our platform also in other country than Finland. The workshop was organized in cooperation with teachers from the secondary school Gdansk, Poland and the gallery personnel. With the teachers and gallery personnel the pedagogical aims were designed. The platform and its usage were described beforehand to teachers and gallery personnel. This enabled teachers to link workshop to school work by asking students to prepare stories already before the workshop. Students were also asked to think about the emotions related to their stories.

Our research question was: can a student get engaged when sharing a personal story with other students. In addition, we wanted to know if our Audio Sharing application hinders or supports the activities. The participants were 30 students from three different classes from a local secondary school. Age of the students was between 13–16 years, which match well to our target group. Our initial plan was as follows:

1. The gallery personnel welcomed the young people and explained the idea of the workshop. This included a discussion about storytelling and what kind of personal experiences students have on storytelling. After this Sound Sharing application was introduced. Finally, students were divided into team of two, each team has a number, and the task was provided for the students (20 min).
2. Each team was pointed out a location in a gallery, where they could find a paper on the wall with a number (same as their team number) and NFC tag. Team locations were planned so that they would not disturb each other and there would be sufficient WLAN coverage. The task was to record both student stories and then listen to stories from two other groups. When listening stories the students were advised to take notes to decide which stories were most impressing. The students were provided a user identifier and password to log into ADAM in order to upload their stories. The students had an Android device provided by us and Sound Sharing application in their use for recording and listening stories (40 min).
3. In the end, most impressing stories were listened and discussed. Feedback of the workshop was provided by the students. Each student filled a questionnaire (Fig. 1) at the end of the workshop (30 min).

Initially we planned a workshop for 20 students as we had only 10 Android phones with us. So it was a surprise when we got 30 students. We modified our plan on the fly by defining the team size to 3 and asking teams to select two stories out of three, which they would record. In the actual workshop both introduction and the recording and listening stories took longer than planned almost hour and a half, which meant that the whole workshop lasted 2 h. We split the students into two different spaces to give them more space when using the mobile application. We had one researcher per space. After 1.5 h the listening of the stories began. Gallery personnel translated these stories afterwards from Polish to English to us. The outcomes were analyzed from the questionnaire data, video and observation notes.

4.2 Results of the First Workshop: Observations and Questionnaire

Observations were conducted by two persons. When analyzing the notes and video taken during the introduction, the following issues came clearly visible: students enjoyed, were interested, concentrated, paid attention and finished the tasks. Enjoyment was observed from the laughter and happiness. Interest could be seen from the willingness to discuss and ask questions. Concentration and attention could be detected from the silence and keen faces when explaining the idea of workshop and demonstrating the application, and on the other hand from relevant questions and serious discussions when it was time for discussions. Topics of discussion were stories, which came to students' minds during the introduction, how emotions are subjective, time and place related, what kind emotions were raised after hearing someone's story. Both researchers had similar observations related the usage of applications. Students were willing to ask questions, were happy and helped each other to accomplish the tasks.

We also noticed hindrances. One of it was when several students could not upload their stories to the system. The students were quite understanding and continued working in a good mood, which might indicate that working with the stories was interesting enough not to bother too much on technical problems. It was agreed with the students that we listen to two stories, which would be told orally by students who did not succeed to upload their stories, and two stories, which were uploaded into ADAM. All these stories were very personal including the emotions related to stories. While one student was telling his/her story all other students were listening carefully. There was no negative behavior during or after the story telling. Neither there were any negative comments. On the contrary, the comments were supportive and positive. Thus, we could see that the students had done the school/home work for the workshop, and as hoped presented their emotionally rich stories. Based on these stories, discussions and the behavior of the participants it was clear that they took the workshop very seriously.

When observing the use of the application it seemed that the students did not have any other problems after they learned where the phone's NFC reader (needed to start the application) is located. This was confirmed by both researchers. Because there was no hesitation in the use and no questions of the usage of the mobile application, we could assume that the application worked smoothly and it was easy to use.

Based on observations and discussions with students it was obvious that the Gallery as an environment had a positive impact on the workshop. Students were excited about the place and at the same time relaxed. They looked at paintings on the walls and video art, but art works did not prevent them from accomplishing their tasks.

The questionnaire provides more detailed information about engagement and some additional information of the application. If we look at the behavioral engagement first, we will see that students were putting effort and paying attention to the workshop most of the time. According to their answers they were concentrating and not just pretending to work. An interesting result is that they did just enough to get work done. This could relate to a cognitive answer where students indicate that tasks were challenging for only some of the time. All in all we could see that students were behaviorally engaged most of the time (Fig. 2B). Emotional engagement related answers indicated that students were most of the time happy, excited and enjoying themselves. Only occasionally did they seem bored. Thus, emotionally they were engaged (Fig. 2E). This confirms the behavior that was observed, laughter, happiness, interest, discussions and relevant questions, no negative comments, and attention. The third component, cognitive engagement was not as positive as the others. It can be seen that they paid attention to task and to some extent to task mastery, but they did not invest much on tasks relating to larger context. As discussed, the level of challenge for completing the tasks was not high, which could be areas on why students were cognitively engaged only for some of the time (Fig. 2C). This assumption is supported by [11] where authors found a relation between challenging tasks and higher behavioral, emotional and cognitive engagement [7].

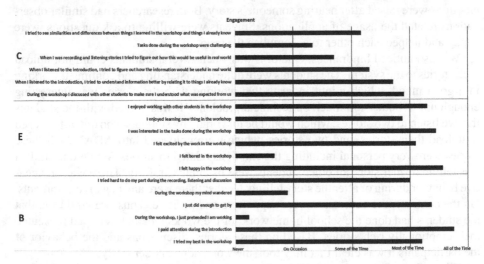

Fig. 2. Audio story engagement

Considering that six users had an iPhone, two users had a feature phone and 23 had an Android phone in their private use, it was expected that users would find the application easy to use – even if most of the users noted that they had never used a similar application. Students indicated that our application was suitable to the task and pleasant to use. Problems with uploading clearly affected the user experience when analyzing student answers on how well the application worked, how many had succeeded in recording their stories, and to some extent also during listening to the stories after recording. In spite of the problems most of the students were able to complete the tasks, and would use similar application elsewhere than this workshop. Almost all students were able to recognize icons (Fig. 3).

Fig. 3. Audio story application functionality (left) and interaction results (right)

4.3 Soundscape Workshop

The second workshop was also organized in the Gdańsk City Gallery. It was more focused, as its main purpose was to study engagement of creating soundscape. In addition, we wanted to know if our soundscape mixer application hinders or supports the activities. We have previously organized two similar workshops in Finland [17]. Thus we had already earlier experience how to define relevant pedagogical aims. We agreed with gallery staff to use the same pedagogical approach and objectives as in Finland. We decided to use SoundSpace application, which is one of the three soundscape mixer applications. We have used SoundSpace also in previous two workshops.

Our research question was: Can a student get engaged when creating soundscapes. In addition, we wanted to know if our soundscape mixer application hinders or supports the activities. The 12 student participants from three classes came from different secondary school this time. Age of students was between 13–16 years. These classes were from Gdansk, Poland. The outline of the workshop was as follows:

1. The gallery personnel welcomed the young people and explained the idea of the workshop. Sound design teacher explained what a soundscape is, and SoundSpace application was introduced. Finally, a task was provided for the students (20 min).
2. The task was to create a soundscape to an image of historical Gdansk. For creating the soundscape the users were provided an image and an adjective that exemplified an atmosphere into the selected image. The users were given a user identifier and password to log into ADAM and a sound collection identifier to choose sounds from. The users had SoundSpace application in their use for creating the soundscape. The devices used were Samsung Galaxy and Nexus phones equipped with headphones. The students created the soundscapes in pairs (30 min).

3. In the end, all the soundscapes were listened and discussed. Feedback of the workshop was provided by the users. Each student filled a questionnaire after creating their final soundscape (Fig. 1) (20 min).

The workshop went as planned. The workshop was bi-lingual in a sense that a short intro was done in Polish and rest of the workshop was in English. This enabled both researchers to observe the workshop in real-time.

4.4 Results of the Second Workshop: Observations and Questionnaire

The observations were conducted by two persons. When analyzing the notes and video taken during the whole workshop, we had similar results compared with the first workshop: students enjoyed, were interested, concentrated, paid attention and finished the tasks. Enjoyment was observed from the laughter. Interest could be seen from the discussions, comments and questions asked. Concentration and attention could be detected from to the point questions and keen faces when explaining the idea of workshop and demonstrating the application. Topics of discussion were sounds and soundscapes, which students experienced on their way to the gallery, how soundscapes are subjective, and how the soundscapes can be time and place related. Students did not have any problems using the application, they were discussing intensively when planning what kind of sounds were needed to create a soundscape which best describes the image and given adjective. They were eager to try out different sounds and helped each other to accomplish the tasks. When it was time to listen to all the soundscapes we decided that each pair displays their image and then we listened the soundscape. After listening the soundscape, other students were asked to guess what the given adjective was. This clearly intensified the listening experience as other students had to concentrate figuring out the adjective. The experienced sound designer researcher was commenting all soundscapes and students were keen to get her comments. Based on her assessment all the soundscapes were creative and proved that students took this task seriously and put effort and creativeness to come up with soundscapes. When observing the usage of the application, it seemed that the students did not have any problems. This was confirmed by both researchers. Because there was no hesitation in the use, no questions of the usage of the mobile application, we could assume that the application worked smoothly and it was easy to use.

The questionnaire provides more detailed information about engagement and some additional information of the application. If we look at the behavioral engagement first, we see that the students were making an effort and paying attention to the workshop most of the time. According to their answers they were concentrating and not just pretending to work, but they did just enough to get the work done. As in the other workshop, this behavior could relate to the cognitive answer where they indicate that tasks were only some of the time challenging. All in all, we could see that students were behaviorally engaged most of the time (Fig. 4B). Answers related with emotional engagement indicated that students were happy most of the time, excited and enjoying themselves. Only on occasion they were bored. Thus, emotionally they were engaged (Fig. 4E). This confirms the behavior that was observed, happiness, interest, discussions on relevant questions, attention and no negative comments. The third component, cognitive engagement was not as positive as the other two. It can be seen that attention was paid to the task and to some extent to task mastery, but not much was invested on relating tasks to larger context. To relate the workshop tasks to a broader context might have needed guidance from teachers. The meta-skill of reflecting in a broader sense is challenging (Fig. 4C). This assumption is supported by other research where they have found a relationship between challenging tasks and higher behavioral, emotional and cognitive engagement [7].

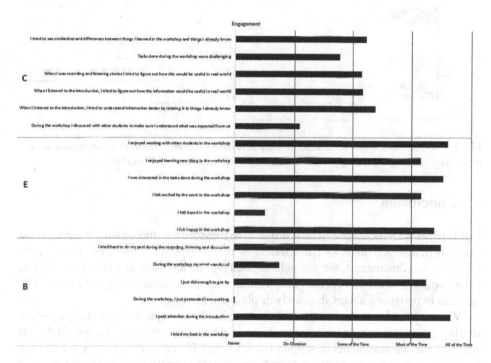

Fig. 4. Soundscape engagement

As four users had an iPhone and eight had an Android phone in their private use, it was expected that using an Android application was easy – even if most users noted that they had never used such application. Students indicated that our application was suitable for the task, pleasant to use and worked well. All of the students were able to complete the tasks, and most of them would use a similar application elsewhere than this workshop. Almost all students were able to recognize icons (Fig. 5). These results are similar to our earlier results collected from two workshops in Finland [17].

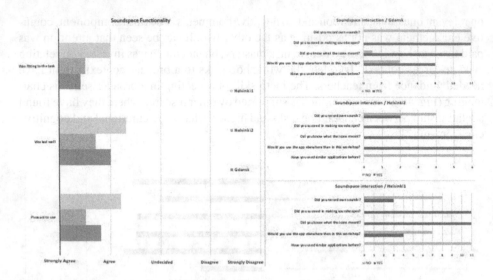

Fig. 5. SoundSpace application functionality results on the left and interaction results on the right. Results from the Gdansk workshop and also from two earlier workshops.

5 Conclusion

In this paper we have described an instrument to measure the student engagement during extra-curricular activities. Our instrument is based on student engagement research. Utilizing this instrument, we are able to analyze engagement in general as well as behavioral, emotional and cognitive engagement components, allowing us to assess how students experienced a workshop and our platform [5, 6].

We organized two workshops with two aims: (1) can a student get engaged when sharing a personal story with other students or when creating a soundscape (2) do our Android applications hinder or support the activities. Based on the findings, we can say that workshops using our platform have been engaging experience for the students, and they were behaviorally and emotionally engaged most of the time. Cognitive engagement was not as positive as the other two - the students paid attention to the task and to some extent to task mastery, but they did not invest much in relating tasks to a larger context. Still, based on the findings we can state that the interaction with audio story sharing and soundscape mixing applications was appreciated.

Acknowledgements. We thank Marta Wróblewska from the Gdańsk City Gallery for workshop arrangement and all the support. Aura Neuvonen has provided valuable advises in the area of soundscapes and participated into implementation of both workshops. We thank also Arto Salonen for his advice and comments during the engagement instrument development. The work is co-funded by EU, Creative Europe Programme, The People's Smart Sculpture project (http://smartsculpture.eu).

References

1. Feldman, A.F., Matjasko, J.L.: The role of school-based extracurricular activities in adolescent development: a comprehensive review and future directions. Rev. Educ. Res. **75**(2), 159–210 (2005)
2. Hatala, M., Wakkary, R.: Ontology-based user modeling in an augmented audio reality system for museums. User Model. User-Adap. Inter. **15**(3), 339–380 (2005). Kluwer Academic Publishers, Netherlands
3. Demiris, A.M., Vlahakis, V., Ioannidis, N.: System and infrastructure considerations for the successful introduction of augmented reality guides in cultural heritage sites. In: Proceedings of the ACM Symposium on Virtual Reality Software and Technology, VRST 2006, pp. 141–144. ACM, New York (2006)
4. Blythe, M., McCarthy, J., Wright, P., Petrelli, D.: History and experience: storytelling and interaction design. In: Proceedings of the 25th BCS Conference on Human-Computer Interaction, BCS-HCI 2011, pp. 395–404. British Computer Society, Swinton (2011)
5. Salo, K., Zinin, V., Bauters, M., Mikkonen, T.: Modular audio story platform for museums. In: Proceedings of the 22nd International Conference on Intelligent User Interfaces Companion (IUI 2017 Companion), pp. 113–116. ACM, New York (2017)
6. Salo, K., Bauters, M., Mikkonen, T.: Mobile soundscape mixer – ready for action. In: Younas, M., Awan, I., Kryvinska, N., Strauss, C., van Thanh, D. (eds.) MobiWIS 2016. LNCS, vol. 9847, pp. 18–30. Springer, Cham (2016). doi:10.1007/978-3-319-44215-0_2
7. Fredricks, J.A., Blumenfeld, P.C., Paris, A.H.: School engagement: potential of the concept, state of the evidence. Rev. Educ. Res. **74**(1), 59–109 (2004)
8. Christenson, S.L., Reschly, A.L., Wylie, C. (eds.): Handbook of Research on Student Engagement. Springer Science & Business Media, New York (2012)
9. Ladeira, I., Marsden, G.: Interactive personal storytelling: an ethnographic study and simulation of apartheid-era narratives. In: Proceedings of the 2014 Conference on Designing Interactive Systems, DIS 2014, pp. 249–258 (2014). doi:10.1145/2598510.2598597
10. Peinado, F., Navarro, Á., Gervás, P.: A testbed environment for interactive storytellers. In: Proceedings of the 2nd International Conference on INtelligent TEchnologies for interactive enterTAINment, INTETAIN 2008, Article No. 3. ICST, Brussels (2008)
11. Marshall, M.T., Dulake, M., Ciolfi, L., Duranti, D., Kockelkorn, H., Petrelli, D.: Using tangible smart replicas as controls for an interactive museum exhibition. In: Proceedings of the TEI 2016: Tenth International Conference on Tangible, Embedded, and Embodied Interaction, pp. 159–167 (2016). doi:10.1145/2839462.2839493
12. Negrini, M., Di Blas, N.: Digital storytelling for cultural heritage: a modular, multi-channel, multi-scenario approach. In: Toniola, L., Boriani, M., Guidi, G. (eds.) Built Heritage: Monitoring Conservation Management, Part IV, pp. 367–375. Springer International Publishing, Switzerland (2014)
13. Jennings, P., Cain, R.: A framework for improving urban soundscapes. Appl. Acoust. Appl. Soundscapes Recent Adv. Soundscape Res. **74**(2), 293–299 (2013)
14. Shepard, M.: Tactical sound garden [TSG] toolkit. In: Proceedings of the 3rd International Workshop on Mobile Music Technology, Brighton, UK (2006)
15. Drechsler, A., Raffaseder, H., Rubisch, B.: Klang.Reise: new scientific approaches through an artistic soundscape installation? In: AM 2012 Proceedings of the 7th Audio Mostly Conference: A Conference on Interaction with Sound, New York, USA, pp. 44–46 (2012)
16. Casu, M., Koutsomichalis, M., Valle, A.: Imaginary soundscapes: the SoDA project. In: Proceedings of the 9th Audio Mostly: A Conference on Interaction with Sound, AM 2014, Article No. 5. ACM, New York (2014)

17. Salo, K., Bauters, M., Mikkonen, T.: User generated soundscapes activating museum visitors. In: Proceedings of the 32nd ACM SIGAPP Symposium on Applied Computing, SAC 2017, pp. 220–227. ACM, New York (2017)
18. Shernoff, D.J., Vandell, D.L.: Engagement in after-school program activities: quality of experience from the perspective of participants. J. Youth Adolesc. **36**(7), 891–903 (2007)
19. Dawes, N.P., Larson, R.: How youth get engaged: grounded-theory research on motivational development in organized youth programs. Dev. Psychol. **47**(1), 259 (2011)
20. Skinner, E.A., Kindermann, T.A., Furrer, C.J.: A motivational perspective on engagement and disaffection. Conceptualization and assessment of children's behavioral and emotional participation in academic activities in the classroom. Educ. Psychol. Measur. **69**, 493–525 (2009). doi:10.1177/0013164408323233
21. Oblinger, D.G.: Leading the transition from classrooms to learning spaces. EDUCAUSE Q. **28**(1), 14–18 (2005)
22. Jamieson, P.: Designing more effective on-campus teaching and learning spaces: a role for academic developers. Int. J. Acad. Dev. **8**(1), 119–133 (2003)
23. Montgomery, T.: Space matters: experiences in managing static formal learning spaces. Act. Learn. High Educ. **9**(2), 122–138 (2008)
24. Bennet, S.: First questions for designing higher education learning spaces. J. Acad. Librianship **33**(1), 14–26 (2007)
25. Vygotsky, L.S.: Mind in Society. The Development of Higher Psychological Processes. Harvard University Press, Cambridge (1978)
26. Hunter, A.B., Laursen, S.L., Seymour, E.: Becoming a scientist: the role of undergraduate research in students' cognitive, personal and professional development. Sci. Educ. **91**(1), 36–74 (2007)
27. Fredricks, J., McColskey, W., Meli, J., Mordica, J., Montrosse, B., Mooney, K.: Measuring student engagement in upper elementary through high school: a description of 21 instruments. Issues & Answers. REL 2011-No. 098. Regional Educational Laboratory Southeast (2011)
28. Fredricks, J.A., Blumenfeld, P.C., Friedel, J., Paris, A.: School engagement. In: Moore, K.A., Lippman, L. (eds.) What Do Children Need to Flourish? Conceptualizing and Measuring Indicators of Positive Development, vol. 3, pp. 305–321. Springer, Boston (2005)
29. Hart, S.R., Stewart, K., Jimerson, S.R.: The student engagement in schools questionnaire (SESQ) and the teacher engagement report form-new (TERF-N): examining the preliminary evidence. Contemp. Sch. Psychol. **15**, 67–79 (2011)
30. Finlay, K.A.: Quantifying School Engagement: Research Report. National Center for School Engagement, Denver (2006)
31. Matthews, K., Adams, P., Gannaway, D.: The impact of social learning spaces on student engagement. Paper presented at the Pacific Rim First Year in Higher Education Conference, Townsville, Australia, May 2009
32. Patton, M.Q.: Qualitative Research and Evaluation Methods, 3rd edn. Sage, London (2002)
33. Johnson, R.B., Onwuegbuzie, A.J., Turner, L.A.: Toward a definition of mixed methods research. J. Mix. Methods Res. **1**(2), 112–133 (2007)

Short and Reliable Path Selection for Automatic Evacuation Guiding Based on Interactions Between Evacuees and Their Mobile Devices

Takanori Hara(✉), Masahiro Sasabe, and Shoji Kasahara

Graduate School of Information Science, Nara Institute of Science and Technology,
8916-5 Takayama-cho, Ikoma, Nara 630-0192, Japan
{hara.takanori.hm8,sasabe,kasahara}@is.naist.jp
http://www-lsm.naist.jp/index.php/top-e

Abstract. When large-scale disasters occur, evacuees have to evacuate to a refuge quickly. For this purpose, there has been proposed an automatic evacuation guiding scheme based on implicit interactions among evacuees, their mobile devices, and networks. In this scheme, an evacuation route is obtained as the shortest path, which may not be safe. In this paper, we propose a short and reliable path selection for existing automatic evacuation guiding, which allows evacuees to evacuate quickly while avoiding encounters with blocked road segments as much as possible. First, the proposed scheme calculates k-shortest ($k \geq 1$) paths from the current location to the destination, with the help of the existing algorithm. Then, it selects the most reliable one from the candidates by taking into account road blockage probabilities, each of which is an estimated probability that the corresponding road is blocked under a certain disaster. Through simulation experiments, we show that the proposed scheme can reduce the number of encounters with blocked road segments with an appropriate value of k, while keeping the average/maximum evacuation time compared with the shortest path selection.

Keywords: Automatic evacuation guiding · Path selection · Path length · Path reliability · Road blockage probability · k-shortest path

1 Introduction

In the 2011 Great East Japan Earthquake, both fixed and mobile communication networks have been unavailable for long time and in wide areas, due to damage of information communication infrastructures. As a result, it has been reported that there were many cases where evacuees and rescuers could not collect and distribute important information, e.g. damage information, evacuation information, and government information [16]. Evacuees quickly have to evacuate to refuges along safe routes to keep their own safety when a large-scale disaster occurs. While they can acquire static information, e.g., map and location of refuges, in usual time, they cannot grasp dynamic information, e.g., blocked road segments, until the disaster occurs.

© Springer International Publishing AG 2017
M. Younas et al. (Eds.): MobiWIS 2017, LNCS 10486, pp. 33–44, 2017.
DOI: 10.1007/978-3-319-65515-4_3

To tackle this problem, Komatsu et al. have proposed an automatic evacuation guiding scheme based on implicit interactions between evacuees and their mobile devices [14], where communication among mobile devices is enabled by Delay Tolerant Networks (DTN) [9]. In this scheme, an application for evacuation guiding tries to navigate an evacuee by presenting his/her evacuation route as a recommended route using information shared between mobile devices and/or between mobile devices and cloud systems. When a large-scale disaster occurs, the application is activated automatically. Note that the application should be pre-installed into his/her mobile device in usual time. The application calculates an evacuation route from the current position to a refuge with map and location detected by Global Positioning System (GPS), and navigates the evacuee by presenting the route. In addition, the application can also grasp the actual evacuation route of the evacuee, i.e., his/her trajectory, by measuring his/her position periodically. The evacuee tries to evacuate along the recommended route. When the evacuee discovers a blocked road segment during his/her evacuation along the recommended route, he/she will take another route by his/her own judgment. As a result of tracing his/her actual evacuation route as the trajectory, the application can detect a blocked road, which makes the difference between the recommended route and the actual evacuation route. The application can automatically estimate and record this road as a blocked road segment. We can expect that the evacuation route can be improved by sharing blocked road segments, which were discovered, when a mobile device can communicate with other mobile devices and/or the remaining communication infrastructures.

In [14], the effectiveness of the automatic evacuation guidance scheme has been evaluated in terms of the average/maximum evacuation time and the ratio of evacuees that have finished evacuating to all evacuees. They, however, do not take into account the safety of evacuation routes and the shortest path is used for the recommended route. In case of earthquakes, an evacuee has to evacuate quickly and safely by avoiding encounters with blocked road segments as much as possible. Recently, we can obtain information to predict such occurrence of blocked road segments, i.e., road blockage probability, from a certain municipality, e.g., Nagoya city in Japan [6]. (See the details in Sect. 4.1). In this paper, we propose a short and reliable path selection for the automatic evacuation guiding by using the information about map and road blockage probabilities. Through simulation experiments, we show the validity of the proposed scheme in terms of the total number of encounters with blocked road segments and the average/maximum evacuation time.

The rest of this paper is organized as follows. Section 2 gives related work. In Sect. 3, we explain the existing automatic evacuation guiding scheme. In Sect. 4, the proposed scheme is presented, and Sect. 5 gives simulation results. Finally, Sect. 6 provides conclusions and future work.

2   Related Work

There are several existing studies on evacuation guiding supported by information and communication technology (ICT) [10,12,14]. Iizuka et al. propose an evacuation guiding scheme which presents evacuees evacuation paths and evacuation timing to avoid traffic jams, by using an ad-hoc network [12]. Fujihara and Miwa propose an evacuation guiding scheme using DTN under the situations of damage to communication infrastructures [10]. Komatsu et al. propose an automatic evacuation guiding scheme based on implicit interactions among evacuees and their mobile devices [14]. In the existing studies, the evacuation route is selected from the viewpoint of speedy evacuation, e.g., route length. In the evacuation, safety is important as well as speediness. In this paper, we propose a short and reliable path selection for the automatic evacuation guiding, which allows evacuees to evacuate quickly while avoiding encounters with blocked road segments as much as possible.

There are several existing studies on the risk analysis after a disaster occurs [4–6]. In Japan, a certain municipality, e.g., Nagoya city, has been evaluating the regional risks, road blockage probabilities, after occurrence of a large-scale disaster [6]. Church and Cova map evacuation risks on transportation networks using a spatial optimization model, called critical cluster model, in which the whole area is divided into multiple small areas and small areas with high ratio of population to exit capacity are regarded as those with high evacuation risk [5]. Since the model in [5] is only based on pre-disaster factors, i.e., population and exit capacity, Chen et al. extend this model by adding post-disaster factors, e.g., spatial impact of disaster and potential traffic congestion caused by evacuation guiding. In this paper, we improve the safety of evacuation guiding by taking into account a pre-disaster factor, i.e., road blockage probability.

The concept of path reliability, which will be explained in Sect. 4.2, is inspired by road network reliability [1,3,11]. There are two kinds of definitions of road network reliability: connectivity reliability and travel time reliability [11]. Connectivity reliability is defined as a probability that there exists at least one route between the source and the destination without heavy delay or road disruption. Travel time reliability is defined as a probability that traffic on the path can reach the destination within a specified time. Iida proposes a method to analyze and to evaluate the connectivity reliability, the travel time reliability, and the reliability of the links composing the road network [11]. Chen et al. analyze a road network with traffic demands by considering the connectivity reliability, the travel time reliability, and the capacity reliability [3]. Ahuja et al. propose a method to calculate the path reliability from the reliability of each link of the path [1].

When a disaster occurs, the road network might not be able to function as usual. Thus, evacuees have to select appropriate evacuation routes by taking into account various aspects: estimated evacuation time, traveling distance, and traffic congestion. There are several studies on a multi-objective path selection [15,17,19]. In [19], Yuan and Wang propose path selection models for emergency logistics management, with the help of an ant colony optimization algorithm [8], in order to select a route that minimizes both total travel time and route complexity. In [15], Lu et al. assume that the available capacities of nodes and edges of the road network may change during evacuation. They model the node capacities and edge capacities as time-series data and propose capacity constrained routing algorithms. Mohammad et al. propose path selection for evacuation planning with the help of a multi-objective evolutionary algorithm, where multiple factors, i.e. the distance from refuges, the capacity of refuges, and the population, are considered [17]. In this paper, we also tackle a kind of the multi-objective path selection, which considers the path length and path reliability.

3 Automatic Evacuation Guiding Scheme

Since the proposed path selection relies on the automatic evacuation guiding scheme [14], we first introduce the overview of that scheme.

3.1 Preliminaries

$G = (\mathcal{V}, \mathcal{E})$ denotes a graph representing the internal structure of target region, where $\mathcal{V}$ is a set of vertices, i.e., intersections, and $\mathcal{E}$ is a set of edges, i.e., roads, in the map. There are N ($N > 0$) evacuees in the region and each of them has a mobile device. $\mathcal{N} = \{1, 2, \ldots, N\}$ denotes a set of the evacuees (devices). Each device $n \in \mathcal{N}$ measures and records its own locations by using GPS at intervals of I_M ($I_M > 0$) just after a disaster occurs.

3.2 Overview

Figure 1 illustrates the flow of guiding evacuee $n \in \mathcal{N}$ to a refuge. Evacuee n has pre-installed an application for evacuation guiding into his/her mobile device before a disaster occurs. The application can obtain static information, i.e., the peripheral map of target region and the location information of refuges, in advance. When a disaster occurs, the application is initiated automatically. The application first finds out nearest refuge $d \in \mathcal{V}$ from location $s \in \mathcal{V}$ of evacuee n. Next, it calculates evacuation route $\widehat{p}_{s,d}$ and presents him/her the route as the recommended route (Step 1 in Fig. 1). Recommended route $\widehat{p}_{s,d}$ between source s and destination d on map G is given by a vector of edges constructing the route.

Evacuee n tries to move along recommended route $\widehat{p}_{s,d}$. When evacuee n discovers a blocked road segment during his/her evacuation along recommended route $\widehat{p}_{s,d}$ (Step 2 in Fig. 1), he/she will take another route by his/her own judgment (Step 3 in Fig. 1). The application can trace the actual evacuation route as a trajectory by measuring his/her positions periodically, i.e., at the interval of I_M. As a result, the application can detect blocked road segment $e \in \mathcal{E}$, which makes the difference between the recommended route and the actual evacuation route. Then, the application automatically records blocked road segment e into a set of blocked road segments, $\mathcal{E}^n_{NG}$ (Step 4 in Fig. 1). The application further recalculates a new evacuation route $\widehat{p}_{s',d}$, which does not

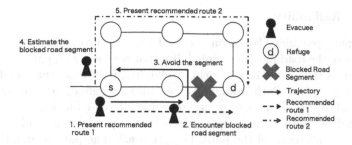

Fig. 1. Flow of evacuation guiding.

include blocked road segments in $\mathcal{E}_{NG}^n$ ($\forall e \in \mathcal{E}_{NG}^n$), and presents him/her the route, from current location s' to nearest refuge d (Step 5 in Fig. 1).

Evacuation guiding finishes when the evacuee reaches the refuge or the application cannot find out any evacuation route to the refuge. In addition to such self-discovery of blocked road segments, the application can also obtain new information about blocked road segments when the mobile device can communicate with other mobile devices and/or the remaining communication infrastructures. The obtained information about blocked road segments is used for route recalculation if the current recommended route contains the blocked road segments which were newly discovered. Thus, we can expect that such information sharing will improve the evacuation guiding and result in shortening evacuation time.

4 Proposed Scheme

In [14], the shortest path is applied as the recommended route for quick evacuation. In case of an earthquake, a main shock and the succeeding aftershocks might make some road segments blocked, due to secondary disasters, e.g., collapse of buildings along the route and fires. Thus, it is also important to achieve safe evacuation by avoiding encounters with such blocked road segments as much as possible. In this paper, we first model reliability of a path according to road blockage probabilities of road segments that compose the path, and propose a scheme to select a short and reliable evacuation path by taking into account the length and reliability of paths.

4.1 Road Blockage Probability

In Japan, a municipality, e.g., Nagoya city, has been evaluating the regional risks, e.g., road blockage probabilities, caused by future large-scale disasters such as Nankai Trough Earthquake [6]. The road blockage probability is an estimated probability that the corresponding road is blocked due to collapse of buildings along the road under a certain disaster. It is calculated based on the degree of collapse and height of each building along the road, and the width of the road.

4.2   Path Reliability

We define path reliability based on the road blockage probabilities. Let p_e ($0 \leq p_e \leq 1$) denote the road blockage probability that road $e \in r$ on path r is blocked. Then, $1 - p_e$ is the probability of road availability, indicating that road e is not blocked but passable. Path availability can also be defined as the probability that all roads $\forall e \in r$ on path r are passable. If road blockage probabilities are independent, path availability is given by the product of road availability probabilities of all roads of the path, $\prod_{e \in r}(1 - p_e)$. The path availability takes a value in the range of $[0, 1]$ and a large (resp. small) value means high (resp. low) availability.

Since the existing shortest-path algorithm, e.g., Dijkstra's algorithm [7], assumes that each road has a cost and that the sum of the road costs composing a path represents the cost of the path, we additionally define path reliability by modifying the path availability as follows:

$$f_p(r) = -\sum_{e \in r} \log(1 - p_e). \tag{1}$$

Note that the path reliability becomes high (resp. low) if $f_p(r)$ is small (resp. large). When a path includes at least one road segment with a high road blockage probability, (1) takes a remarkably high value. Thus, selecting a path according to (1) will enable evacuees to avoid blocked road segments as much as possible.

4.3   Path Selection

The length of path r, i.e., path length, is given by the sum of the length of all roads composing path r:

$$f_d(r) = \sum_{e \in r} d_e, \tag{2}$$

where d_e denotes the length of road $e \in E$. First, mobile device $n \in \mathcal{N}$ calculates candidates of the recommended routes as a set of k-shortest paths, $\mathcal{P}^{n,k}_{s,d}$ ($k \geq 1$), from current location $s \in \mathcal{V}$ to destination $d \in \mathcal{V}$. To enumerate the k-shortest paths, we can use existing algorithms, e.g., Yen's algorithm [18] and Pruned Landmark Labeling based approach [2]. Next, mobile device n selects recommended route $\widehat{p}^n_{s,d}$ with minimum path reliability $f_p(r)$,

$$\widehat{p}^n_{s,d} = \arg \min_{r \in \mathcal{P}^{n,k}_{s,d}} f_p(r). \tag{3}$$

Note that we can control the trade-off between speediness and reliability of evacuation by changing k. The proposed scheme with $k = 1$ is equivalent to the shortest path selection, while that with $k = \infty$ selects a path only based on path reliability.

5   Simulation Results

Through simulation experiments, we evaluate the effectiveness of the proposed scheme in terms of safety and speediness of evacuation.

5.1   Simulation Model

We used The ONE Simulator [13]. We also used the map of 3, 700 [m] × 2, 200 [m] southwest area of Nagoya station in Japan, which was provided by Nagoya city (Fig. 2). This map's internal graph structure is composed of 2,839 vertices and 5,252 directed edges. We assume a hundred evacuees with their own mobile devices. We set the simulation time to be 5, 000 [s]. When the simulation starts, a disaster occurs and the evacuees move from arbitrary points on the map (blue points in Fig. 2) to a refuge located near the center on the map (a green square in Fig. 2) at a speed of 4 [km/h].

We set measurement interval I_M to be 50 [s]. We assume communication ranges for mobile-to-mobile direct communication, e.g., Wi-Fi Direct, to be 100 [m] and communication ranges for communication with infrastructures, e.g., wireless LAN, to be 100 [m]. To focus on the effectiveness of the proposed scheme itself, we assume that mobile devices can finish retrieving information at each contact with other mobile devices and/or communication infrastructures. One wireless LAN access point (AP) is located at the refuge, and 25 AP's are placed in 5 × 5 grid arrangement.

As for disaster scenarios, we set the blocked road segments (red lines in Fig. 2) according to the road blockage probability of each edge on the graph. Nagoya city in Japan provides information of the road blockage probabilities for several classes depending on the degree of damages. In this paper, we use the data of maximum class that considers the possibility of all kinds of disasters. We set the

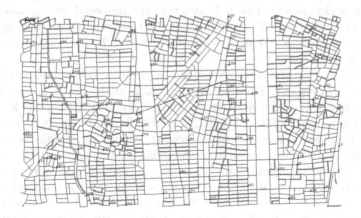

Fig. 2. Simulation area: 3, 700 [m] × 2, 200 [m] southwest area of Nagoya station in Japan. (Color figure online)

number k of the recommended route candidates to be an integer value in the range of $[1, 50]$.

We use two kinds of evaluation criteria. The first one is the total number of encounters with blocked road segments of all evacuees, which is related to the safety of evacuation. The second one is the average (resp. maximum) evacuation time among evacuees, to evaluate the speediness of evacuation. Here, we define the evacuation time as the time interval from evacuation start to the evacuation completion. The succeeding results are the average of 300 independent simulation experiments.

5.2   Evacuation Movements for Evaluation

The performance of the proposed scheme is affected by communication environments. Therefore, we evaluate the following three communication environments: INFRA+MOBILE, MOBILE, and OFFLINE. In case of INFRA+MOBILE, mobile devices can communicate both with other mobile devices and with communication infrastructures. In case of MOBILE, mobile devices can communicate only with other mobile devices. In case of OFFLINE, mobile devices can communicate neither with other mobile devices nor with communication infrastructures.

In order to show the upper bound of the performance of the proposed scheme, we also evaluate ideal evacuation (IDEAL), in which all evacuees know the information about all blocked road segments before the evacuation starts.

5.3   Total Number of Encounters with Blocked Road Segments

Figure 3 illustrates the relationship between the total number of encounters with blocked road segments of all evacuees and the number k of the recommended route candidates. First, we observe that the total number of encounters with blocked road segments monotonically decreases with k, regardless of the communication environments. This indicates that the proposed scheme can improve the safety of evacuation. We also find that the total number of encounters with blocked road segments steeply decreases when $k = 2$ and gradually decreases when $k > 3$.

Next, we focus on the performance of the proposed scheme under each communication environment. The improvement ratio of the result of $k = 10$ (resp. $k = 50$) to that of $k = 1$ becomes 28.4%, 33.2%, and 34.0% (resp. 36.2%, 43.3%, and 47.7%) in case of INFRA+MOBILE, MOBILE, and OFFLINE, respectively. Thus, the proposed scheme is robust against inferior communication environments. In [14], the existing automatic evacuation guiding scheme tries to improve evacuation by sharing information about blocked road segments among evacuees. In addition to this mechanism, the proposed scheme also tries to guide evacuees to refuges along safe routes to avoid encounters with blocked road segments as much as possible. As a result, the proposed scheme can achieve safe evacuation even under inferior communication environments.

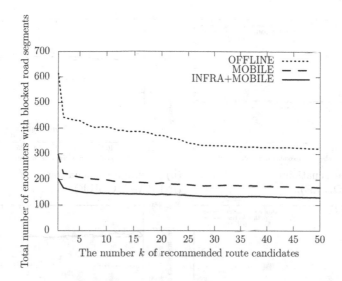

Fig. 3. Total number of encounters with blocked road segments.

5.4 Evacuation Time

In Sect. 5.3, we showed that the proposed scheme with $k \geq 2$ can reduce the number of encounters with blocked road segments by selecting more reliable evacuation routes. Increase of k, however, may also make the evacuation routes longer. In this section, we evaluate the effectiveness of the proposed scheme in terms of average evacuation time and maximum evacuation time.

Figures 4a, c, and e illustrate the transition of average evacuation time when changing k from 1 to 50 in case of INFRA+MOBILE, MOBILE, and OFFLINE, respectively. First, we focus on the impact of communication environments. We observe that INFRA+MOBILE and MOBILE show similar results while OFFLINE presents worse results than them. We also find that the proposed scheme with $k \geq 2$ can keep average evacuation time compared with that with $k = 1$, i.e., the shortest path selection, regardless of the communication environments. Specifically, the increase ratio of average evacuation time with $k \geq 2$ to that with $k = 1$ is not more than 4.8% (INFRA+MOBILE), 1.4% (MOBILE), and 1.8% (OFFLINE). This indicates that the proposed scheme can improve the safety of evacuation while keeping the average evacuation time.

Next, Figs. 4b, d, and f illustrate the transition of maximum evacuation time when changing k from 1 to 50 in case of INFRA+MOBILE, MOBILE, and OFFLINE, respectively. We first observe that the communication environments play an important role in reducing the maximum evacuation time. Next, we focus on the performance difference among path selection schemes in each communication environment. From Fig. 4b and d, the proposed scheme with $k \geq 2$ in case of INFRA+MOBILE and MOBILE can also suppress the increase of the maximum evacuation time as in the case of the average evacuation time. On the contrary,

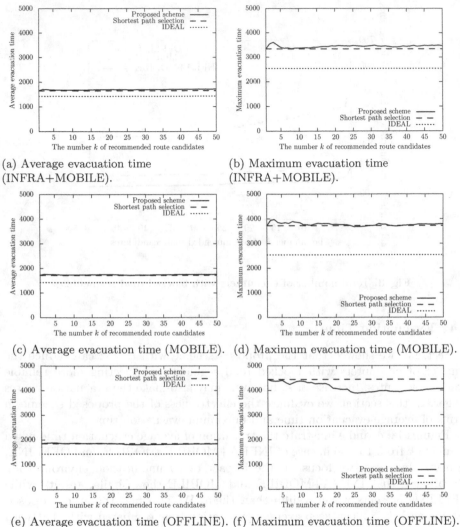

(a) Average evacuation time (INFRA+MOBILE).

(b) Maximum evacuation time (INFRA+MOBILE).

(c) Average evacuation time (MOBILE).

(d) Maximum evacuation time (MOBILE).

(e) Average evacuation time (OFFLINE).

(f) Maximum evacuation time (OFFLINE).

Fig. 4. Relationship between k and average/maximum evacuation time.

in case of OFFLINE (Fig. 4f), the proposed scheme with $k \geq 2$ can shorten the maximum evacuation time compared with the shortest path selection. In case of OFFLINE, mobile devices cannot obtain any information from others and thus selecting reliable evacuation routes becomes more important.

5.5 Appropriate Value of the Number k of Route Candidates

From the results in Sects. 5.3 and 5.4, we find that the proposed scheme can reduce the number of encounters with blocked road segments while keeping the average/maximum evacuation time by increasing k. In our scenario, $k = 25$ seems to be an appropriate value to achieve both safe and speedy evacuation. Note that the appropriate value of k may change depending on the shape of the map and the distribution of road blockage probabilities.

6 Conclusion

When a large-scale disaster occurs, evacuees have to evacuate to the refuge quickly and safely. The existing studies, however, use the shortest path selection for speedy evacuation, and pay less attention to the safety of the evacuation route. In this paper, we first defined the path reliability based on the road blockage probability of each road segment composing the path. Next, we further proposed a short and reliable path selection. The proposed scheme first calculates k-shortest ($k \geq 1$) paths from the evacuee's current location to the destination. Next, it selects the route with the highest path reliability from the candidates.

Through simulation experiments, we showed that the proposed scheme can improve the safety of evacuation in terms of the number of encounters blocked road segments, by increasing k, regardless of the communication environments. In addition, the proposed scheme with $2 \leq k \leq 50$ can keep the average/maximum evacuation time compared with the shortest path, i.e., the proposed scheme with $k = 1$. Thus, we showed that the proposed scheme can achieve both safe and speedy evacuation. As future work, we plan to propose a scheme to determine an appropriate range of k according to the shape of the map and the distribution of road blockage probabilities.

Acknowledgments. This research was partly supported by JSPS KAKENHI (15H04008) and (15K00126), Japan.

References

1. Ahuja, R.K., Magnanti, T.L., Orlin, J.B.: Network Flows: Theory, Algorithms, and Applications. Prentice-Hall Inc., Upper Saddle River (1993)
2. Akiba, T., Hayashi, T., Nori, N., Iwata, Y., Yoshida, Y.: Efficient top-k shortest-path distance queries on large networks by pruned landmark labeling. In: Proceedings of the Twenty-Ninth AAAI Conference on Artificial Intelligence, AAAI 2015, pp. 2–8. AAAI Press (2015). http://dl.acm.org/citation.cfm?id=2887007.2887008
3. Chen, A., Yang, H., Lo, H.K., Tang, W.H.: Capacity reliability of a road network: an assessment methodology and numerical results. Transp. Res. Part B: Methodol. **36**(3), 225–252 (2002)
4. Chen, X., Kwan, M.P., Li, Q., Chen, J.: A model for evacuation risk assessment with consideration of pre- and post-disaster factors. Comput. Environ. Urban Syst. **36**(3), 207–217 (2012). http://www.sciencedirect.com/science/article/pii/S019897151100113X
5. Church, R.L., Cova, T.J.: Mapping evacuation risk on transportation networks using a spatial optimization model. Transp. Res. Part C: Emerg. Technol. **8**(1–6), 321–336 (2000). http://www.sciencedirect.com/science/article/pii/S0968090X0000019X

6. City of Nagoya: Earthquake-Resistance City Development Policy (in Japanese). http://www.city.nagoya.jp/jutakutoshi/cmsfiles/contents/0000002/2717/honpen. pdf
7. Dijkstra, E.W.: A note on two problems in connexion with graphs. Numer. Math. 1(1), 269–271 (1959). http://dx.doi.org/10.1007/BF01386390
8. Dorigo, M., Birattari, M., Stutzle, T.: Ant colony optimization. IEEE Comput. Intell. Mag. 1(4), 28–39 (2006)
9. Fall, K.: A delay-tolerant network architecture for challenged internets. In: Proceedings of SIGCOMM 2003, pp. 27–34 (2003)
10. Fujihara, A., Miwa, H.: Disaster evacuation guidance using opportunistic communication: the potential for opportunity-based service. In: Bessis, N., Dobre, C. (eds.) Big Data and Internet of Things: A Roadmap for Smart Environments. SCI, vol. 546, pp. 425–446. Springer, Cham (2014). doi:10.1007/978-3-319-05029-4_18
11. Iida, Y.: Basic concepts and future directions of road network reliability analysis. J. Adv. Transp. 33(2), 125–134 (1999)
12. Iizuka, Y., Yoshida, K., Iizuka, K.: An effective disaster evacuation assist system utilized by an ad-hoc network. In: Stephanidis, C. (ed.) HCI 2011. CCIS, vol. 174, pp. 31–35. Springer, Heidelberg (2011). doi:10.1007/978-3-642-22095-1_7
13. Keränen, A., Ott, J., Kärkkäinen, T.: The ONE simulator for DTN protocol evaluation. In: Proceedings of the 2nd International Conference on Simulation Tools and Techniques, pp. 55:1–55:10 (2009)
14. Komatsu, N., Sasabe, M., Kawahara, J., Kasahara, S.: Automatic evacuation guiding scheme based on implicit interactions between evacuees and their mobile nodes. GeoInformatica 1–15 (2016). http://dx.doi.org/10.1007/s10707-016-0270-1
15. Lu, Q., George, B., Shekhar, S.: Capacity constrained routing algorithms for evacuation planning: a summary of results. In: Bauzer Medeiros, C., Egenhofer, M.J., Bertino, E. (eds.) SSTD 2005. LNCS, vol. 3633, pp. 291–307. Springer, Heidelberg (2005). doi:10.1007/11535331_17
16. Ministry of Internal Affairs, Communications: 2011 WHITE PAPER Information and Communications in Japan. http://www.soumu.go.jp/johotsusintokei/ whitepaper/eng/WP2011/2011-index.html
17. Mohammad, S., Ali, M., Mohammad, T.: Evacuation planning using multiobjective evolutionary optimization approach. Eur. J. Oper. Res. 198(1), 305–314 (2009). http://www.sciencedirect.com/science/article/pii/S037722170800670X
18. Yen, J.Y.: Finding the k shortest loopless paths in a network. Manage. Sci. 17(11), 712–716 (1971)
19. Yuan, Y., Wang, D.: Path selection model and algorithm for emergency logistics management. Comput. Ind. Eng. 56(3), 1081–1094 (2009). http://dx.doi.org/10.1016/j.cie.2008.09.033

Exploring Behavior Change Features for Mobile Workout Applications

Perin Ünal[1(✉)], Seyma Kucukozer Cavdar[1], Tuğba Taşkaya Temizel[1],
P. Erhan Eren[1], and Sriram Iyengar[2]

[1] Graduate School of Informatics, Middle East Technical University, Ankara, Turkey
perinunal@gmail.com, {kseyma,ltemizel,ereren}@metu.edu.tr
[2] College of Medicine Texas A&M Health Science Center, Houston, USA
iyengar@medicine.tamhsc.edu

Abstract. With the rapid emergence of mobile technologies in recent years, mobile health (m-health) has become fundamental to healthcare. Persuasion strategies and behavior change support features are widely used in m-health applications to increase the effectiveness of these applications on users. However, in the literature, there is a lack of research to analyze the current situation of m-health applications particularly from the perspective of behavior change approaches. In this study, the workout applications in the health and fitness category of Google Play store were selected and explored in terms of the relation of the features with the number of downloads and rating statistics obtained from the store. The findings are expected to be a guideline for application developers in order for m-health applications to be more effective in changing users' behaviors to lead a healthy life.

Keywords: Mobile applications · Mobile health · Behavior change

1 Introduction

Mobile health (m-health) is described as "emerging mobile communications and network technologies for healthcare systems" [1]. With the rapid emergence of mobile technologies in recent years, m-health has becomes fundamental to healthcare. Previous studies [2], show the important function of m-health in healthcare.

In recent years, persuasive technology and behavior change support systems (BCSS) have been increasingly used to raise the effectiveness of m-health applications. Technology that is intentionally designed to change a person's attitude or behavior is called persuasive technology [3]. BCSS are now widely applicable in m-health domain. They are designed to assist users in pursuing their goals in accordance with their needs a [4]. BCSS are also integrated with persuasive technology to increase the effectiveness of the applications.

Due to the growing interest in m-health applications, there is a need to better understand the ongoing situation of m-health applications particularly those that are based on behavior change approaches. So far, very few studies have been conducted to assess m-health applications. Significant features of applications need to be identified for m-health

M. Younas et al. (Eds.): MobiWIS 2017, LNCS 10486, pp. 45–53, 2017.
DOI: 10.1007/978-3-319-65515-4_4

applications to be adapted by a higher number of users and for developers to use these findings according to the needs of users.

Features that were previously mentioned in the literature [5–7] were used in the current study and the whole set was extended through hands-on research by obtaining the mobile physical activity applications from the Turkish and US versions of Google Play store. A total of 46 top workout applications were selected from the health and fitness category. After downloading and installing the applications, the features offered by these applications were classified according to their relativity. Workout applications were chosen mainly because they support behavior change and direct user to perform physical activity; there is a sufficient number of applications in this category to conduct statistical analysis, and the different types of workout applications allowed us to distinguish their specific characteristics.

The main objective of the study was to identify the important features of workout applications and investigate how they affect the number of downloads and rating of the application in the Google Play Store. The findings of the study will contribute to the field of BCSS, in particular by demonstrating the design issues of m-health applications and by providing an insight into the features that need to be included in an m-health application to be more effective in changing user behavior. In addition, the findings of this study can be a guideline for application developers in the m-health domain.

2   Related Work

Ploderer et al. [6] provided a general discussion on the approaches used in BCSS. Liu et al. [8] investigated the status of m-health applications for iOS devices. The authors mainly focused on the developer's perspective rather than the behavior change function of the applications. Similar to the current study, Liu et al. categorized the top 200 applications in Apple Store and provided an analysis of these applications in terms of their architecture, function and user satisfaction.

There are several studies investigating the factors that affect the use of m-health applications or motivate users carry out specific health-related activities through mobile applications. Munson and Consolvo [7] developed a mobile phone application to motivate users to perform physical activity and monitored 23 users over a four-week period. As a result, they found that the application feature that was most favored by all the participants was reminders and the rewards did not produce the expected result in terms of motivating the users. In addition, Munson and Consolvo reported on the limited benefits of sharing one's progress online. Harjumaa et al. [9] investigated ten application features and found self-monitoring, reduction and reminders to be the most motivating of all. In the same study, praise and rewards were only effective in certain cases. In the study by Dennison et al. [10], the users valued the applications providing tools to record and monitor behavior, setting goals and giving advice and information. On the other hand, context-sensing capabilities and social media interactions were considered to be unnecessary and unappealing.

In a similar study, Chang et al. [11] presented a framework that contained the effective factors on affecting user behavior in terms of downloading applications related to well-being. The factors included in this framework were; value, ease-of-use, trust, social support, attractiveness, diffusiveness, and fun and excitement. The authors then conducted a survey with users to evaluate 12 applications in terms of the above-mentioned factors. The results showed that the download and use of an application was highly correlated with needs, excitement, and usefulness.

The current study differs from the previous studies in that it focuses both on m-health applications and behavior change approaches [12]. Furthermore, different from the study by Liu et al. [4], in the current study, Android platform was chosen and the effect of features on the number of downloads and ratings of mobile workout applications were extensively analyzed. In addition, the quantitative analysis method was adopted to assess the features of m-health applications using live user data from the application store.

3   Methodology

In this study, quantitative research methodology was mainly used. The main stages of the study were; data collection, data analysis, and the interpretation of the results. The details about data collection and data analysis are given in the following sub-sections, and the results are discussed in the next chapter.

3.1   Data Collection Process

The scope of this study was to investigate the top workout mobile applications under the health and fitness category of the Android application store, Google Play Store, and to identify the effects of features on the number of downloads and ratings of these applications. Android platform was chosen since the effect of m-health applications in the Google Play Store is increasingly growing [13, 14]. Another reason was that Google Play store is the only application store that provides the download counts for mobile applications.

The US and Turkish versions of Google Play Store were used to obtain the application data. In the Turkish store, top free applications in the health and fitness category were listed using the 'Top Free Apps' button. From this list, the name, number of downloads, and rating information of the top 200 applications were recorded as of 7 December 2014. In Google Play store, the number of downloads is given as a range (for example 10 million – 20 million). Therefore, in the current study, the minimum number of downloads was recorded. The collection of data from the US store was performed in a similar way. However, since this store does not offer a 'Top Free Apps' list, popular applications were not in order. Furthermore, in this version of the store, the top and paid applications were not separated. As a result, a total of seven free workout applications were obtained from the US store.

The applications lists obtained from both stores were assessed in terms of their suitability for the current study using the following two criteria; the application language being English, and the application supporting a behavior change such as directing the user to perform physical activity. Therefore, applications that only provided information and did not motivate users to undertake any physical activity were excluded from the study since they did not support behavior change.

Following the elimination process according to the above-mentioned criteria, a total of 46 top free applications were chosen from both stores. Each application was screened by at least two different reviewers for the extraction of features related to behavior change. In this process, first, one reviewer screened all applications. Then, three other reviewers assessed an equal number of applications. In cases where there was a conflict between the two reviewers, a third reviewer screened the application in question and the decision was made by the majority (2 of 3). As a result of the screening process, a total of 23 features were obtained from the 46 applications. After the installation of the applications on a smartphone using the Android operating system version 4.3, each application was further analyzed in terms of the presence of features presented in Table 1.

Table 1. Descriptive statistics of features for workout applications

Feature	Number of applications with the feature	Number of applications without the feature
Prompt practice	46	0
Provide exercise programs for each sport type	46	0
Provide instruction on exercises	41	5
Prompt for hydration	39	7
Self-reports	25	21
Reminders	23	23
Share on Facebook	23	23
Voice Coach	18	28
Share on Twitter	17	29
Share activity summary via other apps on device	16	30
Share on Google+	11	35
Visualize activity statistics	9	37
Provide a social platform	8	38
Create own workout	8	38
Share with community friends	7	39
Challenge previous performance levels	6	40
Select sport type	5	41
Challenge with community friends	3	43
Prompt specific goal setting	2	44
News feed reporting others' activities	2	44
Message exchanges on a social platform	2	44
Music list	1	45
Link to music player	1	45

3.2 Data Analysis

In order to identify significant features on dependent variables, we performed selection through the Minimum-Redundancy Maximum-Relevance (mRMR) method [15] using the R Project for Statistical Computing. In this study, the mRMR algorithm was chosen to identify the features that best describe the target variable, number of downloads and ratings of the applications.

To explore whether there is a significant difference, first, normality of data is checked using Kolmogorov-Smirnov test. The results revealed that the significance values were lower than 0.05 (D(46) = .44, p < .05; D(46) = .17, p < .05), so the data was not normally distributed. When the data is not normally distributed, based on the rank order of observations, non-parametric tests can be performed by sacrificing some information such as the magnitude of difference. Since the data was not normally distributed, we used the Mann Whitney U Test as the non-parametric test to analyze the relationship between the dependent and independent variables. As suggested by Cohen [16], an ANOVA test requires at least 26 data points to observe large differences between the groups. Therefore, features with a minimum of 20 data points were selected as independent variables. The statistical analysis was performed using Statistical Package for the Social Sciences (SPSS) version 22. The results of the tests are presented in Sect. 4.

4 Results and Discussion

Based on the results of the mRMR algorithm, workout applications' features were ordered by their effect on the number of downloads and rating values. As shown in Fig. 1, the first one, 'message exchanges', has a significant effect on the number of downloads. The average number of downloads for applications offering message exchanges is nearly 5 million whereas those that do not provide it is only about 1 million. The effect of other features is relatively smaller, and in the last two of them ('share activity summary via other apps on device', and 'prompt for hydration'), the average

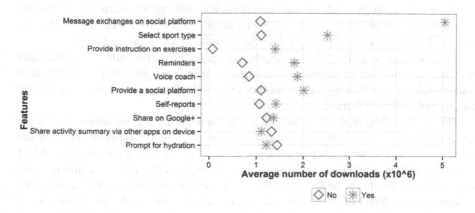

Fig. 1. Differences between the average numbers of downloads of workout applications with and without the given features

number of downloads of applications that do not support these features is even higher than those that do. These two features are plotted in order to show the reduced effect. The remaining features had a non-positive effect on the number of downloads, and therefore were not included in the figure.

The same analysis was performed in the analysis of the rating values of workout applications. Figure 2 presents the significant features of these applications. The first six were found to have a positive effect, which means that if an application had them, then its rating was higher. In order to show the difference in the effect, the last feature, 'Prompt for hydration', was also plotted. The remaining features did not have a positive effect on the rating values.

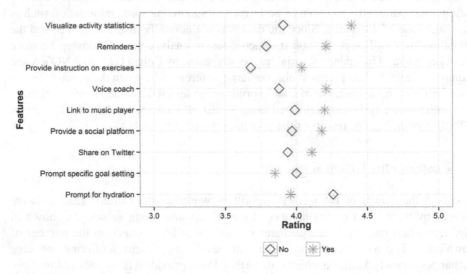

Fig. 2. Differences between the average ratings of workout applications (over 5) with and without the given features

Since only reminders, sharing on Facebook and self-reports features satisfied the minimum number of data points to conduct a statistical test, they were included in the statistical analysis. Table 2 presents the results of the Mann-Whitney U Test.

The results presented in Table 2 indicate that the feature of reminders is significantly related to the number of downloads and rating. Workout applications offering such features have a significantly higher number of downloads and rating than other applications without these features.

The results of the analyses showed that the features of the applications are significantly related with the user behavior in terms of downloading and rating the applications in the store. The features of top workout applications, which were downloaded by minimum 1000 users revealed the significance of features offered in these applications. To our knowledge, this is the first study that used an empirical hands-on research method to determine the effect of the features in workout applications on the number of downloads and user rating levels using live data from users in the application store.

Table 2. The results of the Mann-Whitney U Test to determine the relationship between the selected features/social approaches and the number of downloads/rating (workout applications)

Selected Features		N	Downloads				Rating			
			Mean Rank	U	Z	p	Mean Rank	U	Z	p
Self-reports	Yes	25	25.96	201.00	−1.42	.16	25.88	203.00	−1.32	.19
	No	21	20.57				20.67			
Reminders	Yes	23	30.11	112.50	−3.50	**.00***	30.74	98.00	−3.68	**.00***
	No	23	16.89				16.26			
Share on Facebook	Yes	23	22.02	230.50	−.78	.43	22.28	236.50	−.62	.54
	No	23	24.98				24.72			

One of the three applicable features for statistical analysis, reminders, were found to have a significant effective both on the number of downloads and on rating. This means that if a workout application offers the reminder feature, the number of download and rating of that application is higher than other applications without the same feature. In the literature, reminders were also found to be the most contributing feature to changing user behavior [10].

Significant differences were found in workout applications in terms of the number of downloads and ratings as shown in Figs. 1 and 2. Message exchanges, selecting sport type and providing instruction on exercises were found to be the common three features in terms of the high number of downloads. When the relationship between the features and the ratings of workout applications was considered, the mostly observed three were; visualizing activity statistics, reminders and providing instruction on exercises. One factor on the discrepancy between the relevant features in terms of the number of downloads and rating of workout applications can be related to how the particular characteristics are implemented in terms of the user interface and usability. Our findings clearly show that there is a large discrepancy between the reasons for downloading an application and its final rating. This can be attributed to users not being satisfied with the quality or the implementation of the features that initially attracted them to download the applications. Application developers can use our findings to improve in order to enhance utility and usability of their applications and thereby improve the ratings of their applications.

5 Conclusion and Future Work

In this study, 46 m-health applications obtained from the Turkish and US version of Google Play store were investigated in terms of their behavior change support features. The main aim was to identify the significant features of m-health applications that affect the number of downloads and rating of the applications in the store. For the purpose of the study, several statistical analyses were conducted and visual representations of the results were presented in this paper.

The main contribution of the study was to provide a guideline for the developers of m-health applications. Based on our findings, when designing and developing m-health applications, designers can focus on certain aspects relevant to the specific types of application, such as workouts, to achieve a higher number of downloads and higher ratings. These specific features can be added to applications to build effective BCSS in the health domain, particularly when combined with the guidelines stated in [17, 18]. The theoretical ground can be incorporated into mobile applications with the help of clinicians and experts on health behavior change to develop better applications.

There are few limitations in the study. First, the analysis was limited to the applications in the Google Play store since it is the only application store that provides the download counts. Second, even though both Turkish and USA versions of Google Play store were explored, the analysis was limited to English language applications. Finally, only workout applications of health and fitness category are analyzed in this study. For future research, it is suggested that different sub categories in the m-health domain be investigated.

References

1. Istepanian, R.S.H., Pattichis, C.S., Laxminarayan, S.: Introduction to mobile M-health systems. In: Micheli-Tzanakou, E. (ed.) M-Health: Emerging Mobile Health Systems, pp. 3–14. Springer, New York (2006)
2. Norris, A.C., Stockdale, R.S., Sharma, S.: A strategic approach to M-Health. Health Inform. J. **15**(3), 244–253 (2009)
3. Fogg, B.J.: Persuasive technology: using computers to change what we think and do. Ubiquity **3**(44), 2 (2002)
4. Oinas-Kukkonen, H.: A foundation for the study of behavior change support systems. Pers. Ubiquitous Comput. **17**(6), 1223–1235 (2012)
5. Oinas-Kukkonen, H., Harjumaa, M.: Persuasive systems design: key issues, process model, and system features. Commun. Assoc. Inf. Syst. **24**, 485–500 (2009)
6. Ploderer, B., Reitberger, W., Oinas-Kukkonen, H., van Gemert-Pijnen, J.: Social interaction and reflection for behaviour change. Pers. Ubiquitous Comput. **18**, 1667–1676 (2014)
7. Munson S., Consolvo, S.: Exploring goal-setting, rewards, self-monitoring, and sharing to motivate physical activity. In: Proceedings of the 6th International Conference on Pervasive Computing Technologies for Healthcare, pp. 25–32. IEEE Press, San Diego (2012)
8. Liu, C., Zhu, Q., Holroyd, K.A., Seng, E.K.: Status and trends of mobile-health applications for ios devices: a developer's perspective. J. Syst. Softw. **84**(11), 2022–2033 (2011)
9. Harjumaa, M., Segerståhl, K., Oinas-Kukkonen, H.: Understanding Persuasive System Functionality in Practice: A Field Trial of Polar FT60. In: Proceedings of the Fourth International Conference on Persuasive Technology, PERSUASIVE 2009, Claremont, California, USA (2009)
10. Dennison, L., Morrison, L., Conway, G., Yardley, L.: Opportunities and challenges for smartphone applications in supporting health behavior change: qualitative study. J. Med. Internet Res. **15**(4), e86 (2013)
11. Chang, T., Kaasinen, E., Kaipainen, K.: What Influences users' decisions to take apps into use? A framework for evaluating persuasive and engaging design in mobile apps for well-being. In: Proceedings of the 11th International Conference on Mobile and Ubiquitous Multi Proceeding, MUM 2012, pp. 1–10. ACM New York (2012)

12. Unal, P., Temizel, T.T., Eren, P.E.: An exploratory study on the outcomes of influence strategies in mobile application recommendations. In: 2nd International Workshop on Behavior Change Support Systems, pp. 27–40 (2014)
13. Butler, M.: Android: changing the mobile landscape. IEEE Pervasive Comput. **10**(1), 4–7 (2011)
14. Gavalas, D., Economou, D.: Development platforms for mobile applications: status and trends. IEEE Softw. **28**(1), 77–86 (2011)
15. Peng, H., Long, F., Ding, C.: Feature selection based on mutual information: criteria of max-dependency, max-relevance, and min-redundancy. IEEE Trans. Pattern Anal. Mach. Intell. **27**(8), 1226–1238 (2005)
16. Cohen, J.: A power primer. Psychol. Bull. **112**(1), 155–159 (1992)
17. Oduor, M., Alahäivälä, T., Oinas-Kukkonen, H.: Persuasive software design patterns for social influence. Pers. Ubiquitous Comput. **18**(7), 1689–1704 (2014)
18. Stibe, A.: Advancing typology of computer-supported influence: moderation effects in socially influencing systems. In: MacTavish, T., Basapur, S. (eds.) PERSUASIVE 2015. LNCS, vol. 9072, pp. 253–264. Springer, Cham (2015). doi:10.1007/978-3-319-20306-5_23

Mobile Web - Practice and Experience

Prediction of Conditions for Drying Clothes Based on Area and Temperature Data

Marketa Stastna[1], Jan Dvorak[1], Ali Selamat[1,2],
and Ondrej Krejcar[1(✉)]

[1] Faculty of Informatics and Management,
Center for Basic and Applied Research, University of Hradec Kralove,
Rokitanskeho 62, 500 03 Hradec Kralove, Czech Republic
{marketa.stastna, jan.dvorak}@uhk.cz,
Ondrej@Krejcar.org
[2] Faculty of Computing, Universiti Teknologi Malaysia, 81310 Johor Bahru,
Johor, Malaysia
aselamat@utm.my

Abstract. These days systems for housework automation become more and more popular, as well as a trend of intelligent households develops. This paper deals with description of problems while creating a mobile application intended to facilitate the household care in area of drying clothes. The application uses technology of acquiring user's location by GPS or Wi-Fi module and communication with a web service. This paper focuses particularly on fundamental application functionality, which is a recommendation, whether it is advisable to hang outside clothes that just have been washed and for how long. The calculation of the time when the laundry will be dry depends on many variables, including detected weather in the given area. The problem was solved using a calculation of absorbing water into air, which unwinds of formulas for calculation of water vapour pressure. Therefore the result of the project is an application using the abovementioned calculations for practical simplification of household care.

Keywords: Smart application · Clothes drying · Forecast · Water vapour · Moist air, Android

1 Introduction

Nowadays mobile devices develop more and more, as well as there are widening areas covered by various smart mobile applications. This paper targets the range of household care, which becomes increasingly popular, either in the scope of automation of the household processes, robotisation, intelligent devices, or whole smart systems for household care. Thanks to the various systems and applications working in this area, the users can gain precious free time extra and save their effort connected with housework. The importance of this topic has been notified by a collective of authors from Ryukoku University, who has dealt with classification of different kinds of washed laundry and detection of the laundry condition using video and 3D sensors in the article [1]. In other article [2] authors concern pairing socks by image processing

© Springer International Publishing AG 2017
M. Younas et al. (Eds.): MobiWIS 2017, LNCS 10486, pp. 57–69, 2017.
DOI: 10.1007/978-3-319-65515-4_5

and 3D sensors and they point out to the lack of automatic systems in the area of folding and tidying clothes, which proves that it is still useful to develop new systems in this area. Article [3] offers optimal conditions for prevention of electrostatic charge in clothes using calculation for electrostatic characteristics in laundry during the drying process (Table 1).

Table 1. Data about the clothes

Type	Weight	Weight of the wet	Coefficient	Material
Trousers	560	905	0.6160	cotton
T-shirt 1	210	370	0.7619	cotton
Sock	26	46	0.7692	cotton
Sweat pants	370	520	0.4054	cotton/polyester
T-shirt 2	130	230	0.7692	cotton
T-shirt 3	140	190	0.3571	polyester

The very calculations for the process of drying laundry or any other object are not a simple matter, because they depend on many variables, such as air temperature, air humidity, atmospheric pressure and many others, including air-circulation speed. The problem of moisture saturated air-circulation speed was analysed in article by R. Zakinyan and col. [4], in which there are released new formulas for moisture saturated air-circulation. However, the drying process does not depend just on temperature conditions, but also on the type of the clothes itself, that is on its material and weight, which makes the whole problem even more complicated (Table 2).

Table 2. Results of the experiments

Type	Weight	Expected time to dry	h	min
Trousers	560	1731	28	51
T-shirt 1	210	803	13	23
Sock	26	100	1	40
Sweat pants	370	753	12	33
T-shirt 2	130	502	8	22
T-shirt 3	140	251	4	11

This article deals with creating a mobile application intended to facilitate the household care in the area of drying laundry. The processes in household are generally closely mutually linked and they depend on many other events and conditions. Drying laundry must follow directly after process of washing and it can vary according to a specific household. While in some households there is used automatic clothes dryer, elsewhere clothes are being dried inside the house, whereas other families prefer to dry clothes in the fresh air, which depends on variable outdoor conditions. Exactly for these was created the application described in this article.

The application with this purpose should be user adaptive, so that its results correspond with individual needs of a specific user. The user can apply the application to manage the process of drying clothes, while the clothes may be divided into several batches, where each of them can finish drying in a different time. It's obvious, that the application must take into account the temperature data, on which the process depends. These data relate to the location, in which the user is situated [15]. Therefore it is essential, that the application detects the user's position, and on the basis of this position it inquires about the temperature information in given area (Table 3).

Table 3. Comparison the predicted VS real values

Type of the clothes	h	min	h real	min real
Trousers	28	51	28	30
T-shirt 1	13	23	12	15
Sock	1	40	4	0
Sweat pants	12	33	12	15
T-shirt 2	8	22	8	15
T-shirt 3	4	11	4	0

The application described by this article detects the user's position using GPS module, Wi-Fi and mobile transmitter, which are included in an access to the user's location through Google API [16]. The application also communicates with a web service [12], from which it gains information about temperature, air humidity, wind speed, amount of precipitation or snowfalls. Out of this service it also obtains answers to further time periods, in order to make the calculations the most precise and adequate to the temperature changes. Nevertheless, at the same time it's necessary to consider the possibility of changing the forecast, which is definitely not improbable, and to alert the user about the change appropriately, so that the user takes into account for instance a coming rain, which wasn't considered by the previous calculation.

2 Problem Definition

The objective of this article is to design and implement a mobile application for Android platform, which suggests to the user, whether it is advisable to hang washed clothes outside. This application not only gives the recommendation, but it also displays, in what time a selected batch of clothes will be dried up or whether it is expected that a rain or a snowfall comes during the drying. As it was said already, the goal of this application is to save user's free time and effort that the user would spend for example by unnecessary hanging clothes, while it's about to rain soon. Because the laundry is washed in several batches, the application should enable to manage these batches and information about them. Today there exist two applications for Android platform, which attempt to carry out a similar issue (Table 4).

The first of them is an application Drying Rack [5], which notifies the user, until what period he/she can hang the clothes outside. The user can set up weather

Table 4. Evaluation of our VS other algorithms

	Recommendation	Calculation	Widget	Notification	Batch management
Laundry forecast	✔	✔	✖	✔	✔
Drying days	✔	✖	✔	✖	✖
Drying rack	✔	✖	✔	✔	✖

monitoring, so that the application notifies him/her, whether the rain is coming. However, the application does not even deal with the calculation of the current time to complete drying the clothes, next it is not possible to change type of the hanging clothes, as well as the actually hanging clothes batches could not be tracked. Therefore this application does not meet the defined requirements.

The second solution is an application Drying Days [6]. Although this application uses the current weather detected according to the user's position, on the other side it does not work with the ascertained information to the maximum benefit of the user. Based on the temperature data the application only announces to the user by an evaluation from 0 to 5, whether it is advisable to hang the clothes outside, but it does not even display the time period, when the clothes are going to be dried up. As well as the previous application this one also does not allow to manage different batches of clothes, when a specific batch may dry up in other time than another one (according to the type of material etc.). Therefore this application is unsatisfactory as well.

On Google Play there can be found many applications for the weather forecast, which can also serve to help with planning of drying the clothes. It seems that the best out of these applications for this objective is an application Weather Timeline – Forecast [7]. This one displays the weather clearly in a timeline, whereas it's possible to display the forecast view in intervals of one hour, and on this basis there can be made a conclusion about the right planning for drying. However, the application is still just an application about weather and none of the other requirements (a recommendation, whether it is advisable to hang the clothes outside, displaying the dry-up time etc.) are fulfilled using it.

While designing the application there arose two main problems. The first one is the very calculation of speed of water absorption from clothes into the air, which has to be deduced from physical formulas for absorbing vapour into saturated and unsaturated air. The second problem happens to be the detection of the user's position, which does not have to be absolutely precise though (weather doesn't differ with an accuracy of meter) and assorting an optimal web service, which can utilise this position to provide temperature data in given area, which are needed for the aforesaid calculation.

The specialist article [8] could help to solve the first part, because it focuses on a solution for manual washing and drying clothes by designing a theoretical model and its validation on practical experiments. But closer it aims to physical models for wringing clothes, which are also interesting objects of scientific research, but are not useful for the goal of this project. The article by J. Zemitis and col. [9] deals with production of humidity in a home environment caused by various sources, while it focuses especially on amount of water produced into the air by domestic tasks such as washing or drying clothes. This article provides interesting experiments, such as recording a weight of different kinds of clothes before washing, after washing and in specific time intervals after washing. These data can help while solving the problem of drying clothes velocity, especially while testing the selected algorithm, but only in some limits, because it deals with drying clothes in the indoor environment. Besides, the article does not provide suitable mathematic models to solve the problem.

The article [10] concerns with an effect of humidity on a speed of drying carpet tiles during industrial drying, which depends on temperature of a gas stream and its velocity. However, these calculations are inapplicable, because they can't be used for the outdoor drying. The abovementioned article by J. Zakinyan and col. [4] describes the thermal circulation of moisture saturated air in the lower layers of the atmosphere. This circulation definitely influences the drying process, but while solving our problem it will be sufficient to use influence of the wind speed, which can be easily gained by a web service, in contrast with that detailed functions of the circulation with many hardly obtainable variables that would influence the drying speed only minimally compared to the other variables.

The second part of the problem is to determine the user's position. An automatic function of mobile devices today is GPS module, just as Wi-Fi module and equally it is possible to determine the user's position by a mobile transmitter. For the most perfect and the most stable detection of the user's position it is suitable to use all three of the possibilities together, specifically in the way, that they appropriately complement with each other in the case of failure of one or two of them. That is possible by using Google Location API, which enables to gain the current user's position and return its coordinates.

The problem of assigning the right algorithm for the speed of drying clothes (resp. water absorption) is not satisfactorily solved in the abovementioned articles, because they don't provide the optimal drying model. Therefore it is necessary to build the desired algorithm using the known physical formulas for the pressure of water vapour in saturated and unsaturated air, the experiments with drying clothes and to make a well-balanced consideration to create the optimal drying model for the purpose of this application.

3 New Solution

This chapter concerns with solving the problems described in the previous chapter, particularly the problem of creating the calculation for drying, because the issue of obtaining the user's position can be successfully figured out by Google Location API [16], as it was mentioned above. To create the desired algorithm we take inspiration from previous work [17, 18]. It turned out to be convenient using the physical formulas for pressure of water vapour and relative air humidity, mentioned for example in the article [11]. The empiric formulas for pressure of water vapour at temperature within the limits of the earth's climate is following:

$$p_s = 610.78 * \exp(\frac{t}{(t + 238.3)} * 17.2694),$$

where p_s stands for saturated vapour and t stands for temperature in degrees Celsius. Relative humidity is defined by a correlation

$$RH = \frac{p}{p_s},$$

out of which can be derived actual pressure p. For conversion of water vapour pressure into concentration in units $\frac{kg}{m^3}$ it is possible to use an expression

$$\frac{0.002166 * p}{(t + 273.16)}.$$

This way we can use both information about temperature and information about humidity, yet there remains dependence on the wind speed, which increases (with the increasing wind speed it grows the speed of drying) and was selected on the basis of the consideration. The calculation takes into account given weight of the object (clothes), which is then divided by the calculated concentration. The algorithm expects a simplification of amount of the air surrounding clothes of different sizes to one cubic meter, and at the same time it simplifies the time, in which a certain weight of water in grams is absorbed into the air. The calculation must take into account also the forecast for the next time periods, because all the temperature data change over time. To solve this request it was created the algorithm described by the flow diagram (Fig. 1).

In the beginning the algorithm sets the weight to be absorbed as the initial weight of water in the clothes, which is derived from the weight of the clothes and the type of the clothes material. Then there runs the cycle, where there's consequently calculated the time until the next forecast (the time of the next forecast can vary in dependence on the area) and the weight, which is going to be absorbed over this time. If the water to be absorbed is greater than the already absorbed weight (which means it's still necessary to continue drying), then the already absorbed weight has to be deducted from it and the cycle can continue. But if this time allows absorbing more water than is needed, then it's necessary to end the cycle and count the precise time, over which the residual weight can be absorbed. In the end the time to dry is added together as the sum of all the times from the completed cycles and of the residual time.

To introduce the application functionality closer it was created an indicative flow diagram, which simplifically displays, how the application behaves. First of all when opening the application, it obtains the user's position and on its basis it detects the temperature data in the given area (temperature, humidity, wind speed, rainfalls, snowfalls etc.). If the application is opened for the first time, it pre-sets some default clothes values, which can be consequently simply reset by the user. When the user opens the application already for the second time, the values stay saved from the previous opening. Based on all of these information it's performed the described calculation of the time to dry and the application provides the user with the recommendation, whether it is advisable to hang the clothes outside or not and explains why (it displays the actual temperature data and the information, whether it is going to rain or snow). If it's advisable to hang the clothes outside, then the application displays a possibility to set up a new batch of clothes, that is to start drying such designated

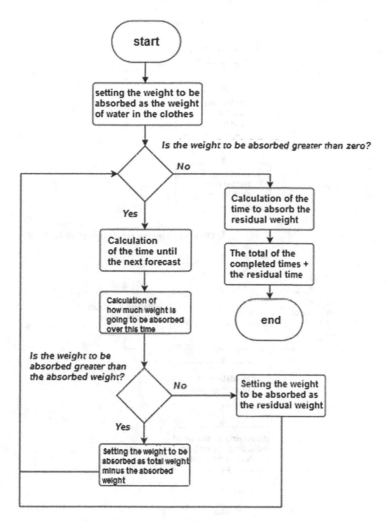

Fig. 1. Algorithm for drying calculation

clothes. After selecting this option the application moves to a screen allowing management of these batches. See the flow diagram (Fig. 2).

The essential part of the application is also a service for informing the user about a change of the forecast. That service is being started always in a specific time, so that it doesn't consume too much system resources, and after performing its job it ends again. For each drying batch the service verifies, whether the forecast in the particular area has changed, and if yes, then it displays a notification about the coming rain or snow.

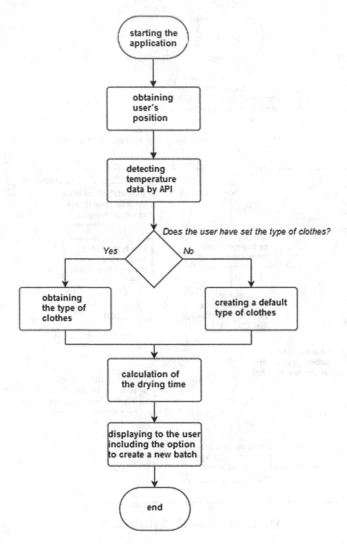

Fig. 2. Flow diagram when starting the application

4   Implementation

This chapter concerns about implementation of the application. As it was aforementioned, to detect the user's position it was selected Google Location API and to determine the drying speed it was implemented the algorithm described above. Also it was necessary to consider saving data that the application needs for running, which means the data about the currently drying batches, the setting of type and material of the user's clothes etc. To store these data it wasn't necessary to use any of the larger databases, it was sufficient to utilize a storage provided by a class SharedPreferences, where it's possible to save the data as couples characterised as key-value.

The drying batches are represented by a list of instances of a class Batch, so it was suitable to save them as objects. That was realized using a library Gson, which allows to convert an object into Json format and consequently to convert this string back to the object Batch. For the notifications it was created a class NotificationService, which is a descendent of a class Service. This class consists of an inner class PollTask. That one is a descendant of an asynchronous task and in the background it takes care of detecting the forecast change.

The regular initializing of the service ones in a certain time is provided by a class AlarmManager. The appearance of the application was selected the easiest and the most comprehensible for the user, as well as its control. It was considered, that the application should be graphically comfortable for the best possible user experience. Out of this reason the design of the application was provided with several pastel colours and with representative icons. The following pictures were taken using an emulator, set for various locations, with a purpose to show all the application's possibilities. The figure (Fig. 3) shows the notification, which displays in the case that the forecast has changed, and it is going to rain. The notification shows the time, when it's going to start raining, and the batch that has to be taken inside.

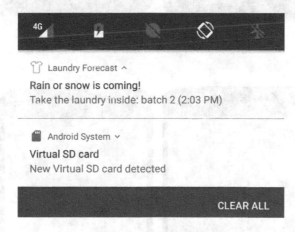

Fig. 3. Notification

In the figure (Fig. 4) you can see the appearance of the main screen of the application – the picture on the left shows the suggestion to hang the laundry outside and the time to dry, the picture on the right notifies about the coming rain. The pictures below show other screens of the application intended for the batch management and setting the preferences.

In the screen (Fig. 5) on the left you can see the screen for the batch management. It provides information about the individual batches, as for example time of hanging out, type of the laundry, location, where the laundry was hanged out, and also the information about possible coming rain or snow. On the left there are also orientation numbers of the batches, which were assigned to the batches for their greater clarity. The batches are listed

Fig. 4. Main screen of the application

Fig. 5. Batch management and setting

consequently according to the starting time of the drying. The most important part of this screen is the right column containing the information, whether the batch is already dried up (Done), or whether the forecast has changed and it's going to rain, and therefore it's necessary to take the laundry inside (Rain), or the batch is just being dried. In that case it displays the time remaining until the end of the drying, which is being actualized every minute. Any batch can be deleted by one long click.

In the figure (Fig. 5) at right there is shown the screen with setting the type of the laundry. Here the user may select from various types of the laundry relevant to a specific weight. If there are more types of the laundry in one batch, it is suitable to use the heaviest type. Equally the user may select the type of material of the laundry. When confirmed with a button, the application returns to the main screen, where it shows the calculation adapted to the new values.

5 Testing of Developed Application

In this chapter there will be tested the selected algorithm for the time to dry. It's not supposed to be perfectly precise, but because the drying itself is not an easy process, but in contrary it depends on many surrounding events, which wouldn't be even pursuant to involve in the application (for example spaces between the individual pieces of clothing on the drying rack, production technology of the clothes). However, it would be appropriate, if the success rate of the forecast was minimally 80%, i.e. only one of the five batches can last more than it was predicted. According to the fact, that in this season in our latitude it's winter and snow, the application suggests not to hang the laundry outside at all, and therefore it is even impossible to test the algorithm in the outside environment. Accordingly it was chosen a method of inner testing, even though it is limited by not existing wind speed and even the temperature doesn't change over time. The testing environment was defined as follows:

- temperature 21, 9°C,
- humidity 47%.

Data about the clothes. The following table determines information about the clothes used in the experiment. Particularly it is important the type of material, which is in relation with a coefficient (the weight of the dry clothes divided by the weight of the wet clothes) and the weight of the clothes. Based on these coefficients there were configured the default coefficients of the different materials in the application.

Results of the experiments. The following table determines the expected results of drying for the aforesaid clothes in the given environment. The column "expected time to dry" states the time returned by the calculation in minutes.

In the table below there are compared the values of the expected time against the real one.

Most of the tested subjects finished the drying a little earlier that the expected time, which signifies a good result. Only one piece of clothing dried up over more than twice longer period than it was expected, which could have been caused by a specific type of fabric.

Comparing the application with the others. The following table compares functionality of the application with the two other mentioned applications on Google Play with the similar orientation.

As you can see, the application Laundry Forecast fulfils the resolved goals. In contrary the other two applications do not consist of the calculation of the time to dry or do not enable the batch management. In contrast to that it would be suitable to complementthe application Laundry Forecast with a widget, which isn't missing in both of the other applications and comes out as a prospective enhancement of this application.

6 Conclusions

The objective of this paper was to create the mobile application that would make the user's household care easier, concretely when drying the laundry. The goal of the application was to provide the user with the recommendation, whether it is advisable to hang the washed laundry outside, and the calculation of the time to dry. Next the application should notify the user about coming rain or snow. For the scope of the application it was created the algorithm for calculation of the time to absorb the water from the laundry into the air, which was consequently tested in the previous chapter in the practical experiments. The algorithm considers prospective weather forecast provided by a web service. This solution saves user's energy and time, because then he/she can plan the processes of the household care more effectively. The solution could be enhanced with a new functionality and consequently applied in new areas, where it's needed the calculation of time to dry of some fabrics or even other objects. The application was created for Android platform and it utilizes the detection of the user's position, by which it locates temperature data of given area. The application accomplishes the specified requirements. Future research for such kind of Smart Applications development will be focussed also on development of Smart application for people with dementia [13, 14] for which can be very useful to have some application for detection of known people faces, because they often forgot their faces due to mentioned diseases.

Acknowledgement. This work and the contribution were supported by project "SP-2102-2017-Smart Solutions for Ubiquitous Computing Environments" Faculty of Informatics and Management, University of Hradec Kralove, Czech Republic.

References

1. Corral, L., Sillitti, A., Succi, G.: Mobile multiplatform development: an experiment for performance analysis. In: Procedia Computer Science, vol. 10, pp. 736–743 (2012). doi:10.1016/j.procs.2012.06.094
2. Daiky, H., Tsutomu, M., Kazuki, M., Avaneysan, K.: A study of laundry tidiness: laundry state determination using video and 3d sensors. Energy Build. **127**(1), 19 (2016). doi:10.1007/978-3-662-46742-8_2

3. Kakuzki, M., Tsutomu, M., Daihi, H., Avanesyan, K.: A study of laundry tidiness: socks pairing using video and 3D sensors. Energy Build. **127**(1), 303 (2016). doi:10.1007/978-3-662-46742-8_28
4. Park, C.H., Chung, S.E., Yun, C.S.: Effect of drying condition on the electrostatic characteristics of the laundry. Fibers Polym. **8**(4), 432–437 (2007). doi:10.1007/BF02875834
5. Zakinyan, R., Zakinyan, A., Ryzhkov, R., Avaneysan, K.: Convection of moist saturated air: analytical study. Atmosphere **7**(1), 8 (2016). doi:10.3390/atmos7010008. [cit. 2017-01-03]
6. Drying Rack (Weather). In: Google Play. Google (2017). https://play.google.com/store/apps/details?id=com.rustedgears.stendipanni&hl=cs. Accessed 03 Jan 2017
7. Drying Days. In: Google Play Google (2017). https://play.google.com/store/apps/details?id=com.tyrell.dryingdays. Accessed 03 Jan 2017
8. Weather Timeline - Forecast. In: Google Play Google (2017). https://play.google.com/store/apps/details?id=com.samruston.weather&hl=cs. Accessed 03 Jan 2017
9. Rahmayanti, H.D., Utami, F.D., Abdullah, M.: Physics model for wringing of wet cloth. Eur. J. Phys. **37**(6), 065806 (2016). 10.1088/0143-0807/37/6/065806
10. Zemitis, J., Borodinecs, A., Frolova, M., Avanesyan, K.: Measurements of moisture production caused by various sources: analytical study. Energy Build. **127**(1), 884–891 (2016). doi:10.1016/j.enbuild.2016.06.045
11. O'Dell, D.R., Carr, W.W.: Effect of humidity on the drying rates of carpet tiles. Text. Res. J. **66**(6), 366–376 (1996). doi:10.1177/004051759606600603
12. Sobeslav, V., Maresova, P., Krejcar, O., Costa Franca, T.C., Kuca, K.: Use of cloud computing in biomedicine. J. Biomol. Struct. Dyn. **34**(12), 2688–2697 (2016)
13. Klimova, B., Maresova, P.: Computer-based training programs for older people with mild cognitive impairment and/or dementia. Front. Hum. Neurosci. **11**(1), 1–9 (2017). ISSN 1662-5161
14. Klimova, B., Maresova, P., Kuca, K.: Assistive technologies for managing language disorders in dementia. Neuropsychiatr. Dis. Treat. **12**(1), 533–540 (2016)
15. Benikovsky, J., Brida, P., Machaj, J.: Proposal of user adaptive modular localization system for ubiquitous positioning. In: Pan, J.-S., Chen, S.-M., Nguyen, N.T. (eds.) ACIIDS 2012. LNCS, vol. 7197, pp. 391–400. Springer, Heidelberg (2012). doi:10.1007/978-3-642-28490-8_41
16. Behan, M., Krejcar, O.: Modern smart device-based concept of sensoric networks. EURASIP J. Wirel. Commun. Netw. **155**, 2013 (2013)
17. Novotny, J., Dvorak, J., Krejcar, O.: User based intelligent adaptation of five in a row game for android based on the data from the front camera. In: Paolis, L.T., Mongelli, A. (eds.) AVR 2016. LNCS, vol. 9768, pp. 133–149. Springer, Cham (2016). doi:10.1007/978-3-319-40621-3_9
18. Novotny, J., Dvorak, J., Krejcar, O.: Face-based difficulty adjustment for the game five in a row. In: Younas, M., Awan, I., Kryvinska, N., Strauss, C., Thanh, D. (eds.) MobiWIS 2016. LNCS, vol. 9847, pp. 121–134. Springer, Cham (2016). doi:10.1007/978-3-319-44215-0_10

Google Glass Used as Assistive Technology
Its Utilization for Blind and Visually Impaired People

Ales Berger[✉], Andrea Vokalova, Filip Maly, and Petra Poulova

Faculty of Informatics and Management, University of Hradec Kralove,
Hradec Kralove, Czech Republic
{ales.berger,andrea.vokalova,filip.maly,
petra.poulova}@uhk.cz

Abstract. Project Google Glass represents the innovative technology developed by Google's X Lab. This smart gadget is built on human interaction with world through Android operating system. Wearable computer with the optical head-mounted display (abbreviated as OHMD) has been developing by Google. Firstly, the primary purpose of Project Google Glass was the hands-free displaying of knowledge presently obtainable to most sensible mobile phone users. Secondly, Google Glass (abbreviated as GG) was allowing interaction with the Internet and the web via basic voice or vision commands. In a basic view, Google Glasses are wearable computers that can easily power mobile devices such as Smartphones or tablets. This paper is focused on the practical utilization of Google Glass for sensually impaired people (in this case it means blind or visually impaired people). Google Glass is easily programmable and helpful technology that can significantly help people, not only the handicapped or impaired individuals, but their benefits can also make easier life for elderly people. Primary purpose of the paper is to provide and test developed application for basic navigation issues, which are usable for daily support of blind or visually impaired people. Second part of research is using Google Glass camera as a basic recognition tool for blind or visually impaired individuals. In this point of view it is possible to call GG as Assistive Technology or device, which helps blind people or people with visual impairment too. Google Glass are currently often used in various domains such as medicine, research, education.

Keywords: Google Glass · Smartphone · Assisting technology · Blindness · Visually impaired people · Voice recognition

1 Introduction

In this chapter are published the basic definitions of Google Glass, as well as its history of development, used technology and advantages. Project Google Glass represents a futuristic gadget, which can be personalized by using different Smartphone's options and Internet connection. Glass is a new first-party hardware product designed by Google. It is a head-mounted computer that sits on a human's face very similarly to a pair of glasses (resting on ears and nose). It has a camera, a display, a touchpad

© Springer International Publishing AG 2017
M. Younas et al. (Eds.): MobiWIS 2017, LNCS 10486, pp. 70–82, 2017.
DOI: 10.1007/978-3-319-65515-4_6

(along the right arm), a speaker, and a microphone. The display is projected into a right eye using a prism, and sound is played into an eardrum from above the ear via bone conduction. While Glass looks very different from any other device, it runs an operating system that is now very common: Android. We can use this technology of your Smartphone, while not use of your hands. It is a bit like alternative device having software package and every one other options that offered in Smartphone. However, the main issue is that it is quicker, wearable and you'll be able to use it whereas doing day to day activities [1].

1.1 Google Project Glass History – The Four Generations of Google Glass

Google has declared the Project Glass in April 2012 to use the wearable technology with the optical head mounted display. Google has started selling Glass in the USA on 15th April 2013 for limited period [2]. The family of Google Glass technology consists of the four Glass Generations:

First Generation Glass
This is a pioneering version of Google Glass, which was focused mainly on using camera.

Second Generation Glass
Sometimes called as "Enterprise Edition". Second Generation was powered by an Intel Processor instead of Texas Instruments.

Third Generation Glass
This generation is working with a new functionality, which is display over both eyes, a possible hint at where the company is taking its eye-worn wearable [3].

Fourth Generation Glass
This group represents the last generation of Google Glass with many modifications. This version of GG is used in presented research.

1.2 Advantages of Google Glass

The most important advantages of Google Glass is that it communicates the requests from user to the computer and informs the conversational partner as to the wearer's use of the machine [4].

Other authors [2] have confronted the challenges and concluded that the fourth and upcoming generations of digital eye glass will prove more fruitful than other technologies as the problem of the clarification of pictures in camera, objects out from the range of laser light were also verified. Another author [5] presents the summary of seven basic advantages provided by Google Glass:

1. It is easily wearable and easy to handle.
2. It is useful technology for all kinds of people.
3. Access the documents, pictures, videos or map is very quickly.

4. There are mainly used: navigation, communication and social networks tools or applications.
5. There is natural voice command language for communication.
6. It is possible to use it with android phone through Wi-Fi.
7. It is an innovative, futuristic technology for technology lovers.

1.3 Technologies Used in Google Glass

This part of article is describing the technologies used in Google's Glass. Some of these technologies were already mentioned in this text, but without providing a precise definition from different authors.

Android Operating System
Android is a software stack for mobile devices that includes an operating system, middleware and key applications. Android is a software platform and operating system (abbr. OS) for mobile devices based on the Linux operating system and developed by Google and the Open Handset Alliance. It allows developers to write managed code in a Java. Unlike other embedded mobile environments, Android applications are all equal, for instance, an applications which come with the Smartphone are no different than those that any developer writes. The framework is supported by numerous open source libraries such as openssl, SQLite and libc. From the point of security, the framework is based on UNIX file system permissions that assure applications have only those abilities that mobile phone owner gave them at install time [6].

Bluetooth
Bluetooth is another type of short range wireless communication. This technology is based on 802.15.1, which is the standard specific for Wireless Personal Area Networks. Similar to 802.11 it works by means of radio signals in the frequency band of 2.4 GHz, but it is different due to the fact it was meant to replace wires among electronic devices. Depending on the class of the device, this technology can provide ranges of up to 100 meters (class 1) [7]. The main advantage of the Bluetooth is fact that this technology is part of every Smartphone, laptop or tablet.

EyeTap Technology
EyeTap is a device which allows, in a sense, the eye itself to function as both a display and a camera. EyeTap is at once the eye piece that displays computer information to the user and a device which allows the computer to process and possibly alter what the user sees. That which the user looks at is processed by the EyeTap. This allows the EyeTap to, under computer control, augment, diminish, or otherwise alter a user's visual perception of their environment, which creates a Computer Mediated Reality [8].

Smart Grid Technology
A smart grid is an electricity network based on digital technology that is used to supply electricity to consumers via two-way digital communication. This system allows for monitoring, analysis, control and communication within the supply chain to help improve efficiency, reduce energy consumption and cost, and maximize the transparency and

reliability of the energy supply chain. The smart grid was introduced with the aim of overcoming the weaknesses of conventional electrical grid by using smart net meters. Many government institutions around the world have been encouraging the use of smart grids for their potential to control and deal with global warming, emergency resilience and energy independence scenarios [9].

Wearable Computer
A wearable computer is a digital device that is either strapped to or carried on a user's body. It is used most often in research that focuses on behavioral modeling, health monitoring systems, IT and media development, where the person wearing the computer actually moves or is otherwise engaged with his or her surroundings. Wearable computers provide constant computer and user interaction. In extreme cases, they serve much like a prosthetic, in that device use does not require users to cease other activities Wearable computers are particularly helpful for application that need a lot of advanced process support than simply hardware coded logics [10].

Wi-Fi Technology
Wi-Fi is an abbreviation for the term Wireless Fidelity. This is popular name for IEEE 802.11 protocol for wireless local megabits per second (Mb/sec). In comparison, standard Ethernet provides maximum data speed of 10 Mb/sec via cables. Wi-Fi operates in the 2.4 Gigahertz (GHz) radio band the same frequency used by most Smartphones and microwave ovens over 11 channels [11].

1.4   Google Cloud

Google Cloud Platform is a set of public cloud computing services established by Google. This platform includes a range of hosted services for data storage, computing or application development that run on Google hardware. Google Cloud Platform services are designed primarily for software developers, cloud architects, data analysts and other IT professionals over the public Internet [12].

Vision API
Google Cloud Vision API is a part of Google Cloud Services. Google Cloud Vision API enables developers to understand the content of an image by encapsulating powerful machine learning models in as easy to use REST API. It quickly classifies images into thousands of categories (e.g., "sailboat", "lion", "Eiffel Tower"), detects individual objects and faces within images, and finds and reads printed words contained within images. You can build metadata on your image catalog, moderate offensive content, or enable new marketing scenarios through image sentiment analysis. Analyze image uploaded in the request or integrate with your image storage on Google Cloud Storage [13]. The scheme of Google Glass and Cloud Platform functionality is shown in Fig. 1.

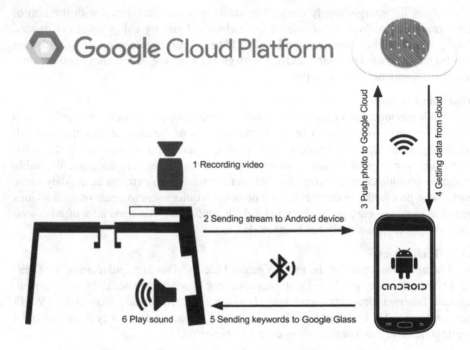

Fig. 1. Scheme of Google Glass and Cloud Platform functionality.

2 Assistive Technology and Devices Used for Blind or Visually Impaired People

Assistive technology is one of the core strategies schools and other organizations use to help with learning and attention issues. Some adaptive tools are low-tech and some are pretty high-tech. Here are some common examples of its utilization:

- Audio players and Recorders,
- Timers,
- Reading Guides,
- Seat Cushions,
- FM Listening Systems,
- Calculators,
- Writing Supports,
- Graphic Organizers.

Technological companies such as Microsoft or Google often recognize that third-party assistive technology products – such as screen readers, magnifiers, and specialty accessibility hardware – are essential for many of their customers. That's why they work closely with providers to support compatibility with Microsoft technology. The following assistive technology providers offer products used by our customers today:

- Vision,
- Learning,
- Dexterity and Mobility,
- Language and Communication [14].

2.1 For What Health Conditions Can Be Used Assistive Technology or Device?

Some disabilities are quite visible, and others are "hidden". Most disabilities can be grouped into four major categories:

1. **Cognitive disability:** intellectual and learning disabilities/disorder, distractibility, reading disorders, inability to remember or focus on large amounts of information.
2. **Hearing disability:** hearing loss or impaired hearing.
3. **Physical disability:** paralysis, difficulties with walking or other movement, inability to use a computer mouse, slow response time, limited fine or gross motor control.
4. **Visual disability:** blindness, low vision, color blindness, visual impairment [15].

2.2 Blindness and Visual Disabilities - Worldwide Overview

More than 80% of information entering the brain is visual [16]. Other scientific studies had shown that when person's eyes are open, our vision accounts for two-thirds of the electrical activity of the brain - a full 2 billion of the 3 billion firings per second - which was the finding of neuroanatomist R.S. Fixot in a paper published in 1957 [17]. Today, there is an estimated 180 million people worldwide who are visually disabled. Of these, between 40 and 45 million persons are blind and, by definition, cannot walk about unaided. They are usually in need of vocational and/or social support. The loss of sight causes enormous human suffering for the affected individuals and their families. It also represent a public health, social and economic problem for countries, especially the developing ones, where 9 out of 10 of the world's blind live. In fact, around 60% of them reside in sub-Saharan African, China and India. Approximately 50% of world's blind suffer from cataract. The majority of the remaining persons are blind from conditions that include, among others, glaucoma, trachoma, onchocerciasis (also known as river blindness) and different conditions of childhood blindness. Despite a half century of efforts, commencing with organized trachoma control activities, and the global burden of blindness is growing largely because of the population growth and ageing [18]. The global trend supported by calculated prediction of the blind people in 2020, was conducted by the World Health Organization (abbreviated WHO) and is shown in Fig. 2.

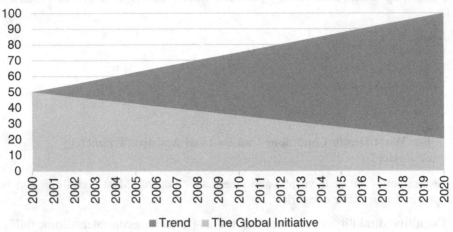

Fig. 2. Global prediction - the total number of blind people in 2020 [18].

A blind person or a person with a low vision is dealing with navigation, orientation and other recognition issues in a daily basis. These problems can be easily solved by learning or using special equipment (e.g., cane etc.), especially in a limited space area, such as in a flat or in a house. But when a blind person wants to visit a doctor, a friend, look for a job or travel few blocks, navigation and orientation in a noisy environment overwhelming with many people, cars and sometimes during night, windy or rainy weather is very demanding and sometimes impossible without a help of a social assistant. Authors of the paper have developed an assistive application, which is using a Google Glass connected via Smartphone in order to help these people and their navigation or recognition issues outdoors as well as indoor. Outdoor navigation is surely the most important problem with which are visually impaired/blind people dealing every day.

3   Methodology

Primary purpose of the paper is to provide and test developed application for basic navigation issues, which are usable for daily support of blind or visually impaired people. Second part of research is using Google Glass camera as a basic recognition tool for blind or visually impaired individuals.

Methods and methodology used in the presented research are based on case study approach. Here the focus of attention is on a particular community (e.g. blind people, visually disabled people), organization or set of documents. The attraction of this kind of research is that it stems from empirical curiosity but is at the same time practical. The whole research may be interested in a wider question but a case study enables researchers to focus on a specific example. A major challenge in case study is connection author's own primary research or re-analysis with the broader theoretical themes and empirical concerns of the existing literature.

Addressed participants were testing the functionality of developed application by using a pair of Google Glass Generation 4 and their own Smartphone with Android OS. Authors aim to provide a GG as assistive technology for visually disabled people. When the results of a presented study show that this devices and app can be successfully established as helpful assistive technology for the participants (can easily substitute social assistant and restore self-esteem/self-sufficiency of participants), it can provide a significant improve and change in their daily living.

3.1 Conducted Experiments and Testing App

Firstly, during the process of testing the app, all blind or impaired users are dealing with basic navigation issues in an open environment (e.g., town, park, hospital etc.). Each participant gets an unknown address in the town and only by using a pair of Google Glass device and developed app in Smartphone is trying to find estimated address as soon as possible. After a series of this navigation experiments the acquired results (first experiment measures time for destination point alone, second with help of social assistant and third by using GG and developed app), obstacles and comments from respondent's deep interview are analyzed as well. Second part of this experiment aims on recognition troubles indoor as well as outdoor. In this experiment, participants were approaching in a front of 30 different kinds of objects, animals and obstacles in order to use the app and GG instead of their eyes for their basic and successful recognition.

3.2 Participants

There were 15 participants participating in the presented study. All of them are dealing with visual disabilities in many varieties and 5 of them are completely blind. There are 8 women (3 of them are blind) and 7 men (2 of them blind). The average age is 45 years.

4 Results and Discussion

In this part are described two conducted experiments and measured data. First experiment is dealing with navigation issue in three different situation. First situation measured total time of participants from start to final destination on their own (without any help from an assistant or a Smartphone). Second situation measured total time from start to final destination with the assistance of social assistant. This data are shown in the table (see Table 1). Second situation provided mostly the shortest time in the first experiment, because blind/visually impaired people can walk fluently and without any troubles or obstacles in their route. They are guided by specialized assistant, who is helping them with navigation and orientation in unknown environment. There is only one disadvantage - blind/visually impaired people are trying to be as much independent

Table 1. Data and time from experiment no. 1.

Person	Alone [1]	With assist [2]	GG & SP [3]	Change [4] ([1]–[2])	Change [5] ([1]–[3])
1.	69.15	55.03	58.22	+ 14 min	+ 10 min
2.	45.01	41.12	42.50	+ 3.5 min	+ 3 min
3.	35.18	34.46	33.10	+ 1 min	+ 2 min
4.	28.33	25.54	25.14	+ 3 min	+ 3 min
5.	38.26	32.14	30.35	+ 6 min	+ 8 min
6.	56.20	51.11	50.20	+ 5 min	+ 6 min
7.	39.59	35.32	37.55	+ 4.5 min	+ 2 min
8.	35.09	33.10	32.15	+ 3 min	+ 3 min
9.	40.01	37.55	38.01	+ 2 min	+ 2 min
10.	25.59	24.17	23.20	+ 1.5 min	+ 2.5 min
11.	75.45	69.35	69.55	+ 6 min	+ 6 min
12.	61.47	59.22	62.11	+ 2 min	– 0.5 min
13.	53.35	45.13	43.02	+ 10.5 min	+ 10.5 min
14.	30.58	28.50	26.39	+ 4 min	+ 4 min
15.	36.45	31.59	32.30	+ 4.5 min	+ 4 min
AVG	**44.55**	**40.22**	**41.25**	**+ 4.5 min**	**+ 4.36 min**

as possible. Third situation provided Google Glass and connected Smartphone with App for better navigation. This situation is testing assistive technology (GG) in order to sustain people's independency without any additional support.

4.1   1st Experiment - Navigation Issue

First conducted experiment is dealing with the most crucial navigation issue among blind or visually impaired people. Blind people are often depending on social assistant's help or on other people's help in order to get to unknown address in their town. Visually impaired people are more self-sustaining, but this part of daily living is for them very stressful too. The average time to reach the final destination was about 45 min on their own. The two oldest participants were the slowest ones and got 75.45 and 69.15 min (see Table 1). Second situation changed the total time to average time, covered by 40.22 min. The variance of average time with assistant and without assistant is about 4.5–5 min. Third situation (using GG & SP) provided the average time 41.25 min, which is 3.5 min shorter than the measured time without the GG and SP. Average variance between the total time without assistance and with using a GG is 4.36 min. In this point of view we can call Google Glass and developed Smartphone app as assistive technology, because they are helping participants to get to any place faster, easier and without assistance. Developed app with utilization of Google Glass is very promising and authors are working on another testing and experiments in order to get more data for upgrading this application.

4.2   2nd Experiment - Obstacles Recognition

Second experiment deals with recognition troubles indoor as well as outdoor. In this experiment, participants are approaching in a front of 30 different kinds of objects, animals and obstacles in order to use the app and GG instead of their eyes for their basic and successful recognition. The developed application connected with GG must recognize more than 60% of tested obstacles in order to be successful. Each participant tests 15 obstacles located indoors and 15 outdoors. The most frequently mentioned obstacles by our participants are: fences, pylons, boards, billboards, uncared trees (and its long branches), bushes, cars/motorbikes/bikes parked on the pavement, dustbins, running dogs, porches, restaurant's porch railings, holes in pavement, people standing on pavement/station in queues and unmarked stairs or glass doors etc.

Tested Android application with GG recognized successfully more than three fourths of tested obstacles (covered by 75%). The downside of this experiment is fact that there were few obstacles, which could not be recognized properly by GG and App. These obstacles are: small billboards, advertising boards, restaurant's porch railings and some types of pylons or lamps. Participants were asked to mention three different obstacles or barriers, which are the most frequently present during their walk in a town. Results are illustrated in Fig. 3. The worst are pylons (99%) and trees/bushes (95%), which marked the majority of visually impaired/blind people. Next research could improve the recognition process of these obstacles in larger participants sample with focus on mentioned obstacles and their various forms.

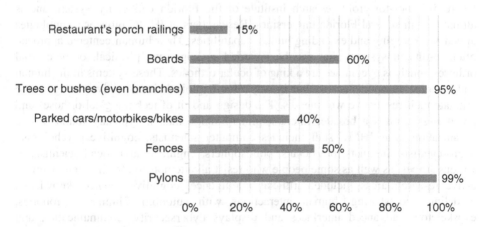

Fig. 3. The most frequently mentioned obstacles in a town

5   Conclusion

Google Glass represents a great opportunity not only for business enterprises, but also for medical organizations, education institutions and social services. Primary goal of this paper is to provide and mainly test developed application for basic navigation issues, which are usable for daily support of blind or visually impaired people.

Secondly, authors aim their attention to utilization of the app as a basic recognition tool for visually impaired people. In this point of view we can call Google Glass and developed Smartphone app as assistive technology, because they are helping participants to get to any place faster, easier and without assistance. Developed app with utilization of Google Glass is very promising and authors are working on another testing and experiments in order to get more data for upgrading this application. Conducted experiment no. 1 shows that the total time to reach destination using GG and SP is almost the same as with help of social assistant. Author's data shows that tested application is focused on two main functionalities: the first one is navigation and the second deals with recognition of 30 different objects, which are mainly addressed as obstacles for visually impaired people. Next upgraded functionality can be also a localization tool in this developed application, which will be published in a following research. Tested Android application with GG recognized successfully more than three fourths of tested obstacles (75%). The worst obstacles are pylons (99%) and trees/bushes (95%), which marked the majority of visually impaired/blind people. Next research is aimed to improve the recognition process of these obstacles in larger participants sample with focus on mentioned obstacles and their various forms.

Acknowledgement. This work and the contribution were also supported by Students Grant Agency — FIM, University of Hradec Kralove, Czech Republic (under ID: UHK-FIM-SP-2017-2108).

The Institute for Human and Machine Cognition (abbr. IHMC)

The Google's Glass used in presented research was kindly provided for free by IHMC. IHMC is a not-for-profit research institute of the Florida University System and is affiliated with several Florida universities. Researchers at IHMC pioneer technologies aimed at leveraging and extending human capabilities. Their human-centered approach often results in systems that can be regarded as cognitive, physical, or perceptual orthoses, much as eyeglasses are a king of ocular orthoses. These systems fit the human and machine components together in ways that exploit their respective strengths and mitigate their respective weaknesses. The design and fit of technological orthoses and prostheses requires a broader interdisciplinary range than is typically found in one organization, thus IHMC staff includes computer scientists, cognitive psychologist, neuroscientists, linguists, physicians, philosophers, engineers and social scientists of various stripes, as well as some people who resist all attempts to classify them. Current active research areas include: artificial intelligence, cognitive science, knowledge modeling and sharing, human interactions with autonomy, humanoid robotics, exoskeletons, advanced interfaces and displays cybersecurity, communication and collaboration, linguistics and natural language processing, computer-mediated learning systems, intelligent data understanding, software agents, expertise studies, work practice simulation, knowledge representation, big data and machine learning, as well as other related areas. IHMC faculty and staff collaborate extensively with industry and government to develop science and technology that can be enabling with respect to society's broader goals. IHMC researchers receive funding from a wide range of government and private sources. IHMC research partners have included: DARPA, NSF, NASA, Army, Navy, Air Force NIH, IARPA, DOT, IDEO, Raytheon, IBM, Microsoft, Rockwell Collins, Boeing, Lockheed, and SAIC, among others [19]. IHMC also offers opportunity to collaborate on various projects with Faculty of Informatics and Management students. It helps students to explore real projects while studying [20].

Authors thank to IHMC in Florida and mainly to Niranjan Suri for providing Google Glass device for free, which was very important for our research. Google Glass device will be also used in next step of our research.

References

1. Freeman, J.: Exploiting a bug in a Google's Glass. http://www.saurik.com/id/16
2. Deshpande, S., Uplenchwar, G., Chaudhari, D.N.: Google Glass. Int. J. Sci. Eng. Res. **4**(12) (2013)
3. Solomon, K.: Google Glass 3.0 could be the oculus rift you can wear to work. http://www. techradar.com/news/portable-devices/other-devices/google-glass-3-0-could-be-the-oculus-rift-you-can-wear-to-work-1246018
4. Lyons, K.M.: Improving support of conversations by enhancing mobile computer input. Ph.D. thesis, Georgia Institute of Technology (2005)
5. Pathkar, N.S., Joshi, N.S.: Google Glass: project glass. Int. J. Appl. Innov. Eng. Manage. (IJAIEM) **3**(10), 031–035 (2014)
6. Nimodia, C., Deshmukh, H.R.: Android operating system. Softw. Eng. **3**(1), 10–13 (2012). ISSN:2229-4007 and ISSN:2229-4015
7. Sosa, A.: Personnel tracking system using a Bluetooth-based epidemic protocol. The University of Texas at El Paso (2007)
8. Mann, S.: Google eye, supplemental material for through the glass, lightly. IEEE Technol. Soc. **31**(3), 10–14 (2012)
9. Techopedia Inc. What is a Smart Grid? Definition from Techopedia. Where IT and Business Meet. https://www.techopedia.com/definition/692/smart-grid
10. Techopedia Inc. What is a Wearable Computer? Definition from Techopedia. Where IT and Business Meet. https://www.techopedia.com/definition/16339/wearable-computer
11. Corral, L., Fronza, I., Ioini, N., Janes, A., Plant, P.: An Android Kernel Extension to Save Energy Resources Without Impacting User Experience. In: Younas, M., Awan, I., Kryvinska, N., Strauss, C., Thanh, Dv (eds.) MobiWIS 2016. LNCS, vol. 9847, pp. 3–17. Springer, Cham (2016). doi:10.1007/978-3-319-44215-0_1
12. Google Cloud Computing, Hosting Services & APIs. Google Cloud Platform. Google. https://cloud.google.com/
13. Google Developers. Google Cloud Vision API Documentation. https://cloud.google.com/vision/docs/
14. Morin, A.: 8 Examples of Assistive Technology and Adaptive Tools. https://www.understood.org/en/school-learning/assistive-technology/assistive-technologies-basics/8-examples-of-assistive-technology-and-adaptive-tools
15. Microsoft. Assistive technology providers. https://www.microsoft.com/en-us/accessibility/assistive-technology-partners
16. Jensen, E.: Brain-Based Learning: The New Paradigm of Teaching. Corwin Press (2008)
17. Fixot, R.S.: American Journal of Ophthalmology (1957)

18. Blindness. Vision 2020 - The Global Initiative for the Elimination of Avoidable Blindness. http://www.who.int/mediacentre/factsheets/fs213/en/
19. IHMC. Institute of Human and Machine Cognition Story. https://www.ihmc.us/about/aboutihmc/
20. Berger, A., Maly, F.: Smart Solution in Social Relationships Graphs. In: Younas, M., Awan, I., Kryvinska, N., Strauss, C., Thanh, Dv (eds.) MobiWIS 2016. LNCS, vol. 9847, pp. 393–405. Springer, Cham (2016). doi:10.1007/978-3-319-44215-0_33

An Approach of Solid Waste Monitoring with Smart Dumpsters and Disposal

Pınar Kirci[1(✉)], Lutfu Çagatay Agca[2], and Muhammed Fatih Aksu[3]

[1] Istanbul University, 34010 Istanbul, Turkey
pkirci@istanbul.edu.tr
[2] Turkcell Technology R&D, Istanbul, Turkey
[3] Turk Telekom, Istanbul, Turkey

Abstract. Today, it is inevitable to consider recycling and quality of recycling because of the natural source insufficiency and environmental pollution. It is obvious that technology and recycling have to be integrated to provide high-quality and innovative recycling. In the paper, with the presented smart trash dumpster project, it is considered to produce smart waste containers. Also, real time state monitoring of smart waste containers together with providing quick and economical collection and disposal process when they become 95% full are the other considered topics in the project. In addition to this, with utilizing the cheap and easy use of mobile technologies, it is aimed to attract the attention of the population who live in big cities to recycling and environmental pollution.

Keywords: Smart trash dumpster · Monitoring · Sensor · Disposal

1 Introduction

Producing smart waste containers and smart recycling dumpsters are the main aims of this type of studies. With mounted sensors and connection providing tools, transmitting data to a database and processing the arriving data are the steps of innovative smart waste container systems. In addition to these technological steps, the application part differs according to the usage areas.

In [1], smart waste containers are used for chemical wastes and for their recycling. In [2], good solutions are presented for the waste and recycling problem in hotels and other areas. For some hotels the waste rates differ according to the seasons. But garbage compactors have regular service schedules, twice per week thus compactors mostly are not full in some seasons when picked up by a hauler. Big variation occurs in waste volumes generated in different seasons. And the hotel staff have not a definite method to measure the compactor fullness level. To improve the compactor usage, a remote electronic monitoring system is mounted. The system, calls the service when the compactor becomes 75% full. Consequently, many redundant compactor pickups were disposed together with big amounts of annual savings. In addition to this, because of decreasing the amount of truck trips, the carbon emissions are also diminished.

Nowadays, widespread technologies make things easier about the improvement in recycling management with providing identification at the recycling dumpster by radio

© Springer International Publishing AG 2017
M. Younas et al. (Eds.): MobiWIS 2017, LNCS 10486, pp. 83–89, 2017.
DOI: 10.1007/978-3-319-65515-4_7

frequencies. Thus, with the convenient applications of the technologies, it is possible to compute and store the waste amounts in containers, monitoring them with RFID based cards and the integration of web based server transmission. Hardest problems of recycling process were solved eventually. The first problem was informing the manager when the waste containers are full to provide transmission of the waste. And the second one was grouping process [3].

In the year of 2012, United Arab Emirates, recycled 3% of its waste amounts. It is a small step when compared to Europe and America but it is a good value for Middle East. To become a *smart city*, Dubai proposes some projects. One of these projects was based on recycling with gamification. To encourage the users for recycling, the gamification method is used in [4].

Our presented system plans to propose a technological infrastructure with utilizing sensors, for real time monitoring of location and the compactness ratio of some waste containers. In the next step, the best route will be planned for the garbage trucks to collect only the 95% full waste dumpsters with considering real time traffic parameters. Also, at the user side a gamification method will be used for smartphone users to attract the attention of people. Thus, people will be encouraged for recycling with individual recycling. Consequently, the proposed project is a kind of social responsibility project.

The rest of the paper is organized as follows. In Sect. 2, smart waste recycling in Turkey is given. Proposed system is presented in Sect. 3. The paper ends in conclusion by proposing concluding remarks.

2   Smart Waste Recycling in Turkey

Recycling technology is still a developing topic in Turkey. In most of the applications, some devices were mounted at waste dumpsters. Smart dumpsters including applications that are based on reward system is developed by ISBAK as presented in Fig. 1 [5]. A solid waste collecting system is presented in [7]. It is experienced in the city of Bursa's Kestel county in Turkey.

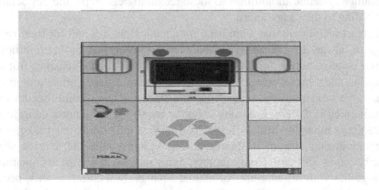

Fig. 1.   Reward based smart container that is developed by ISBAK [5, 6]

Natural sources are consumed very fast because of the needs of people who live a modern life. And when the used products' expiration date reach then great amounts of waste are produced, thus people encounter with a vital waste problem.

As a result of this, people need to find urgent solutions for ever increasing waste problem. The natural resources of the world are waste away because of the environmental destruction and environmental pollution. And, ever growing consumption of people cause different kinds of wastes. At first, the produced wastes need to be stored and this fact emerges the need of vast waste storage areas. Next, they have to be destroyed and the extermination process is provided with high costs. These storage and cost problems lead people to find new solutions for using the sources as optimum as possible, decreasing the waste amounts and recycling.

In the optimum utilization of the sources, main aims are rehandling, reprocessing and reusing of sources to consume less natural sources. In the paper, waste decreasing and recycling methods are examined in Turkey, especially in Istanbul [8–21].

3 The Proposed Structure

The presented system has lower cost, simple and functional structure with easy implementation. Our main aim is to produce a local system which suits our country's needs and circumstances. Investments about recycling proceed but there are not enough products and solutions produced in Turkey, thus wastes are processed and destroyed with inefficient methods. In our paper, we will improve the recycling process with technological and effective methods. At First, the user will login the page with his user name and password as illustrated in Fig. 2.

Fig. 2. Login page of the presented mobile application

Firstly, we consider to determine the fullness of the dumpsters with sensors and also we utilize Arduino platform. We decided to use Arduino because it contains many modules and shields for many technologies and sensors. In the system, for communication there is a Wi-Fi Shield and a GPS module which is connected to that Wi-Fi Shield on Arduino Uno R3. An ultrasonic sensor is used for determining the fullness and depth of the waste dumpsters as shown in Fig. 3.

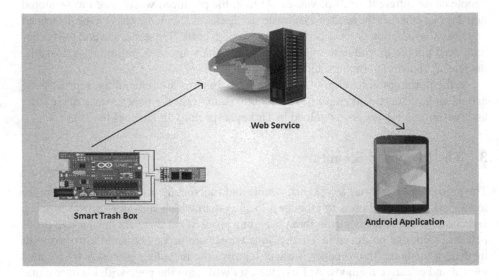

Fig. 3. Main structure of the system

Next, the connection will be provided and the collected data will be sent to a database with a remote server and a MySQL platform on remote server.

All of the locations of the considered waste dumpsters are shown on the google map in Fig. 4. Every one of the waste dumpsters' location addresses are given with the last waste pick up date and hour data. Also, some of the main waste types and amount of each type can be monitored: glass (in Turkish as cam), paper (in Turkish as kagit) or plastic (in Turkish as plastik). In Fig. 4, the considered dumpster is composed of 20% glass material, 10% paper material and 15% plastic material. And, the fullness rate of the waste dumpster can always be monitored with a given rate. In Fig. 4, the considered dumpster is 15% full. By the way, to receive the location data, GPS module will be used because GPS utilizes satellites to determine locations.

Waste dumpsters' locations and the shortest path between the full dumpsters that need to be picked up will be presented by Maps API (Application Programming Interface). Maps API enables to illustrate the positions of the dumpsters on the map with latitude and longitude data together with generating the needed route between considered dumpsters as a ready property. And, the position data of the dumpsters will be received from the database then the positions will be illustrated on the map. Next, route will be determined for the full dumpsters as presented in Fig. 5.

Fig. 4. Illustrating the locations of waste dumpsters on the mobile application

Fig. 5. Determining the routes on mobile application

4   Conclusion

Solid waste collection systems are very important for nowadays social structure and urbanization. Expensive systems are utilized in the cities but they do not provide effective and high quality service [7]. In the paper, high quality presenting and low cost owning smart waste dumpster system is proposed for cities. Also, the smart solid waste collecting system design, application steps are presented.

Acknowledgement. This work has been supported by Scientific Research Projects Coordination Unit of Istanbul University within the Scientific Activity Attendance Support 26109.

References

1. Recyclesmart main page. http://recycle-smart.ca/. Accessed 1 Apr 2016
2. Recyclesmart: Case-study: Large resort hotel. http://recycle-smart.ca/project/compactor-monitor-resort-hotel/. Accessed 1 Apr 2016
3. Abd Wahab, A.M.H., Kadir, A.A., Tomari, M.R., Jabbar, M.H.: Smart recycle bin: a conceptual approach of smart waste management with integrated web based system. In: International Conference on IT Convergence and Security (ICITCS), vol. 1, no. 4, pp. 28–30 (2014)
4. Schafer, V.: Smart cities smart recycling: RecycleBeacon integrates smartphone technology with smart recycling bins to accelerate recycling efforts, BushSystems. http://en.envirocitiesmag.com/articles/sustainable-smart-cities/smart-cities-smart-recycling.php. Accessed 3 Apr 2016
5. Smart container. http://isbak.istanbul/?page_id=555. Accessed 5 Apr 2016
6. Akıllı Konteyner. http://www.akillikonteyner.net/index.php/dokumanlar/urun-katalogu. Accessed 19 Jan 2017
7. Çavdar, K., Köroğlu, M., Akyıldız, B., Akyıldız, M.: Katı atık toplama amaçlı bir akıllı sistemin tasarımı ve uygulaması. Niğde Üniversitesi Mühendislik Bilimleri Dergisi, 3(2) (2014)
8. Lüy, E., Varınca, K.B., Kemirtlek, A.: Katı atık geri kazanım çalışmaları; istanbul örneği. In: AB Sürecinde Türkiye'de Katı Atık Yönetimi ve Çevre Sorunları Symposium, Turkey (2007)
9. Yousuf, T.B., Rahman, M.: Monitoring quantity and characteristics of municipal solid waste in Dhaka City. Environ. Monit. Assess. **135**(1), 3–11 (2007)
10. Arebey, M., Hannan, M.A., Basri, H., Begum, R.A., Abdullah, H.: Integrated technologies for solid waste bin monitoring system. Environ. Monit. Assess. **177**(1), 399–408 (2011)
11. Raharjo, S., Matsumoto, T., Ihsan, T., Rachman, I., Gustin, L.: Community-based solid waste bank program for municipal solid waste management improvement in Indonesia: a case study of Padang city. J. Mater. Cycles Waste Manage. **19**(1), 201–212 (2017)
12. Pandyaswargo, A.H., Onoda, H., Nagata, K.: Energy recovery potential and life cycle impact assessment of municipal solid waste management technologies in Asian countries using ELP model. Int. J. Energy Environ. Eng. **3**(28) (2012)
13. Ezebilo, E.E., Animasaun, E.D.: Households' perceptions of private sector municipal solid waste management services: a binary choice analysis. Int. J. Environ. Sci. Technol. **8**(4), 677–686 (2011)

14. Srivastava, V., Ismail, S.A., Singh, P., Singh, R.P.: Urban solid waste management in the developing world with emphasis on India: challenges and opportunities. Rev. Environ. Sci. Bio/Technol. **14**(2), 317–337 (2015)
15. Cifrian, E., Coz, A., Viguri, J., Andrés, A.: Indicators for valorisation of municipal solid waste and special waste. Waste Biomass Valoriz. **1**(4), 479–486 (2010)
16. Miezah, K., Obiri-Danso, K., Kádár, Z., Heiske, S., Fei-Baffoe, B., Mensah, M., Meyer, A.S.: Municipal solid waste management in a low income economy through biogas and bioethanol production. Waste Biomass Valoriz. **8**(1), 115–127 (2017)
17. Zis, T., Bell, M.G.H., Tolis, A., Aravossis, K.: Economic evaluation of alternative options for municipal solid waste management in remote locations. Waste Biomass Valoriz. **4**(2), 287–296 (2013)
18. Kularatne, R.K.A.: Erratum to: case study on municipal solid waste management in Vavuniya township: practices, issues and viable management options. J. Mater. Cycles Waste Manage. **17**(1), 206 (2015)
19. Braguglia, C.M., Gianico, A., Mininni, G.: ROUTES: innovative solutions for municipal sludge treatment and management. Rev. Environ. Sci. Bio/Technol. **11**(1), 11–17 (2012)
20. Bidlingmaier, W., Sidaine, J.-M., Papadimitriou, E.K.: Separate collection and biological waste treatment in the European Community. Rev. Environ. Sci. Bio/Technol. **3**(4), 307–320 (2004)
21. Shi, W.: Webalert of waste management. Rev. Environ. Sci. Bio/Technol. **10**(187) (2011)

Intelligent Notepad for Windows Phone that Uses GPS Data

Milan Kostak[1], Jan Dvorak[1], Ali Selamat[1,2], and Ondrej Krejcar[1(✉)]

[1] Center for Basic and Applied Research, Faculty of Informatics and Management,
University of Hradec Kralove, Rokitanskeho 62, 500 03 Hradec Kralove, Czech Republic
{milan.kostak,jan.dvorak}@uhk.cz, Ondrej@Krejcar.org
[2] Faculty of Computing, Universiti Teknologi Malaysia, 81310 Johor Baharu, Johor, Malaysia
aselamat@utm.my

Abstract. This work deals with the solution of the problem of notepad applications specializing in location based notifications for mobile devices. First, there is the explanation about the motivation for creating this kind of application. Afterwards, the problems and flaws that current applications struggle with are described. Based on that, a new solution is designed and later implemented. The testing proves that the new solution is better than the current solution and that the application can solve the assigned problems very well. Owing to that, there are many options of actual application and use in real life.

Keywords: Notes · GPS · Location-based application · Task reminder · Windows phone

1 Introduction

In the current modern world, there are barely any people that can imagine living without the ubiquitous electronics. Almost each of us carries around some kind of a smart phone. Only a few years ago, people only needed their phone to call, receive text messages and have a few usually off-line applications [9]. With the advancement of minimization of hardware components, the mobile phones have become more efficient, and therefore able to perform more complex operations. That led to the implementation of different special sensors that enable everyone to use not only mobile phones, but generally all mobile devices on a whole different level. Since then, a big amount of different sensors was integrated into the so called smart phones [11, 12]. Those sensors allow the creation of seemingly very intelligent applications that can enable some of the daily activities.

In this world glutted with information, it is sometimes difficult to organize our own ideas, tasks and duties. There is a big amount of information aimed at us from everywhere and it is important to have the ability to somehow record the relevant ones [10]. With respect to the omnipresence of mobile phones arises an option of creating applications enabling this kind of classification of information.

The existing applications usually focus only at time notifications that are characterized by notifying at a certain time of certain information, at times even with the possibility of periodical repetition. That can prove to be sufficient in many situations.

© Springer International Publishing AG 2017
M. Younas et al. (Eds.): MobiWIS 2017, LNCS 10486, pp. 90–103, 2017.
DOI: 10.1007/978-3-319-65515-4_8

However, sometimes the information is important in a certain location. For example, the notification of having to do shopping on the way home from work would be difficult to set as only a time notification, because the time of the person passing the shop is difficult to set. [1] Therefore, the problem does not consist in remembering all the information, but in assigning it to the right places and in the right moment recall the relevant ones.

The concept of localization is nothing new nowadays [13]. There are many methods of localizing the device. One of them is GPS ("Global Positioning Systems"), which is created by a network of 24 satellites. Outside of the buildings, it can determine the location with the accuracy of up to 5 meters, which is also considered its biggest advantage. The disadvantage is the necessity of direct visibility of the satellites and the necessity of having a special hardware in the device. [2] However, that does not represent such a problem these days, because almost every phone is equipped with this kind of chip.

At this moment, a problem could arise concerning the constant run of the application, which is necessary because of the notifications, but would negatively affect the battery life in the device. Battery is one of the most valuable sources that are in the phone, especially now, when some of the phones require charging every day. An increased use of energy would be uncomfortable and could discharge the battery in several hours. The mobile operating systems fortunately provide different methods of solution that are necessary to employ here [3].

In the case of Windows Phone platform, the application wanting to notify the user only registers itself to the central service that arranges the collection and displaying of information. There are three types of notifications: "toast", "tile" and "raw". All of them work with the information on a similar principle. They differ mostly in the way of displaying [3].

"Live Tiles" can function not only as shortcuts for running the applications, but can also display any data even without the application running and that way attract the users to open the application [4].

"Toast" notification is a kind of notification that displays in the upper part of the screen and it contains only one-line information about what is happening. It can be tapped and the given application opens and the user can react to the displayed notification. It serves mostly for urgent notifications, because in its activation, there is a sound response, or vibration of the device, depending on the user settings. The unseen notifications are saved to the notification center.

The data backup cannot be forgotten, because they are very valuable, sometimes the value is even higher than the value of the device where they are stored, therefore the backup cannot be underestimated. In the case of Windows Phone operating system, it is possible to back up the data in the storage One Drive, where all the data are backed up automatically.

2 Problem Definition and Related Works

The notepad application is not a new invention. For all the mobile platforms, there is a wide array of applications. Even though, the application stores are overflowing with all kinds of applications of different quality and functionality, it is a problem to find an application that would offer at least some basic and functional equipment.

The available applications can be divided into three categories. The most basic ones offer only a storage space for text, or for lists and similar solutions. It cannot be denied that some users need more than this functionality or may be unsatisfied with it. Equally as someone still needs only a pen and paper; some users need just a place to save some text. Nevertheless, the aim of this work is to propose an automatic solution that would work with information in a better way.

The second category of applications includes applications that provide time notifications as something extra. As it has been mentioned in the previous chapter, this solution has its shortcomings too, which is a problem. Most of the applications restrict themselves only to this basic functionality and do not endeavor to use the potential of phones that contain many options and opportunities to create functionally rich applications nowadays. The third category could include applications that truly use modern possibilities of current phones, especially the wide array of sensors that are included in the phones, from GPS to a detector of surrounding illumination or magnetometer (electronic compass).

The solution introduced in the article [1] describes the possibilities of improvement of user's location detection in areas with no GPS signal accessible, because direct satellite visibility is necessary for it. These places are usually interior spaces of the buildings. However, the stated solution is for most of the situations too complicated. Nowadays, the Wi-Fi connection or the data services from the operator are used constantly by many people; therefore it is possible to use only current maps APIs in the phones that can provide the data from these additional sources. In the case of not being able to get the current location, there is always the last known location available that can, despite its outdatedness, provide quite accurate data for most possibilities of use.

The application "My Notes" could be considered as an altogether decent solution of a notepad application. With its more than 3 million downloads, it belongs among the most popular applications in Windows Store. Like many similar applications, besides the standard notes, it supports lists of tasks, shopping lists and events. It is possible to add time notifications to the notes. It allows locking the application or specific notes with a password and synchronizing the data with OneDrive storage. Contrary to its competition, it contains wide choice of settings. It allows adjusting the size of the text, setting the rules for ordering the notes and lists, the tile design, the application theme and many others [5].

The article [6] introduces "Place-Its" application. The aim of the project was to create an application that would enable creating notes and notifications based on the current location of the device, and subsequently to conduct testing with real users for two weeks. The application was aimed at phones with Symbian operating system. These phones do not usually feature the possibility to track GPS signal, therefore the location detection was implemented using GSM signal. With current models of the phones, it is not necessary to be burdened with something like this, because the operating systems as such provide an interface for access to device location information. For the purposes of simplification, we implemented in this project the location based notification without the option of time notification. Another reason for this decision was to make the tested subject use the location based notifications. The created application gives quite a good perspective on how a properly created notepad application with location based notification system could look. Its main problem is mostly the outdatedness of used technologies and procedures. The article presents one very interesting function which is a possibility to create a notification for leaving a selected area. The applications usually allow only creating notification for entering an area, but it is possible to imagine a range of situations where leaving certain area would be a suitable starting mechanism for displaying a note or a task.

The application "Daily Notes" opposed to other similar application, allows working with solved and unsolved notes. The unsolved notes can be moved to the following day. The live tile shows the number of unsolved notes for the current day. Some users will surely appreciate the ability to display unsolved notes on the lockable display thanks to which they can have an immediate overview on what is necessary to finish. Equally as other similar application, it supports entering new notes using voice command and backing up notes in One Drive [7].

The application "Secure Notes" stands out among the mass of regular applications. As the name suggests, apart from classical functions, it allows more advanced protection, specifically the option of protecting individual notes with a password. Otherwise, like other applications, it does not offer more advanced possibilities of administration of the notes. Besides the password protection, it only provides the possibility to set time notifications [8].

However, none of the stated approaches addresses the defined problem in a way that it would be necessary nowadays. Most of the applications do not take into account the possibility of notifying based on the location, even though it is a very accessible and easily implemented way of a significant improvement of this kind of applications. Many applications can serve only as an inspiration concerning additional functionalities. Therefore, it is necessary to think about the optimal way of creating notes and notifications using current location of the user. The following chapter will discuss the ways and possibilities of implementation.

3 New Solution

As it was described in the previous chapters, the aim is to design and implement a mobile application for administration of notes using time notification and location based notification. The main focus of the project is above all implementing location based notifying, because it can move the final application to a completely different level [14].

It is essential to have the access to the location of the device in the application for this kind of purpose. There should be no problem with that. Nowadays, it would be difficult to find a mobile device with current operating system that would not have a GPS module. To access and to process GPS data directly in the application does not present a big problem. The following demonstration of C# code shows the way of acquiring the current location. It can be seen that there are only few lines of code necessary and the rest is taken care of by corresponding API that can solve, for example, even the way of acquiring data. That means that if the device cannot get a signal from the satellites (usually inside of the buildings), it can attempt to get the location by connecting to the internet. Alternatively, it can restore the last known location from the moment that the information was accessible. Even this kind of inaccurate information is usually sufficiently reliable for most of the situations.

As it was described in the previous chapters, the aim is to design and implement a mobile application for administration of notes using time notification and location based notification. The main focus of the project is above all implementing location based notifying, because it can move the final application to a completely different level.

It is essential to have the access to the location of the device in the application for this kind of purpose. There should be no problem with that. Nowadays, it would be difficult to find a mobile device with current operating system that would not have a GPS module. To access and to process GPS data directly in the application does not present a big problem. The following demonstration of C# code shows the way of acquiring the current location. It can be seen that there are only few lines of code necessary and the rest is taken care of by corresponding API that can solve, for example, even the way of acquiring data. That means that if the device cannot get a signal from the satellites (usually inside of the buildings), it can attempt to get the location by connecting to the internet. Alternatively, it can restore the last known location from the moment that the information was accessible. Even this kind of inaccurate information is usually sufficiently reliable for most of the situations.

```csharp
private async Task findCurrentPosition()
{
    Geolocator geolocator = new Geolocator();
    geolocator.DesiredAccuracyInMeters = 50;
    try
    {
        Geoposition pos = await geolocator.GetGeopositionAsync(
                maximumAge: TimeSpan.FromMinutes(5),
            timeout: TimeSpan.FromSeconds(7)
        );
        currentPosition = pos.Coordinate.Point;
    }
    catch (UnauthorizedAccessException)
    {
        // the app does not have the right capability or
        // the location master switch is off
        currentPosition = null;
    }
}
```

An inseparable part is "geofencing". It is a setting out of virtual areas around one spot. It is important, mostly because it would be impractical and inapplicable to activate an event in the application only when the user visits a specific location spot.

The activation has to run when the phone is located in a wider marked area that is created based on one known location spot. There are comfortable functions right in the programming languages that can be used equally for geofencing, just as they are for locating (Fig. 1).

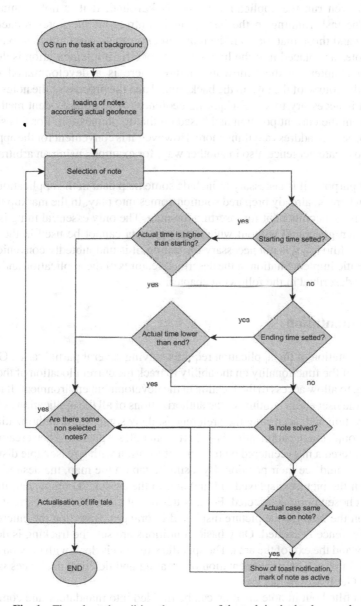

Fig. 1. Flowchart describing the course of the task in the background

In the application, the areas and the optional conditions of launch are to be predefined – typically the entry or leaving the area, or a minimal time of staying in the area before sending the notification. Subsequently, the application has to register itself to the global service that will notify the application about changes that are relevant for it. The operating system then administers tracking of the areas for all the applications at once and notifies the related areas when meeting their conditions. The operating system can even run the application in the background, if it is not running at the moment. The task running in the background controls all the notes related to the current area and those that meet all the requirements create toast notifications. Moreover, the notes are placed into the live tile. The specific implementation is described in the next chapter. In the following picture, there is a developmental diagram describing the course of the task in the background and the process of the notes control.

Then, it is necessary to solve acquiring geofences. The most evident method is to deduce it from the current position and based on that to delineate it. For this situation, it is not necessary to address anything more. However, it is convenient for the application to be able to create geofence also in another way, for example, using an arbitrary point in the map.

For that purpose, it is necessary to include some map data in the application. Fortunately, even here an already prepared solution comes into play. In the markup language XAML, there is a component for inserting the map. The only essential thing is to have a unique token generated without which the map data cannot be used in the finished application. Although it is not necessary for testing, it is undoubtedly convenient.

The specific implementation of the described features of the application and the used methods are described in the following chapter.

4   Implementation

The implementation of the application requires solving several partial tasks. Given the dependency of the functionality on the ability to track the current location of the device, it is essential to allow access to the location in the development environment. It is carried out, so that the user could administer the authorizations of all the applications within the operating system and, according the preferences, deny some of the authorizations.

The key object in the application is – apart from notes – places. When creating them, the user is offered a map centered on the current location with a reasonable distance, so that the user could see their position. By a simple tap on the map, the desired position is chosen (in the picture displayed in blue) and in the associate component, the radius around the chosen point is selected. For a better orientation, there is a current location displayed on the map (in the picture displayed in orange). Based on the entered information, a geofence is created. Only basic conditions are set, the tracking is done only for the entry and the exit of the area. The specific situation is dealt with only on the level of individual notes. The implementation of creating and deleting geofences is located in the class GeofencesHelper.cs.

The data filled out in note creating can be divided into mandatory and complementary. The mandatory fields are only the title and the text of the note. The area selection is not one of them. This was decided in order for the application to be least troublesome in use. For the user that only wants to create a text that cannot be classified anywhere, the makeshift solution could be that the location would be created somewhere on the other side of the world and the notes would be assigned there. However, that would be an inconvenient and poor solution.

There is a wide range of additional data that can be filled out. The previously mentioned data is location that has already been described above. The selection is carried out using "combobox" components. Connected to the location, there are events for entering and exiting it. They define whether the notification should be activated for the given note when entering the chosen location or exiting. Both can be selected, however, only entering is selected as default (Fig. 2).

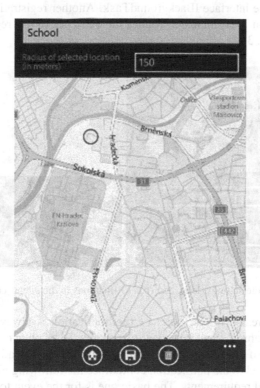

Fig. 2. Selection of the position on the map

Aside from that, it is possible to set time notifications. The starting time setting causes the notifications for the note to be sent only starting from the set time. Setting the ending time does the exact opposite. The notifications stop to be sent after the set time of ending. Both of the possibilities can be combined. This functionality complements perfectly the location based notification. The use is simple to imagine. The classic example could be a situation of a user that regularly goes to a certain place, but wants to be notified only one certain day when entering the location. Furthermore, without having to be concerned about it, the note is deactivated for the following days and the user can delete or edit it later during some bulk control.

Another necessity is creation of notifications that have already been mentioned several times. It is important for them to run even in situations when the application is not running, which is in real situation undoubtedly most of the time. It is essential, because the user needs to be notified for the active notes that would lead to opening the application. Otherwise, there is no reason for the user to open the application. Within the application, another special project that can be run in the background is created. Even here, it is necessary to make a registration in the development environment and to set the trigger point and the type of situation for the application to start running in the background. The trigger point is represented by the class NoteLocationTask.cs, which has to implement the interface IBackgroundTask. Another registration has to be done in the application run. It is suitable to control the existence of this registration in every application run (Fig. 3).

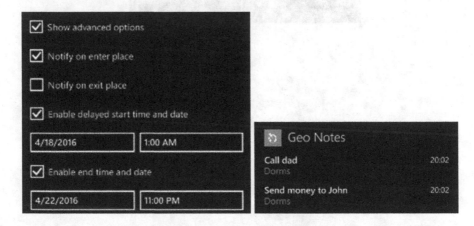

Fig. 3. (a) Note settings (left), and (b) Notifications in the events center (right)

The specially created trigger point of the application is always activated in the moment when the defined event in the settings occurs. Displaying of toast notifications in the code is caused if the notes meet the requirements for the activation. The unclaimed notifications are saved to the notification center (see the following picture).

There are several requirements. The basic one is for the event to correspond to the attributes of the note. That might mean that when leaving the area, the notes taken into account are only those that are set to be run when leaving an area. Another requirement is time. If the specific time was defined, the current time would have to be between the defined times in the note. At the same time, the note cannot be marked as done. The necessary information about meeting the time requirements and the requirements about being marked as done can be found in the detail of the note in the application as it is depicted in the following figure (Fig. 4a).

Fig. 4. (a) Detail of the note, and (b) Live tiles (middle and right)

The notifications are connected to the live tiles that are in their own way also a type of notification. Their implementation and operation is also very simple and can be found in the class TilesHelper.cs. The specific solution that has been selected in the application displays only those notes that are in the given moment marked as active. This setting is taken care of by the application in a different place. It is necessary to set separately all three sizes of tiles, because for each of them, there are different templates of the content. The tiles that support "badge" values are chosen in this case; therefore, the content can be entered only into the big tile. The title of the note and also the place the note is related to are displayed (see figure (Fig. 4b) Live Tiles). All the tiles display "badge" value that shows the number of current notes. The value displayed is also implemented on the locked screen; thereby a quick overview of something necessary to attend is achieved. The user only needs to go to the phone settings and choose the application as the one able to display this information.

The update of the Live Tile is done, apart from the events in the background, also in the front part of the application. These are situations when the user marks some active notes as inactive or done and it is necessary to delete them from the tile, so that it would provide the most up-to-date information solely about the active notes.

Data storage is realized using SQLite database, which provides a sufficient solution. The application works with only two tables that are mutually interconnected. These are tables for saving notes and user defined locations that the geofences are derived from.

The "Pivot" component was chosen to display the main application page. It allows the application page to be divided into several movable pages. The pivot items were implemented for the list of all notes, the list of all locations and the list of currently active or other relevant notes. The latter corresponds with the notes displayed on the live tile and their number with the "badge" value. Through the "flyout" menu, it is possible to use some basic function directly from the list of the items even without switching to another page. The specific form of one pivot item also with the "flyout" menu is displayed in the following figure (Fig. 5).

Fig. 5. Page with active notes

5   Testing of Developed Application

In the previous chapters, a new solution of notepad application that focuses on location based notifying was introduced. Afterwards, a specific implementation of the solution was explained. In this chapter, the testing of the solution will be carried out and the results will be compared with other solutions.

The tests examined two basic features of the application. The first one was the speed of the reaction on entering the areas. The second one was the accuracy of notifications. That means whether the correct and not incorrect notes were displayed. For this test, this application was compared with the "Place-Its" application, which was described in the second chapter. e speed reaction cannot be measured automatically by the program, because it cannot be detected when the timer sets off. If the application could detect it, it would run the action itself with its delayed reaction. For that reason, a semiautomatic measuring was created. The notes were created and subsequently assigned to an area that was edited in the end. Right afterwards, the phone was locked. The starting point of the timer was the process of saving the location, because in that moment the old geofence was deleted and the new one was created. Since that moment, there was an area registered in the system where the device was situated and the timer was measuring the interval of time before the system ran an area control and the application created a notification that data. Due to the big dispersal of the values, they were rounded to whole seconds for a clearer arrangement. They are presented in Table 1 in the column named "1st test". The second test consisted in creating a location in a specifically defined spot. According to the position and radius, a circle that divided the area was ascertained. Then, one specific place was measured out where a manual stopwatch was used for measuring, since it was not possible to apply any kind of semiautomatic measuring for the reasons stated above. In the beginning of the measuring, it was necessary to wait for the moment when the device registered the area as entering. Then, it was physically taken out of the area. During the act of carrying it away, the stopwatch was started in the place, where the area was supposed to end according to the measuring. In the moment when the phone registered that it was out of the area, the measured value was noted and the device was carried back to the area. When crossing the measured end of the area, the stopwatch was started again and the moment for the phone to register being in the area again was awaited. The measured time was noted again and the procedure was repeated several times. The phone was locked and placed in the pocket during the whole time of the test, so that it would resemble a real situation as possible.

Table 1. Measuring of the reaction speed on the areas

1st test	2nd test – exit	2nd test – enter
60 s	43 s	77 s
79 s	71 s	88 s
63 s	99 s	80 s
100 s	79 s	86 s
96 s	58 s	85 s
82 s	95 s	86 s
102 s		
96 s		
92 s		
86 s	**74 s**	**84 s**

When looking at the data, it is necessary to take into account the fact that this was a manual measuring that has its own inaccuracies. Moreover, the limit of the area was determined approximately and the specific calculated coordinates that the device works with when determining the area are unknown. For these reasons, just as in the first test, the measured numbers are rounded to the whole seconds. They are presented in Table (Table 1) in the columns named "2nd test".

As it can be seen in the table, the average values in all the columns are around 1 min and 20 s. These are quite nice numbers taking into consideration the fact that the device has to check constantly its location and at the same time try to save its battery as much as possible.

The basis of the test of the notification accuracy is to find out, whether the device gives accurate results in notifying. That means, whether the geofence always corresponds to its real equivalents. The testing has been run during a period of one week and a total of 54 notifications were called out. Only two of them were erroneous. In both of the cases, it covered the same area that was physically around 45 km far. The specific reason for the failure is unknown. A comparison was carried out with the solution in the application "Place-Its" and from 34 events, 4 were erroneous. The values can be compared in the following table (Table 2).

Table 2. Measuring of notification accuracy

	Correct	Incorrect	% error
Place-Its	30	4	13,3%
New solution	52	2	3,8%

The measuring suggests that the new solution gives better results. In the article describing implementation of the application "Place-Its", the authors state that the given solution had bigger problems notifying at the exit of defined areas. In the new solution proposed in this article, there is nothing to reproach in the speed of reaction or error rate. The main difference lies in the type of event.

Apart from the accuracy, the speed is also important. It would be unsuitable, and in many situations unusable, if the notifications were displayed with a notable time delay. From the data in the table "Measuring of the reaction speed on the areas" it can be noted that regarding problems with time delay, the new solution is good. Most of the values are ranging between 60 and 100 s, which are very acceptable time intervals.

Generally, the testing ended up very well and it verified that the proposed and implemented solution can do well in the actual use.

6   Conclusions

The purpose of the project was to design and implement a better approach to developing a notepad application with a solution using GPS. Gradually, the disadvantages of many present solutions were described and the new solution was proposed, later even implemented. The result is an application that solved the assigned problem very well. It emerged from the testing, that it provides both sufficient correctness and notification speed. The applicability of the proposed solution could be significant. It can provide a relief for its users, so they can simply forget about the notifications. The application notifies the user about the notes itself. In the future, the application could be supplemented with more supporting functionalities. Therefore, it would be convenient to transfer it to other mobile platforms.

Future research at this project will be focussed on development of Smart application for people with dementia [10, 11] for which can be very useful to have some application for detection of known people faces, because they often forgot their faces due to mentioned diseases.

Acknowledgement. This work and the contribution were supported by project "SP-2102-2017 - Smart Solutions for Ubiquitous Computing Environments at Faculty of Informatics and Management, University of Hradec Kralove, Czech Republic.

References

1. Lin, C.Y., Hung, M.T.: A location-based personal task reminder for mobile users. Pers. Ubiquit. Comput. **18**(2), 303–314 (2014)
2. Bharat, R., Manakakis, L.: Evolution of mobile location-based services. Commun. ACM **46**(12), 61–65 (2003). doi:10.1145/953460.953490
3. Lee, H., Chuvzrov, E.: Beginning Windows Phone App Development: Push Notifications. 3rd ed., pp. 405–444 (2012)
4. Liberty, J., Japikse, J., Galloway, J.: Pro Windows 8.1 development with XAML and C#: Push Notifications, pp. 405–444. Apress, Berkeley (2014)
5. Jarawa, S.: -My Notes-: Application for Windows in Microsoft Store

6. Sohn, T., Li, Kevin A., Lee, G., Smith, I., Scott, J., Griswold, William G.: Place-its: a study of location-based reminders on mobile phones. In: Beigl, M., Intille, S., Rekimoto, J., Tokuda, H. (eds.) UbiComp 2005. LNCS, vol. 3660, pp. 232–250. Springer, Heidelberg (2005). doi: 10.1007/11551201_14
7. Kobr, A.: Daily Notes: Application for Windows in Microsoft Store. Microsoft Store
8. Iamchadan. Secure Notes: Application for Windows in Microsoft Store
9. Klimova, B., Maresova, P.: Computer-based training programs for older people with mild cognitive impairment and/or dementia. Front. Hum. Neurosci. **11**(1), 1–9 (2017). ISSN 1662-5161
10. Klimova, B., Maresova, P., Kuca, K.: Assistive technologies for managing language disorders in dementia. Neuropsychiatric Dis. Treat. **12**(1), 533–540 (2016)
11. Behan, M., Krejcar, O.: Adaptive graphical user interface solution for modern user devices. In: Pan, J.-S., Chen, S.-M., Nguyen, N.T. (eds.) ACIIDS 2012. LNCS, vol. 7197, pp. 411–420. Springer, Heidelberg (2012). doi:10.1007/978-3-642-28490-8_43
12. Novotny, J., Dvorak, J., Krejcar, O.: User based intelligent adaptation of five in a row game for android based on the data from the front camera. In: Paolis, L.T., Mongelli, A. (eds.) AVR 2016. LNCS, vol. 9768, pp. 133–149. Springer, Cham (2016). doi:10.1007/978-3-319-40621-3_9
13. Benikovsky, J., Brida, P., Machaj, J.: Proposal of user adaptive modular localization system for ubiquitous positioning. In: Pan, J.-S., Chen, S.-M., Nguyen, N.T. (eds.) ACIIDS 2012. LNCS, vol. 7197, pp. 391–400. Springer, Heidelberg (2012). doi:10.1007/978-3-642-28490-8_41
14. Hustak, T., Krejcar, O., Selamat, A., Mashinchi, R., Kuca, K.: Principles of usability in human-computer interaction driven by an evaluation framework of user actions In: Younas, M., Awan, I., Mecella, M. (eds.) MOBIWIS 2015. LNCS, vol. 9228, pp. 51–62. Springer, Cham (2015). doi:10.1007/978-3-319-23144-0_5

Calculating the Optimal Price of Products in an Online Store

Ondrej Sukala[1], Petra Maresova[2], Jan Dvorak[1], Ali Selamat[1,3], and Ondrej Krejcar[1(✉)]

[1] Faculty of Informatics and Management, Center for Basic and Applied Research,
University of Hradec Kralove, Rokitanskeho 62, 500 03 Hradec Kralove, Czech Republic
{ondrej.sukala,jan.dvorak}@uhk.cz, Ondrej@Krejcar.org
[2] Department of Economy, Faculty of Informatics and Management,
University of Hradec Kralove, Rokitanskeho 62, 500 03 Hradec Kralove, Czech Republic
Petra.Maresova@uhk.cz
[3] Faculty of Computing, Universiti Teknologi Malaysia, 81310 Johor Baharu, Johor, Malaysia
aselamat@utm.my

Abstract. This article focuses on the problem of mass optimisation of the prices in online stores. Each year, the number of online stores in the Czech Republic grows, as well as their turnover and the number of offered products. The original solution which consists of manual adaptations of the products' prices is nowadays insufficient. Therefore, an application was created, that uses data from multiple sources and on their basis automatically calculates the optimal price of a product. This new solution considerably simplifies and accelerates the calculation of the new prices. Moreover, the automatic calculation has also a positive impact on the quality of the resulting prices due to the fact that no mistakes and typing errors are expected to be made in an automatized solution.

Keywords: Optimization of prices · Online store · Competition monitoring · Shopping channels · Product price

1 Introduction

Smart industries bring acceleration of many processes and sustainable economic growth. E-marketing is one of the recent but commonly used sales tools which requires precise knowledge of the customer's preferences and attaches great importance to price determination [7, 8, 10].

The number of online stores in the Czech Republic has stabilised itself in the last few years at approximately 37 300. Due to this amount, Czech Republic is often labeled as the online world power. Each year, a few thousand online stores are born and another few thousand die out [1]. In this case, the correct adjustment of the product price has a significant impact on the success of online stores.

The oprimalisation of the prices is a time-consuming activity which is also needed to be done regularly – sometimes even a few times per day. Some e-shops pay employees to monitor the prices of the competition and accordingly manually adjust the prices in

© Springer International Publishing AG 2017
M. Younas et al. (Eds.): MobiWIS 2017, LNCS 10486, pp. 104–114, 2017.
DOI: 10.1007/978-3-319-65515-4_9

their systems. Current online shops usually have even thousands of products and advertise on more retail channels at the same time [2].

Czech e-shops have the choice of many different services through which they can advertise their goods. The products' comparing websites (Heureka.cz, Zbozi.cz, Google shopping, etc.) often use for offers'comparison the information about availability, users' shop rating and other parameters. However, the most important parameter is the sale price which defines the ranking of the advertisement.. It is not always true that the lowest price leads to the highest number of customers. This is due to the fact that a too low price can seem untrustworthy. Classic PPC systems (Google Adwords, Sklik.cz, ...) are in comparison to the websites mentioned above less concentrated on the price. The success of the offer is decided mainly on the advertisement's text and the offered price per click. Due to the higher prices of conversion, these sold products are usually more expensive than when other advertising methods are used.

Second hand stores and advertising servers are mainly intended for nonrecurring sale of damaged or used goods. The sale price can be often below the purchase price.

The social networks (Facebook, Twitter, Pinterest, ...) are not suitable for direct sale [13]. However, customers can be obtained through addressing their problems in the discussion groups or by creating an interesting input. In this case it is difficult to judge, how big of an impact has the price of the product.

Each retail channel offers various requirements, competition and occurring customers. Due to these reasons, the optimal prices of products can differ depending on the chosen retail channel.

By creating the automatized solution for this task, the e-shop supervisor saves a significant amount of time, considering it consists of routine, time consuming, as well as very uninteresting work. It is possible to achieve even better results than during manual adjustment of prices by creating sufficiently complicated application. Compared to the manual adjustment, the automatized solution does not make unnecessary mistakes and realises the calculations always in the same quality, if the quality of the entry data is not changed.

2 Problem Definition and Related Works

The choice and implementation of pricing strategy is often described as an optimization problem where the firm chooses the most profitable pricing strategy given certain external determinants [9, 11, 12]. Main factors affecting price determination of product are: 1. product cost 2. the utility and demand 3. extent of competition in the market 4. government and legal regulations 5. pricing objectives 6. marketing methods used. The optimization of the price is a process of searching for the highest price which the customer is willing to pay in order to shop in the given online store.

- COST ORIENTED PRICE CREATION
  The calculation is realized by adding the charge to the overall costs of the product. [4]. There are several possibilities of cost embedding into price:
  - Costs Plus – price is based on costs and an increase price for the specific profit.
  - Target Return Method

– Profit Maximizing (marginal revenue (MR) = marginal costs (MC))
– Breakeven Analysis
- VALUE ORIENTED PRICE CREATION
  This method sets the price of the products according to how the customer perceives the value of the product. Even though, the method brings good results, the conducting of customer surveys can be very cost-demanding.
- DEMAND ORIENTED PRICE CREATION
  In order to calculate the demand oriented price creation, it is at first necessary to obtain a sufficient amount of data which concentrates on the number of goods that was sold at a specific product's price. The setting of the price is dependent on the customer's judgement. The needed data can be obtained from customer questioning or rating the history of orders [5].
- COMPETITION ORIENTED PRICE CREATION
  Some online stores directly copy the prices of the competition or slightly adjust them. The average of the competition price is calculated and the result price is set above or below this average according to the advantages and disadvantages of the own offer [3].

All of the above mentioned solutions have significant imperfections. Some solutions do not provide sufficiently qualitative results, others are on the other hand too difficult to process. For the needs of a common internet store which has thousands of items it is necessary to find an easy solution with a sufficient quality of a result.

2.1 Problem of More Prices

In the case, in which e-shop sells goods over more retail channels, more optimal prices – for each retail channel – may be created.

1. SOLUTION 1 – MORE PRICES
   Some online stores offer their customers various prices according to the source from which they access their website. This method is more complicated for implementation and cannot insure a reliable solution. From the technical side, it is not possible to identify the specific user on the web with certainty, as this user can use multiple devices at the same time or on the other side, more users can share one device. In these cases the customer can notice the price change and damage the name of the store for example on the social networks.
2. SOLUTION 2 – MORE E-SHOPS
   Another common solution is the creation of more online stores. The operator and the offered products do not change, only the price and the online store are different.
3. SOLUTION 3 – MERGING OF PRICES
   More ethical solution is provided by the merging of different prices into one. This solution does not enable the achievement of maximal profit on all retail channels, but is simpler for execution and more favourable for online store customers.

The new solution combines all previous methods. The user of the application decides about the price merging in the last step and has the possibility to decline it.

3 New Solution

The new solution offers a collective creation of optimal prices without conducting difficult surveys, also intended for e-shops which do not have any history. The advantage of this solution is the possibility to repeat the price calculation more often than for example with the solution concerning conducting customer surveys.

Necessary data for price creation
New solution requires the database with the following data:

1. products
   a. name
   b. purchase price
   c. recommended retail price
   d. VAT
   e. availability
2. supplier
   a. supplier's name
3. retail channels
   a. retail channel's name
   b. URL for product's interconnection
   c. store's name
   d. store's rating

These are low requirements, considering that most of these data are already available to the online stores for other purposes.

Selection of the supplier
The product can be delivered by more suppliers. Due to this, it is necessary to find the lowest purchase price before the calculation of the retail price. For this calculation, the recommended retail price may be also needed, according to which some suppliers create the bottom retail price level.

Position Search
Every product manually receives a URL address which refers to the profile of these products within the retail channel (e.g. product's detail on the price of goods comparison website). By parsing the assigned profile, the information about competition is obtained. For each offer, these following data are investigated:

- end price (retail price with VAT including all extra charges)
- products' availability (warehouse, delivery within 3 days, etc.)
- possibility of delivery (the cheapest type of transport)
- e-shop rating (unified rating format and number ratings)

All of these data have an impact on the comparison of the individual positions. Their weight can be adjusted in the application's settings. The algorithm gradually passes through all offers from the first (best) position and compares offers of the monitored e-shop with competitors' offers.

Prices adjustment

After the finding of the competition offer, against which it is possible to compete, the position can be obtained by slight decrease of the offer. The value for decrease is set according to how significant is the difference among monitored offers. It is not only the difference in price, but also other data are used, as well as their weight.

Merging of more prices

In the case when the offers are placed on multiple channels, more prices are created that are necessary to be unified. Some online stores use more prices for one product at the

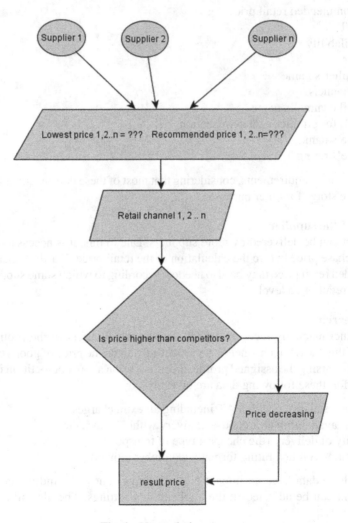

Fig. 1. New solution process

same time. The price is then set according to from which source the customer comes. This process is not suggested as the customer can easily recognize these adjustments (Fig. 1). Due to this reason, the application offers some functions for price unification:

- manually – all possibilities are shown and the user can choose himself the most suitable offer
- price average – the average price is calculated from all recommended product's prices
- always the lowest price
- always the highest price
- rating – the best rated offer is chosen

4 Implementation

The implementation of the solution is in the type of a web application. NETTE Framework and PHP Simple HTML DOM Parser library were chosen for the development of the application. The resulting application is written in PHP language, as it is the most common programming language for creation of web applications [3]. The services of Shoptet.cz, Heureka.cz are also developed in PHP and therefore it is easier to connect to them [6].

4.1 Settings

- Store
  - The price of the cheapest type of transportation serves for the comparison of offers according to the transport price
- Products
  - Extra charge (percentage) – the percentages which set the minimal retail price without VAT are added to the purchase price without VAT
  - Extra charge (amount) – the amount which sets the minimal retail price without VAT is added to the purchase price without VAT
  - Type of price unification
    Lowest price
    Highest price
    Average price
    Best rating
- Impact of data on comparing of offers is set using the values in interval <0;1>, the sum of all values has to be 1
  - Rating of the store
  - Delivery
  - Price of delivery
  - Price of product

4.2 Adding of Products

The new solution offers two different types of adding products. The connection to an e-shop is the most suitable solution for long-time usage of this application. After the connection of the e-shop, it is necessary to adjust the structure of the e-shop's database in order to comply with this application's database structure. The second solution is the adjustment of classes in the models directory of this application.

For one time usage of the application or testing, it is possible to import products from XML file. XML file can be found in the import directory:

<PRODUCT> - characteristics of individual products, file can contain more products at the same time
<NAME> - name of the product
<RECOMMENDED_PRICE> - suggested retail price without VAT
<RETAIL_PRICE> - retail price without VAT
<VAT> - VAT (most commonly 0.21 or 0.15)
<DELIVERY> - delivery (number of days)
<SUPPLIER) – characteristics of the supplier, one product can have more suppliers at the same time
<SUPPLIER_ID> - unique supplier's identifier
<WHOLESALE_PRICE> - purchase price without VAT
<CHANNEL> - characteristics of the retail channel, one product can be offered on multiple retail channels at the same time
<CHANNEL_ID> - unique identifier of the retail channel
<URL> - URL address which specifies product within the retail channel, in case of the stone stores this entry is empty.

4.3 Adjustment of Products, Suppliers and Retail Channels

- Basic data
  - Name of the product
  - Recommended price without VAT
  - Retail price without VAT
  - VAT
  - Delivery
- Suppliers
  - Name of the supplier
  - Wholesale price without VAT
- Retail channels
  - Name of the channel
  - URL address of the product within the retail channel
  - Recommended price – mostly it is automatically calculated using price optimization
  - Position of the offer within the retail channel – most of the time, it is automatically discovered using price optimization
  - Rating of the offer is mainly automatically calculated using price optimization

- Name of the store serves for store removal from the offers' comparison. It is not suitable to compare with the own offer if it already exists on the given retail channel
- Store rating – serves for comparing of offers according to the rating.

4.4   Actualization and Price Calculation

By pushing the button 'Data actualization' the download of the data from all retail channels and further offers' rating is conducted in price optimization section. The automatic merging of process is done according to the chosen method in the settings section. For chosen offers, it is possible to avoid automatic merging and manually select the most suitable offer. The prices of all shown products are adjusted by selecting the chosen offers and pushing the button 'Accept the changes' (Figs. 2 and 3).

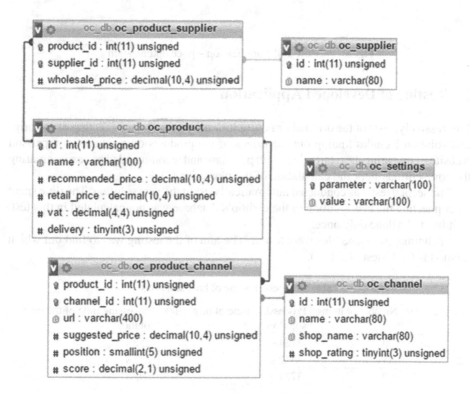

Fig. 2. Data model

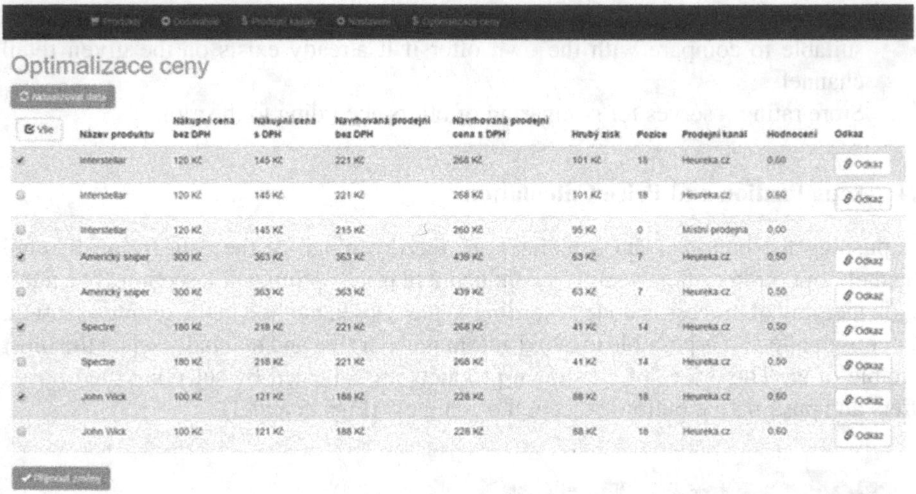

Fig. 3. Preview of the application – price optimization

5　Testing of Developed Application

Progressively, tests of the original or new solution were conducted. Testing of the original solution includes finding out the prices of the products on products' comparison websites, comparing the retail prices with purchase and recommended prices, comparing the competition offers and calculation of the new price [3].

The second test was conducted automatically using the new solution. The time spent by connecting the new solution to the e-shop's database was not calculated in this test, as it has to be done only once.

Each time, two same files were tested. The aim of the testing was to find out which method is the fastest (Table 1).

Table 1. Speed testing of both solutions

Test number	Number of items	Processing time of original solution	Processing time of the new solution
1	50	3124 s	252 s
2	55	3342 s	277 s
3	60	3731 s	298 s

Testing consisted of three independent attempts which proved that the new solution is 12 times faster as the original one.

Even though, the tests were not focused on the quality measurement of the price calculation, it was already during these tests visible that when using manual calculation of the price, mistakes often happen.

6 Conclusions

The new solution is more than 12 times faster than the manual adjustment of the products' prices. The result was proven by testing. The new solution is significantly less time-demanding and therefore, the costs of price optimization in online stores are decreased. Moreover, another advantage of the new solution is that it provides a reliable and precise price calculation. Finally, it is also possible to repeat the price calculation without repeating some activities (products' price search, obtaining of information about competition's offers, etc.).

Future research will be focused on inclusion of other factors influencing pricing such as: customer's demand and government and legal regulations for market in Europe.

Acknowledgement. This work and the contribution were supported by project "SP-2102-2017 - Smart Solutions for Ubiquitous Computing Environments" Faculty of Informatics and Management, University of Hradec Kralove, Czech Republic.

References

1. Oplustil, O.: Shopexpo 2015 – e-shops from whole country Czech at one place. Markething, 9 June 2015. http://www.markething.cz/shopexpo-2015. Accessed 9 June 2016. ISSN 1805-4991
2. Baker, W., Kiewell, D., Winkler, G.: Using big data to make better pricing decisions, 1 June 2014. http://www.mckinsey.com/insights/marketing_sales/using_big_data_to_make_better_pricing_decisions. Accessed 2 Jan 2016
3. Maresova, P., Sobeslav, V., Krejcar, O.: Cost–benefit analysis – evaluation model of cloud computing deployment for use in companies. Appl. Econ. **49**(6), 521–533 (2017)
4. Kotler, P., Armstrong, G.: Marketing. Grada, Prague (2004). 855 p. ISBN 978-80-247-0513-2
5. Wohe, G., Kislingerova, E.: Introduction into Company Economy, 2nd edn. C.H. Beck (2007). Accessed 2 Jan 2016. ISBN 978-80-7179-897-2
6. Hustak, T., Krejcar, O., Selamat, A., Mashinchi, R., Kuca, K.: Principles of usability in human-computer interaction driven by an evaluation framework of user actions. In: Younas, M., Awan, I., Mecella, M. (eds.) MOBIWIS 2015. LNCS, vol. 9228, pp. 51–62. Springer, Cham (2015). doi:10.1007/978-3-319-23144-0_5
7. Maresova, P., Klimova, B.: Economic and technological aspects of business intelligence in european business sector. In: Park, J., Jin, H., Jeong, Y.S., Khan, M. (eds.) Advanced Multimedia and Ubiquitous Engineering. Lecture Notes in Electrical Engineering, vol. 393, pp. 79–84. Springer, Singapore (2016)
8. Mundere, L., Marešová, P.: Potential of ICT Industry for Economic Growth in Developing Countries - A Case Study of the Republic of Rwanda. Adv. Sci. Lett. (2016). ISSN 1936-6612
9. Hallberg, N.L.: The micro-foundations of pricing strategy in industrial markets: a case study in the European packaging industry. J. Bus. Res. **76**, 179–188 (2017)
10. Zhoua, Y.-W., Caoa, B., Tangb, Q., Zhou, W.: Pricing and rebate strategies for an e-shop with a cashback website. Eur. J. Oper. Res. **262**(1), 108–122 (2017)
11. Baye, M.R., Morgan, J., Scholten, P.: Temporal price dispersion: evidence from an online consumer electronics market. J. Interact. Mark. **18**(4), 101–115 (2004). New Trends of Intelligent E-marketing Based on Web Mining for E-shops

12. Cellary, W., Rykowski, J.: Pens the author workspace challenges of smart industries – privacy and payment in visible versus unseen internet. Gov. Inf. Q. (2015). doi:10.1016/j.giq.2015.08.005
13. Maresova, P., Klimova, B., Tucek, V.: Use of social networks in banking: a study in the Czech Republic. Appl. Econ. 47(57), 6155–6169 (2015)

Smart Security System Based on Android Platform

Pavel Zubr[1], Jan Dvorak[1], Ali Selamat[1,2], and Ondrej Krejcar[1(✉)]

[1] Faculty of Informatics and Management, Center for Basic and Applied Research,
University of Hradec Kralove, Rokitanskeho 62, 500 03 Hradec Kralove, Czech Republic
{pavel.zubr,jan.dvorak}@uhk.cz, Ondrej@Krejcar.org
[2] Faculty of Computing, Universiti Teknologi Malaysia, 81310 Johor Baharu, Johor, Malaysia
aselamat@utm.my

Abstract. Protection of property is very important in today's world both for households and for companies because of quite high crime rates. Existing cheap and widespread security systems are no more sufficient, because most of them cannot be configured or automatically activated/deactivated, eventually enhanced or integrated into IoT. People can either buy a more expensive solution or create their own a lot cheaper systems, which can be enhanced according to their requirements. People also don't want to worry, whether they did activate the security system in their house or office. While implementing the security system it may be sufficient to use cheap platforms such as RaspberryPi and Arduino. The solution is an autonomous system, able to encode itself and to alert the owner in the case of an intrusion attempt into a building.

Keywords: Security system · Arduino · Smartphone · Android · Geo-fence · Python · Pir sensor, infrared sensor · Alarm

1 Introduction

Protection of property is obviously a current topic nowadays around the entire world, because in the society still occurs a high level of crime. The most widespread security systems happen to be the systems using a passive infrared sensor for movement detection. Today there appear interesting projects concerning with securing the property and connecting the systems even with the internet [1], while increasing investments into cloud computing solutions increasing also security issues [9].

First of all it's necessary to say, that security systems can be found often in public spaces and companies, but in many households this type of preventive safety system against the burglars is still missing.

This paper deals with automation and modularisation of a home safety system. The commonly available cheap systems, often based on the movement detection using the passive infrared sensor, are not able to be configured or to make their operation easier for the users or to gain various overviews of their functionality or status.

In the case that a person decides to purchase such cheap alarm, which can be seen in the picture below, it's possible, that while using it to protect the property, it fails, because the volume of the alarm siren is around 100 dB and the owner has no chance to

© Springer International Publishing AG 2017
M. Younas et al. (Eds.): MobiWIS 2017, LNCS 10486, pp. 115–128, 2017.
DOI: 10.1007/978-3-319-65515-4_10

find out, that someone burgles in his real estate at the moment, because if the alarm is situated inside the building, no one aside the burglar doesn't have to hear it.

In the case people really want to protect their property, they will have to either invest huge sums of money (many thousand crowns) into more sophisticated systems or create their own system.

Fortunately the systems, which can alert the owner about the fact that someone intruded into the building in the real time, expand abundantly lately, reaching so far, that they are even low energy intensive [2].

The objective of this work is creating a simple, configurable and extensible security device at a low total cost (not exceeding 125 USD), which is based on Arduino platform and uses the passive infrared sensor. The server part will be based on the platform RasbperryPi and the whole system will be configurable by a created interface. RaspberryPi will also serve as a broker for sending messages between the server and the end devices.

By configurations it's meant for example a possibility to let the application inform the user by SMS, that someone tries to intrude into the building. Next possible configuration is an option, whether the alarm siren shall be turned on or not. Also it is possible to configure telephone numbers, which will have the access to lock/unlock the building, and PIN codes, which will enable to lock/unlock the building.

In the case someone already owns a security system it often happens, that the person worries, whether he really did activate the alarm. The only possibility to check, whether the alarm in the building is/isn't activated, is really to physically go there. That's why there will be implemented a possibility of an automatic alarm activation/deactivation. This function is aimed to be a fundamental function of the whole system. Automation of such basic activities that people perform daily is certainly important for the mankind, because people will be able to concern with the important problems and not such common activities as it's indeed for example driving a car – even today there are already available autonomous vehicles [3].

Today, many people own a smartphone, which was selected as a suitable instrument for detecting, whether the system shall be activated or deactivated. The application for smartphone will be implemented for Android platform out of reason of its proliferation and low prices of the devices based on this platform.

2   Problem Definition

Contemporary security systems are non-configurable at all in the most cases, or the devices, which can be configured, represent an investment in thousands crowns in the case one decides to purchase them. The cheap, commonly available solutions are either unsatisfactory for its absence of option to inform the real estate owner about the actual situation in the building, or because the purchased system is not configurable at all. Also it is missing the possibility of the autonomous decision to activate/deactivate the security device and therefore people must still think about whether they performed the activation or not.

In the following paragraphs there will be briefly described the systems chosen with regard to their price – therefore there will be described the cheaper and also the more expensive solutions that are commonly available to be purchased.

Nowadays it may be purchased the system [4], which contains a remote control and a sensor unit that consists of an integrated alarm siren. By using the remote control the system can be activated or deactivated. The given solution is inapplicable out of the reason that its owner has to bring the remote control with him/her all the time and also it's absolutely impossible to send to the owner any information about an eventual intrusion attempt into his real estate.

I praxis there also occur more sophisticated expensive systems [5], which can be unlocked and locked either using a set code or by a remote control or even using a mobile phone by sending an SMS. Unfortunately, the request to lock and unlock the alarm automatically can't be fulfilled by such system, because the system is not able to decide autonomously, whether the object shall be secured or not.

We can also even come across very sophisticated devices [2], based also on Arduino platform, but unfortunately it does not enable neither the required configuration nor the automatic switching the sensor on/off.

Very successful position on the Czech market in the field of selling safety equipment belongs to Jablotron company, which produces high-level products and provides their support as well. Jablotron company has perfectly processed and controllable the most of its systems, such as for example this one [6], in various ways – by both SMS, and direct entering password into the safety unit.

Within its systems Jablotron company also offers the option to control the safety equipment from anywhere using the internet, which means a certain security risk. A problem of the Jablotron systems is certainly their price, because not everyone can afford them. And furthermore these systems don't offer the required automated system activation/deactivation.

Almost all of the abovementioned approaches do not accomplish the configurability requirements and certainly none of them fulfils the possibility to automatically activate/deactivate the system in a building, office, or apartment – the place where the system will be used. Likewise, these devices, except for some Jablotron products, do not support connecting the system with a home network (they're not IoT friendly). It should be noted, that these devices also cannot inform the user, what daytime he most frequently stays home. It will be necessary to create a new method, whereby the safety equipment decides, whether the system in the building will be activated or not.

The fundamental problem comes up to be certainly creating the method, whereby the system in the building decides, whether the system shall be automatically activated/deactivated. This way the owner doesn't have to think of the activation/deactivation in order to avoid the situations, when the owner often doesn't realize, whether he did really activate the system, wondering all day, whether he didn't forgot to activate it accidentally, and if he wanted to make sure, he would have to check it by going there physically.

The implementation method of this solution will certainly have to be designed, because there are more possibilities how to check the alarm activation in the building and also how to activate/deactivate the alarm automatically.

Next it will have to be designed the configuration interface, whereby it will be possible to set the telephone numbers, to which will be send eventual alerts in the case of an intrusion attempt into the secured building. The system will definitely support the possibility to switch off the siren in the case of activating the system alarm (the silent mode), which may trick the burglar, because he doesn't recognize, that the alarm was triggered (he can't hear the siren), the owner obtains an SMS about the burglary/triggering the alarm and so the burglar may be awaited by the police outside the house.

The whole system will be modular in design for possibility of a further enhancement with other sensors (modules) that would fulfil additional functions, which security systems offer, such as for example detection of smoke, gases or fire.

The sensor, which will be used for securing the object, is so-called passive infrared sensor, which is commonly being used in the security systems. This sensor's short title is PIR, from an English Passive Infrared Detector [7]. The PIR sensing device operates on the principle of a pyroelectric phenomenon, when a temperature change is used to deform a crystal lattice of dielectrics. Generally this phenomenon can be defined as an ability of material, when the material is able to generate a temporary electric potential while changing its temperature. The PIR sensing devices consist of more components and one of them is optics. The function of the optics in the PIR sensing devices is to concentrate signals form the detection zones into the PIR element, which is the basic functional component of the passive infrared detector. Next important part is a method of processing the signal, which can be either analogue or digital. It should be noted, that all the PIR detectors have to be calibrated and the signal can be distorted by for example inconvenient sensor position – opposite to a window, a radiator, because the warm flowing air may distort the scanning [8].

3 New Solution

A central component of the system will be the router, while its network will be separated from a common home network. The single system elements will be connectable to the network by a cable (to the Switch), as it's displayed in the picture, or it will be possible to implement a solution, which will interconnect the single elements by Wi-Fi. SSID of the Wi-Fi will certainly not be transmitted, in order to prevent unnecessary attacks on the concerned Wi-Fi. The router will contain a special configuration – the static IP for the server and the DHCP for the rest devices. Also there will be implemented a whitelist of MAC addresses (the authorized MAC addresses), which will have the permission to communicate through the network (Fig. 1).

The RaspberryPi [18] server will serve as a MQTT broker for transmitting messages between the single network devices. The operating system (OS), which will be installed on the RaspberryPi, is Raspbian. This OS will also appropriately serve to host a web application, where the configurations will be executed. The configuration will support the possibility of sending the SMS about the intrusion attempt to any set telephone numbers, and besides, it will be possible to set, whether the alarm siren shall blare. The last option to configure will be setting PINs and the telephone numbers, whereby it will

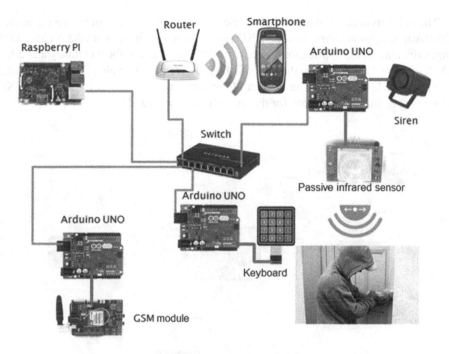

Fig. 1. Structure of the security system

be possible to activate/deactivate the alarm in the building. Likewise, the server will contain a database to save all the data, which will be applicable for various evaluations.

MQTT is now a communication standard for the IoT (Internet of Things, that means connection of embedded devices with the internet). Commonly people would say that HTTP/2 protocol [10] will be a suitable and sufficient communication protocol for needs of the embedded devices, but this protocol is non-trivially implemented in the basis. The HTTP communication is also inconvenient in terms of its design, because the server isn't able to send one message to more clients – while using HTTP, only one client can request the message from the application on the server and the server forwards it to him, that's why MQTT is a lot more effective. The MQTT communication carries out on a principle "publish – subscribe". Published and subscribed are so-called topics on the basis of their title. The topics can be also classified hierarchically, it's possible to use wildcards to subscribe more topics. In the MQTT communication the broker serves as a mediator that takes care of providing a communication N:N. One message can be received by more subscribers at ones and one message (resp. one topic) can be also sent by more publishers at once. In the picture below you can see a basic diagram of the MQTT communication. The contents of the following paragraphs were drawn from [11, 12].

Another component of the system is going to be the GSM module, which is going to take care of sending the SMSs in the case of an intrusion into the secured building. This module will be able to receive the SMSs and then to deactivate the alarm in the building by this functionality. The GSM module is going to be any cheap GSM module capable of sending SMSs using AT commands [13].

The GSM module, as well as the keyboard, siren and PIR is going to be connected with the development board Arduino UNO [14], which is equipped with the ATMega328 chip, sufficient for the application's needs. It contains 32 KB of flash memory and 2 KB RAM. Arduino UNO contains the total of 14 digital I/O pins, 6 analog pins and executes on the voltage level of 5 V. The number of the inputs and outputs of the Arduino UNO device will be fully satisfactory for the security system (Fig. 2).

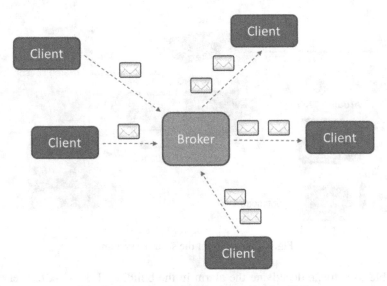

Fig. 2. Scheme of MQTT communication [12]

All the Arduino UNO boards will be equipped by Ethernet shield [15], which is an additional module to Arduino UNO, to which can be connected RJ45 connector. As an alternative to that it can serve a cheap Wi-Fi module, for example ESP8266 [16].

Another system component is Arduino UNO connected to the keyboard, whereby it will be possible to enter the PIN allowing the activation/deactivation of the alarm in the building. The PIN codes will be stored in the configuration on the server, which will authorize and log all the executed actions.

Next option to activate/deactivate the alarm is already mentioned new solution, which activates/deactivates the alarm in accordance with the owner's position. There will be created the Android application, working with geo-fencing [17], which means, that along with the owner's position it determines, whether the security equipment shall activate/deactivate itself. For example the building alarm activates itself, when the owner (resp. smartphone) is far enough, which means outside the geo-fence. It will be required to apply a rule, that the user must have GPS and data turned on, which is already common today. While entering the geo-fence there will be sent the SMS in a certain format to the telephone number of the SIM card in GSM module, the GSM module will consequently send a message about activation/deactivation of the security system.

The last component displayed in the (Fig. 1) is Arduino UNO connected to the alarm siren and to the passive infrared sensor. In the case the PIR detects a movement and the system will be in activated mode, it will send the information about the movement to the server, and if the siren is on, the server instructs Arduino to let the siren blare.

The whole system will be implemented modularly, in order to make it possible to enhance it with further sensors (resp. movement sensing devices), therefore the individual sensing devices will have to be indicated by unique identifiers, whereby they will be recognized. Here you can see the advantage of the MQTT protocol, which can send a command to all the sensing devices in the particular part of the building (using the topic with the wildcards) to get activated/deactivated, for example in the situation the building was divided into more parts and the user would decide to let the alarm activated in one of them.

In the production environment it will be appropriate to supply a backup power for the whole system in order to ensure the security system operates constantly, even in the case of power outage. For this purpose it will be sufficient to use common UPSs – backup powers, which manage powering the particular system components in the order of hours or days.

4   Implementation

The respective project implementation consists of installation and configuration of the RaspberryPi server, configuration of the router, implementation of the web configuration application, Android geo-location application, programming and connecting the Arduino with the GSM module, the Arduino with the keyboard and finally the Arduino with the passive infrared sensor and the siren.

First of all there was installed the operation system Raspbian [18] on the RaspberryPi. This operation system is based on linux distribution Debian and offers more than 35 000 packets to be installed, including a webserver – lighttpd, a mysql server and a MQTT broker Mosquitto, which were installed on RaspberryPi.

The MQTT broker has to be compiled separately instead of an easier installation from the repository [19]. The web application will be implemented in PHP; therefore PHP will be installed on the server as well. Further there has to be programming language Python on the server and its library paho-mqtt [20], because in this programming language will be implemented server utility scripts, which means for example creating the impulse for sending the SMS, for deactivation etc.

The next step happens to be the router configuration. To the server (RaspberryPi) it will be assigned static IP address 192.168.1.100 and the other network devices will have the IP addresses assigned dynamically by DHCP. The router interface will get address 192.168.1.1. During the configuration the Wi-Fi was ultimately completely turned off, because the devices were cable connected, so the turned-on Wi-Fi would present an unnecessary safety risk. Also there were authorized only the MAC addresses that take place in the system (MAC address of the RaspberryPi and all the Arduino devices). Likewise it is possible to authorize MAC address of the PC, whereby the configurations will be executed.

The web configuration application is created in PHP – concretely in Yii framework, which is suitable for modular applications development. Here it is possible to configure the telephone numbers, on which will be send the alert in the case of triggering the alarm, the possibility to turn off the siren and the authorisation codes for access into the building and also the telephone number, whereby it will be possible to unlock the building. The user has to make the respective authentication and authorisation before performing an action, of course. User passwords are being hashed using a strong enough algorithm bcrypt.

All the Arduino devices communicate through MQTT protocol, as it was mentioned several times, that's why there were defined the topics (resp. their templates), which will be used for the communication.

All the prototype components are being connected on a non-solder contact field, suitable for creating prototypes of the systems like this one.

The first Arduino is connected to the GSM module. It was selected GSM module Neoway M590 [21], which is very cheap and reliable. The entire communication with the GSM module is being realized using AT commands. The Arduino has to be connected with the GSM module by a converter 3.3 V – 5 V, important for a voltage transmission, because the GSM module operates with the maximum logic voltage 3.3 V level for Rx (receiving) a Tx (transmitting) pins, whereas the Arduino operates on the 5 V level. The voltage transmission has to be bidirectional, because the communication is being carried out also from the side of GSM module to the Arduino – the GSM module sends the answers and the received SMSs to the Arduino. Then there's only needed to interconnect the voltage supply of 5 V and GND with the GSM module.

There has to be charged a satisfactory credit on the SIM card, or (as it is implemented in the project) there has to be a monthly tariff, so that it could send the SMSs. With this Arduino together with the GSM module it's connected the abovementioned Ethernet Shield, which provides the network communication with the server, resp. MQTT broker.

The next Arduino desk is connected to the keyboard with a layout of 4x4 keys using eight digital pins. The keyboard operates on the 5 V level, therefore it's not needed to convert the voltage levels. During the implementation to the Arduino there was connected a seven-segment display, which can display 4 digits, therefore it is possible to view the entered 4-character PIN also on the display. While pressing key "*", entering the PIN is being reset. The PIN consists of 4 numbers 0–9. The PIN assignment is being confirmed by key "#". This Arduino desk is also connected with the Ethernet Shield to provide the network communication.

The last Arduino, which belongs to this prototype, is interconnected with the siren by a digital pin and GND. The siren intensity in the project is 85 dB, while in the production environment there are being used louder sirens. The Arduino is also in inter-connection with the fundamental component of the project – the passive infrared sensor. The passive infrared sensor is interconnected with the Arduino by 5 V pin, GND and one digital pin, from which the data are being sent to the Arduino.

The last, but an important component of the prototype, is a very simple Android application, where the user sets a GPS location of the object he wants to secure. He also sets the distance in meters from the given point, which characterizes a circle range of the geo-fence, and when the user passes it, the security system is activated/deactivated, resp. it is sent an SMS in a specific format to the telephone number of the SIM card used in the security system.

The first system scenario is following – the whole system is activated, the passive infrared sensor detects a movement of a person, it sends a signal to the Arduino, the Arduino sends the message to the broker using MQTT and eventually turns on the siren, the message is forwarded to the GSM module, which loads the telephone numbers, to which it sends the SMS saying that the sensor detected the movement. Everything is logged on the server in the database.

A different possibility of running the system is sending activation/deactivation SMS from the Android application. The SMS is delivered to the configured telephone number of the Arduino interconnected with the GSM module, the message is delivered to the server, where it's authorized and consequently the server generates a message to activate/deactivate the system. Equally the system deactivation can be achieved by direct entering password on the keyboard. Consequently the Arduino sends a message, which is received by the server and the system is activated/deactivated on the basis of the correctly entered password.

The last figure (Fig. 3) is a snapshot of the created Android application. Here it is possible to configure the building (resp. system) location and the distance from the building location (system location), within which the system will stay deactivated. Also it is possible to configure the telephone number, which is inserted into the GSM module. Last but not the least the system can be manually locked/unlocked by two buttons at the bottom.

Fig. 3. Snapshot of the Android application [author]

5 Testing of Developed Application

The solution couldn't be compared with the other systems, because there wasn't found any similar available system for comparison; therefore the system testing was divided into several steps listed below:

- Testing the web application
- Testing the mobile application
- Testing the server scripts
- Testing the data persistence
- Testing the MQTT communication
- Testing the GSM module – sending and receiving the SMSs
- Testing the system security
- Overall test of the system

Outcomes of the testing are going to be conclusions, which will confirm the summary of sufficient functionality, eventually deficiencies of the individual system components.

First of all it was tested the web application, created in the programming language PHP. There were tested the single configuration actions; existence of links, functionality of forms and logging into the application, and also the overall application speed. The first testing of the web application indicated, that responses of the PHP scripts are rather sufficient, the performance was increased after implementing yiilite.php class instead of the classic yii.php class, which can be found, as well as the yiilite, in the framework root folder. The yiilite is suitable for production environment. While using the default setting of MySQL server, the database operations indicated marked deceleration in comparison with a classic MySQL server that runs on the large servers – that was quite expected though. Acceleration of work with the database was then achieved by using connection from the PHP application by the socket instead of by TCP/IP, which in the default configuration status of MySQL on Raspberry is situated in/var/run/mysqld/mysqld.sock. The application was evaluated as sufficient in terms of performance and speed.

Next it was tested the mobile Android application. While testing there were unveiled minor mistakes, which were eliminated, and the application has no problem with storing all the entered values. Sending the SMSs works partially, because the GPS was tested only in the building with a low set geo-fence distance circle, therefore in the production environment it will be necessary to adjust this application, eventually to re-implement it to achieve a higher user-friendliness by Google Api Client and by implementing GeofencingApi [22].

Further there were tested the server scripts implemented in the programming language Python. The Python scripts were executed very quickly with no long response. The testing data were recorded to a console and saved into the database.

In this step there was tested also the persistence of data in MySQL. As it was above-mentioned, PHP actions, working with the database, appeared to be slower, whereas database operations, initiated from Python scripts, were executed on the contrary very quickly.

The next step was testing the MQTT communication between the single system units. The MQTT broker and Arduino worked without any problems and black-outs, so the messages were delivered quickly and with a low response. The advantage of the system is certainly the fact that the system units were interconnected by a cable instead of using Wi-Fi network, which could potentially be disrupted by the intruder/burglar. In the production environment the cables should be placed in the walls to eliminate the chance of cutting the wire. In the testing environment the cables were not placed in the walls (Table 1).

Table 1. Tests results [author]

Test	Evaluation 1–5	Notes
Testing the web application	3	It would be appropriate to achieve acceleration of the database operations
Testing the mobile application	3	The application is simple, it would be more appropriate to implement a more user-friendly application Possibility of having the mobile phone stolen and the alarm deactivated
Testing the server scripts	1	–
Testing the data persistence	2	The speed of DBMS should be increased
Testing the MQTT communication	1	–
Testing the GSM module – sending and receiving the SMSs	3	The signal strength is not always sufficient
Testing the system security	3	Prevent the possibility of MAC spoofing
Overall test of the system	3	Implement a back-up power, for which it didn't remain enough resources in the prototype

Afterwards it followed the testing of the GSM module – receiving the SMSs and forwarding them to the server. The selected GSM module is one of the cheapest on the market. During the first test it was found out a reverse wiring of the zener diode, which was revealed very quickly after getting requested wiring diagram of the GSM module components. Then the module operated rather reliably. It would be useful to illustrate the signal strength of the GSM module for example in the web configuration application, so that the user could see, whether he installed the GSM module in the correct place, because the mobile signal at some places doesn't have to be sufficient. Therefore, neither sending the alert SMS nor automatic activation/deactivation would work. Sending the SMSs at the sufficient signal strength operated without any problems.

In the penultimate step it was tested the system security. The router is secured sufficiently; the main aspect is a strong enough password and a suitably chosen firmware, which should be without any exploit. A detected risk part is the MAC address, which can be duplicated, and this way, if the MAC address of one system part is discovered, it is possible to get connected with the separate network of the security system.

The last test was the overall system test according to the scenarios from the end of the previous chapter. Both of the presented tests were carried out without a problem.

In the table below you can see an evaluation of the individual system parts (1 – passed excellently, 5 – didn't pass) with notes that represent the critical parts that could be threatened (Table 2).

Table 2. Components prices [author]

Component	Price/pc (USD)	Number of pcs	Total cost (USD)
Raspberry Pi B2+	40	1	40
Arduino Uno (clone)	3	3	9
Ethernet Shield	5	3	15
Keyboard	0.6	1	0,6
Seven-segment display	0,8	1	0,8
Siren piezzo	1,6	1	1,6
PIR	1,2	1	1,2
GSM shield Neoway M590	2,7	1	2,7
Router	24	1	24
Total cost	**90 USD**		

6 Conclusions

This article describes the process of creating the new method of implementing security systems, which can become partially autonomous. The new solution involves a certain risk that the system could be abused by an intruder, therefore it will be continued on the system's development and it will be emphasised on securing the system and treating the error conditions.

The advantage of the new system, except its autonomy, is for example the fact that all the situations are being recorded on the server, therefore the owner may utilize the data afterwards for example for various evaluation. In the case that the user makes the web application available over the internet, he can execute the configurations remotely even when he's away from home.

In the future the system can be enhanced with an unlimited number of sensors that doesn't have to be used just for the security system. Accordingly, this system can serve as a basis of system for the household automation.

Finally, below you can see a price list of the single components.

Acknowledgement. This work and the contribution were supported by project "SP-2102-2017 - Smart Solutions for Ubiquitous Computing Environments" Faculty of Informatics and Management, University of Hradec Kralove, Czech Republic.

References

1. Bhagwat, C.N., Krishnan, Y.N., Badrinath, K.: Cloud based intruder detection system. In: 2nd International Conference on Electronics and Communication Systems (ICECS), pp. 1244–1245 (2015)
2. Huzaimy, J.M.: Wi-Fi and GSM Based Motion Sensor for Home Security System Apllication. IOP Conference Series: Materials Science and Engineering, vol. 99, conference 1, pp. 2–6. doi:10.1088/1757-899X/99/1/012010
3. Stanchev, P., Geske, J.: Autonomous cars. History. State of art. Research problems. In: Vishnevsky, V., Kozyrev, D. (eds.) DCCN 2015. CCIS, vol. 601, pp. 1–10. Springer, Cham (2016). doi:10.1007/978-3-319-30843-2_1. ISBN 978-3-319-30843-2
4. Palmat s.r.o. PIR ST205 (2016). https://www.elektro-paloucek.cz/komunikace/alarmy-a-hlasice/alarm-s-pohybovym-cidlem-pir-st205. Accessed 1 Oct 2017
5. Krejcar, O., Mahdal, M.: Optimized solar energy power supply for remote wireless sensors based on IEEE 802.15.4 standard. Int. J. Photoenergy, **2012**, Article ID 305102, 9 p. (2012). doi:10.1155/2012/305102
6. CIP Trading, Oasis Plus House with GSM (2017). https://www.zabezpecovaci-zarizeni.cz/profesionalni-kvalitni-alarmy-jablotron/bezdratovy-oasis-plus/bezdratovy-zabezpecovaci-system-oasis-plus-house-s-gsm-%5Bset603%5D. Accessed 1 Nov 2017
7. Ada, lady. How PIRs Work. adafruit, 28 January 2014. https://learn.adafruit.com/pir-passive-infrared-proximity-motion-sensor/how-pirs-work. Accessed 1 Nov 2017
8. Michalec, L.: PIR detector, 19 March 2013. http://vyvoj.hw.cz/automatizace/pir-cidlo-skvely-sluha-ale-zly-pan.html. Accessed 1 Nov 2017
9. Maresova, P., Klimova, B.: Investment evaluation of cloud computing in the European business sector. Appl. Econ. **47**(36), 3907–3920 (2015)
10. Krejcar, O., Jirka, J., Janckulik, D.: Use of mobile phones as intelligent sensors for sound input analysis and sleep state detection. Sensors **11**(6), 6037–6055 (2011). doi:10.3390/s110606037
11. MQTT developers. MQTT community wiki. github (2017). https://github.com/mqtt/mqtt.github.io/wiki. Accessed 1 Dec 2017
12. Behan, M., Krejcar, O.: Modern smart device-based concept of sensoric networks. EURASIP J. Wirel. Commun. Netw. **155**, 2013 (2013)
13. Telit. Datasheets. sparkfun, 4 Srpen 2006. https://www.sparkfun.com/datasheets/Cellular%20Modules/AT_Commands_Reference_Guide_r0.pdf. Accessed 1 Dec 2017
14. Drabek, A., Krejcar, O., Selamat, A., Kuca, K.: A smart arduino alarm clock using hypnagogia detection during night. In: Fujita, H., Ali, M., Selamat, A., Sasaki, J., Kurematsu, M. (eds.) IEA/AIE 2016. LNCS, vol. 9799, pp. 514–526. Springer, Cham (2016). doi: 10.1007/978-3-319-42007-3_45
15. Drabek, A., Krejcar, O., Selamat, A., Kuca, K.: Arduino Ethernet Shield 2. Arduino (2013). https://www.arduino.cc/en/Main/ArduinoEthernetShield. Accessed 1 Dec 2017
16. Machacek, Z., Slaby, R., Vanus, J., Hercik, R., Koziorek, J.: Non-contact measurement system analysis for metallurgical slabs proportion parameters. Elektronika ir Elektrotechnika, **19**(10) (2013). ISSN: 1392-1215
17. Benikovsky, J., Brida, P., Machaj, J.: Proposal of user adaptive modular localization system for ubiquitous positioning. In: Pan, J.-S., Chen, S.-M., Nguyen, N.T. (eds.) ACIIDS 2012. LNCS, vol. 7197, pp. 391–400. Springer, Heidelberg (2012). doi:10.1007/978-3-642-28490-8_41
18. Raspberry Pi Foundation. Raspbian. Raspberry Pi (2017). https://www.raspberrypi.org/downloads/raspbian/. Accessed 13 Leden 2017

19. Novotny, J., Dvorak, J., Krejcar, O.: User based intelligent adaptation of five in a row game for android based on the data from the front camera. In: Paolis, L.T., Mongelli, A. (eds.) AVR 2016. LNCS, vol. 9768, pp. 133–149. Springer, Cham (2016). doi:10.1007/978-3-319-40621-3_9
20. Python Software Foundation. paho-mqtt 1.1. Python, 1 Feb 2015. https://pypi.python.org/pypi/paho-mqtt/1.1. Accessed 13 Jan 2017
21. Neoway. Neoway M590 Hardware Design Manual. mirifica Europe (2008). http://docs.mirifica.eu/Neoway.com/archive/M590/Neoway%20M590%20Hardware%20Design%20Manual%20V1.1.pdf. Accessed 14 Jan 2017
22. Machaj, J., Brida, P.: Performance comparison of similarity measurements for database correlation localization method. In: Nguyen, N.T., Kim, C.-G., Janiak, A. (eds.) ACIIDS 2011. LNCS, vol. 6592, pp. 452–461. Springer, Heidelberg (2011). doi:10.1007/978-3-642-20042-7_46

Mobile Health Application Running on Public Cloud During Hajj

Ibtehal Nafea[⊠]

College of Computer Science and Engineering, Taibah University,
AlMadinah, Medina, Saudi Arabia
inafea@taibahu.edu.sa

Abstract. Cloud computing is the key of supporting big data analytics field by storing and accessing data and programs over the Internet. Big data analysis can be lever-aged for diseases prevention during Hajj. In a previous work, we presented an approach to Hajj Health Control (HHC) to handle big data issues and avoid da-ta loss, which will lead to improved healthcare and assist with disease prevention systems during the Hajj period. In order to allow more flexibility and reliability in our system, we characterize the report of pilgrim to encompass social networks from mobile's health application running on public cloud to handle our system in more efficient and economical way. By combining big data and cloud computing it deliver a high availability of storage and computation in reasonable price. The chosen cloud vendor is Amazon whose AWS (Amazon Web Services) and S3 (Simple Storage Services) capabilities would be recruited.

Keywords: Hajj · Big data model · Healthcare · Cloud computing · Saudi Arabia

1 Introduction

About two to three million Muslims from over 180 countries travel to Saudi Arabia each year for the Hajj. They spend about two weeks of physical movement from place to place and are in close contact with each other in two holy places (the cities of Makkah and Madinah) as well as spending one day collectively in close contact in Mina's camps. They also all stay together in Arafat for the following half-day from sunrise until sunset and return to Mina to stay there for three days before traveling back home. The month of Ramadan is the peak time for performing Umrah, and the number of participants can be as high as during the Hajj. The mass gathering at the Hajj or Umrah has been associated with the risk of communicable diseases due to pilgrims being in close contact with each other in the same place and at the same times. Both specific event conditions and specific patient pathological conditions are common causes of serious diseases contracted through large gatherings. Returning pilgrims may spread the diseases to their unvaccinated household contacts or even to the community at large. Hajj represents a major challenge to the Saudi Ministry of Health (MOH) in addressing infection control at this big gathering.

© Springer International Publishing AG 2017
M. Younas et al. (Eds.): MobiWIS 2017, LNCS 10486, pp. 129–136, 2017.
DOI: 10.1007/978-3-319-65515-4_11

The Saudi government allocates a lot of money to the budget of integrated services for the pilgrims during their stay and their movement between the sacred places. For example, a total of SR 3.242 billion (about $800 million) was spent to build an efficient network of smooth roads for cars and buses and shaded roads for pedestrians [1]. Hajj represents a major challenge to the Saudi Ministry of Health in addressing infection control at this big gathering.

The Saudi government allocates multiple resources for the health of the pilgrims that includes qualified personnel, health facilities, logistics and materials to serve the Hajj pilgrims. For instance, many permanent and seasonal health facilities are distributed in Mecca and the sacred places [2]. These include 25 permanent and seasonal hospitals, 44 permanent and 114 seasonal health centers, and around 96 cooling units for heat fatigue and stroke management. A total of 458 of intensive care beds and 4141 hospital beds were prepared in Mecca, sacred places and Medina for regular and emergency cases during the Hajj seasons. These numbers are subject to annual increase as needed based on the expected number of pilgrims and the high-risk groups [1].

These are a huge range of health services provided by Saudi MOH during the influx of more than 2 million pilgrims during the Hajj. Hundreds of conditions are treated here, and it leaves a vast amount of stored big data that could be managed, analyzed and utilized to provide a better understanding of disease spread, prevention and for improving early warning and response to infectious disease outbreaks. Cloud computing is naturally a good fit for storing and processing that big data or computing resources accumulated from such operations. In other words, Big Data represents content, and Cloud Computing is infrastructure. Big data becomes affordable for most enterprises in the presence of rented commodity server. For health care providers Cloud-based big data solutions can be shared to provide access to patients' information. According to a report by research firm Markets and Markets, cloud computing market in healthcare will grow to $5.4 billion by 2017 [3]. Many businesses adopt cloud computing because cloud computing is a model of providing IT services and resources, that are available on demand and with dynamic scalability. Also, the human interaction is low due to automatic provisioning of resources. Furthermore, with cloud computing, if you've got an internet connection you can access to the large pool resources. The data centers for high companies such as Google, Facebook and Amazon provide sources for additional business revenues by making use of and hiring empty computational resources already available to the company. Therefore, data centers became known as "clouds", where clients can submit requests to the cloud provider, specifying the number of resources they need to perform certain tasks and computational services without having to know where to perform its task and without purchasing standalone software or hardware. These clouds gathered thousands of servers with infrastructure complementary networks, storage, and cooling units. Many vendors such as Amazon and Google provide cloud servers and clients can benefit with high flexibility and scalability. Social networks allow pilgrims to communicate with each other creating vast information that provides a spatial and temporal data. Also, they can share their impressions from the Hajj with the world in real time. Social networks are not the only help available to pilgrims during their Hajj, but the pilgrims also get benefits from different services offered by authorized ministries. This paper illustrates how big data analysis can be leveraged for disease prevention. It suggests a plan for the management of the big data of pilgrims so that it can be analyzed and utilized for disease prevention and control during the Hajj as well for assisting in health policy planning for future Hajjes and for the exchange of information to be used at global, regional and country level. This work presents link architecture between three main ministries that deal with pilgrims and is presented as a mobile application running on cloud-based infrastructure to handle our system in more efficient and economical way. In this work, Big Data technology and Cloud computing are combined to deliver a high availability of storage and computation in reasonable price. Also, the three main ministries of Saudi will have better control to each pilgrim's need and can provide customized health care in this way. Our approach will benefit both the pilgrims and the ministries since the pilgrims will be able to run their applications anywhere anytime with accurate results and the ministries will be able to share resources and get cooperation in handling the extra load.

1.1 Cloud and Mobile Paradigm

The cloud is an enabler of the mobile applications and salient data management technologies such as the big data. The paradigm of the model proposed in this paper is a cloud computing model where the relevant data, information, and software resides on the cloud hosted servers and facilitate the proposed mobile application. The cloud model facilitates the anywhere, anytime access to data and information and all that is required is an internet connection. The incorporation of the mobile technology and the underlying mobile application facilitates the surpassing of geographical boundaries and connecting different users into a single group through the mobile based application. The mobile application communicates with the cloud-hosted applications, uploads data and receives relevant information.

In this paper, we present related works. Then we outline details about the suggested architecture. Finally, we conclude our work and state our future work.

2   Related Works

Cloud Computing offers many services supported with multiple benefits such as cost effectiveness, reliability, availability, and flexibility. Cloud computing and big data are considered as a new generation of the business platform.

A survey on Big Data Computing in Clouds and future research directions for the development of analytics and visualization tools in several domains of science, engineering, and business is considered by [4].

In the healthcare industry, cloud computing is a fast growing area of development as providers understand how the cloud can help in their different operations. There are many types of research considering cloud and big data in healthcare domain. For example, [5] has presented a smart health system assisted by cloud and big data that has three main features. (1) a unified data collection layer for the integration of public medical resources and personal health devices, (2) a cloud-enabled and data-driven platform for multisource heterogeneous healthcare data storage and analysis, and (3) a unified API for developers and a unified interface for users. The results of that study show that the technologies of cloud and big data can be used to enhance the performance of the healthcare system so that users can enjoy various smart healthcare applications and services.

In [6] there is an approach that enables various cloud providers to cooperate to execute, together, common requests. They extended the Hadoop framework by adding provisions for hardware acceleration with Field Programmable Gate Arrays (FPGAs) within the cloud, for multi-cloud interaction, and for global cloud management. The results illustrated the great advantage of using hardware acceleration while processing massive amounts of data.

In [7] Ahmad et al. proposed a context-aware framework that offers a set of cloud-based services to support crowds during the Hajj and Umrah. The framework considered e-health services through mobile sensors and produces an alarm in case of emergency. In our proposed framework, we focus on health services using a magnetic card based on a coding system that is used for registering in our Hajj Health Control (HHC) system. Moreover, a cloud-based architecture is developed by combining a set of services offered by three ministries. We give attention to the social network as a part of our proposed system that runs on the public cloud. Most of the studies concern about security during Hajj rather than consider social networks, some of the research focus on the behaviors of pilgrims when they use social networks in [8] they analyze the behaviors based on spatial proximity information. In this work, they used a proximity system to identify pilgrims' social networks and applied social network analysis to three observations. (i) Estimate the participation of the pilgrims and distinguish leaders and followers, (ii) observe how different groups of pilgrims are formed during prayers and (iii) identify intensity peaks and track group formation over time. They implemented two types of peer-to-peer proximity sensor nodes, using smartphones with BT and ANT+technology. The proposed methods in their study were applied on data collected from 41 different participants during a period of eight days in a real-life scenario.

2.1 Novelty of Approach

The proposed system is unique in itself as it combines the power of cloud computing, mobile applications and social networks to collect data regarding the disease outbreaks during the Hajj. The data would be directly matched to the patients for the reported diseases. The background and demographic information of the patients along with the disease details would facilitate in a proper analysis of disease outbreaks and further planning relevant interventions. The approach unlike other approaches it utilizes the resources and support of the three ministries and makes use of a magnetic card that would collect all patient data on a first-hand basis, thereby adding higher credibility to the collected data. The patient-centric data would also help in classification of the big data analysis of the collected data. Another remarkable system feature is that it utilizes the benefits of social networks and that would help in a higher usage of the application as users during the Hajj would be able to be in connect with their groups and family members.

3   System Architecture

Our system is extended from previous work [9] as an agile modeling techniques are used for the prototype of the data-gathering approach. It shows sufficient management of data in health centers distributed in three main locations (Mina, Arafat, and Muzdalifah).

Figure 1 shows the system platform with new cloud technique and social networks that developed as a personal enterprise to offer Hajj and Umrah services through Facebook, Twitter, and others.

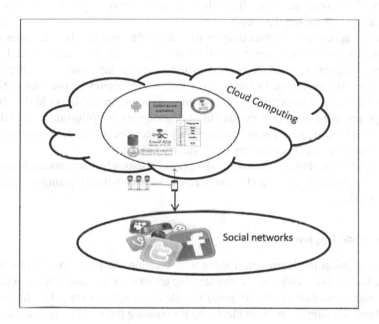

Fig. 1. HHC system platform

It connects the three main ministries as described before, and each pilgrim should use his/her mobile device and the magnetic card. This system suggests using valid information from Ministry of Interior (MOI) and provides a unique magnetic card that includes ten digits for each pilgrim based on a coding system for specific demographic and history of health profile data. More valuable information and details can be found in the previous work of [9]. There will be three centric elements i.e. the patient, the report and the disease, that will be exchanged between three different ministries. The report will describe one or more disease for a single patient. It is also possible that one disease may be reported by several different health facilities. Therefore, we have a network relationship between a disease and the report. The record of disease is supposed to collect all information about one disease supplied by all reports covering this disease. Each disease is associated with one patient, so the record of disease contains a link to a patient record. As the disease record collects all the data about the diagnosis, treatment and outcome of the disease (treated and alive or died) in the incoming reports from health facilities, the patient record contains all information retrieved from the magnetic card of each patient.

Sensors in mobile phones act as a body sensor network, which provides health information related to the human such as pulse rate, heartbeat and blood pressure, and records in the patient health record as presented in [1]. User context modeling is similar to the one used in [7].

The storage and retrieval of big data are delivered from the cloud infrastructure. Cloud computing plays a large part in improving social networks. Cloud computing is not just used in storing heavy multimedia content for social networks, but it is also an ideal infrastructure for big data analysis.

Pilgrims can use their mobile devices to contact the available health center and via social networks and it can generate reports about all disease transactions for each pilgrim that visited different health facilities classified based on information of diseases and patients from the healthcare facilities. This information could be used on the spot to implement immediate health measures and interventions. An action could then be taken to manage, prevent and control the spread of disease between pilgrims at their different residences and during movement between holy places during the Hajj, and this action could be recorded and controlled by the Ministry of Hajj.

At the end of the Hajj, an international report of diseases by contents could be written and used at a global, regional and country level to assist in health planning, policy, and decision-making.

3.1 Technical Implementation

The basic technical implementation starts with creating use cases for the product. The identification of cloud vendor and the underlying technology is required for moving ahead with the implementation of the proposed mobile cloud application [11]. The following technical specifications have been identified for building the mobile application.

Cloud Vendor: Amazon Web Services (AWS)
Cloud Storage: Amazon S3 (Simple Storage Service)
Mobile Development Platform: Android SDK and Android Development Tools /iOS
Cloud Deployment Model: Hybrid Cloud
Cloud Stack: IaaS (Infrastructure as a Service), PaaS (Platform as a Service), DBaaS (Database as a Service) and SaaS (Software as a Service)

Figure 2, shows a typical mobile cloud computing model that utilizes the cloud computing infrastructure, mobile networks and everything is seamlessly connected through the internet. The internet acts as the backbone for facilitating the mobile-cloud applications [10].

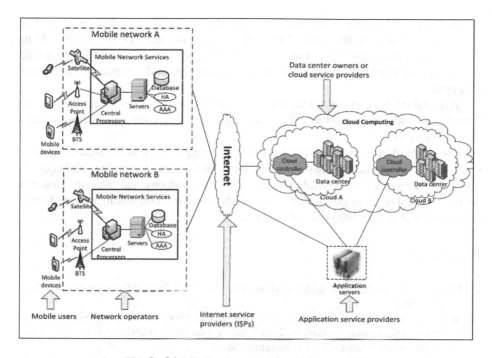

Fig. 2. Mobile cloud computing architecture [10]

3.2   Implementation Issues and Concerns: Security, Integrity, Cost, and Feasibility

A major challenge for cloud-based implementations is security and reliability of the underlying applications and the user data. Most of the public cloud implementations have a model which is tenant-based that is same space is shared across different users though it is logically separated. In such cases, the integrity of the hosted application data is of utmost concern [10]. Cost is another factor as public cloud implementations tend to be cost effective. However, private cloud implementations are expensive and required in-house setup of IT teams for administration and management [11]. However, with the present scenario and multiple vendors, the cloud and mobile technology have evolved, and the feasibility of implementation is simple and fast.

4   Conclusion

Big data and cloud computing are new generations of many business platforms. In healthcare, they play a potentially critical role in preventing diseases. This paper is extended from our previous work that has suggested a plan for the management of the big data of pilgrims so that it can be analyzed and utilized during Hajj for disease prevention and control. As well as for assisting in health policy planning for future Hajjes and the exchange of information for use at global, regional and country level.

The proposed system links large data sets from different ministries using mobile applications, cloud computing, social networks and specific cards. Then it draws patterns from these links to control spread of diseases during Hajj. This work combines big data and cloud computing to deliver high availability of storage and computation in reasonable price.

In the future, we can add middleware through abstraction layer to dissimulate the complexity of accessing and processing the data stored on different points from various cloud developers.

The technical implementation and feasibility of the proposed mobile-cloud application is not a complex task given the enhancements in the cloud technology and competitive support provided by multiple vendors. However, security and integrity concerns are there as Hajj receives pilgrims from across the world some of whom are very particular about their private and personal information.

References

1. Eltahir, A.: Development of health services in Hajj season. J. Family Community Med. 7(1), 13–14 (2000)
2. Nafea, I., Bhairy, M.N., Zeidan, Z.A.: Health tracking framework for hajj pilgrims using electronic health records for Hajj. In: 2014 IEEE International Conference on Bioinformatics and Biomedicine, Belfast, UK, 2–5 November 2014
3. Horowitz, B.: Cloud computing in health care to reach $5.4 billion by 2017: report. eWEEK. http://www.eweek.com/news/cloud-computing-in-health-care-to-reach-5.4-billion-by-2017-report. Accessed 8 Jun 2017
4. Assuncao, M.D., Calheiros, R.N., Bianchi, S., Netto, M., Buyya, R.: Big data computing and clouds: trends and future directions. J. Parallel Distrib. Comput. (JPDC) 79(5), 3–15 (2015)
5. Zhang, Y., et al.: Health-CPS: healthcare cyber-physical system assisted by cloud and big data. IEEE Syst. J. (2015)
6. Mershad, K., et al.: Cloud providers collaboration for a higher service level in cloud computing. In: 2013 Third International Conference on Communications and Information Technology (ICCIT). IEEE (2013)
7. Ahmad, A., et al.: A framework for crowd-sourced data collection and context-aware services in Hajj and Umrah. 2014 IEEE/ACS 11th International Conference on Computer Systems and Applications (AICCSA). IEEE (2014)
8. Muaremi, A., et al.: Understanding aspects of pilgrimage using social networks derived from smartphones. Pervasive Mobile Comput. 15, 166–180 (2014)
9. Nafea, I.: Utilizing big data analysis for diseases prevention and control during Hajj. In: International Conference on Open and Big Data (OBD). IEEE (2016)
10. Dinh, H.T., Lee, C., Niyato, D., Wang, P.: A survey of mobile cloud computing: architecture, applications, and approaches. Wirel. Commun. Mobile Comput. 13(18), 1587–1611 (2013)
11. Claybrook, B.: Private cloud implementation: cloud strategies for mobile devices. Search Cloud Applications (2012). http://searchcloudapplications.techtarget.com/feature/Private-cloud-implementation-Cloud-strategies-for-mobile-devices. Accessed 8 Jun (2017)

Mobile Devices and Mobile Applications Used in Parkinson's Disease

Blanka Klimova[1,2(✉)]

[1] University of Hradec Kralove, Rokitanskeho 62, Hradec Kralove, Czech Republic
blanka.klimova@uhk.cz
[2] University Hospital Hradec Kralove, Sokolska 581, Hradec Kralove, Czech Republic
blanka.klimova@fnhk.cz

Abstract. Current demographic trends indicate that there is a growing number of older population groups worldwide, which is associated with an increase of chronic neurological disorders such as Parkinson's disease, which burden the country's healthcare system. Therefore there is an urgent call for developing efficient strategies which could reduce the healthcare costs and meet the demand of older ill people at affordable cost. One of such approaches is the use of mobile devices and applications. The purpose of this study is to explore mobile devices and/or mobile applications which are used in the assessment, management and treatment of Parkinson's disease. The methods used in this study include a literature review of available sources found in the world's acknowledged databases Web of Science, Scopus, PubMed, and ScienceDirect, as well as the methods of comparison and evaluation of the findings from the selected studies were applied. The findings show that mobile devices and smart-based apps can serve as an appropriate assessment, diagnostic, monitoring and treatment tools for patients with PD since they are relatively cost-effective, reliable and non-invasive. However, more research has to be done in the area of their use in the treatment of PD symptoms, as well as more randomized controlled trials with larger samples of subjects should be conducted.

Keywords: Mobile devices · Mobile apps · Parkinson's disease · Randomized clinical trials · Benefits

1 Introduction

Current demographic trends indicate that there is a growing number of older population groups worldwide, which is associated with an increase of chronic neurological disorders such as dementia. At present, there is about 47 million people living with dementia and this number almost doubles every 20 years. [1]

One of the common types of dementia is Parkinson's disease (PD) which affects 10 million people all over the world. Although its incidence rises with the age, 4% of people are diagnosed with PD before they are 50 years old. [2] It is caused by the loss of dopamine-producing neurons and by the accumulation of a protein into Lewy bodies in neurons in the area of midbrain, in the so-called pars compacta substantia nigra. Before

© Springer International Publishing AG 2017
M. Younas et al. (Eds.): MobiWIS 2017, LNCS 10486, pp. 137–143, 2017.
DOI: 10.1007/978-3-319-65515-4_12

this disease begins, there is a loss of 60–80% of dopaminergic neurons. [3] The symptoms of PD involve overall tremor, especially in hands, slowness of movement, rigidity of limbs, and balance difficulties. [4] Sometimes these symptoms are illustrated by acronyms TRAP (Tremor, Rigidity, Aknesis and Posture instability). [5] Apart from the motor symptoms, in the course of the development of PD patients might acquire other disorders known as non-motor symptom complex which comprise cognitive difficulties; neuropsychiatric symptoms such as depression, anxiety, hallucinations or apathy; autonomic symptoms such as low blood pressure, constipation, difficulties in swallowing, increased sweating or sexual dysfunction; sleep disorders; or loss of smell [2].

All the chronic neurological disorders, including PD, burden the country's healthcare system. [6, 7] Therefore there is an urgent call for developing efficient strategies which could reduce the healthcare costs and meet the demand of older ill people at affordable cost. One of these strategies includes the use of the Internet in healthcare to provide patients with relevant health information, services and support. In fact, this corresponds to the well-established concept of electronic health, the so-called e-Health [8], respectively mobile Health, the use of mobile devices, especially mobile phones and tablets, to provide healthcare and health information [9], which are now exploited by most of older people. [10] In addition, older people take an advantage of mobile applications which can maintain and improve their health. [9] Sanchez Rodriguez et al. [11] classify mobile health applications in the field of neurological disorders into five groups:

- *healthy lifestyle applications* which concentrate on the improvement of the patients' lifestyle by promoting a healthy and balanced diet, adequate hydration, and regular exercise.
- *information applications* providing information about a specific medical condition or other medical topics.
- *assessment applications* aimed at the diagnosis, assessment, and/or follow-up of patients by providing data for healthcare professionals.
- *treatment applications* which can be used by healthcare professionals to treat patients.
- *specific applications* addressing specific neurological disorders, based on the team's own criteria or needs; they should promote the education and participation of patients and their families by providing relevant data on treatment and home assistance, as well as how to find self-help groups, or healthcare professionals.

Researchers [12] also draw attention to the concept of the Internet of Things (IoT) which is the connection of any physical object such as a mobile device to the Internet. [13] For example, Pasluosta et al. [12] present that real time motion metrics in PD can be then acquired in virtually any scenario by placing lightweight wearable sensors into the patient's clothes and connecting them to a medical database via a mobile device.

The purpose of this study is to explore mobile devices and/or mobile applications which are used in the assessment, management and treatment of Parkinson's disease.

2   Methods

The methodology of this study reflects Moher et al. [14] The methods include a literature review of available sources found in the world's acknowledged databases Web of Science, Scopus, PubMed, and ScienceDirect. The search was based on the key words: *mobile devices* and *Parkinson's disease*, *mobile applications/apps* and *Parkinson's disease* in the period of 2000 till the end of 2016. As Sanchez Rodriguez et al. [11] state, 2000 can be the benchmark for the proliferation and normalisation of healthcare tools in society.

Furthermore, methods of comparison and evaluation of the findings from the selected studies were applied. The study was included if it were written in English; if it were a randomized clinical trial focused on the use of mobile devices and/or mobile applications in PD; and if it matched the corresponding period, i.e., from 2000 till 2016.

Altogether 2,081 studies were detected, most of them were identified in Science-Direct (1,720 articles), followed by Scopus (273 articles), PubMed (44 articles) and Web of Science (43 articles). The analysis was done by identifying the key words and checking duplication of available sources in the databases mentioned above. Afterwards, the studies were assessed for their relevancy, i.e. verification on the basis of abstracts whether the selected study corresponds to the set goal. After the exclusion of such studies, 25 sources were analysed and 20 eventually excluded.

3   Results and Their Discussion

Although there was a sufficient number of studies concerning the mobile devices and apps, most of them were descriptive or observational studies, e.g. [15–20] Only five controlled clinical trials [21–25] were detected and their overview is presented in Table 1 below. The studies are listed in the alphabetical order of their first author.

As the findings in Table 1 show, all the studies focus on the assessment and diagnostics of the symptoms, especially the gait and tremor in PD. This is no surprising since more than half of patients with PD suffer from falls. The mobile devices are usually connected with sensors [21–24], which reflects the concept of IoT that appears to be becoming an efficient healthcare platform for the chronic neurological diseases, respectively PD. The data which are collected from wearable sensors are used to quantify the patient's gait. This is usually done in three phases: gait segmentation, gait parameter extraction and gait parameter analysis. [12] As Ferrari et al. [22] state, the findings from the gait analysis are then applied in practice in monitoring PD patients, for example, their falling, freezing of gait, functional ability, or physical activity. Although there is ongoing research on wearable technology in free-living environments for people with PD, there has not been fully validated system to monitor clinical features or activities in these environments yet. [15] As Pasluosta et al. [12] argue, major delays of home monitoring systems for patients with PD result from the lack of long-term reliability of hardware and software capable of coping with large inter-patient variability.

Table 1. Selected controlled clinical trials

Study	Objective	Number of subjects	Type of mobile devices/apps/ wearable sensors	Benefits
Ellis et al. [21]	To test and show a potential of a smart-based mobile app SmartMOVE used in the assessment of gait and gait variability in PD.	12 PD patients and 12 age related healthy controls.	Smartphone, heel-mounted footswitch sensors, sensor-embedded walkway.	Findings indicate that the new smart-based app can serve as an appropriate assessment methods of gait to conventional gait analysis.
Ferrari et al. [22]	To describe and test a new method for estimating spatio-temporal gait parameters.	16 PD patients and 12 age related healthy controls.	Smartphone, shoe-worn inertial sensors.	Results show that wearable sensors can be an appropriate diagnostic tool for gait and a promising tool for tutoring and guiding gait execution in PD.
Kostikis et al. [23]	To propose a practical smartphone-based tool to accurately assess upper limb tremor in PD patients.	25 PD patients and 20 age related healthy controls.	Smartphone accelerometer and gyroscope.	Findings suggest that the proposed method should be effective in assisting doctors in the hospitals, remotely evaluate patient's conditions and communicate results to the doctors.
Marx et al. [24]	To transfer findings from the restricted stationary video-oculography to a wearable head-mounted devices.	10 Progressive Supranuclear Palsy patients (PSP), 11 PD patients and 10 age related healthy controls.	EyeSeeCam.	Findings show that EyeSeeCam is a simple, rapid and reliable tool to differentiate clinically established PSP patients from PD patients and healthy adults; the use of wearable eye-tracking in patients can help with uncertain diagnoses.
Ozinga et al. [25]	To determine whether kinematic data measured by hardware within a tablet device, was of sufficient quantity and quality to characterize postural stability.	17 PD patients and 17 age related healthy controls.	Tablet with the motion capture system.	Results indicate that the hardware in the tablet provides data of sufficient accuracy for the quantification of postural stability in patients with PD.

Source: author's own processing

As it has been already stated above, majority of the studies analyzed by the author of this study aim at the assessment of the PD symptoms and a possibility of monitoring the patients with PD thanks to mobile devices and IoT. However, there are only a few studies which would deal with the treatment applications for people with dementia. One of them is the study by Lopez et al. [26], which presents a glass system with a portable auditory device with the Listenmee app® offering over 100 different sounds and an adjustable metronome to individualize the cueing rate as well as its smartwatch with accelerometer to detect magnitude and direction of the proper acceleration, track calorie count, sleep patterns, steps count and daily distances. Although the experiment was performed with seven PD patients, the findings showed considerable improvements in gait performance over three major dependent variables: walking speed in 38.1%, cadence in 28.1% and stride length in 44.5%. Fortunately, there is another research going on in the area of smart-based medication adherence of PD patients. [27]

The limitations of this study consist in the small sample of the selected studies and their large variability which may provide ambiguous results.

4 Conclusion

In conclusion, mobile devices and smart-based apps can serve as an appropriate assessment, diagnostic, monitoring and treatment tools for patients with PD. The objectivity, portability, and ease of use of mobile devices make it ideal for use in clinical environments lacking sophisticated biomechanical systems. In addition, they are relatively cost-effective, reliable and non-invasive. However, more research has to be done in the area of their use in the treatment of PD symptoms, as well as more randomized controlled trials with larger samples of subjects should be conducted.

Acknowledgments. This review study is supported by the SPEV project 2017, Faculty of Informatics and Management, University of Hradec Kralove, Czech Republic. The author thanks Josef Toman for his help with the data collection.

References

1. Dementia statistics (2017). https://www.alz.co.uk/research/statistics
2. Parkinson's Disease Foundation, Statistics on Parkinson's (2017). http://www.pdf.org/en/parkinson_statistics
3. Chang, E.: Parkinson's and Alzheimer's diseases: similar but very different (2012). http://www.alznyc.org/nyc/newsletter/fall2012/06.asp#.VZ5-x7dT85s
4. Houghton, D., Hurtig, H., Metz, S., Brandabur, M.: Parkinson's disease: medications (2015). http://www3.parkinson.org/site/DocServer/Medications.pdf?docID=185
5. Blanchet, P.: Speech disorders in individuals with Parkinson's disease (2015). http://www.nysslha.org/i4a/pages/index.cfm?pageid=3519
6. Klimova, B., Maresova, P., Kuca, K.: Non-pharmacological approaches to the prevention and treatment of Alzheimer's disease with respect to the rising treatment costs. Curr. Alzheimer Res. **13**, 1249–1258 (2016)

7. Maresova, P., Klimova, B., Novotny, M., Kuca, K.: Alzheimer´s disease and Parkinson´s diseases expected economic impact on: Europe – a call for a uniform European strategy. J. Alzheimer´s Dis. **54**, 1123–1133 (2016)
8. Bujnowska-Fedak, M.M., Pirogowicz, I.: Support for e-health services among elderly primary care patients. Telemed. J. E-Health **20**(8), 696–704 (2014)
9. Klimova, B.: Mobile health devices for aging population groups: a review study. In: Younas, M., Awan, I., Kryvinska, N., Strauss, C., Thanh, Dv (eds.) MobiWIS 2016. LNCS, vol. 9847, pp. 295–301. Springer, Cham (2016). doi:10.1007/978-3-319-44215-0_24
10. de Veer, A.J.E., et al.: Determinants of the intention to use e-health by community dwelling older people. BMC Health Serv. Res. **15**(103), 1–9 (2015)
11. Sanchez Rodriguez, M.T., Vazquez, S.C., Martin Casas, P., Cano de la Cuerda, R.: Neurorehabilitation and apps: a systematic review of mobile applications. Neurologia (2015). pii:S0213–4853(15)00233-9
12. Pasluosta, C.F., Gassner, H., Winkler, J., Klucken, J., Eskofier, B.M.: An emerging era in the management of Parkinson's disease: wearable technologies and the Internet of Things. IEEE J. Biomed. Health Inf., 2168–2194 (2015)
13. Gabbai, A.: Kevin Ashton describes the internet of things: the innovator weigs in on what human life will be like a century from now. Smithonian (2015)
14. Moher, D., Liberati, A., Tetzlaff, J., Altman, D.G.: The PRISMA group. Preferred reporting items for systematic review and meta-analysis: the PRISMA statement. PLoS Med. **6**, e1000097 (2009)
15. Del Din, S., Godfrey, A., Mazza, C., Lord, S., Rochester, L.: Free-living monitoring of Parkinson's disease: lessons from the field. Mov. Disord. **31**(9), 1293–1313 (2016)
16. Kefaliakos, A., Pliakos, I., Charalampidou, M., et al.: Wireless monitoring for patients with cardiovascular diseases and Parkinson's disease. Stud. Health Technol. Inf. **226**, 87–90 (2016)
17. Szydlo, T., Konieczny, M.: Mobile and wearable devices in an open and universal system for remote patient monitoring. Microprocess. Microsyst. **46**((A)), 44–54 (2016)
18. Dai, H., Zhang, P., Lueth, T.C.: Quantitative assessment of Parkinsonian tremor based on an inertial measurement unit. Sensors **15**(10), 25055–25071 (2015)
19. Carignan, B., Daneault, J.F., Duval, C.: Measuring tremor with a smartphone. Methods Mol. Biol. **1256**, 359–374 (2015)
20. Rossi-Izquierdo, M., Basta, D., Rubio-Rodriguez, J.P., Santos-Perez, S., Ernst, A., Sesar-Ignacio, A., et al.: Is posturography able to identify fallers in patients with Parkinson's disease? Gait Posture **40**(1), 53–57 (2004)
21. Ellis, R.J., Ng, Y.S., Zhu, S., Tan, D.N., Anderson, B., Schlaug, G., et al.: A validated smartphone-based assessment of gait and gait variability in Parkinson's disease. PLoS One **10**(10), e0141694 (2015)
22. Ferrari, A., Ginis, P., Hardegger, M., Casamassima, F., Rocchi, L., Chiari, L.: A mobile Kalman-filter based solution for the real-time estimation of spatial-temporal gait parameters. IEEE Trans. Neurol. Syst. Rehabil. Eng. **24**(7), 764–773 (2016)
23. Kostikis, N., Hristu-Vasakelis, D., Arnaoutoglon, M., Kotsavasiloglou, C.: A smartphone-based tool for assessing Parkinson hand tremor. IEEE J Biomed. Health Inform. **19**(6), 1835–1842 (2015)
24. Marx, S., Respondek, G., Stamelou, M., Dowiasch, S., Stoll, J., Bremmer, F., et al.: Validation of mobile eye-tracking as novel and efficient means for differentiating progressive supranuclear palsy from Parkinson's disease. Front Behav. Neurosci. **6**, 88 (2012)
25. Ozinga, S.J., Machado, A.G., Miller Koop, M., Rosenfeldt, A.B., Alberts, J.L.: Objective assessment of postural stability in Parkinson's disease using mobile technology. Mov. Disord. **30**(9), 1214–1221 (2015)

26. Lopez, W.O., Higuera, C.A., Fonoff, E.T., Souza Cde, O., Albicker, U., Martinez, J.A.: Listenmee and listenmee smartphone application: synchronizing walking to rhythmic auditory cues to improve gait in Parkinson's disease. Hum Mov. Sci. **37**, 147–156 (2014)
27. Lakshminarayana, R., Wang, D., Burn, D., Chandhuri, K.R., Cummins, G., Galtrey, C., et al.: Smartphone– and internet-assisted self-management and adherence tools to manage Parkinson's disease (SMART-PD): study protocol for a randomized controlled trial (v7; 15 August 2014). Trials **15**, 374 (2014)

Security and Mobile Network Systems

An Authentication Mechanism for Accessing Mobile Web Services

KamalEldin Mohamed[(✉)], Duminda Wijesekera, and Paulo Cesar Costa

George Mason University, 4400 University Dr., Fairfax, VA 22030, USA
kmohamed@gmu.edu

Abstract. Port knocking is a method of externally opening ports on a firewall by generating a connection attempt on a set of prespecified closed ports in order to prevent attackers from discovering and exploiting potentially vulnerable services on a network host while allowing authenticated users to access these services [19]. We extend the implementations of secure port knocking systems from traditional servers and desktop clients to mobile client/server applications as an authentication technique to securely protect resources hosted by mobile servers. More specifically, our research objective primarily focuses on developing a secure authentication framework, utilizing secure port knocking techniques coupled with Open Authorization (OAuth) standard, for accessing smart mobile devices while acting as Web service providers/hosts that are located behind and protected by the Internet Service Provider (ISP) perimeter firewall; that way the mobile clients have to be authenticated by two different authentication mechanisms/layers that are independent from each other before these clients are granted access to the protected resources.

Keywords: Mobile Web services · Mobile hosts, port knocking · OAuth 2.0

1 Introduction

Port knocking is a stealth method to externally open ports that, by default, the firewall keeps closed. It works by an external requester attempting to connection attempts (so called knocks) to a series of predefined closed ports. When the correct sequence of knocks is received, the firewall opens certain port(s) to allow a connection [5]. The simplest type of port-knocking authentication process involving transferring a set of packet numbers predefined at both the client and the server. For example, a client computer, as a port-knocker, starts the knocking process and the process that is expected to be completed after transferring four TCP synchronization attempts with packet numbers (say 2981, 6534, 2397, and 9056) to a server. Meanwhile, a port-knock daemon that sits on the server buffers and checks the sequence when completed. If the port order is similar to the predefined sequence, then the action is triggered on the server side based on the request of the user. This request could be a request for SSH or HTTP. Therefore, the port that is assigned to them opens temporarily and close again on receiving another knock sequence [10].

© Springer International Publishing AG 2017
M. Younas et al. (Eds.): MobiWIS 2017, LNCS 10486, pp. 147–162, 2017.
DOI: 10.1007/978-3-319-65515-4_13

Port knocking has been used in complex authentication mechanisms. Methods using port knocking for authentication fit into three categories: those that transmit (1) a plain-text authentication token, (2) a cryptographic proof of knowledge of an authentication token and (3) a one-time authentication token. Examples of such systems include Krzy-winski's [14] port knocking system that can be configured to use either plain-text or encrypted authentication tokens, Doyle's [13] knockd/knockd that sends an encrypted token, and Spread-spectrum TCP, by Barham et al. [17] that uses a one-time token stream. All three types authenticate based on the knowledge of some secret key and assume that key exchange is conducted by some out-of-band mechanism. Although port knocking has been referred to as providing security through obscurity, and in some cases, a well-implemented port knocking system used in conjunction with strong authentication can be a secure authentication mechanism.

On the other hand, Open Authorization (OAuth) is an authentication standard used by social sites such as Facebook and Twitter to protect their APIs and federate identification across domains. OAuth seeks to resolve the shortcomings of propriety authentication protocols by creating a universal, interoperable authorization mechanism shared between services. OAuth uses a bearer token instead of the username-password pair. It allows a third-party service to access user data on another service without disclosing the login credentials for that service. For example, a user can authorize HP's online photo-printing service "PrintPho" to access their images on their Facebook account without giving "PrintPho" their Facebook password [3, 8].

The security features and authentication mechanisms used by OAuth to authenticate users could be effectively utilized as an authentication layer for accessing protected resources hosted by mobile servers allowing them to indirectly authenticate their clients without the need to know and/or to store their access credentials locally.

In this paper, we propose an authentication framework for securely accessing mobile Web services. The framework uses Port Knocking (PK) authentication mechanism coupled with Open Authorization (OAuth 2.0) to authenticate mobile Web service clients before granting their access to Web services hosted by mobile Web services hosts. Section 2 introduces the Hybrid Port Knocking (HPK) system that uses Cryptography and Steganography to perform mutual authentication between the port knocking server and the port knocking clients. Section 3 presents the Hybrid Port Knocking system that we ported into the mobile devices' environment. Section 4 discusses the implementation's topologies of our proposed authentication framework. Section 5 presents the integration of Open Authentication (OAuth 2.0) into the proposed framework. Sections 6 states the security features provided by the proposed framework. Section 7 discusses the experimental tests we conducted on the proposed framework. A conclusion is in Sect. 8.

2   The Hybrid Port Knocking System (HPK)

The HPK system or Tariq is a hybrid port-knocking technique that uses Cryptography, Steganography, and Mutual Authentication to develop another security layer in front of any service that needs to be accessed from the public and/or private networks. The HPK system consist of two modules, namely the "HPK Server" module and the "HPK Client" module that they collectively carryout the following processes in order to securely and dynamically open or close a firewall port and/or execute a command at the destination server/network [1, 2]:

- Traffic Monitoring: the port knocking server is installed to be located behind the network firewall in such a way that it will continuously monitor and check the traffic incoming to the firewall public network interface.
- Traffic Capturing and Analyzing: the port knocking server is designed to only capture the traffic that is carrying an image as the payload for further processing.
- Image Processing: the pork knocking client encrypts the message it needs to send to the port knocking server using the server's GnuPG public key, it then uses Stega-nography to hide/encode the encrypted message into a PNG image, chops the image and sends it over to the server using the proper port knocking sequence. The port knocking server, on the other hand, extracts the payload (image) from the received packet.
- Client Authentication: after receiving the port knocking traffic with the proper sequence from the client, the port knocking server will further authenticate the client by sending back a challenge value encrypted using the client GnuPG public key. The client will then use its GnuPG private key to decrypt the challenge and sends the decrypted value back to the port knocking server.
- Server Authentications: upon receiving the correct challenge response back from the client, the port knocking server will now know it is communicating with a legitimate client, it will then unhide/decode the encrypted port knocking PNG image payload it initially received from the client. It then decrypts the encrypted message using its GnuPG private key.
- Request Execution: once the mutual authentication between the port knocking server and the client is successful, the port knocking server will then executes the client request that it decrypted initially. The client request to be executed could be either opening/closing a specific firewall port or executing a certain command at the port knocking domain network.

3 Porting the Hybrid Port Knocking System (HPK) into the Mobile Devices Environment

After porting the Hybrid Port Knocking (HPK) system into the mobile devices' environment, we ended-up having three main components; the "Mobile Port Knocking Client", the "Port Knocking Server" and the "Firewall Agent". Our main contributions beside the porting of the original HPK client/server applications, are the development of the "Firewall Agent" as well as strengthening the overall security features of the original HPK system. We further discuss these added security features in Sect. 6. In the following subsection, we provide a description for each of these components:

3.1 The Mobile Port Knocking Client

It is responsible for encrypting a request message to be sent to the mobile port knocking server, hiding the encrypted message in a PNG picture using steganography, splitting the PNG picture into equal chucks and then using specific ports for performing the knocking sequence along with sending each chunk as a payload over UDP.

3.2 The Port Knocking Server

It is responsible for unhiding and decrypting the request message that was sent by the client, authenticating the mobile port knocking clients and making sure they are legitimate before opening/closing firewall ports and providing Web services access accordingly. The port knocking server is designed to be capable of running on both, the mobile/Android platforms when acting as a server or from a traditional server machine.

3.3 The Firewall Agent

The HPK system, besides utilizing encryption and message hiding technique to secure the communication between the port knocking server and its clients, it also requires the use of privileged user access (such as 'root') to the firewall in order to be able to execute and update the dynamic IPTABLES rules in the firewall [7, 11]. In the mobile devices environment, the only feasible way to implement this particular requirement directly from the mobile device is through rooting the mobile device itself from its default original image in order to be able to execute shell commands such as IPTABLES. To avoid modifying the mobile device native image, which could impact the overall operation of the mobile device, causes instability and could potentially render the mobile device unusable; we therefore developed a 'Firewall Agent' software component to accomplish the execution of IPTABLES requirements accordingly. The 'Firewall Agent' is designed

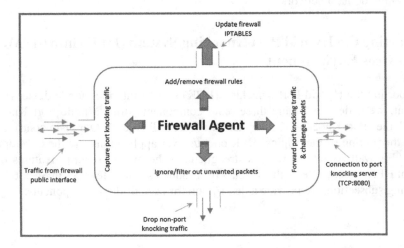

Fig. 1. Port knocking firewall agent

to be installed, configured and run as a daemon service in any standalone server that is separate from the firewall, in the same server as the OS-type firewalls, or as an Open-Write plug-in package in the appliances-type IPTABLES firewalls (Fig. 1).

The following are the key responsibilities and functionalities of the 'Firewall Agent':

Packet Capture. The firewall agent uses packet capturing techniques (libpcap) in order to capture/sniff only the interesting port knocking traffic from the firewall outside inter-face and delivers it to whichever entity that is acting as the port knocking server (a mobile server or a traditional server) that is connected to the inside network interface [21].

Secure Transmission Channel. The firewall agent is also designed to accept incoming TCP connections from the port knocking servers (including the Android servers when acting as port knocking servers) only over the internal network interface; these connec-tions are mainly used for delivering the port knocking related traffic to the appropriate port knocking server in order for the port knocking traffic to be further analyzed of whether the requesting client is legitimate for establishing a connection and accessing the protected web services accordingly. These connections are considered to be as secure since they are only allowed to take place from the inside/trusted network as well as each connection is password protected.

Challenge Transport. The firewall agent also facilitates the transport of the 'chal-lenge' packet sent by the port knocking server for authenticating the requesting client before it decides of whether the requested firewall ports should be opened or closed accordingly. The firewall agent also transports the 'challenge response' from the client back to the server after which the port knocking server could decide if the requesting client is authentic or not. It's important to note that, during the port knocking process, the firewall agent acts only as a relay between the port knocking client and the port knocking sever for transporting the port knocking traffic as well as the challenge traffic; where the contents of these packets do not get changed while in transit; instead, the firewall agent ensures the traffic is getting delivered to the proper destination whether it is to the port knocking server or to the client.

Manage Firewall Dynamic IPTABLES Rules. After the mobile port knocking client and the port knocking server successful mutual authentication, the firewall agent shall then execute the necessary IPTABLES commands (as a 'sudo' user) based on the instructions it receives from the port knocking server to either open or close the requested firewall ports [11].

3.4   Port Knocking Client/Server Protocol Flow

Figure 2 below shows the ported HPK protocol flow between the 'Mobile Port Knocking Client', the 'Firewall Agent' and the 'Port Knocking Server' while explaining how these components interact together to perform a secure port knocking authentication flow:

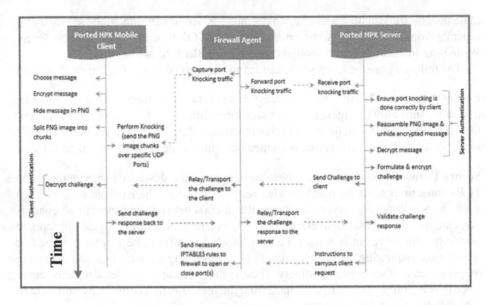

Fig. 2. The ported HPK protocol flow

4   Port Knocking Implementations in Mobile Devices

As described in the Sect. 3, after porting the Hybrid Port Knocking System (HPK) in the mobile devices, we ended up having three main modules/components, the 'Port Knocking Client', the 'Port Knocking Server' and the 'Firewall Agent'. Accordingly, the following subsections provide detailed description of how these modules could be put together for the implementations of the proposed ported port knocking framework in the mobile devices' environment while considering different network topologies.

4.1   Implementation (1): The Android Web Services Host as The Port Knocking Server

In this architecture, the 'Android Client' uses the port knocking client application to act as the port knocking client, whereas the 'Android Server' itself (beside being a Web services host) is also hosting the port knocking server application and therefore acting as the port knocking server. The 'Firewall Agent' is running from the same server as the firewall and will be listening on TCP port 8080 (or any other TCP custom port > 1024) on the firewall inside interface so that the Android port knocking server connects to it in order to receive the port knocking client candidate traffic to be further analyzed. It's important to note that, at the time of the port knocking and when the client has not been authenticated yet; rather than directly communicating with the server, all interactions between the client and the server during the port knocking process have to be facilitated by the 'Firewall Agent'; therefore, the same TCP (port 8080) socket connection between the 'Firewall Agent' and the Android port knocking server is also used by the port knocking server for authenticating the client thereby sending the encrypted 'challenge' to the client and receiving the client response accordingly. Once the port knocking client is successfully authenticated and determined to be legitimate and upon instructions from the mobile/Android port knocking server, the 'Firewall Agent' will place the necessary firewall rules into the firewall after which the client should be able to 'directly' communicate with the Android Web services host (Fig. 3).

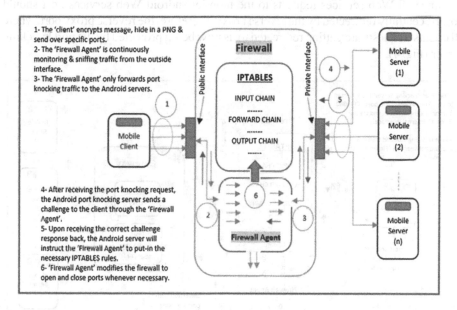

Fig. 3. The mobile/Android Web services host as the port knocking server

The main characteristic of this architecture is the fact it is a platform-independent, where the Mobile/Android devices themselves (client and server) do not rely, for the most part, on any additional third party application(s) or device(s) to perform an end-to-end port knocking authentication. This architecture could also be suitable to implement in situations where the mobile servers are directly connected to the ISP firewall without any intermediaries in between.

4.2 Implementation (2): The Reverse Proxy as The Port Knocking Server

In the second implementation, the 'Android Client' continued to use the port knocking client application to act as the port knocking client. However; the 'Android server' is acting as the Web services host, whereas a new reverse proxy server has been introduced to act as the port knocking server as well as reverse proxying the Web services requests from those Android clients after being successfully authenticated via port knocking. The reverse proxy is built to be located in the inside network between the ISP firewall and the Android Web services hosts. Also, in this implementation, the 'Firewall Agent' still resides alongside the firewall in the same server.

The connection between the 'Port Knocking Server' and the 'Firewall Agent' remains the same as in the first implementation above (for example, via TCP port 8080) where the port knocking server daemon at the reverse proxy will establish the necessary TCP connection with the 'Firewall Agent' from the inside network through which it receives the port knocking traffic and interacts with the port knocking client accordingly throughout the port knocking authentication process.

Since all Web services requests to the mobile/Android Web services host should now be centrally redirected by the reverse proxy; therefore, the reverse proxy port, where all clients' requests are getting redirected to, is now being protected by the port knocking server (Fig. 4).

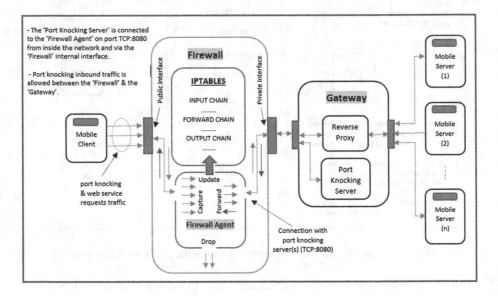

Fig. 4. The reverse proxy as the port knocking server

A main characteristic of this architecture is the added security feature that the mobile/Android Web services hosts and their protected resources are no longer directly exposed to the public interface, instead they are only accessible via the reverse proxy server in such a way that all Web services requests to the Android Web services hosts should now being centrally managed and redirected by the reverse proxy to the appropriate Android server and therefore all related connection attempts could be easily monitored and administered as well as any potential risks and/or attacks could be relatively easily identified and quickly counter- measured.

4.3   Implementation (3): The Reverse Proxy as The Port Knocking and The Firewall Agent Server

The third implementation is similar to the second implementation (described in Subsect. 4.2 above) except that, the 'Firewall Agent' is moved from the firewall server to the reverse proxy server. That is, both the 'Firewall Agent' and the 'Port Knocking Server Daemon' are now residing and running from the same server as the reverse proxy. The connection between the 'Firewall Agent' and the 'Port Knocking Server Daemon' also remain the same and via TCP port 8080, but this time this connection is being established and maintained from/with the same server. However, in this architecture, since the 'Firewall Agent' no longer exists in the same server as the firewall, the following design constraints have been added to this architecture in order to accommodate this change and ensure the port knocking process is being handled properly and as securely:

- The port knocking UDP traffic is now being redirected by the firewall to the inside interface where the 'Firewall Agent' is listening and capturing port knocking traffic accordingly. After capturing the interesting traffic, the 'Firewall Agent' will continue to forward it to the port knocking server daemon that resides in the same server.
- The 'Firewall Agent' in this implementation is residing in a remote server outside the firewall server; it is therefore designed to have the ability to establish a secure SSH connection with the firewall using 'Root' privileges through which, the 'Firewall Agent' interacts with the firewall for putting-in or removing the necessary IPTABLES rules requested by the 'Port Knocking Server Daemon' (Fig. 5).

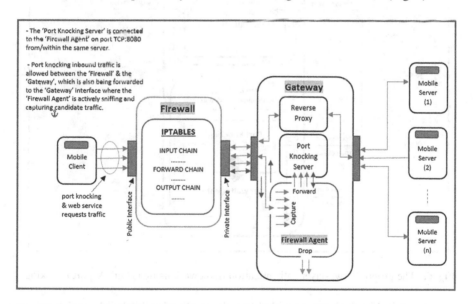

Fig. 5. The reverse proxy as the port knocking and the firewall agent server

This architecture has the same features as the second implementation (described in Subsect. 4.2 above), in addition to the fact that the 'Port Knocking' and the 'Firewall Agent' components are now both located in the reverse proxy server and that gave an additional benefit of freeing up the firewall server to be running as an independent server/device.

5   The Integration and Implementation of OAuth 2.0

Integrating OAuth 2.0 to our port knocking authentication framework results in an enhanced and a more secure dual authentication framework where mobile clients have to be authenticated by each authentication layer independently before access to the protected resources is granted. In our implementation for integrating OAuth 2.0 to the proposed port knocking authentication framework, we implemented the 'Password Authorization Grant' OAuth flow and utilized Membrane open source as the authorization server for validating requests and issuing access token, the mobile port knocking client will act as an OAuth client as well as a port knocking client, and the mobile server will act as the token validator beside being a Web services host. Membrane is a full featured OAuth 2.0 implementation written in Java that can act as an authorization server, client and/or proxy for a resource server [15].

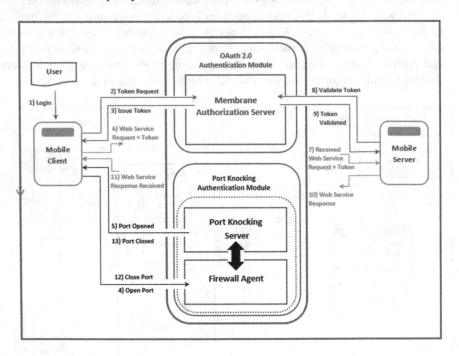

Fig. 6. The proposed two-layer authentication framework using OAuth & port knocking

As shown in Fig. 6 above, provided that the application is already registered with OAuth 2.0 authorization server (Membrane), the user of the mobile port knocking client will login to the application using his/her OAuth registered credentials to request an access to a particular protected resource that is hosted by the Android Web services host, after which the user/client authentication will be carried-out as follows:

- The client (acting on behalf of the user) while following OAuth 2.0 'Password Authentication Grant' flow, starts the authentication process by requesting an access token from the OAuth 2.0 authorization server (Membrane).

- Membrane authorization server will then validate the client request as well as ensures the requesting client itself is legitimate based on the information provided during the initial registration. Membrane will then issue the access token to the client accordingly [15].
- Since the port for accessing the Android server resources is closed at this stage, the client will then have to authenticate via port knocking to get the necessary port open accordingly.
- Once the Android server port is open for access after the client successfully authenticate via port knocking, the client will then present the access token along with the Web services request for accessing the Android server resources.
- Upon receiving the client request, the Android server (while acting as an OAuth token validator) will further communicate with the Membrane authorization server to validate the access token presented by the client and once validated, access to Android server protected resource(s) is granted accordingly.

6   The Security Features of the Proposed Framework

The proposed framework continued to use the same security features that are provided by the original Hybrid Port Knocking system (HPK); in addition, the following security enhancements to the port knocking framework (after being ported into the mobile/ Android device environment) have been successfully implemented in order to further strengthen the overall security of the framework while implementing in the mobile devices' environment:

- Supports Symmetric and Asymmetric Cryptography: the ported framework uses Advanced Encryption Standard (AES) or symmetric key encryption with 128-bit encryption key for the encryption and decryption of all messages exchanged between the Android port knocking client and the Android port knocking server. In addition, the framework encryption engine includes the implementation of RSA Public Key Cryptography with a key length of 2048-bit for the Android server and the Android client. The framework now supports both, asymmetric as well as symmetric encryption for the mutual authentication between the server and the client.
- Better Secret Concealment: Instead of using a single PNG picture, more PNG pictures have been added to the framework (currently a total of five different PNG pictures). The Android port knocking client is now choosing a PNG picture that is different from the previous one it used for hiding the encrypted message request before sending it over to the port knocking server. The main purpose of using multiple and different PNG pictures versus a single PNG picture for carrying the secret, is the fact that it looks more normal for the client to be sending multiple/different pictures instead of sending the same picture repeatedly which could potentially appeal to traffic monitoring hackers. Rather, our technique could make the protocol looks like a picture exchange application which may not attract hackers' attention.
- Transmitting Port Knocking Traffic More Naturally: in most port knocking implementations, the closed ports that are used to communicate the knocks are typically TCP ports. Using a knock sequence of TCP SYN packets to known closed ports could

look anomalous to anyone monitoring especially if it is used repetitively. In addition, traditional TCP SYN knocks rely on the packets arriving in the correct order; something that cannot be guaranteed without establishing a connection. In our implementations of port knocking for mobile devices, rather than using the TCP SYN for preforming the knocks, we used a secret message as a payload in PNG chucks over UDP. As stated, we also varied the PNG picture when performing different knocks.

- Ability to Capture Interesting Traffic Only: Instead of listening and capturing each and every single incoming packet to the firewall public interface, the packet capturing listener has been developed to focus only on capturing and feeding the firewall agent with UDP packets from which the port knocking traffic is a subset. The firewall agent will in turn forwards the UDP potential port knocking traffic to the port knocking server for further analysis to determine whether the correct knocking sequence is made and the source/sending client is legitimate. With this new feature added, the framework is now more efficient and therefore works with better performance on how to handle incoming traffic.

- Protection Against DoS Attacks: A new security feature has also been added to the framework to prevent against denial of service (DoS) or network flooding attacks, in such a way that when a certain number of packets/second that are sent from a single source are detected to exceed a pre-set threshold value, the framework packet capturing agent (Firewall Agent) will then start to ignore capturing such packets from that particular source for a pre-specified period of time. This added security feature has proven to be effective to counter-measure and prevent denial of service attacks.

7   Experimental Results

7.1   The Performance of the Proposed Framework

Our proposed port knocking framework has been experimented in a test bed with the following specifications:

- The Physical/Host Machine: has Intel Core i5-6400 CPU @ 2.7 GHz and a total of 12 GB memory with Oracle VirtualBox version 5.1.4 and Genymotion version 2.8.0 for provisioning virtual Android devices.

- Two virtual Ubuntu-16.04 servers with 2.7 GHz processor and 2 GB memory each. One acting as IPTABLES firewall and the other as NGINX reverse proxy.

- Virtual Samsung Galaxy S6 (with Android 6.0 "Marshmallow" OS): a virtual Android acting as a Web services host and another virtual Android acting as a Web services client. Each virtual Android has 2.7 GHz processor and 2 GB memory.

- Web Service Test Candidate: we developed a "Dictionary" client/server mobile Web service in Java as our Web service testing candidate, where the "Words and their Meanings" are stored in a SQLight database in the Android Web services host that are exposed as a Web service from the Android host.

For the performance test, we measured the ability of the proposed port knocking framework on how well/fast it performs when servicing port knocking clients' requests for opening and/or closing the firewall ports. After performing several opening and closing port requests using the port knocking client, our experimental results clearly indicate that all the implementations of our proposed port knocking framework are capable of servicing clients' requests with high performance. Figure 7 below shows the average response time (in milli-seconds) for the port opening/closing requests for all the proposed port knocking implementations. As expected, port knocking implementation (3) has the best average response time (while using both AES and RSA) compared to the other proposed implementations; this is because the port knocking server and the firewall agent are both in the same server (the reverse proxy) that could enable the interaction between the two to be faster compared to the other proposed port knocking implementations where the port knocking server and the firewall agent are not in the same device/server. Also, as shown in Fig. 7 below, our experimental results show that in all the proposed port knocking implementations the symmetric encryption (AES) is always faster than the public key encryption (RSA) by an average value of 37.3 ms approximately. This is also an expected result since by design, RSA is more computationally expensive compared to AES.

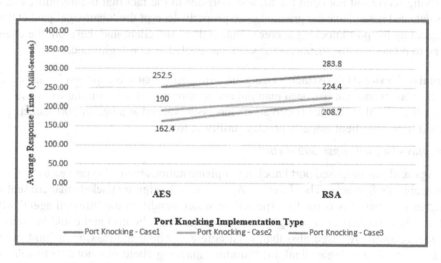

Fig. 7. Performance testing results for the proposed framework

7.2   Replay and Denial of Service Attacks

In order to ensure the Hybrid Port Knocking System (HPK) continued to be immune against Denial of Services (DoS) and replay attacks after being ported into the mobile devices, we carried out a replay and DoS attacks on all of the proposed port knocking implementations as described below:

Replay Attack. During an active session between a legitimate Android port knocking client and an Android server, the entire session traffic was captured using 'tcpdump' utility. This traffic has been further filtered using Wireshark to include only the TCP traffic that is needed to perform the replay and the DoS attacks; essentially this traffic includes all the port knocking traffic along with the Web services requests traffic that was originated/sent by the client [16, 21–23].

Using the 'tcpwrite' utility [22], the header information for the captured packets 'trace-replay.pcap' was then manipulated in such a way that it looks as if it was coming from another client with different source IP address and different source MAC address:

tcpwrite -i trace-replay.pcap –outfile=trace-replay-tcpwrite.pcap –srcipmap=
10.10.10.62:10.10.10.63 –enet-smac=08:00:27:04:08:11

The resulting manipulated packets that are written into the "trace-replay-tcpwrite.pcap" file could now be used to lunch the reply attack using the tcpreplay utility as follows [23]:

tcpreplay -i eth0 trace-replay-tcpwrite.pcap

After carrying-out the above replay attack, all of the port knocking proposed implementations (described above) are proven to be resilient against replay attacks. The port knocking server did not open the firewall port due to the fact that the intruding client was detected not to have the private key to properly decrypt the 'challenge' packet that was sent by the port knocking server to authenticate the client and therefore the client failed to properly authenticate and as such was treated as non-legitimate.

Denial of Service (DoS) Attack. Using the same packet that was captured for the replay attack (above) and that has been manipulated to appear as if it is coming from another client, the Denial of Service (DoS) attack has been lunched at a rate of 300 packets per second from one client using 'tcpreplay' utility as follows:

tcpreplay –loop=0 –pps=300 -i eth0

Again, all the proposed port knocking implementations were also proven to be resilient against DoS attacks. The 'Firewall Agent' started to ignore packets that are sent at a higher rate than it is normally expected, in which condition the 'firewall agent' will assume these packets are coming from a non-legitimate client(s) and could be treated as such accordingly. Note also that, even before reaching the maximum limit of 50 packets/sec. from a single client, the intruding/attacking client was not able to authenticate since it does not have the proper private key to respond to the port knocking 'challenge' request.

8   Conclusion

The proposed mobile client/server framework extends port knocking authentication systems to be included in and utilized by mobile clients/servers as well. Our framework is modular and flexible, and could be used by those applications that mandate access only whenever it is needed and should not last for more than it is needed; an example of such applications includes accessing one's medical records. Further, the proposed framework is at least as secure as the original Hybrid Port Knocking system (HPK) for providing mutual authentication and resiliency to the replay and the denial of service (DoS) attacks. Moreover, it offers added security features such as the ability to use symmetric encryption as well as public key encryption. Rather than using a single PNG picture as in the original HPK system, the proposed framework is capable of using multiple PNG pictures for encoding/hiding the payload in transit, which made its transmission look like a normal PNG exchanged between two. Additionally, rather than transporting the PNG picture payload over TCP SYN packets, we used the UDP protocol, that is faster and a more common way of sending images. Additionally, the proposed framework 'FirewallAgent' has the ability to detect and ignore DoS- suspicious packets as well as being able to ignore additional packets from the same DoS-suspicious source for a preconfigured time. Lastly, our experimental results have shown that all the implementations of the proposed port knocking framework have high performance when servicing port knocking clients' requests.

References

1. Hadi, A., Al-Bahadili, H.: A hybrid port-knocking technique for host authentication. IGI-Global Knowledge Disseminator (2012)
2. Hadi, A., Al-Bahadili, H.: Network security using hybrid port knocking. IJCSNS Int. J. Comput. Sci. Netw. Secur. **10**(8), 8–12 (2010)
3. Gibbons, K., O'Raw, J., Curran, K.: Security evaluation of the OAuth 2.0 framework. Inf. Manage. Comput. Secur. **22**(3), December 2014. ISSN: 0968-5227
4. DeGraaf, R., Aycock, J., Jacobson, M.: Improved port knocking with strong authentication. Department of Computer Science, University of Calgary, Calgary, Alberta, Canada (2005)
5. ArchLinux: Port Knocking (2016). https://wiki.archlinux.org/index.php/Port_knocking. Accessed Dec 2016
6. Vasserman, E., Hopper, N., Tyra, J.: SilentKnock: practical, provably undetectable authentication. Int. J. Inf. Secur. **8**, 121–135 (2009). Springer-Verlag (2008)
7. Fideloper: Managing the Iptables Firewall (2013). http://fideloper.com/iptables-tutorial. Accessed Nov 2016
8. Internet Engineering Task Force (IETF): The OAuth 2.0 Authorization Framework. Request for Comments: 6749 (2012). https://tools.ietf.org/html/rfc6749
9. Ellingwood, J.: How to choose an effective firewall policy to secure your servers (2015). https://www.digitalocean.com/community/tutorials/how-to-choose-an-effective-firewall-policy-to-secure-your-servers. Accessed Nov 2016
10. Boroumand, L., Shiraz, M., Gani, A., Khan, S., Shah, S.: A review on port-knocking authentication methods for mobile cloud computing. Center for Mobile Cloud Computing Research (C4MCCR), Faculty of Computer Science and Information Technology, University of Malaya, Kuala Lumpur, Malaysia (2014)
11. Linux Firewall Tutorial: IPTables Tables, Chains, Rules Fundamentals. http://www.thegeekstuff.com/2011/01/iptables-fundamentals. Accessed Nov 2016
12. Demircioglu, M.: Analysis of port knocking mechanism. A master's Thesis in Computer Engineering, Atilim University (2009)
13. Doyle, M.: Implementing a port knocking system in C. Physics Honor Thesis, The University of Arkansas (2004)
14. Krzywinski, M.: Port knocking: network authentication across closed ports. SysAdmin Magazine **12**, 12–17 (2003). http://www.portknocking.org/docs/krzywinski-portknocking-sysadmin2003.pdf

15. Membrane OAuth Authentication. http://membrane-soa.org/service-proxy-doc/4.2/security/oauth2. Accessed Sept 2016
16. Shrestha, N.: Wireshark – network protocol analyzer tool for RHEL/CentOS/Fedora (2016). http://www.tecmint.com/wireshark-network-protocol-analyzer-tool-for-rhelcentosfedora. Accessed Nov 2016
17. Barham, P., Hand, S., Isaacs, R., Jardetzky, P., Mortier, R., Roscoe, T.: Techniques for lightweight concealment and authentication in IP networks. Intel Research, Technical report IRB-TR-02-009, 25 July 2002
18. Port Knocking: Port knocking implementations (2013). http://www.portknocking.org/view/implementations. Accessed June 2016
19. Port Knocking. https://en.wikipedia.org/wiki/Port_knocking. Accessed June 2016
20. Nelson, R.: Reverse proxy using NGINX Plus (2014). https://www.nginx.com/blog/reverse-proxy-using-nginx-plus. Accessed Nov 2016
21. TcpDump & LibPCap. http://www.tcpdump.org. Accessed Oct 2016
22. TCPWrite. http://tcpreplay.synfin.net/tcprewrite.html. Accessed Oct 2016
23. TCPReplay, PCap Editing & Replay Tools for *NIX. http://tcpreplay.synfin.net/wiki/tcprewrite. Accessed Oct 2016

Aspects of Application Security for Internet of Things Systems

Aneta Poniszewska-Maranda$^{(\boxtimes)}$ and Bartosz Wieczorek

Institute of Information Technology, Lodz University of Technology, Łódź, Poland
aneta.poniszewska-maranda@p.lodz.pl, wieczorek.bartosz20@gmail.com

Abstract. Year by year the solutions associated with the idea of Internet of Things (IoT) gaining in popularity. Internet of Things is a term describing the concepts of network connections between objects that may directly or indirectly collect, process and exchange data via computer networks. It is important to establish new standards of data management as well as create mobile and IoT applications extending the functionalities of IoT systems to enable the users to benefit from the newest technological advances. Addressing these tendencies the paper presents some sensitivities of mobile applications that could compromise the safety of IoT and several methods of dealing with these problems.

1 Introduction

The Internet is a powerful tool used in all kinds of the information systems. The network is available almost anywhere, at home, at work, also on mobile devices (phones, watches). People start to think to connect the Internet to almost all devices of everyday use, so they can communicate with each other by taking simple decisions for people and helping them in their life. Such idea is called the *Internet of Things (IoT)*.

Recent tendencies in the field of application development indicate the more and more significant role which mobile applications fulfil in everyday live of the rapidly growing number of smartphone users. It is important to establish new standards of data management as well as create mobile and IoT applications extending the functionalities of their existing systems to enable the users to benefit from the newest technological advances [27].

The number of devices used in systems based on the concept of Internet of Things increases. The development of such systems may cause that their number may reach a very high value. The average person will be surrounded by a number of devices that will aim to assist him and make certain decisions, facilitating his life. To be able to do it, they have to store, exchange and transfer the data among the set of different devices and systems.

At the consumer level, user interaction or control of IoT devices is most often accomplished via mobile device applications. Basing on potential aims that the attackers want to gain an access to one can deduce that the most vulnerable parts of the application will embrace the data storage points, the permission

M. Younas et al. (Eds.): MobiWIS 2017, LNCS 10486, pp. 163–176, 2017.
DOI: 10.1007/978-3-319-65515-4_14

management policy, the application file system and any kind of configuration files that may be stored within the device.

The problem presented in the paper concerns the security of IoT which is a big issue, over which the solution many professionals work around the world. This paper shows some of sensitivities of mobile applications that could compromise the safety of IoT. It also presents several well-known methods of dealing with these problems.

The presented paper is structured as follows: Sect. 2 gives the outline of Internet of Things concept. Section 3 deals with the chosen aspects of IoT security threats. Section 4 presents the chosen solutions of communication security of IoT while Sect. 5 describes the application security.

2 Concept of Internet of Things

The concept of Internet of Things appeared several years ago and in that time has evolved into one of the pillars of new technologies sector. There is no clear definition of this concept in the literature. In many cases, the definitions are complementary, creating a more accurate description of the problem. This concept is also often associated with the concept of ubiquitous computing. But the idea of IoT is more complicated than just a simple statement, and can often be misinterpreted. The following paragraphs present the most common definitions of IoT.

The Internet of Things is a vision, in which objects become part of the Internet, where every object is uniquely identifiable and accessible on the Web. These objects may directly or indirectly collect, process or exchange data via data communications network. This concept can be described by a simplified equation [1]:

$$physical\ objects\ +\ sensors\ and\ microprocessors\ =\ IoT$$

Another, shorter and more general definition says that it is a concept in which digital and physical devices are connected to appropriate infrastructure, where can provide a wide range of new applications and services. This definition does not specify the fact addressing infrastructure devices or even not talking about infrastructure [2].

One of the first attempts to define this concept was pretty simple concept. The Internet of Things is all objects in everyday life, which are equipped with wireless identifiers and so that they can communicate with each other and be managed by a computer [3].

The shortest definition, which may describe the concept of the Internet of Things shows that it is clearly identification of objects and their representation in the structure of the Internet. This is the most general definition that may expresses the most important elements concerning the issue of IoT [4]:

"Internet of Things is a term that ignites the imagination of people around the world. Some see it as a chance to "better tomorrow", others fear the ongoing and increasingly ubiquitous digitization of life. However, it can't be denied, that the number of different devices connected to the network is increasing every year, bringing to significant changes in the functioning of factories, intelligent buildings, everyday objects, as well as ourselves."

On the basis of all above definitions of the issues of IoT and taking into account its important aspects, the concise and yet comprehensive definition of this concept was created. Thus,

Internet of Things is a concept, where clearly identifiable and smart objects can communicate with each other in a defined environment to make autonomous decisions by analysing and processing the data collected from the environment.

The environment can be the Internet or only a portion (e.g. local area network and the devices used only at home). Additionally, there may be mentioned also that the interconnected devices provide the user with various number of applications and services which enable it to communicate with them. To take the autonomous decisions, except to analyse the collected information, objects may use generally understood knowledge, that is, for example, elements related to the habit of the user in some aspect, so that the object will be able to make the better decisions.

3   Threats of IoT Security

Preventing the threats connected with development of IoT applications and vulnerabilities characterizing this concept is not a task which can be realized by a single targeted solution. Some attempts have been made to establish the policy of securing the IoT applications each of them embracing different regions of security breaches [27].

Indeed, the number of devices connected to the Internet of Things is increasing rapidly, it is estimated that this number will exceed 25 billions by 2020 year. Beside the increase in the number of various devices available on the market also the interesting solutions incorporating the ideas of IoT in various areas of human activity are produced – starting from the industry, production, transport, energy, urban, residential, health and life [5,6].

The idea of IoT solutions comes down to devices often equipped with sensors collecting the data. IoT communication devices are done through two main vectors, radio frequency (RF) and internet gateway devices. Both avenues of communication offer a variety of attack vectors against IoT. IoT RF communication protocols include 802.11 ("WiFi"), Bluetooth, Zigbee, ZWave, Near Field Communication (NFC) and 433MHz – all are susceptible to RF signal intercept by *software defined radio* (SDR) or other similar devices. Each standard does, however, carry a different level of over-the-air security capabilities (Fig. 1) [7].

At the customer level, user interaction or control of IoT devices is most often accomplished via mobile device applications. Control interface applications offer many additional attack vectors. Because most customer mobile device control applications do not speak directly to the IoT device, they must communicate

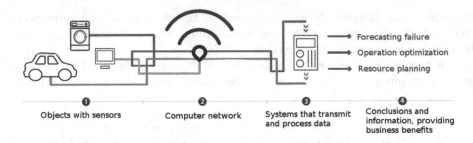

①	②	③	④
Objects with sensors	Computer network	Systems that transmit and process data	Conclusions and information, providing business benefits

Fig. 1. Idea of functioning of IoT solutions

through an intermediary server or service connected via Internet, thus creating additional attack surfaces for attackers.

For example, imagine the functioning of a simple system consisting of a number of devices equipped with temperature sensors. These devices send the collected data via the network to a system whose function is to process the received data and decide to reduce or increase the temperature in the room. And then send a message to the ventilation devices to make appropriate action and send the averaged data to mobile devices so that the user with the application will be able to display them and control the temperature in the room (Fig. 2).

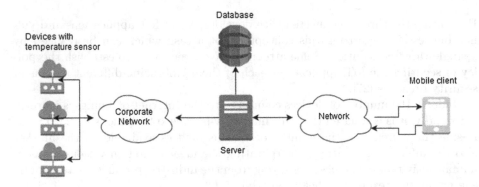

Fig. 2. Example of IoT system

An example which is shown above is of course to present the idea of the Internet of Things in practice. But also allows to see that the IoT is associated with a continuous exchange of data between the various components of the whole system such as the above mentioned devices with sensors, servers processing received data from sensors and client applications. It requests the question of the security of these data and the security of the entire system. How big an impact on the entire ecosystem sensitivity has the client applications?

4   Communication Security

We can observed few areas of attack related to communication between a client mobile and other system components of IoT, starting from the direct communication between devices collecting data and mobile application. In this case, the communication can be carried out using several available means of communication such as WiFi, NFC, Bleutooth (Fig. 3). With each of the available methods of communication between sensor and mobile application several sensitivities are linked. For example, there is a risk of man in the middle attack to intercept transmitted data in the case of use of WiFi networks.

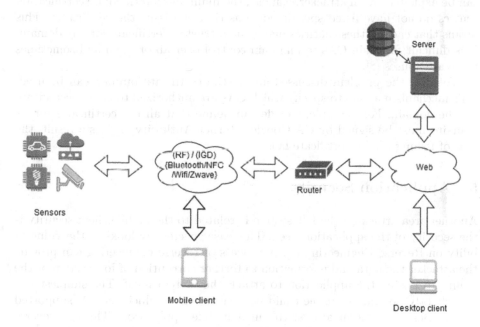

Fig. 3. Communication in IoT system

Another example may be the measuring devices that use a NFC or Bluetooth as transmission technology. There is a risk of an attacker posing as the device. In the case of devices that communicate via NFC the attacker having an open access to signal transmitting NFC chip is able to reprogram it, that could lead to execution of malicious actions on end device. In the case of devices that are equipped with Bluetooth Low Energy of which the best example is the beacons growing on popularity, the risk of posing the device is bind with the capture of device ID by the attacker. The length of the identifier depends on the used communication protocol (iBeacon, Eddystone), however the capture process is often not complicated, but there are Beacons on the market that already providing encryption communication and "shuffle id". "Shuffle id" gives the ability to change the IDs in time.

Another already mentioned area attack associated with communication taking place with the mobile client is communication with a remote server. Here, the risk of various types of attacks including a man in the middle also exist, to intercept transmitted data, for which it is so important to remember the encryption of transported data.

One obvious solution is to use SSL, which is a network protocol used to secure Internet connections. An SSL certificate ensures the confidentiality of data transmitted over the Internet. Secure connections using HTTPS are one of the basic building blocks of today's Internet. Nevertheless, it has also be remembered that, despite of many advantages of SSL there is also a flaw that can be exploited by an attacker. Namely, the main and intermediate certification centres do not have listed specific domains that can issue the certificates. This means that each of these entities may issue a trusted certificate for any domain. It is difficult for main CAs to maintain control over all of them and sometimes there are abuses [8].

To solve the problem discussed above, the certificate pinning can be used. This mechanism allows to specify which CAs are authorized to issue a certificate for the domain. For example, Google can define that all the certificates for its domains must be signed by CA Google Internet Authority G2. As a result, the case of issuing a false certificate fails.

5   Application Security

Another area attack on the IoT system is related to the mobile client security is the security of the application itself. This case specifically looks at the vulnerability on Reverse Engineering [5]. A process of reverse engineering can provide the attacker the data and information to further corruption of IoT system or the ability to posing the application to attack the system itself. The simplest but also slightly abstract example could be a situation in which the IDs supported by the Beacons system are "sewn" in a mobile application. Through reverse engineering an attacker would be able to obtain them, what in the long term would result in the ability of posing the Beacons.

In the situation where Beacon serves as the trigger for the display of marketing content problem seems to be insignificant harm. However, when the Beacon is used in transport, for example to calculate the amount of travel the problem becomes a bit more serious.

Another example of application sensitivity may be the use of reverse engineering tools to decompile the applications, finding the code responsible for communication with a remote server, and in order to obtain information for an attack aimed directly at it. Opportunities and information that an attacker can gain by making reverse engineering applications are limited only by the skill and cleverness of attacker. It is important to take the actions to protect the applications against easy data access and modification by reverse engineering. The basic method aimed at securing the application against the possibility of making reverse engineering is obfuscation.

Obfuscation is a very large topic, because they are constantly being created subsequent publications on new techniques or theirs modifications – there are many tools that allow us to automatically darkening the created code. It should also be remembered that, as with other methods of securing the code – they have to slow down the attack, not preventing it. In addition to obfuscation techniques there are also at the same time the algorithms designed to automatically reverse this process which in itself can be an interesting source of new ideas used in the process of obfuscation. Obfuscation takes place at three levels [12, 14, 15]:

- transformations *source code* to *source code*,
- transformations *bytecode* to *bytecode*,
- transformations *machine code* to *machine code*.

Transformations "*source code* to *source code*" allow the conversion of our readable code to code very difficult to read (Fig. 4).

```
{
    static String a(byte[] paramArrayOfByte)
    {
        int i = 0;
        StringBuffer localStringBuffer = new StringBuffer();
        String[] arrayOfString = { "00", "01", "02", "03", "04", "05", "06", "07", "08"
        while (i < paramArrayOfByte.length)
        {
            localStringBuffer.append(arrayOfString[(0xFF & paramArrayOfByte[i])]);
            i++;
        }
        return localStringBuffer.toString();
    }

    public final byte[] a(String paramString)
    {
        String str = getResources().getString(2130968577);
        try
        {
            MessageDigest localMessageDigest2 = MessageDigest.getInstance("SHA-256");
            localMessageDigest1 = localMessageDigest2;
            localMessageDigest1.reset();
            localMessageDigest1.update(str.getBytes());
            return localMessageDigest1.digest(paramString.getBytes("UTF-8"));
        }
        catch (NoSuchAlgorithmException localNoSuchAlgorithmException)
        {
            while (true)
```

Fig. 4. Example of code obfuscation

The advantage of this solution is that after such transformation we can use any compiler, because the code is still valid, only looks more exotic. In addition, despite the fact that the resulting code has a strange structure, we can debug it, seeing the source.

Transformations *"bytecode* to *bytecode"* operate on the code during compilation (Figs. 5 and 6). The most common current method is based on LLVM project (*Low Level Virtual Machine*, e.g. compilator *clang*). The core of LLVM is the intermediate representation (IR) – a low-level programming language similar to assembly. The work principle of compilers based on LLVM is as follows [10,11,13]:

– replace source code for indirect representation,
– pass the LLVM IR by the optimization modules,
– replace LLVM IR on processor machine code in the chosen architecture.

```
public static int sum(int iarry[]) {
        int result = 0;
        for (int i = 0; i < iarry.length; i++) {
                result += iarry[i];
        }
        return result;
}
```

Fig. 5. Example method *sum()* in its original Java source code

Compilation for the indirect representation is similar to the code compilation for Java or C# – the whole program is translated into commands similar to Assembler – but LLVM does not have a virtual machine able to execute such program, therefore at the end, the intermediate code is translated entirely into machine code for the target architecture. LLVM intermediate code is not so flexible, and depends on the target architecture – it will be slightly different, e.g. for x86 and ARM. From our point of view, the most interesting is the moment of optimization, because of regardless of language input in this place we have always deal with "assembler" LLVM, so we can add our plugin, which instead of optimize the code – it will be a mix of them. Then we do not have also to worry about the architecture of the target, as the result of our transformation will take care the module responsible for the final translation of LLVM IR into machine code.

Transformations *"machine code* to *machine code"* – this type of obfuscation is the most insidious and depends on the processor architecture, file format and even the compiler options used to create the binary file. It is also difficult to influence on placement of machine instructions, because the manipulation of one of them can lead to a whole chain of changes, but with a little patience and perseverance, we can get very interesting effects of obfuscation greatly hindering the process of reverse engineering (Figs. 7 and 8).

There are many methods used during the obfuscation [10–12,14,15,24]. Of course, any combination of techniques and modifications are possible and most

public static int sum(int[]);	public static int sum(int[]);
0: iconst 0	0: iconst 0
1: istore 1	1: istore 1
2: iconst 0	2: iconst 0
3: istore 2	3: istore 2
4: iload 2	4: **goto** 8 // side-step return
5: aload 0	address pop when falling-through
6: arraylength	7: pop // if coming from jsr at #23,
7: if icmpge 22	pop return address
10: iload 1	8: iload 2
11: aload 0	9: aload 0
12: iload 2	10: arraylength
13: iaload	11: if icmpge 26 // jump to jsr at
14: iadd	#26
15: istore 1	14: iload 1
16: iinc 2, 1	15: aload 0
19: **goto** 4	16: iload 2
22: iload 1	17: iaload
23: ireturn	18: iadd
	19: istore 1
	20: iinc 2, 1
	23: jsr 7
	26: jsr 29
	29: pop // pop return address off
	from jsr at #26
	30: iload 1
	31: ireturn

Fig. 6. Example method *sum()* in bytecode form before (left) and after (right) obfuscation

0	00000000: b802000000	MOV EAX, 0x2
1	00000005: b906000000	MOV ECX, 0x6
2	0000000a: 01c8	ADD EAX, ECX
3	0000000c: 85c0	TEST EAX, EAX
4	0000000e: 7405	JZ 0x15
5	00000010: 83f808	CMP EAX, 0x8
6	00000013: 75eb	JNZ 0x0
7	00000015: c3	RET

Fig. 7. Sample code in its original form

often used in obfuscators. All of them have the same goal – to change the look of the program so that the understanding of principles of its operations took a lot of time, while not changing its functionality. Some of the available methods used during the obfuscation are as follows [11,13–15]:

- Renaming – one of the basic methods involving the swapping of names of variables and functions.
- Control flow flattening – the purpose of this method is to completely flatten the control flow graph of a program.
- Dummy code – this technique is designed to add more amount of code and not to modify the functionality of the transformed function.
- Random sequence of blocks.
- Opaque predicates – is an obfuscated condition, that, followed with a conditional operation, will make the analysis harder and in some cases impossible

until the code is actually executed until that condition is evaluated. This is
used to disrupt static analysis or emulation.
- Combining functions.

Adduced herein sensitivities of mobile applications are not a finite list of all
of them that can be used by potential attackers on the IoT system. As the risk
connected with actions of malware and botnet attacks, there are software based
attacks. In the case of attacks, the attacker can create malicious codes such as
Worms, Trojans and viruses to infect and control the smart devices to extract
their information. Another example is blackmailer or activist endeavors to mess
up or terminate the network by launching the Denial of Service (DoS) attack.
DoS attack is a particular attack on a network or a computational resource, and
the effect of DoS attack may contribute to the reduction in network capacity.

There are two categories of DoS attacks in IoT: *Distributed Denial Of Service (DDoS)* and *Ordinary Denial Of Service (ODoS)* [16,17]. For common DoS
attack, a tool is required to send packets to an intended system that crash the
network or sometimes force the system to restart. Meanwhile, DDoS can be a
single attacker but not powerful as a proxy attacker. From that, the impact of
this attack not only disabled the network but also prevent it to be accessible to
a very large network [18–20].

```
0   00000000: b837272a61    MOV EAX, 0x612a2737      38  0000007f: eb52            JMP 0xd3
1   00000005: eb3a          JMP 0x41                 39  00000081: d8
2   00000007: eb2f          JMP 0x38                 39  00000082: eb27            JMP 0xab
3   00000009: 81c06de78ae1  ADD EAX, 0xe18ae76d      40  00000084: f7
4   0000000f: eb16          JMP 0x27                 40  00000085: eb09            JMP 0x90
5   00000011: 81e87daf9577  SUB EAX, 0x7795af7d      41  00000087: 81e93cdbac3f    SUB ECX, 0x3facdb3c
6   00000017: e994000000    JMP 0xb0                 42  0000008d: ebd9            JMP 0x68
7   0000001c: 83                                     43  0000008f: ea
7   0000001d: eb08          JMP 0x27                 43  00000090: 81c0c757b8d5    ADD EAX, 0xd5b857c7
8   0000001f: bb0089c4e5    MOV EBX, 0xe5c48900      44  00000096: eba0            JMP 0x38
9   00000024: eb53          JMP 0x79                 45  00000098: ea
10  00000026: 68                                     45  00000099: ebf5            JMP 0x90
10  00000027: ebe8          JMP 0x11                 46  0000009b: dc
11  00000029: f7                                     46  0000009c: eb09            JMP 0xa7
11  0000002a: eb0c          JMP 0x38                 47  0000009e: 81c388775b66    ADD EBX, 0x665b7788
12  0000002c: 81e9699dec08  SUB ECX, 0x8ec9d69       48  000000a4: ebaf            JMP 0x55
13  00000032: e9ab000000    JMP 0xe2                 49  000000a6: d8
14  00000037: 83                                     49  000000a7: eb00            JMP 0xa9
14  00000038: 81c038e2d5f6  ADD EAX, 0xf6d5e238      50  000000a9: eb05            JMP 0xb0
15  0000003e: ebc9          JMP 0x9                  51  000000ab: 74cb            JZ 0x78
16  00000040: d8                                     52  000000ad: eb21            JMP 0xd0
16  00000041: eb56          JMP 0x99                 53  000000af: d8
17  00000043: eb4b          JMP 0x90                 53  000000b0: 81c0dc665268    ADD EAX, 0x685266dc
18  00000045: eb05          JMP 0x4c                 54  000000b6: eb09            JMP 0xc1
19  00000047: 75b7          JNZ 0x0                  55  000000b8: 81c396e99ded    ADD EBX, 0xed9de996
20  00000049: eb2d          JMP 0x78                 56  000000be: eb9d            JMP 0x5d
21  0000004b: e9                                     57  000000c0: 83
21  0000004c: b995f3fde5    MOV ECX, 0xe5fdf395      57  000000c1: eb09            JMP 0xcc
22  00000051: eb1a          JMP 0x6d                 58  000000c3: 81f14ffbe7e8    XOR ECX, 0xe8e7fb4f
23  00000053: eb13          JMP 0x68                 59  000000c9: ebbc            JMP 0x87
24  00000055: 81ebef03dbd0  SUB EBX, 0xd0db03ef      60  000000cb: d8
25  0000005b: eb08          JMP 0x65                 60  000000cc: eb1d            JMP 0xeb
26  0000005d: 39d8          CMP EAX, EBX             61  000000ce: eb12            JMP 0xe2
27  0000005f: e98f000000    JMP 0xf3                 62  000000d0: 53              PUSH EBX
28  00000064: 81                                     63  000000d1: eb09            JMP 0xdc
28  00000065: eb51          JMP 0xb8                 64  000000d3: 81eb3c8f5c2d    SUB EBX, 0x2d5c8f3c
29  00000067: ea                                     65  000000d9: ebc3            JMP 0x9e
29  00000068: 01c8          ADD EAX, ECX             66  000000db: 81
30  0000006a: eb06          JMP 0x72                 66  000000dc: e93effffff      JMP 0x1f
31  0000006c: d8                                     67  000000e1: e8
31  0000006d: ebbd          JMP 0x2c                 67  000000e2: 81c1e1c939fa    ADD ECX, 0xfa39c9e1
32  0000006f: 81                                     68  000000e8: ebd9            JMP 0xc3
32  00000070: eb13          JMP 0x85                 69  000000ea: da
33  00000072: 85c0          TEST EAX, EAX            69  000000eb: e95cffffff      JMP 0x4c
34  00000074: eb0c          JMP 0x82                 70  000000f0: 83
35  00000076: eb01          JMP 0x79                 70  000000f1: eb00            JMP 0xf3
36  00000078: c3            RET                      71  000000f3: 5b              POP EBX
37  00000079: 81ebeb56863b  SUB EBX, 0x3b8656eb      72  000000f4: e94effffff      JMP 0x47
                                                     73  000000f9: da
```

Fig. 8. Sample code after obfuscation

6   Conclusions and Future Research Issues

Good direction in work on the problem of IoT system security is an attempt to create an effective method of detecting the malicious behaviour in the system – method which most likely be based on the mechanisms of artificial intelligence, because so far the most common strategy was a response to the attack, the method and patching gaps in the system.

Biologically inspired models for security have been more flourishing to put up the wonderful defence in securing ad hoc networks. Because of the features of ad hoc network, they require a strong, decentralized security mechanism. The similarities between the biological phenomenon's and the operations of the network make bio inspired approach a interesting field for research [21].

Biologically inspired approaches can be used because of numerous similarities between the nature and computer world. The characteristics of a biological system include [9, 22]:

- Adaptive to their environment, which ensures their survival in the harshest conditions.
- Capacity to heal, remain strong and resilience against failures caused by many factors.
- Capacity to accomplish very intricate tasks using a limited set of basic rules.
- Efficient in learning, resolving and regenerating themselves when exposed to new conditions.

Due to the development in the computer world there has been a paradigm shift from a giant centralized system to independent decentralized and adaptive system. This system has to address numerous other challenges, such as [23]:

- Density of the network is immense because of strong connectivity. Hence scalability is a major issue. Since the network is open, any number of nodes can be dynamically added into it.
- Early systems were static, with single transmitter and receiver and a fixed communication channel. Such systems did not have to deal with varying dynamics of the world. Today's dynamic networks have to deal with varying behaviour resulting from traffic, bandwidth, multiple channels and network conditions.
- Effective management of resources to manage a cost effective network.
- Self organization, self evolution and survivability.

Comparing the characteristics of the biological system with the computer networks, it is evident that bio inspired techniques can be used to solve these challenges. For example there is a model described by Yaser and Azween to provide security in mobile ad hoc network inspired by biological processes [20]. The model is based on the features of immune system such as imperfect detection, anomaly detection, memory response, diversity and adaptive detection. The essence of immune system is the ability to differentiate between self and non self. To secure ad hoc networks the proposed model uses the intelligent agents of which two are static and others are mobile. The mobile agents that carry out the security mission are:

1. Manager agent monitors the network configuration periodically to identify the changes in the routing tables.
2. Monitor agent identifies self patterns and blocks others. In case of self pattern, packets are accepted and transferred normally. Otherwise the packets are blocked and the monitor checks the database if it is not a new pattern that generates an update, else the monitor informs the manager about the new pattern.
3. Replicate agent starts a new task whenever it creates a new entry for a new node or updates an entry of an existing node.
4. Recover agent provides a restore point to the corrupted nodes.

Heena et al. [25] explained an idea which uses machine learning techniques to differentiate between good and fraudulent node in a wireless network. It derives an inspiration from human immune system to use virtual antibodies in the system to disable fraudulent nodes. Machine learning based biologically inspired system can be divided into three essential blocks:

- machine learning algorithm to classify data into fraudulent or legal nodes,
- generation of virtual antibodies,
- trust rating.

The wireless network is divided as clusters; the data received from nodes is classified as fraudulent or legal data. If a fraudulent data is received the cluster heads will generate virtual antibodies. Finally the gateways will generate trust rating for the nodes. These trust ratings will be used to disable a fraudulent node.

The authors of [26] present a threat analysis of IoT and use an Artificial Neural Network (ANN) to combat these threats. A multi-level perception, a type of supervised ANN, is trained using internet packet traces, then is assessed on its ability to thwart Distributed Denial of Service (DDoS/DoS) attacks. The detection was based on classifying normal and threat patterns. The ANN model was validated against a simulated IoT network demonstrating over 99% accuracy. It was able to identify successfully different types of attacks and showed good performances in terms of true and false positive rates [26].

In conclusion, unsecured mobile applications that are part of the IoT, can be a serious problem for the security of the entire system. There are many possibilities of obtaining data allowing exposure of the system components. Of course on the other side there is a fairly large arsenal of application and communication security methods. Nevertheless, the risks are very real, so it is important that both programmers and system architects makes best efforts to increase the level of security of the entire IoT system, by securing each component.

The analysis of opportunities and attempt to create solutions of self-adaptive mechanism protecting the system is a very good direction as evidenced very promising research.

References

1. McEwen, A., Cassimally, H.: Designing the Internet of Things. Wiley, Chichester (2014)
2. da Costa, F.: Rethinking the Internet of Things. A Scalable Approach to Connecting Everything. Apress Open, Berkely (2013)
3. An Introduction to the Internet of Things (IoT). http://www.lopezresearch.com/
4. Arsénio, A., Serra, H., Francisco, R., Nabais, F., Andrade, J., Serrano, E.: Internet of intelligent things: bringing artificial intelligence into things and communication networks. In: Xhafa, F., Bessis, N. (eds.) Inter-cooperative Collective Intelligence: Techniques and Applications. Studies in Computational Intelligence, vol. 495, pp. 1–37. Springer, Heidelberg (2014). doi:10.1007/978-3-642-35016-0_1
5. Ruggieri, M., Nikookar, H., Vermesan, O., Friess, P.: Internet of Things: Converging Technologies for Smart Environments and Integrated Ecosystems. River Publishers, Aalborg (2013)
6. Gartner: Gartner Says 4.9 Billion Connected "Things" Will Be in Use in 2015 (2014). http://www.gartner.com/newsroom/id/2905717
7. Devito, M.: A security assessment of Z-Wave devices and replay attack vulnerability (2016). https://www.sans.org/reading-room/whitepapers/internet/security-assessment-z-wave-devices-replay-attack-vulnerability-37242
8. Misra, A., Dubey, A.: Android Security: Attacks and Defenses. Auerbach Publications, Boca Raton (2013)
9. Barak, B., Goldreich, O., Impagliazzo, R., Rudich, S., Sahai, A., Vadhan, S., Yang, K.: On the (Im)possibility of obfuscating programs. In: Kilian, J. (ed.) CRYPTO 2001. LNCS, vol. 2139, pp. 1–18. Springer, Heidelberg (2001). doi:10.1007/3-540-44647-8_1
10. Wroblewski, G.: General method of program code obfuscation. In: Proceedings of the International Conference on Software Engineering Research and Practice, SERP 2002, USA, pp. 153–159 (2002)
11. Ceccato, M., Di Penta, M., Nagra, J., Falcarin, P., Ricca, F., Torchiano, M., Tonella, P.: The effectiveness of source code obfuscation - an experimental assessment. In: Proceedings of the 17th IEEE International Conference on Program Comprehension, ICPC, pp. 178–187. IEEE Computer Society (2009)
12. Madou, M., Anckaert, B., De Bus, B., De Bosschere, K.: On the effectiveness of source code transformations for binary obfuscation. In: Proceedings of the of International Conference on Software Engineering Research and Practice, SERP 2006, pp. 527–533 (2006)
13. Canetti, R., Tauman Kalai, Y., Varia, M., Wichs, D.: On symmetric encryption and point obfuscation. In: Micciancio, D. (ed.) TCC 2010. LNCS, vol. 5978, pp. 52–71. Springer, Heidelberg (2010). doi:10.1007/978-3-642-11799-2_4
14. Bitansky, N., Canetti, R.: On strong simulation and composable point obfuscation. In: Rabin, T. (ed.) CRYPTO 2010. LNCS, vol. 6223, pp. 520–537. Springer, Heidelberg (2010). doi:10.1007/978-3-642-14623-7_28
15. Canetti, R., Dakdouk, R.R.: Obfuscating point functions with multibit output. In: Smart, N. (ed.) EUROCRYPT 2008. LNCS, vol. 4965, pp. 489–508. Springer, Heidelberg (2008). doi:10.1007/978-3-540-78967-3_28
16. Patra, L., Rao, U.P.: Internet of Things - architecture, applications, security and other major challenges. In: Proceedings of the 3rd International Conference on Computing for Sustainable Global Development, INDIACom, New Delhi, pp. 1201–1206 (2016)

17. Billure, R., Tayur, V.M., Mahesh, V.: Internet of Things - a study on the security challenges. In: Billure IEEE International Advance Computing Conference, IACC, Banglore, pp. 247–252 (2015)
18. Shifa, A., Asghar, M.N., Fleury, M.: Multimedia security perspectives in IoT. In: Proceedings of the 6th International Conference on Innovative Computing Technology, INTECH, pp. 550–55 (2016)
19. Xi, W., Ling, L.: Research on IoT privacy security risks. In: International Conference on Industrial Informatics - Computing Technology, Intelligent Technology, Industrial Information Integration, ICIICII, Wuhan, pp. 259–262 (2016)
20. Ahamed, J., Rajan, A.V.: Internet of Things (IoT): application systems and security vulnerabilities. In: Proceedings of the 5th International Conference on Electronic Devices, Systems and Applications, ICEDSA, pp. 1–5 (2016)
21. Banu, R., Ahammed, G.F.A., Fathima, N.: A review on biologically inspired approaches to security for Internet of Things (IoT). In: International Conference on Electrical, Electronics and and Optimization Techniques, ICEEOT, Chennai, pp. 1062–1066 (2016)
22. Meisel, M., Vasileios, P., Lixia, Z.: A taxonomy of biologically inspired research in computer networking. Elsevier Comput. Netw. J. **54**(6), 901–916 (2009)
23. Dressler, F., Akan, O.: A survey on bio-inspired networking. Elsevier Comput. Netw. J. **54**(6), 881–900 (2010)
24. Mohamed, Y.A., Adbullah, A.B.: Biologically inspired Model for Securing Hybrid Mobile Ad hoc Networks. IEEE (2008)
25. Rathore, H., Jha, S.: Bio-Inspired Machine Learning Based Wireless Sensor Network Security. IEEE (2013)
26. Hodo, E., et al.: Threat analysis of IoT networks using artificial neural network intrusion detection system. In: International Symposium on Networks, Computers and Communications, ISNCC, pp. 1–6 (2016)
27. Michalska, A., Poniszewska-Marańda, A.: Security risks and their prevention capabilities in mobile application development. Inf. Syst. Manag. **4**(2), 123–134 (2015). WULS Press

Track & Trace System with Serialization Prototyping Methodology for Pharmaceutical Industry in EU

Josef Horalek and Vladimir Sobeslav[(✉)]

Faculty of Informatics and Management, University of Hradec Králové, Rokitanskeho 62, 50003 Hradec Králové, Czech Republic
{josef.horalek,vladimir.sobeslav}@uhk.cz

Abstract. This paper provides principles and proposals of the Track & Trace system for purposes of serialization integration in drug identification in pharmaceutical industry. Common principles of industrial product marking are introduced with special part of 2-D Data Matrix code which has been recommended by GS1 consortium for pharmaceutical purposes. The principles of saving production data during whole supply chain between manufacturer and customer to local authority systems will be shown as well. Later chapters uncover some overlooked problems of T&T implementation process and describe suitable methods that minimize risks of failures of final implementation project. Following the theoretical analysis of technology Track & Trace and serialization will be processed as practical methodology.

Keywords: Pharma · Track and Trace · Serialization · GMP · GS1 · Product identification

1 Introduction

The demand for information is rising across individual market segments. Pharmaceutical industry is highly restricted by the requirements of the local authorities (national agencies established by legislation of the given state) as well as supranational agencies that are defined by international contracts, agreements and legislation (as for example the central authority in the scope of European Union). Considering the widespread illicit trade with counterfeit medications, their smuggling and general illegal handling, it is necessary to pursue detailed and unique labelling of such drugs. These labels have to be registered by a local authority in a centralized database [1]. It is necessary to implement well-arranged methods that convert aforementioned presumptions into the practice in order to secure exact and unchangeable labelling. The labelling methods for individual parts of a package have to be retrospectively re-validated and components that do not meet the standards have to be returned to production before their release into the distribution chain [2]. The presumptions must be fulfilled on the grounds of potential high sanctions that are threatening the producers in case of failing to comply with the mandatory regulations [1].

© Springer International Publishing AG 2017
M. Younas et al. (Eds.): MobiWIS 2017, LNCS 10486, pp. 177–186, 2017.
DOI: 10.1007/978-3-319-65515-4_15

2   Why to Use Unique Codes in Pharmaceutics

Pharmaceutical products are coming into the focus of criminal organizations all around the world in the recent years. A large amount of forged drugs is appearing on markets. WHO estimated that there were sold 75 billion dollars' worth forged medical products in 2010 [3]. The risks, to which the potential consumer is submitted, can be serious. A forged drug can contain same type of active substance, but in different (possibly non-homogeneous) therapeutic dosage, it can contain no active substance at all or different active substance (generic substitute). It can also be contaminated by different substances. Counterfeits can succumb to decay because of poor storing and distribution (neglected temperature and humidity during the transport and storage). The risks can be divided into the categories in perspective of the aforementioned overview:

- Threat to a producer – lost profits, an injury to the producer's reputation, a market position loss.
- Threat to a patient – overall influence on the population health state.
- Threat to a health-care system – insurance companies cover ineffective healing agents and they are facing the risk of costs for additional treatment of the patients under the influence of ineffective (counterfeit) healing agents at the same time.

3   Industrial Product Marking

A large number of different machine-readable codes can be utilized for the industrial products labelling. Basically, we can divide the codes into one-dimensional linear codes, two-dimensional barcodes and electronic codes (e.g. RFID). Each of the aforementioned types of product markers can be used for the labelling according to relevant legislation [1]. The initial demands on unambiguity, error proofness, flexibility and the amount of stored data in such a code play important role. At the same time, it is necessary to keep in mind the price and the final size of the given product labelling [4]. The content of mandatory information for the labelling of products adjusted by law and other generally binding regulations can be exactly specified. The labelling of most common products contains only GTIN (Global Trade Identification Number), for example the European Article Number (EAN). EAN is usually represented by one-dimensional linear barcode that can be read by common laser readers. This code is error proof (it contains a control sum) and allows upside down reading [5]. EAN is a code belonging to the code family of GS1 Consortium organization, which standardizes also the advanced 2-D Data Matrix utilized in pharmacy. In case of necessity to utilize more information embedded into one code, a more complex representation needs to be implemented.

4   Advanced 2-D Data Matrix Code

2-D Data Matrix was developed as highly resilient code with the ability of easy scanning with no regards to its position in relation to reading device. It allows coding of up to 2 335 alphanumeric characters with given code size of 144 × 144 points (a minimal code has size of 10 × 10 characters and it allows to code 3 alphanumeric characters). It also provides high robustness against damage (damage up to 40% does not necessarily impact the readability) and it can be merged into clusters in order to increase the amount of encoded information [6]. The advanced version of 2-D Data Matrix GS1 ECC 200 allows utilization of application identifiers (AI) and thus it offers the possibility to carry for example EAN 13 or other linear codes [8]. This predestines it for the utilization in the pharmaceutical industry. Basic unit is 8-bit code word, where the value 1 is filled with black colour, the value 0 with white. The coloured squares are arranged into the pattern shown on the Fig. 1. Individual code words blocks are merged into the code matrix with additional correction blocks.

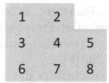

Fig. 1. 8-bit code word [6].

During the scanning it figures the algorithms by means of the defragmentation and reconstruction of individual data words. In order to correctly identify the code, determine its spatial position in relation to the reading device and consequently read the individual data matrix points there are implemented auxiliary mechanisms "L" Finder Pattern a Clock Track [6].

"L" Finder Pattern is an algorithm for seeking of right-angled pattern in the shape of L created by full lines. The pattern determines turning of the code in relation to scanner. By the evaluation of the information the code is correctly positioned, which ensures the data readability in the correct order with no regard to its position in relation to a reading device [8].

Clock Track is reading timing of the data matrix made up from right-angled system of dashed lines. The main purpose is to create right-angled grid, where the reader searches for individual bits (0 or 1) in the intersections with the given margin of error. The proper grid creation is necessary for flawless code readability and counts among the critical code quality parameters. The data are located only in sectors 1, 2 and 3, because the other sectors are used for the damaged code correction according to

Fig. 2. "Track & Trace" text encoded in 2-D matrix code.

Solomon-Reed's error correction algorithms. Detailed information regarding the issue can be found in [9] (Fig. 2).

4.1 Application Identifiers for 2-D Matrix Codes

If 2-D Data Matrix GS1 ECC 200 code will be used, it is necessary to tell to the reading electronics the type of its content. In order to do so, there is so called FNC1 character (Function Code). Even though it does not appear in the final string, it is extremely important. Without FNC1 this code will be encoded as a standard DM code, outcome of which is mere line string. The prefix of an application identifier defines the data type and has fixed amount of positions that follow it. For example, the prefix 01 and following 14 positions are dedicated for GTIN. Then there can be another prefix and matching data field. The order of prefixes is not important. From the aforementioned information it is possible to deduce that by using AI it is possible to accommodate major portion of linear codes in the 2-D Data Matrix ECC 200 [8].

It is obvious from the stated characteristics that within this code can be located a large amount of data on small space while simultaneously, the reading speed can be increased, as well as orientation dependence and high robustness against errors.

4.2 Code Clusters

2-D Data Matrix code of GS1 ECC 200 standard can "grow" in terms of size depending on the amount of stored data, both within the individual matrix or so called cluster. The aforementioned algorithms allow merging of two codes by their adjacent edges and creation of a rectangular matrix, alternatively of four codes and creation of square matrix. The final code has identical properties with the properties of the codes, from which the cluster was made. The demands on the reading device are in no way increased and the reading can be done with the majority of common reading devices.

4.3 Evaluation Parameters of 2-D Data Matrix GS1

According to the standard ISO 15415 the basic evaluation parameters can be enumerated as axial non-uniformity, grid non-uniformity, "L" Finder error, Clock Track fixed pattern damage or different pixels per element error [10].

Other observed parameters are decoding level, correction algorithms usage level, level of contrast against background and many others. All the evaluated parameters are scaled A to F (without E), ranked as A (best), F (worst) parameter value. Acquired values are statistically processed by calibrated reader and the final code value cannot be worse than C from the point of view of overall acceptability of the code [10].

5   Track & Trace and Serialization Principles

The T&T and serialization with the assistance of Tamper-Evident product protections are trying to find out adequate answers to mentioned problems. Similar rules for usage, as stated by the source [1], are determined by the regulations of the European commission in delegated authority (EU) 2016/161 from 2nd October, 2015, that supplement the Directive 2001/83/ES of the European Parliament and of the Council by detailed rules specification for safety features stated on the packages of humane healing drugs. In this context the Directive 2011/62/EU of the European Parliament and of the Council in the article 54 letter o) states that the healing drugs with the exception of radiopharmacs and other healing drugs stated on the Whitelist have to have safety features on the package, which allows the distributors and the people qualified to distribute medicinal products to:

- Verify the authenticity using the unique identifier (UI).
- Identify individual packages using the unique identifier (UI).
- Verify whether the outside package has been manipulated with (ATD).

In the T&T system the producer makes the documentation in the electronic form and consequently transfers the data into the place of destination via data networks. The shipper receives an identifier (token) which reports the package delivery after the arrival into the place of destination. On the ground of the information it is possible to perform a shipment check in the destination, while the distribution participant obtains information of the shipment whereabouts. The main purpose of the T&T is the real time response on questions regarding the shipment state, its whereabouts, time of status changes or competencies [11]. The T&T separates the material flow and the data flow into two (or more) channels and prevents physical manipulation with the data or the product. It is a cross-check control. In order to store the data, EU HUB was established. It is a central European storage, from which the information is transferred into national storages [1]. Using the public and non-public networks it is possible to trace the history and the route of a product on all levels of manipulation depending on assigned user permissions. The main principle of the serialization is providing every individual package of medicinal

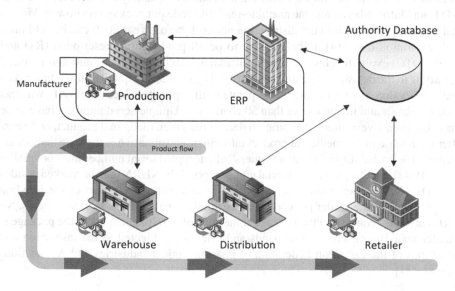

Fig. 3. "Track & Trace" text encoded in 2-D matrix code [12].

products with its own serial number, which serves as unique production number, and HRI data in such a way that creates unique identifier (UI). A suitable encryption is recommended regarding the serial number in order to make impossible any estimates about the extent of production or distribution batch. The serialization is actually T&T on the lowest level that allows traceability of each individual medicinal product package from its production, storage, distribution, dispensation (in the pharmacy) or consumption (in the health-care facilities), discharge (after the expiration date) and possibly withdrawal from distribution [12]. This chain is also demonstrated by Fig. 3.

The described process is not so clearly structured in common practice. Owing to the distribution and storage, or possible withdrawal from certain markets, where the product is oversupplied, and its redistribution to the markets, where the product is in shortage, the aggregation and disaggregation occur. The operations also have to be monitored in detail and they always have to leave traceable inspection trace [11].

6   Formal Requirements for T&T with Serialization

In the time of the study processing following data and procedures were mandatory according to [13] that specify duties for producers, distributors and final retailers of medicinal products integrated in serialized T&T environment. Firstly, mandatory fields of the identification code have to contain GTIN (prefix 01), Batch Number (prefix 10), Expiry Date (prefix 17, RRMMDD format), Serialised Number (prefix 21) and National Healthcare Reimbursement Number, if it is required by the target country [6].

6.1   Obligations for the Medical Product Manufacturer

Demands are also placed on the medicament producers. Namely product labelling with 2-D Data Matrix where only one machine-readable code per package is allowed. Medicinal products released into the distribution network before year 2019 can be sold until their expiration date [14]. Labelled have to be all products on prescription (Rx) and others (OTC) explicitly classified on the Blacklist. Tamper-Evident solution is required according to the decision of national authority. The readability quality must attain maximally "C" value. Code structure must operate with application identifiers (AI), whereas code blocks should not be longer than 50 characters. Unique serial numbers have to be traceable even 1 year after the expiration date of the given medicinal product, or 5 years after the release of the medicinal product into sale (determinative is the state that occurs earlier). The probability of a random "guess" of encrypted serial number must be smaller than 1/10000 [6]. Only GTIN and serial number (possibly NHRN) can be marked besides the 2-D code, the other readouts can be placed on different parts of the package. Reading response time of the reader per code must be smaller than 300 ms in 95% of cases. No HRI readout is required on the package if the sum of two longer sides of the package is smaller than 10 cm. Previous demands and rules are subjected to the inspection and objections of the European Federation of Pharmaceutical Industries and Associations regulator [1].

6.2 Vertical Model and Tamper-Evident Package

Figure 4 demonstrates vertical model of typical system architecture for coordinated T&T processes. A single production process was for this purpose simulated on a production line taking into account option for serialization and aggregation.

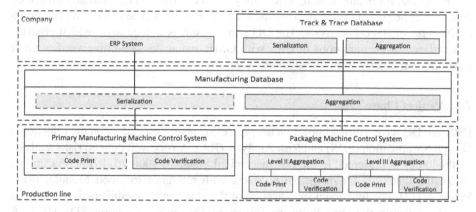

Fig. 4. T&T system vertical model with serialization and aggregation.

Printing and control mechanisms on individual machines, data transfers towards the production databases and their subsequent transfer into ERP systems are obvious from the lowest level of the model. Corporate databases primarily intended for the communication with local authority are on the same level as ERP systems.

The Tamper-Evident solution is suitable addition for serialization. The main purpose of the Tamper-Evident package is to strengthen the package authentication by prevention of opening of the package and consecutive utilization of the package for the forgery insertion, or the possible alternation of the package content. Similarly, in a potential product warranty claim the producer must be sure that the product in question is truly his own. There is a suitable solution in the Tamper-Evident category even for such a purpose. It is possible to recommend considering Tamper-Evident solution already in the phase of T&T implementation preparation [16].

7   Track & Trace Implementation

T&T implementation and serialization is demanding on correct organization of individual steps, responsibility assignment for their fulfilment, accompanying documentation creation and intermediate tests execution. There is a lot of possible approaches for the task fulfilment, including own unique solutions. One of the most effective solution is to use recommended processes based on GAMP 5 standards – Good Automated Manufacturing Practice – developed by International Society for Pharmaceutical Engineering (ISPE). Methods are focused primarily on project's individual life cycle phases and regulate system steps and recommendations in order to achieve maximal efficiency of employed procedures [11].

7.1 Conceptual Phase

The conceptual phase is one of the most difficult project parts. It can be divided into User Requirements Specification (URS) and Design Qualification (DQ) [12]. It is important to deal with Quality Assurance control and to mitigate the risks by means of GMP method, for example using GAP analysis, in the URS phase. Suitably presented conclusions help responsible decision-making management. The results can be shown in the form of SWOT analysis. The DQ phase result is a document, which controls concordance of presumptions in URS with GMP and at the same time verifies other relations, particularly from the suppliers' side.

7.2 Project Phase

URS and DQ have a direct impact on the projection phase, especially on the Functional Design Specification (FDS) and Risk Analysis (RA). A very well defined risks analysis methodology is presented in the Pharmaceutical Standard 9000:2011 (Pharmaceutical packaging materials for medicinal products with reference to Good Manufacturing Practice) [12]. The functional specification of the plan can be documented by means of Function Specification (FS), Software (Hardware) Design Specification (SDS, HDS). A very important step is the new validation by means of updated RA (with regard to GMP) and possible DQ completion [12]. If all the requirements are fulfilled, the ordering party and the supplier can proceed to the Factory Acceptance Test (FAT), which results in test protocol. If the FAT is not accepted, it has to be revised according to SDS, HDS, URS and FS documents.

7.3 Operational Phase

Project phase completion verifies that the project fulfilled all the acceptance criteria in required extent and that it can be operated while maintaining all the qualitative and quantitative indicators. It creates prerequisites for the production processes repeatability given the same conditions. Following Process Qualification should verify where the borderline of the process stability in extreme scenarios is.

7.4 End-of-Life Phase

Project Retirement phase is a period when it is obvious that the production facility is no longer capable of providing output in a given quality and quantity. It can be planned or caused by external influences. It can be caused by technical wear and tear, moral or legislative obsolescence or decline of the facility operation objective.

8 Conclusion

The serialization in the pharmaceutical industry is one of the biggest challenges of the present day. The legislative pressure transferred on the producers in an effort to prevent forgery spreading into the medicinal product market does not permit any hesitation. In case of non-fulfillment, or even just a partial fulfillment, of the requirements the producers face the loss of the market, good reputation and especially of the income that is necessary for financially healthy company.

It is possible to claim, that there is inexhaustible amount of technologies on the market that can successfully solve the serialization issue. However, it is necessary to point out the fact that every pharmaceutical production has its particularities which, or more precisely their knowledge, are the key for properly selected medicinal product serialization technologies. It is essential to strongly point out the monitoring of the European legislation by one's own sources within the GAP analysis, because the relevant legislation is effective from the release date of the given European Union administrative body, not from the release date of a local translation by a national authority. This places new requirements on pharmaceutical corporations' personnel department and creates the demand for new specialists focused on the legislation.

Acknowledgments. We would also like to thank to Ondrej Horning and Ladislav Balik, doctoral students who were helping with the simulation tests in laboratories. This work and the contribution were also supported by project of specific science, Faculty of informatics and Management, University of Hradec Kralove, Czech Republic.

References

1. Lundqvist, B.: EU Competition Law and Ip Rights in the Pharma and Biotech Sectors. Oxford University Press, New York (2016)
2. Kongar, E., Haznedaroglu, E., Abdelghany, O., Bahtiyar, M.O.: A novel IT infrastructure for reverse logistics operations of end-of-life pharmaceutical products. Inf. Technol. Manage. **16**(1), 51–65 (2015)
3. Burns, W.: WHO launches taskforce to fight counterfeit drugs. Bull. World Health Organ. **84**(9), 689–690 (2006)
4. Lawrence, X.Y.: Pharmaceutical quality by design: product and process development, understanding, and control. Pharm. Res. **25**(4), 781–791 (2008)
5. Dai Shuguang, X.Y.J.X.: Improved algorithms based on EAN-13 barcode identifying. Comput. Digit. Eng. **7**, 038 (2011)
6. GS1 DataMatrix Guideline. GS1 AISBL, version 16.0, 438p. (2016)
7. Kato, H., Tan, K.T.: Pervasive 2D barcodes for camera phone applications. IEEE Pervasive Comput. **6**(4), 76–85 (2007)
8. ISO/IEC 16022:2006: Information technology – Automatic identification and data capture techniques – Data Matrix bar code symbology specification. International Organization for Standardization, 132p. (2014)
9. Lacan, J., Roca, V., Peltotalo, J., Peltotalo, S.: Reed-Solomon forward error correction (FEC) schemes. The Internet Engineering Task Force (2009). (No. RFC 5510)
10. ISO/IEC 15415:2011. Information technology – Automatic identification and data capture techniques – Bar code symbol print quality test specification – Two-dimensional symbols. International Organization for Standardization, 43p. (2011)
11. Sultanow, E., Chircu, A.M.: Improving healthcare with data-driven track-and-trace systems. In: Strategic Data-Based Wisdom in the Big Data Era, vol. 65 (2015)

12. Mallesh, D.A., Sawhney, R., De Anda, E.M.: Implementation of serialization and traceability in a pharmaceutical packaging company. In: Proceedings of the IIE Annual Conference, p. 1. Institute of Industrial Engineers-Publisher (2015)
13. European Medicines Verification System (EMVS). European Pack Coding Guidelines. European Federations of Pharmaceutical Industries and Associations (2013)
14. Krähenbühl, C., Oberleitner, B., Manetto, A., Murphy, P., Lambrinos, K.: Pharmacy (2016)
15. Cordon, C., Garcia-Milà, P., Vilarino, T.F., Caballero, P.: Serialization in the pharmaceutical industry. In: Strategy is Digital, pp. 47–64. Springer, Cham (2016)
16. Kelepouris, T., Theodorou, L., McFarlane, D., Thorne, A., Harrison, M.: Track and Trace Requirements Scoping. University of Cambridge, London (2006)

Visual Moving Objects Tracking Using Shape Detectors and Object Models

Yin-Tien Wang[✉] and Chin-An Shen

Tamkang University, Tamsui, New Taipei City 25137, Taiwan
ytwang@mail.tku.edu.tw

Abstract. This paper presents an algorithm of robot visual moving-object tracking (MOT) based on the probabilistic object model with a pedestrian detector. Three major research topics investigated in the study include the combination of moving feature detection and pedestrian detection, the improvement of probabilistic object model, and the tuning mechanism of object model training. The developed MOT was further integrated with the visual simultaneous localization and mapping (vSLAM) to form a simultaneous localization, mapping, and moving object tracking system. The extended Kalman filter (EKF) was used to estimate the system states and the speeded-up robust features (SURFs) were employed to represent the visual environment map. Experiments were carried out in this research to validate the performance of the developed systems.

Keywords: Visual simultaneous localization and mapping (vSLAM) · Object model · Pedestrian detectors · Visual moving object tracking

1 Introduction

This paper presents an algorithm of robot visual moving-object tracking (MOT) [1] based on the probabilistic object model with the pedestrian detector. Major research topics include the combination of moving feature detection and pedestrian detection [2], the improvement of probabilistic object model, and the tuning mechanism of object model training. Firstly, the moving feature detection was integrated with a pedestrian detector to set the location boundaries of image features belonged to an object. Therefore, different groups of moving features will be trained as separated moving objects. Secondly, the representation of the probabilistic object model [3, 4] was modified to ensure the robustness of moving object tracking. Instead of using the image features from multiple image frames, the image features of one frame were used to train the object model for the purposes of computational efficiency as well as on-line training. Finally, the feedback of the recognition and tracking of moving objects was utilized to tune the training condition for the object model. The tuning mechanisms were designed based on fixed values, expert table, and fuzzy rules.

© Springer International Publishing AG 2017
M. Younas et al. (Eds.): MobiWIS 2017, LNCS 10486, pp. 187–192, 2017.
DOI: 10.1007/978-3-319-65515-4_16

The developed MOT was integrated with the visual simultaneous localization and mapping (vSLAM) [5] to form a simultaneous localization, mapping, and moving object tracking (SLAMMOT) system. The extended Kalman filter (EKF) [6] was used to estimate the system states and the speeded-up robust features (SURFs) [7] were employed to represent the visual environment map. Two experiments were carried out in this research to validate the performance of the developed systems.

2   SLAMMOT System

The proposed SLAMMOT system is shown in Fig. 1. The MOT (moving object tracking) block includes the functions: object data association, pedestrian detection, probabilistic object model, as well as moving object recognition and tracking. The probabilistic object model is expressed as

$$p(o_i \mid s, l) = \sum_j p(o_i \mid s, C_j, l) p(C_j \mid s, l) \tag{1}$$

where o_i is the ith object; the known information includes the description vector s and the pixel coordinates l of an image feature. The shape model, called codebook C_j [3], of the object was first trained in the object model buildup process. The object model is then created based on known codebooks. The shape model was usually created offline [3] using several image frames. An online training process was developed in reference [8]. In the recognition process, the object and its location x were detected according the following expression:

$$\begin{aligned}
p(o_i, x \mid s, l) &= \sum_j p(o_i, x \mid s, C_j, l) p(C_j \mid s, l) \\
&= \sum_j p(o_i, x \mid C_j, l) p(C_j \mid s)
\end{aligned} \tag{2}$$

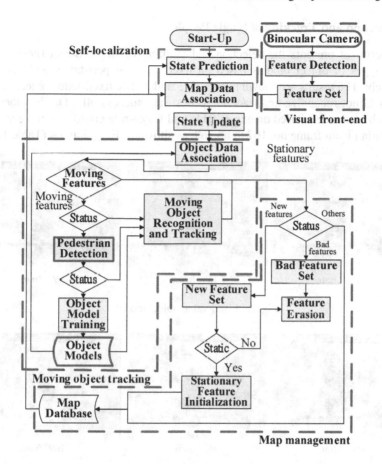

Fig. 1. The integration of moving object tracking (MOT) with the simultaneous localization and mapping (SLAM)

3 Tuning Mechanism of Object Model

Three types of tuning mechanism were designed including fixed values, expert table, and fuzzy rules for the object model. The design concept was to determine the working conditions of function blocks: pedestrian detection and object model training, in Fig. 1.

4 Experimental Results

Two experiments were carried out to verify the proposed algorithms. The tuning mechanisms based on fixed values, expert table, and fuzzy rules, respectively, were validated in the experiments.

4.1 Detection and Tracking of Single People

First experiment presents the detection and tracking of single object (people) using different types of object models based on fixed-value, expert-table, and fuzzy-rule, respectively. The results are shown in Figs. 2, 3 and 4. The fixed-value object model in Fig. 2 could not recognize and track the pedestrian, successfully. On the other hand, both the object models based on expert-table and fuzzy-rule could recognize and track the pedestrian from frame no. 167 to no.169, as shown in Figs. 3 and 4 (Table 1).

167th frame   168th frame   169th frame

Fig. 2. Fixed-value object model

167th frame   168th frame   169th frame

Fig. 3. Expert-table object model

167th frame   168th frame   169th frame

Fig. 4. Fuzzy-rule object model

Table 1. Object models

	Fixed-value	Expert-system	Fuzzy-system
No. of successive tracking frames (%)	250 (48.9%)	362 (70.8%)	362 (70.8%)

4.2 Detection and Tracking of Heterogeneous Objects

Second experiment presents the detection and tracking of heterogeneous objects (people). Each of the pedestrian no. 1 and no. 6 has its object combination, as shown in Fig. 5(a). These two pedestrians walked approach and cross over each other, as shown in Figs. 5(b)–(d). The results showed that two pedestrians could be successfully identified when they are approach, crossing over, and leaving each other.

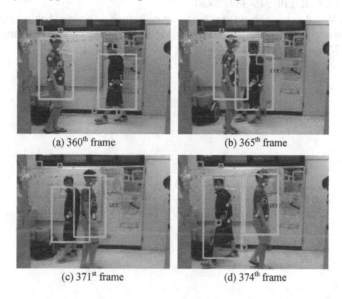

(a) 360th frame   (b) 365th frame

(c) 371st frame   (d) 374th frame

Fig. 5. Detection and tracking of two people.

5 Conclusion

The study presents an improved probabilistic object model for detection and tracking of moving objects. Three types of tuning mechanism for the object model were proposed to regulate the parameters of the object model. The experimental results showed that the tuning mechanisms based on expert table and fuzzy rule can improve the number of successive tracking frames. The results also showed that two different pedestrians could be successfully identified when they are approach, crossing over, and leaving each other.

References

1. Choi, W., Pantofaru, C., Savarese, S.: A general framework for tracking multiple people from a moving camera. IEEE Trans. Pattern Anal. Mach. Intell. **35**, 1577–1591 (2013)
2. Dalal, N., Triggs, B.: Histograms of oriented gradients for human detection. In: Proceedings of the IEEE Conference on Computer Vision and Pattern Recognition (2005)
3. Leibe, B., Leonardis, A., Schiele, B.: Robust object detection with interleaved categorization and segmentation. Int. J. Comput. Vision **77**(1–3), 259–289 (2008)

4. Ess, A., Leibe, B., Schindler, K., van Gool, L.: Robust multiperson tracking from a mobile platform. IEEE Trans. Pattern Anal. Mach. Intell. **31**(10), 1831–1846 (2009)
5. Davison, A.J., Reid, I.D., Molton, N.D., Stasse, O.: MonoSLAM real time single camera SLAM. IEEE Trans. Pattern Anal. Mach. Intell. **29**(6), 1052–1067 (2007)
6. Wang, Z., Huang, S., Dissanayake, G.: Simultaneous Localization and Mapping. World Scientific Publishing Co. (2011)
7. Bay, H., Ess, A., Tuytelaars, T., Van Gool, L.: SURF: speeded-up robust features. Comput. Vis. Image Underst. **110**, 346–359 (2008)
8. Shen, C.A.: Visual moving object tracking using pedestrian detector and object model. Master thesis, Department of Mechanical and Electro-Mechanical Engineering, Tamkang University, Taiwan (2015)

Research of the Mobile CDMA Network for the Operation of an Intelligent Information System of Earth-Moving and Construction Machines

Tatyana Golubeva[1]([✉]), Viktor Pokussov[2], Sergey Konshin[1], Boris Tshukin[3], and Evgeniy Zaytcev[1]

[1] Almaty University of Power Engineering and Telecommunications, Almaty, Kazakhstan
ya_nepovtorimaya@mail.ru, {ots2,evgeniy.zaitcev}@yandex.com
[2] National Innovation Centre, Almaty, Kazakhstan
v@victor.kz
[3] National Research Nuclear University MEPhI, Moscow, Russia
tsh-k22@mail.ru

Abstract. In papers, the mobile CDMA network was experimentally researched for organizing the operation of an intelligent information system of earth-moving construction machines. Reliable and high-quality operation of the intelligent information system of earth-moving and construction machines is ensured by data transmission from various sensors, video cameras, control signals to smart objects, and other information. In addition, it is necessary to organize the storage of all operational information and its processing. In papers, various parameters of data transmission using a mobile network were researched.

Keywords: Mobile · Intelligent information system · Smart objects · Earth-moving and construction machines

1 Introduction

In previous researches on the organization of reliable management by smart objects of the intelligent information system of earth-moving and construction machines, the authors performed mathematical modeling [1]. In [2–7], the authors considered the results of mathematical modeling and development of entire structure of an intelligent information system of earth-moving and construction machines, as well as individual components of the system.

Many investigators are engaged in close directions. For example, article [8] deals with location-based services (LBS) in the context of Industry 4.0 and Internet of Things (IoT) to provide new opportunities to optimize many processes in the application of earth-moving and construction machines and their intellectualization. The optimization of ways to find the most efficient route on the construction site to ensure the delivery and subsequent tracking of cargo is considered. This article proposes a wireless sensor network with low power consumption in combination with a network of wireless sensors with a high update rate. The article [9] deals with the smaRTIproject aimed at developing

© Springer International Publishing AG 2017
M. Younas et al. (Eds.): MobiWIS 2017, LNCS 10486, pp. 193–205, 2017.
DOI: 10.1007/978-3-319-65515-4_17

of an autonomous material flow using intelligent transport elements, using autoID technologies and the concept of the Internet of things. And in [10], the measurement problems for monitoring the process of using thermoelectric generators for powering wireless sensor modules are investigated. Wireless data transmission to a central base station, where more fifty sensor modules share one radio channel is considered.

2 Formulation of the Problem

In previous papers [2–7], the authors mainly researched operation of an intelligent information system of earth-moving and construction machines and its parts in quarries located separately from cities. However, an intelligent information system of earth-moving and construction machines should be universal and at the same time to operate reliably in urban conditions, transmitting various information and managing smart objects in the city.

In previous studies, radio communication was carried out practically without the influence of other communication systems. This is due to the fact that mining quarries are located far from populated areas, where there are no other radio communication systems. The proposed work explores the operation of radio channels in urban conditions. Urban conditions are very different from ones in previous studies, since a large number of radio systems for various purposes are already operating in cities.

For the operation of an intelligent information system of earth-moving and construction machines, the research was carried out as part of a pilot project for the introduction of the mobile network CDMA 2000 1x EV-DO in the largest city of Kazakhstan - Almaty.

When implementing a mobile network, it was necessary to conduct frequency and territorial planning of the mobile network.

3 Theory

The CDMA 1x EV-DO standard provides a peak data rate of up to 2.4 Mbit/s in the forward channel and 153.6 kbps in the reverse channel. It allows to provide a variety of data services.

To organize the operation of an intelligent information system of earth-moving and construction machines, it is necessary to transmit such operational data as information from sensors of positions of various working bodies of earth-moving and construction machines, video information from digital video cameras, reverse control signals to the executive mechanisms of various working bodies of earth-moving and construction machines (smart objects) and the like.

In Kazakhstan, Huawei actively introduces CDMA2000 1X/1xEV-DO based on the BTS3606 station. The station supports both CDMA2000 1X, and CDMA2000 1x EV-DO.

To upgrade the basic configuration of the BTS3606 1x EV-DO, you need to install the EV-DO CECM module (see Fig. 1). Once the module is installed, users can upgrade stations remotely. The system can return to the original version if the update was not fully downloaded. The BTS3606 provides auto boot function. If the software versions of the existing boards and the new board are different, the software of the new board can be upgraded automatically through the auto load function.

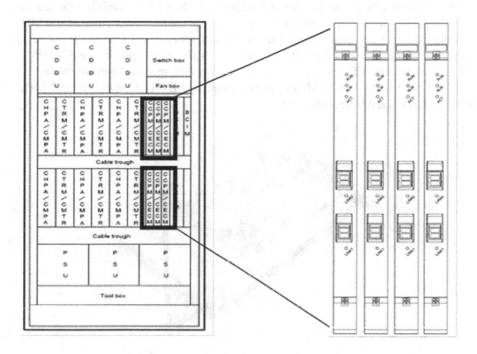

Fig. 1. Location of CECM modules on BSC3606

The compact base module of the EV-DO channel (CECM) is a board that processes CDMA2000 1x EV-DO signals. The module processes the service data 1x EV-DO, Completely changing channels. CECM is applicable to BTS3606 and BTS3606A.

There are two types of CECM:

- CECM with two optical interfaces;
- CECM without optical interface.

A base station consisting of a single cabinet can be configured with a maximum of eight CECM modules to provide the maximum number of service channels.

To add subscribers to a mobile cell, two cabinets can be used on one site to support the configuration of more than two carriers/three sectors.

4 Experimental Results

The experiments were carried out within the framework of the project, which included the import, installation and configuration of CECM channel cards supporting EV-DO services, the installation and debugging of the BSC6600 base station controller software, the BTS3606 base station and other devices required for operation of base station in EV-DO mode.

The base station of the BTS 3606 model with the Huawei CECM channel card was installed and integrated into the existing network of the Kazakhstan mobile company ALTEL, for what the connection to the BSC 3606 via the 4 E1 channels is arranged. For the pilot project, a frequency band of 2.49 MHz within the frequency range of 800 MHz, assigned to ALTEL, was allocated. The receive frequency band of the test BS occupies a radio spectrum area of 829,095 … 831,585 MHz, the transmit one-874,095 … 876,585 MHz. Two CDMA channels are assigned in the specified band of the test BS: №157 (829,71 MHz–874,71 MHz) - carrier frequency EV-DO, №199 (830,97 MHz–875,97 MHz) - carrier frequency 1X.

Fig. 2. Appearance of the Huawei EC 500 PCMCIA-EVDO modem

To date, there are many models of mobile phones, modems and stationary devices that support the CDMA 2000 1x EV-DO standard. For data transfer, CDMA USB modems, which provide the ability to access the Internet at a speed of 2.4 Mb/s from anywhere in the city or the suburbs, are widely used. Also wireless (PCMCIA-EVDO-modem) modems for laptops and devices equipped with PCMCIA interface, are used.

Table 1. Main characteristics of the Huawei EC 500 modem

Modem name	Huawei EC 500
Weight	about 50 g
Size	88,4 × 54 × 5 mm
Talk time	not limited (powered by a laptop)
Waiting time	not limited (powered by a laptop)
Standard	CDMA 800 MHz 1X & EV-DO
Transmitter output power	not more than 0.2 W
External connections	PCMCIA Type II
Transfer data rate	Up to 2.4 Mbps
Standards	1x, EV-DO Service (IS-856)

When working with a laptop, the modem allows you to make calls, receive/send sms. For the tests, a Huawei EC 500 PCMCIA-EVDO modem was used (see Fig. 2). The characteristics of the modem are shown in Table 1.

The task of synthesis of superimposed network EV-DO is to find such network parameters, which at given hardware and time-frequency resources, meet the quality of customer service requirements at the hour of greatest load.

In the process of planning the superimposed radio access network, the features of EV-DO technology are taken into account, the main ones of which are:

- in the reverse channel, the code division of channels is used, consequence of which is the link between the capacity of the network and the coverage area through the allowable level of intra-system interference;
- in the reverse channel there are no restrictions on blocking the call, due to the appearance of the so-called "soft" capacity;
- the time division of channels is used in the forward channel and the base station (BS) transmitter power is consumed only for information transmission;
- in the forward channel, interference at the input of the subscriber station receiver is generated by neighboring base stations;
- in the system there is traffic, which is characterized by different transmission rates, the probabilities of errors at receiving and time delays while transmitting data;
- the information transfer rate depending on the communication conditions on the forward and reverse channels varies discretely within acceptable limits;
- the asymmetry of the data streams in the forward and reverse channels takes place in the network, so the requirements for the energy parameters of these channels, provided equal coverage areas will be different. The alignment of the coverage areas in the forward and reverse channels of the superimposed network is achieved by controlling the power of base station transmitters;
- the results of testing are influenced by the speeds of the subscribers' movement, the multipath of the receiving signals, the speed and accuracy of the power control of transmitters of mobile radio stations, the parameters of handovers.

During the experiments a number of tests of various services were carried out in the real working conditions of the pilot network and active networks of other mobile operators.

In the beginning, video on demand (VOD) was tested.

The purpose is to check whether BSC supports on-line video playback and what will be the average speed of this service, what will give information about the speed of the direct mobile data transmission channel of the intelligent information system of earth-moving and construction machines.

Description - the subscriber terminal is connected and registered with the AAA. A USB cable is used to communicate with the computer. Real Player is installed on the computer to play video files.

Figure 3 shows the average speed of the Video on Demand service, which was 1.5 Mbps.

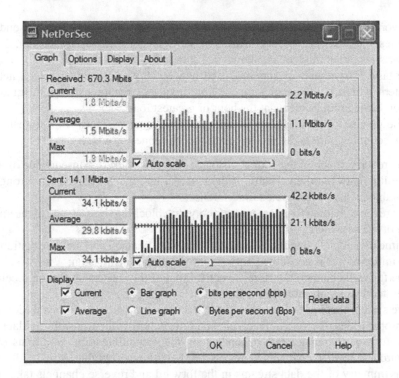

Fig. 3. Video on Demand Service Testing (VOD)

Table 2 shows the stages of testing and the expected results.

Table 2. Video on Demand Service Testing (VOD)

Procedure	Expected result
On the computer connected to the subscriber terminal connect Dial-up, enter the user name and password	Connection successful
Go to the website, which allows you to play on-line video/audio	Login Successful
Play streaming video (for example, a video file)	Video played successfully

Then testing of video call services was carried out, since it is possible to transmit control signals of the intelligent information system of earth-moving and construction machines within the framework of this mobile service.

The goal is to check whether BSC supports on-line video playback and what the average speed of this service will be.

Description - two subscriber terminals are connected and registered with the AAA. For communication with computers, USB cables are used, or instead of phones there is a pcmcia card. On computers, the Flexit program is installed, to make a video call. Web cameras are connected to computers.

Since in EV-DO the speed in the reverse channel is a maximum of 153 Kbit/s, and the video speaking provides for commensurate quality of both the called and the calling subscriber, the average speed of the received video stream is 127.9 Kb/s, and the average speed of the sent video stream is 101.3 Kbit/S (see Fig. 4).Table 3 shows the testing steps and expected results.

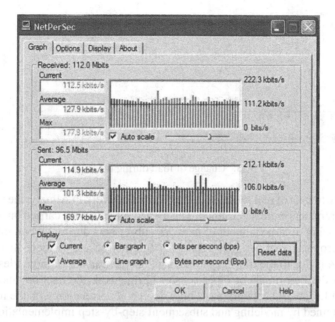

Fig. 4. Ilustration of the data transmission rate for a video call service

Table 3. Testing the video call service

Procedure	Expected result
On the computer connected to the subscriber terminal connect Dial-up, enter the user name and password	Connection successful
Press the call button, wait for connection with the called subscriber	Connection successful
Video speaking	Video speaking was successful

When optimizing the network, it is necessary to know the daily load on the base stations, to determine the hours of the greatest load on the network, to identify the areas in which communication deteriorate significantly when the number of subscribers increases.

The amount of transmitted data begins to drop quite sharply after midnight, however, the data transfer does not stop completely even at night and in the morning (see Fig. 5).

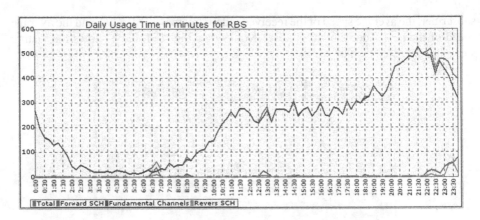

Fig. 5. Change of load during the day

According to data of real sessions in the EV-DO network in Almaty, the mean values of session parameters were determined. The measurements were carried out on the basis of data processing of large number of network subscribers during several busy daytime hours. The proportion of sessions related to Internet access is more than 95%. The remaining 5% is due to the transfer of data such as the transfer of large files or transfer of data from POS terminals or other sensors. In general, the data obtained on a real CDMA 2000 1x EV-DO network has a high degree of correlation with the forecast data that were obtained by modeling and subsequent step-by-step implementation.

With the help of the M2000 server from the base station controller, statistics were obtained not only of the load changes during the day, but also the information about the distribution of the radiated power was obtained (see Fig. 6).

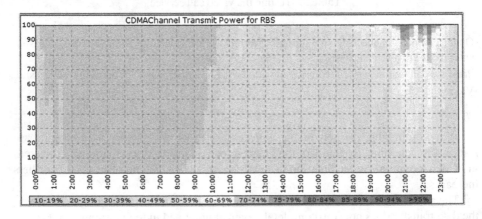

Fig. 6. Distribution of radiated power

According to the distribution of radiated power, it can be seen that the largest part of subscribers uses the services of 1x and EV-DO mainly from 11:00 to 24:00. It is important that during the maximum load there will be a minimum amount of communication interruptions and the data transmission rate remains stable. The algorithm for determining network parameters is based on an estimating the throughput of the reverse EV-DO channel, that determines the number of served subscribers. Estimating the throughput of the direct channel EV-DO characterizes the quality of serving of subscribers taken for maintenance.

Also, in the course of the experiments, testing of data loading from the HTTP serer, where it is supposed to store various data sets necessary for the operation of an intelligent information system of earth-moving and construction machines, was carried out.

Table 4 shows the stages of testing and the expected results.

Table 4. Testing of data transmission from HTTP server

Procedure	Expected result
On the computer connected to the subscriber terminal connect Dial-up, enter the user name and password	Connection successful
Go to the website, which allows you to play on-line video/audio	Login Successful
Play streaming video (for example, a video file)	Video played successfully

The purpose of the test is to check whether BSC supports on-line video playback and what the average speed of this service will be. Test description - the subscriber terminal is connected and registered in the AAA. A USB cable is used to communicate with the computer. Real Player is installed on the computer to play video files. The average download speed from the FTP server was 2.0 Mbps.

To achieve maximum receiving/sending rates, the condition of fixed-state of mobile terminal is necessary. Since the test was carried out while driving at a speed of 40–60 km/h, the signal transmission data in the forward channel when connected via HTTP (see Fig. 7) and FTP (see Fig. 8) is understated.

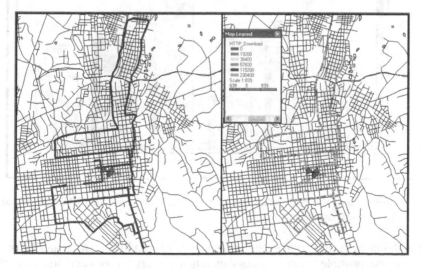

Fig. 7. Route of testing and the data rate through the HTTP server in the forward channel, bit/s

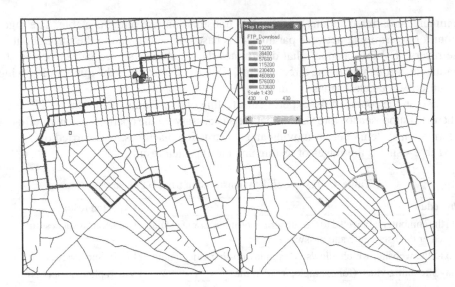

Fig. 8. Route of testing and the data transmission rate via FTP server in forward channel, bit/s

Distribution of rate streams is considered based on the obtained data, (see Fig. 9)

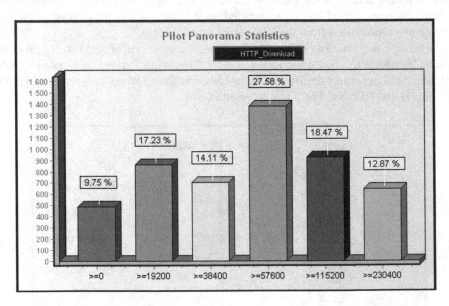

Fig. 9. Distribution of the rate streams requested by the mobile terminal when connected via HTTP, in the forward channel

In addition, in the course of experiments, testing of data loading from an FTP server, where it is also possible to store various data sets necessary for the operation of an intelligent information system of earth-moving and construction machines, was carried out.

The purpose of the test is to check what speed of file transfer (uploading, uploading) via FTP will be and whether it will be supported by the BSC (see Table 5). Test description - the subscriber terminal is connected and registered with the AAA. A USB cable is used to communicate with the computer. The average download speed from the FTP server was 2.0 Mbps.

Table 5. Testing of transmitting data from an FTP server

Procedure	Expected result
On the computer connected to the subscriber terminal connect Dial-up, enter the user name and password	Connection successful
Logging on to FTP server	Login Successful
Downloading a 15 MB file from the FTP server	File downloaded from FTP server successfully
Uploading a 1 MB file to the FTP server	File uploaded to FTP server successfully

5   Conclusions

The analysis of the data download experiments from the HTTP server and the FTP server showed that the data transmission rate when connecting to FTP is much higher (Fig. 10).

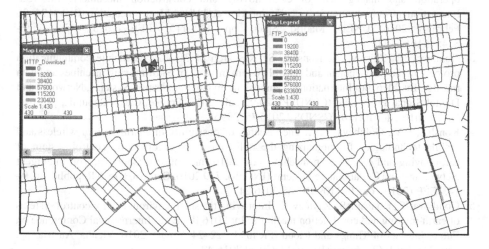

Fig. 10. Comparison of data rates in a forward channel when connected via HTTP and FTP

This is due to a simple connection topology: the mobile terminal establishes a connection to the FTP server via BTS, BSC and PCF. When connecting via HTTP, it is necessary to connect to the host via PDSN, Gateway, a certain number of routers, etc. In addition, the host can be located in another country, on another continent and each trunk that connects the intermediate nodes of the equipment has its own limited throughput.

The average rate is calculated only at the moments of real data transmission. It should be noted the nature of the average rate in the sector (in fact, throughput) - the value of about 600 kbit/s varies little with the increase of load on the sector.

Thus, the research of the mobile CDMA network for the operation of an intelligent information system of earth-moving and construction machines showed its full potential for use for these purposes.

Moreover, as the research showed, for the operation of an intelligent information system of earth-moving and construction machines using the mobile CDMA 1xEV-DO network, it is most expedient to create FTP servers with the most requested information. The creation of FTP-servers will significantly increase the data transmission rate and will provide resources for organizing any multimedia services in a mobile CDMA network.

References

1. Kayim, T.T., Golubeva, T.V., Kaiymov, S.T.: Mathematical and computer modeling of movement of the executive mechanism of the adaptive multipurpose operating part of earth-moving and construction machine. In: The IRES -12th International Conference on Innovative Engineering Technologies (ICIET), Prague, 27 September 2015
2. Golubeva, T.V., Konshin, S.V.: Improving of positioning for measurements to control the operation and management of earth-moving and construction machinery. In: 13th International Conference on Remote Engineering and Virtual Instrumentation (REV)/ 24–26 February 2016, UNED, Madrid, Spain, pp. 112–115. IEEE (2016). 978-1-4673-8245-8/16/$31.00
3. Golubeva, T., Zaitsev, Y., Konshin, S.: Research of 3G-324 M mobile communication protocol in the management and control system of work of earth-moving machines and data transfer. In: 201610th International Symposium on Communication Systems, Networks and Digital Signal Processing (CSNDSP), 20-22 July 2016, Prague, Czech Republic, pp. 1–3. IEEE (2016). doi:10.1109/CSNDSP.2016.7573995
4. Konshin, S.V., Golubeva, T.V.: The research of possibility of sharing use of wireless and mobile technologies for organizing the radio channels of operation control system of earthmoving and construction machines. In: 2016 International Conference on Intelligent Networking and Collaborative Systems (INCoS), 7–9 2016, Ostrava, Czech Republic, pp. 9–14. IEEE (2016). doi:10.1109/INCoS.2016.24
5. Golubeva, T., Konshin, S., Zaytcev, E.: Improving the smart environment for control systems of earth-moving and construction machines. In: 2016 IEEE 4th International Conference on Future Internet of Things and Cloud (FiCloud), 22–24 August, 2016, Vienna, Austria, pp. 240–243. IEEE (2016). doi:10.1109/FiCloud.2016.42
6. Golubeva, T., Zaitsev, Y., Konshin, S.: Research of electromagnetic environment for organizing the radio channel of communication of operation control system of earthmoving. In: 19-th International Symposium on Electrical Apparatus and Technologies (SIELA 2016), Bourgas, Bulgaria, 29 May–1 June 2016, pp. 1–4. IEEE (2016). doi:10.1109/SIELA.2016.7543006

7. Golubeva, T.V., Zaitsev, E.O., Konshin, S.V.: Research of WiMax standard to organize the data transmission channels in the integrated control system of earth-moving machines. In: 2016 17th International Conference of Young Specialists on Micro/Nanotechnologies and Electron Devices (EDM), June 30–July 4, 2016, Novosibirsk, Russia, pp. 91–95. IEEE (2016). doi:10.1109/EDM.2016.7538701

8. Hartmann, F., Worms, K., Pistorius, F., Wanjek, M., Stork, W.: Energy aware, two-staged localization concept for dynamic indoor environments. In: Smart SysTech 2016, European Conference on Smart Objects, Systems and Technologies, VDE Conference Publications, pp. 1–6 (2016). ISBN: 978-3-8007-4229-5. http://ieeexplore.ieee.org/document/7750889/

9. Stockmann, M., Anderseck, B., Hille, A.: Unleashing the power of events out of smart transport items. In: Smart SysTech 2014, European Conference on Smart Objects, Systems and Technologies, pp. 1–5 (2014). doi:10.1109/SmartSysTech.2014.7156023. http://ieeexplore.ieee.org/document/7156023/

10. Boegel, G., Meyer, F., Kemmerling, M.: Wireless sensor system for industrial applications powered by thermoelectric generator. In: Smart SysTech 2014, European Conference on Smart Objects, Systems and Technologies, pp. 1–5. (2014). doi:10.1109/SmartSysTech. 2014.7156017. http://ieeexplore.ieee.org/document/7156017/

11. Budilovsky, S.: Evolution of CDMA2000 1x EV-DO standard and 3G accessibility from Intertelecom, 3 July 2014. http://ru.gecid.com/netlan/cdma2000_1x_ev-do_intertelekom/?s=all

Mobile and Wireless Networking

Blaubot – Hassle-Free Multi-device Applications

Peter Barth[✉] and Henning Groß

Hochschule RheinMain, Kurt-Schumacher-Ring 18, 65197 Wiesbaden, Germany
peter.barth@hs-rm.de, mail.to@henning-gross.de

Abstract. Blaubot is a middleware that supports channel-based communication among many Android devices forming a local group. It abstracts from the underlying networking infrastructure supporting at least Bluetooth and WLAN configured as star network using point-to-point connections with automated master selection. A flexible beacon-based connection management discovers, (re-)connects, and merges local groups automatically using several independent network infrastructures including protocols such as Multicast, Bluetooth, and NFC concurrently. This allows for dynamic expanding and shrinking of the group during program execution, but sacrifices guaranteed delivery. An easy to use API allows to post prioritised messages on queue-based channels, that are delivered to all subscribed group members.

Keywords: Mobile middleware · Bluetooth · Message distribution

1 Introduction

In many scenarios smartphones need to communicate among a local group of devices. Such scenarios include multi-device games, chats, electronic signs, etc. On the one hand, devices may share a stream of acceleration or other sensor data with soft real time requirements, on the other hand they may transfer binary data such as images. In these scenarios a local group of devices should be formed and they communicate among themselves without requiring a central server for coordination. All smartphones support Bluetooth or WLAN, which are adequate to meet most messaging requirements regarding bandwidth and latency.

However, forming local groups of devices to communicate among themselves is cumbersome at best. While connecting two paired Bluetooth devices is straightforward, connecting more than two is not. The Bluetooth API provides only a single bidirectional connection, the application developer must either connect all devices directly using a quadratic number of connections or dispatch via a master. Implementing a master in a hub and spoke architecture is a viable alternative, but demanding to implement. In addition, some devices may join, others may leave the group dynamically during program execution. Connection management becomes a nightmare, recovering from a master failure is tricky to implement. If a heavyweight Bluetooth discovery does not cause others to disconnect, it may still take dozens of seconds to find potential peers. With WLAN, devices routinely connect to access points, but then most applications require a

© Springer International Publishing AG 2017
M. Younas et al. (Eds.): MobiWIS 2017, LNCS 10486, pp. 209–223, 2017.
DOI: 10.1007/978-3-319-65515-4_18

fixed server to process and distribute messages. Thus, these applications have to follow and implement a client/server architecture with a dedicated server running e.g. on a PC. Mobile applications, that form groups among peers, do not fit the client/server architecture. When a local group is formed and connections are established, they have to be shared to transmit messages with different characteristics. For example, in game or simulation scenarios, messages may contain sensor information from e.g. the acceleration sensor, gyroscope, or magnetic compass requiring many small messages with soft real time constraints. A common rate is 50 Hz with 12 byte payload (three floats) each. Intermittently, large binary media data, such as sound bites or camera images, may have to be transmitted, which requires few large messages without timing constraints. Posting an image of around 100 KByte should from a developer perspective be a single API call. Note, that transmitting such an image via Bluetooth may take a second. Sensor data does not even consume one percent of available bandwidth, but requires single digit millisecond round trip time. Mixing both message types may significantly delay sensor messages or may block image transmission indefinitely. A scenario with soft real time constraints is sharing finger-tracking data as in Fig. 1. A local group of seven devices serves simultaneously as input and output device using Blaubot. Each device posts touch-points on a shared channel, reads posted touch-points and visualises them with a different colour per device.

Fig. 1. Sample Blaubot-application sharing finger tracking data

First, we briefly review communication infrastructure and middleware for locally connecting mobile devices. Then, we introduce the Blaubot architecture, that covers announcement, discovery and management of connections as well as distributing messages over established connections. Main contributions are the protocol for forming local groups called kingdoms and the technological independent beacons to share state and connection parameters. We detail the state-based protocol establishing master/client relationships in a local group borrowing ancient nomenclature using *king*, *prince*, *peasant*, and *free* to form *kingdoms*. An independent beacon protocol offers information about connection parameters and state. We shortly introduce channel-based messaging and its configuration. Finally, we evaluate the infrastructure with help of sample applications, introduce debug views, and conclude.

2   Communication Infrastructure and Middleware

We design a middleware to exchange information among a group of smartphones forming a Mobile Ad-Hoc Network (MANET) [14]. There shall not be a central coordinating instance to form the local group. We may use combinations of technologies available in many (Android) smartphones. Forming a MANET always includes a discovery phase, where potential partners are found, and a phase where the network is established and used to transfer messages between devices, potentially via many hops [12,14].

It quickly becomes obvious, that WLAN and Bluetooth are the only widely supported communication technologies on smartphones, that may serve as messaging backbone. They work well within a range of 10 m and provide single digit millisecond latency and one to two digit MBit/s bandwidth. Both support many connections. Bluetooth is limited to seven because scatter-net is not supported [2,14]. Both Bluetooth and WLAN are a natural choice to form the backbone of the wireless communication middleware. Bluetooth only works reliably with bidirectional connections (RFCOMM). Although standards extending WLAN may allow forming MANETs, such as Multicast and Wi-Fi Direct [3], they are often not supported on the device, the router, or explicitly turned off due to security considerations. Therefore, a widely usable messaging backbone is bound to rely on bidirectional connections.

For the discovery protocol there is a wider array of options but lacking consistent support across devices and infrastructure. Bluetooth's Service Discovery Protocol (SDP) can be used to discover devices and services. However, Bluetooth discovery is time consuming, may interfere with smartphone health, and pollutes the radio environment [4]. Modern approaches such as Bluetooth Low Energy (BLE) [10] are a better fit for discovery if configured for quick interconnection. WLAN technologies often support discovery protocols such as Wi-Fi Direct Discovery, Universal Plug and Play, or Multicast DNS Service Discovery [3,14]. For the discovery phase it seems prudent for a practically useful middleware on top of existing smartphones and environments, to combine many different technologies, that can be used concurrently.

Most available middlewares and protocols that help to form MANETS require control over the deployed hardware, get aided by a central coordinating server, or focus on either a specific application context or network technology. A central organising instance is required for example in WASP [9]. Dedicated leadership election algorithms for multi-hop environments are available, as for example [11,13], but not necessary in our case. Complex routing of data from one device to any other is handled by protocols such as AODV [13], ROMA [5], or DSDV [6], which again is only necessary in multi-hop environments. Technologies that form a MANET directly, without additional middleware are lacking consistent support in available smartphones [15]. Consequently, developers started to emulate the necessary behaviour on the application layer [1] focusing mostly on WLAN or using these technologies for a dedicated application only, for example to share an internet connection [16].

3   Blaubot Architecture

To form local groups, we implement a star network using point-to-point connections on top of Bluetooth or WLAN. The announcement and distribution of connection parameters is independent and may use different communication technologies such as WLAN Multicasting or NFC. To this end, Blaubot orchestrates core components for announcement and discovery, connection management, and messaging as depicted in Fig. 2. The *beacons* take care of announcing a device, more precisely an instance of an application running on that device, as potential member of a local group and discovering other potential members. To this end, the beacons publish an application ID set by the application developer, which identifies each device as potential member of the same local group. In addition, beacons publish the communication parameters to connect to the group using either WLAN or Bluetooth, but always the same communication technology for each device within a local group of the same application. Apart from that initial decision the application should not be aware of the underlying communication technology for messaging. Beacons should disseminate connection information as well as read such information and propagate discovery events to the connection management. Beacons may be implemented using any communication technology including one-to-many technologies for announcement. Several beacon implementations can be used concurrently, which may provide a more stable and faster knowledge transfer among potential group member candidates.

The *connection management* establishes and manages all point-to-point connections of a device, in case of the master many and in all other cases one. Based on the discovery events of the beacons, it decides independently without further exchange with other devices, which is the master device and tries

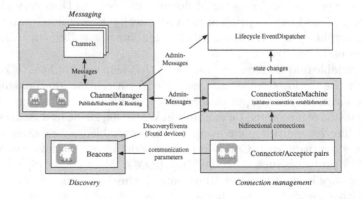

Fig. 2. Blaubot architecture

to either connect actively (client) or let others connect (master) using connector/acceptor pairs. The connector/acceptor pairs abstract from the underlying communication technology for point-to-point communication and currently support Bluetooth (RFCOMM) and WLAN (TCP sockets). In addition to TCP sockets, we also support WebSockets to interoperate through proxies. Connector/acceptor pairs produce a bidirectional point-to-point connection, whose only requirement is to transfer chunks of binary data. The connection management relies on an elaborate protocol to elect and reelect a master even in case of failure. We use an finite state automaton to implement the state changes and call the formed and reformed local groups *kingdoms*. Each change in the connection management, which mainly focuses on newly joined or leaving devices as well as network loss, is made available to the developer.

The developer may not use the connections directly, but benefits from a channel-based publish and subscribe messaging API. Channels, identified by short integers, can be subscribed and/or posted to. The *channel manager* takes care of duplicating messages if necessary and distributing them to subscribed devices. Each channel embodies a queue with optional priority and configuration to constrain for example rate or size. Channels finally post on one connection queue, that sends messages onto the one connection of the client, or each relevant connection queue of the master. The connection queue is not visible to the developers, but used by Blaubot to communicate state such as communication parameters to all members of the kingdom to update their beacons.

4   Kingdoms – Form Local Groups

To form local groups, we use the information disseminated by beacons, without needing a central server known to every potential group member. Additionally, there is no guarantee on the order in which announcements through beacons come in, nor on whether the information is still valid when the device acts upon it. Such an independent protocol is likely to form small local groups, that need to be merged to one larger local group later. Note, that we do not care which device is the master. We provide a protocol based on state transitions that eventually decides which device is master and that flexibly handles failure, even of the master, and supports merging of groups.

The protocol on each device follows a series of state transitions in order to form a maximally large local group. A device may be in one of four states, *king*, *prince*, *peasant*, or *free*, as depicted in Table 1. We call a local group *kingdom* and the master of that local group *king*. In order to quickly recover from failure, each kingdom has a standby candidate known to every other member, the *prince*, taking over in case the king dies[1]. A stable kingdom is any group of devices with at least two members, one is king, the other prince. There may be just one single king for a short period of time. While the king is busy distributing messages, the prince takes care of seeking and guiding new potential members through beacons and looks out for other kingdoms as potential merger candidates. Members of

---

[1] The king is dead, long live the king.

a kingdom, that do not have a special role, are *peasants* and may be asked for guidance. There are no stable kingdoms with one member. Devices that are not member of a kingdom are *free* and are always eager to form kingdoms by actively asking for guidance. Each device runs through the states given in Table 1 depending on events triggered by either information from beacons or from members of the kingdom as well as from establishing or loosing point-to-point connections. All possible state transitions are visualised in Fig. 3. Once Blaubot is started on a device in an application instance, it starts out in *free* state. The device activates its configured beacons to disseminate and receive other beacon information. As soon as beacon information is received, it acts on one of the possible three cases: found a superior *free*, an inferior *free* or a *king* through a *prince*. If it finds another *free*, it starts to form a kingdom. We have to devise a reliable mechanism to decide which of the two *free* will become *king*. We choose the superior *free* to become king by comparing their unique device ID. Note, that we do not care which *free* becomes *king* as long as the decision coincides if both parties exchange their beacon information in one go. The unique device ID is supplemented by the connection parameters used to join the kingdom. If the device decides it is *king*, it activates its acceptor and waits for peasants to join. For a brief period of time, a *free* can be *king* without *peasant*. If the *free* realises its inferiority, it becomes a *peasant* and tries to connect to the other former *free*, which should have pronounced himself king in the meantime. This only works, if both devices "exchange" information. If the new *peasant* fails repeatedly to connect to the elected *king*, he becomes *free* again. If the new *king* remains alone for a configurable period of time, he becomes *free* again. When two free devices meet, success is depicted in Fig. 4 (a) and failure in (b). As soon as a *king* welcomes its first peasant, he will remain *king* for the time being. Each time a *peasant* joins, a new *prince* may be elected by the *king*. The *king* chooses the most superior *peasant* following the king election procedure closely. All members of the kingdom are informed by the *king* who the *prince* is through the established network. If there is a newly appointed *prince*, the existing *prince* becomes *peasant* again. Note, that only the *prince* actively advertises connection information for other *free* to join the king and thus the kingdom. This reduces load on the king and traffic in stable local groups, which may otherwise negatively impact throughput or stability in case similar radio frequencies are used.

Table 1. Devices states

State	Icon	Description
king		master, handling all connections and distributing messages
prince		client member, beacons actively scout for free and other kingdoms
peasant		client member, may respond to beacon inquiries
free		no member of a kingdom, start state, eager to go to other state

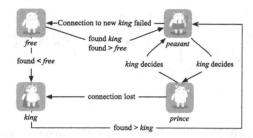

Fig. 3. States of a device

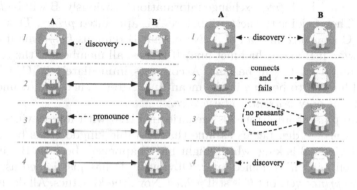

Fig. 4. Two *free* (a) connect successfully (b) fail to connect

If any *free* finds a *prince* of a kingdom, it connects to that kingdom as a *peasant* enlarging the kingdom. If that does not work, or an existing member looses the connection, then that *peasant* or *prince* will become *free* again and the search for a kingdom continues anew. Obviously, if the *prince* is lost, the *king* appoints a new *prince*. In case the *king* dies, all members of the kingdom try to connect to the *prince*, who will appoint himself *king* in due time. Timing issues are fought with exponential back off and finally timeout failure, which always results in the *free* state for the affected device.

There is still one problem. Small kingdoms may emerge that need to be merged to one larger kingdom. In case two small kingdoms meet, they meet via their respective *princes*. Each *prince* learns about the other kingdom and his *king* via the beacon. This information is relayed to the *king*, who can then without further consultation decide whether he is superior or not. The inferior *king* informs all his members about a new *king* they should connect to, then abdicates and bows himself down to the other *king* by connecting as *peasant*. The information to whom to connect is the last message distributed in the to be dissolved small kingdom. The superior *king* just expects new members, but does not trigger any life cycle event. We present a typical walk through with three devices A, B, and C as shown in Fig. 5. We use lexicographical order to determine superiority; the most powerful being C. Let us assume, that first A

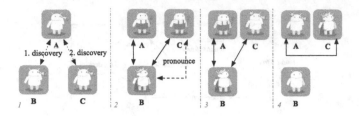

Fig. 5. Typical walk through with three devices

and B, which are both *free*, exchange information. Obviously, B will be *king* and A *peasant*. Then C joins the network before A is appointed *prince*. This causes B to appoint C as *prince* instead of A. Note, that B remains *king* even if C would have been *king* if B and C had met first. If B dies, all members of the remaining kingdom know that C will be *king*. A connects immediately to C, which has proclaimed himself to be *king* in the meantime. After a successful connection C appoints A, his only *peasant*, to be *prince*.

Next, we present an erroneous scenario in Fig. 6 with four devices where a *king* and its *prince* die. Let us assume that a stable kingdom has been formed with four devices. B is king, which might have happened, because B met A first and C as well as D have joined later. Obviously, D has just joined as it is not promoted to *prince* yet, but C is still *prince*. Now, the king dies. All devices want to connect to C. However, assume that C dies as well. Then only A and D are left and both try to connect to C, which they think is the new *king*. However, they cannot connect. Note, that if C would have been alive, then a kingdom could have been quickly resurrected. If both important nodes, the *king* and its *prince* die, then there is no kingdom any longer. However, things will recover eventually. First, after a timeout, A and D will become *free* again. As these are the only devices left, they will eventually find each other. Then D will become *king* and A his *peasant* and almost immediately afterwards A will become *prince*. If now C and B recover, they start as *free* and may find A who tells them to connect to their new *king* D. Both C and B will then become *peasant*. The next step, not shown in the figure, is that D will assign C as its new *prince*.

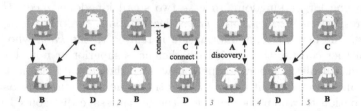

Fig. 6. King dies with four devices

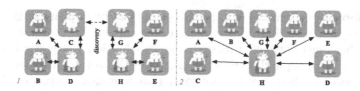

Fig. 7. Two kingdoms merge

Finally, we show an example, where two small kingdoms merge in Fig. 7. There are two kingdoms. First, there is A, B, C, and D with D being *king* and C being *prince*. In addition, there is E, F, G, H with H being *king* and G being *prince*. Eventually, C and G exchange information and they will find out about the other kingdom. Both *princes* will relay that information to their respective *king*. Thus, D knows about H and vice versa. In that case, D must act and informs all his members to connect to H as their new *king*. Finally, he abdicates freeing all connections and bows down himself as *peasant* by connecting to H. All other members follow their former *king*.

5   Beacons – Share State and Connection Parameters

Blaubot uses beacons to exchange state with other devices that are eager to join or form a kingdom. The beacon information is exchanged in one go, there is no complicated handshake procedure enforced by the protocol. After the exchange each beacon partner must have enough information to decide its next step as explained in Sect. 4. Therefore, the information contains all parameters that enable any interested party to connect to an acceptor of a king.

The communication technology to exchange information is independent of the communication technology used to establish the point-to-point based messaging network. The only requirements are, that the communication parameters are transmitted and that corresponding events are triggered. Note, that the communication parameters are not fix throughout a session, as kings may die and new kings may be elected, but typically this information does not change often. However, in case things change, that information needs to be current, thus there must not be any caching. In contrast to the point-to-point communication technology, the protocol does not limit the exchange to use only one technology or one beacon per device. There can be any number of technologies and beacons each triggering their respective events on which the network reacts. This allows, for example, to form a Bluetooth network, where one device joins because of a Bluetooth SDP, the other based on a NFC exchange and one may even just consume relevant information via a QR-code. all of which may trigger the connection phase to join a kingdom. This allows to avoid the costly and most often for network and Bluetooth adapters damaging Bluetooth SDP altogether, while still forming a reliable Bluetooth star network.

In order to realise a beacon technology only a few features need to be implemented. Besides a start and stop there is a discovery phase finding other beacons and an information exchange. We encourage any beacon implementation to react to a *passive/active* setting. This may limit the capabilities of a beacon regarding reach, but must not hinder its exchange capabilities, which is still necessary for the initial forming and merging of kingdoms. However, this allows to avoid using heavyweight discovery technologies, that may adversely affect hardware and network, in a passive state. We only want to form networks of devices running the same application. To this end, the beacon always send an application specific unique ID that will be computed from information given by the application developer. Only beacons with identical application ID trigger events. In case it is not possible to transmit the application ID, e.g. due to size limits, all discovered devices may be eligible, but will be filtered later during the connection phase. Beacon implementations are not constrained to follow a specific approach. However, most scan for devices and for eligible devices an exchange is attempted. Application developers may preset the devices with which an exchange should be attempted. For example, with Bluetooth we might only want to try to connect to paired devices, which works very well in a laboratory setting, where always the same collection of devices should form a Blaubot network as these may be used for a controlled sensor experiment. As usual, there should be an exponential back-off strategy employed while trying to exchange beacon information and eventually devices are temporarily removed from the list if they do not react.

Blaubot brings a series of beacon implementations, that allow the application developer to use different networking and discovery technologies. A subset of beacon implementations is given in Table 2. With *Bluetooth classic* we denote standard Bluetooth connections. We avoid Bluetooth SDP as it may negatively impact Android device health. Instead we rely on a list of already paired devices retrieved from Android at application start, which works well in lab environments or other fixed setups. The beacon exchange is based on an RFCOMM socket connection. Obviously, a beacon exchange is only attempted, if these devices are not yet in the local group. *UDP-Multicast* and *mDNS-SD* work well if Android devices are connected using WLAN over a local router. Both use Multicast over the established network to find peers and then exchange information using TCP-socket connections. *UDP-Multicast* tends to find peers faster, but pollutes the radio environment. With *mDNS-SD* it is vice versa, but still acceptably fast. The *NFC* implementation enables users to perform a unidirectional as well as a bidirectional discovery interaction by performing the intuitive physical gesture

Table 2. Beacon implementations

Network tech.	Characteristic	Latency	Remark
Bluetooth classic	Heavyweight	High	No discovery
NFC	Lightweight	Low	Physical interactions required
UDP-Multicast	Heavyweight	Low	Requires Multicast enabled IP-Network
mDNS-SD	Lightweight	Low	Requires Multicast enabled IP-Network
Wi-Fi Direct	Heavyweight	High	Unstable on Android, not usable

of holding the device against each other. While *Wi-Fi Direct* would be a perfect fit for beacons, its lacking support on current devices prevents its use.

6   Channels – Publish and Subscribe Prioritised Messaging

Once a network is established, Blaubot uses the king as message multiplier and dispatcher. However, the connections are not visible to the application developer, but abstracted away by channels. Each device, that listens on a channel, receives all messages posted to that channel by any connected device. Each device can send to any channel without necessarily being subscribed to it. A channel is identified by a positive short integer number. The application developer does not need to cope with the underlying star network and can focus exclusively on using channels. Unidirectional communication to a device can be achieved by one device sending on a channel, on which only the chosen recipient has subscribed. Blaubot supports life cycle events whenever a device has joined or left the local group. We do not make channel subscriptions available to the application developer. Internally, all devices of the network are known by all devices of the network and know all subscriptions. The *king* copies messages it receives to every subscribed device and serves as a switch with potentially many recipients. The application developer is not aware of whether the device is *king* or not, nor if the message was sent by himself or not. It is only by the discretion of Blaubot to not send messages back from the central dispatcher if they originate from the receiving device. Note, that the *king* may experience lower latency, as its messages are short circuited. Each channel uses a queue to collect and distribute messages as depicted in Fig. 8. The connection itself is also protected by a queue where all channel queues post to. The connection queue sends the messages over the single connection. Having a dedicated queue per channel opens the possibility to configure channels and specify dedicated behaviour adhering to specific requirements. For example, each channel may have set a priority, which the central queue, a priority queue, respects. Note, that internal messages, such as announcement of a prince or keep alive messages, have always priority over any user defined content.

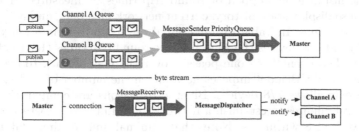

Fig. 8. Channel implementation

Further channel configuration include possibilities to restrict the capacity of a channel queue and implement the typical selection strategies such as discarding oldest or newest or only sending messages, that have been delivered to the channel within a fixed time frame. Obviously, posting to a channel is an asynchronous operation. The channels accept byte arrays as message payload. The message size in bytes is restricted by a 31 bit integer, but messages are split into chunks limited by 16 bit integers. Thus, one huge low priority message in transfer will not block high priority messages unduly.

Note, while there is no guaranteed delivery of messages in the Blaubot network, messages are seldom lost. The underlying protocol uses reliable communication and if no network failure occurs (a disconnect of the device or a failure of the *king*) no messages will be lost. In particular, the subscriptions survive disconnects and messages will flow back in as soon as a device rejoins. Even messages sent to the kingdom will be queued according to channel policies until the network is restored. However, as the *king* may die, some messages can still be lost. The details of the binary message format and the messaging capabilities of Blaubot can be found in [7,8].

7   Evaluation

A working Hello World application transmitting a message to many devices with Blaubot consumes ~20 lines of code [7]. A Bluetooth local chat example with UI and boiler plate code ~500, similar to finger tracking of Fig. 1. Using WLAN the BlaubotMedia example distributes both walkie talkie sound bites as well as a series of camera still images. The sound bites have priority over the still images, which allows to continue using it as walkie talkie, while images are held back or are dropped based on channel configuration. The asynchronous and distributed nature of MANETs reduces developer support to tracking and tracing of specific program flows on each involved device. Blaubot provides built-in tools for application debugging by tracing their states visually as well as the possibility to simulate errors, that are otherwise difficult to reproduce such as connection loss of particular devices or heavy network load. Examples of these integrated debug views are shown in Fig. 9. We see a debug view attached to a Blaubot king, which manages multiple connections to a direct Blaubot server. Connections can be cut, the instance be stopped or round trip times be measured. The debug view may also display state history, current network members, and active point-to-point connections. In Table 3 we measured the setup to form a kingdom of 2 devices (A) and 7/8 devices (B) as well as the round trip times (RTT) of a small message (89 byte) sent from one peasant over the master back to every other peasant repeatedly. Blaubot imposes no limit on the number of nodes, however Bluetooth only allows 7/8 devices. Bluetooth beacons are comparatively slow, taking several minutes to establish a network and Multicast is fastest establishing a network of 8 within 8 s. Note, that minimal and maximal latency may spread widely, while there is not a huge difference in latency independent on the beacon or communication network technology.

Fig. 9. Blaubot (a+b) Media configuration and transmission with priority to audio (c+d) Integrated debug views showing a king (scrolled)

Table 3. Time to create a networks and latency in established network

Beacons	Adapter	#	A [s]	B [s]	min/∅/max RTT [ms]		
Multicast	TCP-Sockets	8	.45	7.65	6	17	48
Bonjour	TCP-Sockets	8	7.96	8.59	6	36	88
Bluetooth	TCP-Sockets	7	38.12	15.10	7	19	148
Bluetooth	RFCOMM	7	20.23	115.47	29	60	138
Multicast	RFCOMM	7	2.93	30.70	12	59	500
Multicast	WebSockets	8	0.80	9.20	12	38	183
Bonjour	WebSockets	8	7.97	11.92	11	27	121
Bluetooth	WifiAp	8	111.40	∞	3	32	160

8 Conclusion

With Blaubot we connect a set of smartphones to form a local group. To that end, we use a wireless infrastructure, which is inherently many-to-many, to build a star network of point-to-point connections to simulate a many-to-many environment. Although this may sound weird at first, it is due to practical considerations. Bluetooth and WLAN infrastructures are very good at establishing reasonably fast and reliable point-to-point connections despite their many-to-many radio characteristics. We build on this reliability to form a practically usable channel-based Multicast MANET infrastructure in practice. To the knowledge of the authors, there is no other possibility that would work with the majority of existing Android smartphones.

We provide a reliable infrastructure that provides acceptable low latency and high bandwidth. Thus, the envisaged scenarios combining sensors of many devices for games have been possible to realise as demonstrated with the finger tracking example. In addition, the distribution of large binary message, as in the distributed media scenario have been possible and shown to work in practice with up to ten devices. The API is straightforward and can easily be used to implement dedicated scenarios, where groups of a few smartphones need to exchange information independently of a server. Although not presented here, Blaubot also supports a server, but not for coordination of network set up, but solely as group member to integrate server applications. Thus, we do not rely on a server to form a local group and local groups continue to work and restructure themselves despite the loss of connection to a central server.

The highly abstracted API is easy to use and allows for further improvement. For example, Blaubot may reduce messaging overhead by including compression filters or provide shortcuts such as direct radio links in the future, without compromising the API.

Blaubot is open source and has been made available via Maven and Gradle lowering the barrier for application developers to employ groups of local devices for their scenarios. New technologies enter the mobile world, such as Wi-Fi Aware and BLE Peripheral-Mode, fitting well as beacon technology. Thus, we hope to make connection loss just a short nuisance and continuously improve Blaubot without changing the developer API. Therefore, more and more applications may employ the power of several smartphones and maybe other mobile appliances to better support local scenarios with soft real time requirements.

References

1. Aguiar, A., Soares, E., Brandão, P., Magalhães, T., Fernandes, J.M., Oliveira, I.: Demo: wireless IP mesh on android for fire-fighters monitoring. In: 9th ACM MobiCom Workshop on Challenged Networks, CHANTS 2014, pp. 89–92. ACM, New York (2014)
2. Beutel, J.: Fast-prototyping Using the BTnode Platform. In: Conference on Design, Automation and Test in Europe, DATE 2006, pp. 977–982. European Design and Automation Association, Leuven (2006)
3. Camps-Mur, D., Garcia-Saavedra, A., Serrano, P.: Device-to-device communications with Wi-Fi Direct: overview and experimentation. IEEE Wirel. Commun. **20**(3), 96–104 (2013)
4. Android Bluetooth Discovery. developer.android.com, BluetoothAdapter.html
5. Dhananjay, A., Zhang, H., Li, J., Subramanian, L.: Practical, distributed channel assignment and routing in dual-radio mesh networks. In: ACM SIGCOMM 2009 Conference on Data Communication, SIGCOMM 2009, pp. 99–110. ACM, New York (2009)
6. Gohs, R.S., Gunnarsson, S.R., Glenstrup, A.J.: Beddernet: application-level platform-agnostic MANETs. In: Felber, P., Rouvoy, R. (eds.) DAIS 2011. LNCS, vol. 6723, pp. 165–178. Springer, Heidelberg (2011). doi:10.1007/978-3-642-21387-8_13
7. Groß, H.: Blaubot project site. http://blaubot.hgross.eu
8. Groß, H.: Mobile Multi Peering. Thesis, HSRM, Wiesbaden, July 2015
9. Kaplan, M., Zheng, C., Monaco, M., Keller, E., Sicker, D.: WASP: a software-defined communication layer for hybrid wireless networks. In: Tenth ACM/IEEE Symposium on Architectures for Networking and Communications Systems, ANCS 2014, pp. 5–16. ACM, New York(2014)
10. Jia, L., Canfeng, C., Yan, M.: Modeling neighbor discovery in bluetooth low energy networks. IEEE Commun. Lett. **16**(9), 1439–1441 (2012)

11. Malpani, N., Welch, J.L., Vaidya, N.: Leader election algorithms for mobile ad hoc networks. In: 4th International Workshop on Discrete Algorithms and Methods for Mobile Computing and Communications, DIALM 2000, pp. 96–103. ACM, New York (2000)
12. Mian, A.N., Baldoni, R., Beraldi, R.: A survey of service discovery protocols in multihop mobile Ad Hoc networks. IEEE Pervasive Comput. 8(1), 66–74 (2009)
13. Perkins, C., Belding-Royer, E., Das, S.: Ad Hoc On-Demand Distance Vector (AODV) Routing (2003)
14. Ververidis, C.N., Polyzos, G.C.: Service discovery for mobile Ad Hoc networks: a survey of issues and techniques. IEEE Commun. Surv. Tutor. 10(3), 30–45 (2008)
15. Wirtz, H., Heer, T., Backhaus, R., Wehrle, K.: Establishing mobile ad-hoc networks in 802.11 infrastructure mode. In: 6th ACM Workshop on Challenged Networks, CHANTS 2011, pp. 49–52. ACM, New York (2011)
16. Yang, Y., Kiesel, S., Previdi, S., Roome, W., Shalunov, S., Woundy, R.: Open Garden (2014)

Overhead Analysis of Inter-domain Mobility Management in Multicasting-Supported FPMIPv6 Networks

Hanjun Cho and Jongpil Jeong$^{(\boxtimes)}$

Department of Smart Factory Convergence, Sungkyunkwan University,
Suwon, Gyeonggi-do 16419, Republic of Korea
{jhj0955, jpjeong}@skku.edu

Abstract. Multicast service will be an important form of communication requiring interruption-free delivery of multicast service in mobile networks increasing MNs. The proposed fast multicast handover procedure in inter domain optimizes multicast management by using the context of the MNs. We evaluate the proposed fast multicast handover procedure compared to the one based through the developed analytical models and confirm that introduced fast multicast handover procedure provides reduced service interruption time and total network overhead compared to the one based during handovers.

Keywords: Multicasting · PMIPv6 · FPMIPv6 (Fast PMIPv6) · Inter-domain mobility management · Overhead analysis

1 Introduction

Recently, IETF (Internet Engineering Task Force) proposed a mobility management technique based on the standardized network through PMIPv6 (Proxy Mobile IPv6) protocol [1]. PMIPv6 is similar to host-centric mobility management protocol [2]. However, it also has the important difference that it does not require MN (Mobile Node) for any processing as to mobility. It provides MN IP mobility by introducing new mobile agents such as MAG (Mobile Access Gateway) and LMA (Local Mobility Anchor). MAG within the domain in PMIPv6 recognizes the motion of MN and recognizes L2 connection notification. Moreover, it also performs the role of sending and registering PBU (Proxy Binding Update) at LMA. LMA performs the role of HA (Home Agent) to manage all MNs registered in PMIPv6 domain that was given by the receiving PBU message. LMA resends PBA (Proxy Binding Ack) including HNP (Home Network Prefix) for MN to MAG. MN that accessed MAG forms its own address and pHoA (Proxy Home of Address) based on HNP received from MAG. When MN runs handover through new network, MN reacquires HNP and HNP acquired from the previously accessed network will be acquired from MAG of newly accessed network. PMIPv6 shows better performance than the conventional host-centric mobility management protocol [3].

However, the previously developed multicast technique cannot be applied to PMIPv6. Furthermore, it is even more difficult to apply the multicast technique

© Springer International Publishing AG 2017
M. Younas et al. (Eds.): MobiWIS 2017, LNCS 10486, pp. 224–236, 2017.
DOI: 10.1007/978-3-319-65515-4_19

between domains. On this account, this paper proposes two PMIPv6 multicast handover techniques for an MN that moves in high speed between LMA domains when multicast service is running. The first proposed PMIPv6 multicast handover technique is to reduce latency through buffering by forming a tunneling between MAGs of LMA through which MAG of LMA has MN and MN's attempt to move. The second proposed PMIPv6 multicast handover technique is to reduce latency through buffering by forming a tunneling between LMA having MN and LMA that is willing to move.

This paper implemented mathematical modeling of the PMIPv6 multicast network proposed by IETF, the latency of multicast handover procedure of the proposed two techniques and the entire network overhead and performed a performance evaluation of these. In the case of latency, IETF's proposed PMIPv6 multicast network increases latency in the linear form due to an increase in the number of hops. However, the proposed two multicast networks maintain fixed value of 85.6 ms based on the analysis of results. That is, it shows that the number of hops does not affect them at all. Moreover, IETF's proposed PMIPv6 multicast network was found to have a difference of at least two times in the case of the entire network overhead.

This paper is organized as follows. In Sect. 2, we will explore related researches. Section 3 will describe a proposed hierarchical modeling system. Section 4 presents performance evaluation of the proposed system modeling. Finally, we will describe the conclusions in Sect. 5.

2 Related Work

MN does not require any specific functionality of a related type. This requirement is a reflection of the concept of a network-based mobility management. Multicast Listener Discovery (MLD) Proxy function is required to support MLD Membership Report sent from MN and send a multicast communication to MN [4]. Designated multicast router functionality is required to manage a multicast forwarding state of MN and send a multicast communication to MN. In some cases, MLD Proxy function needs more dependence on MLD Membership Report. Conceptually, LMA is connected to multicast routing infrastructure by its output interface. At the same time, the input interface is connected to MAG. MAG connected to MN receives the multicast communication via the established tunnel between MAG and LMA.

With the expansion of PMIPv6, FPMIPv6 (Fast PMIPv6) [5] was recently announced as an enhancement of the handover performance of PMIPv6. However, this is designed to optimize unicast communication, and not multicast communication. In other words, because the lack of contribution to the multicast group management, benefits of FPMIPv6 cannot affect to the multicast communication. FPMIPv6 multicast handover procedure optimizes the multicast group management by using MN roaming context. Context passed from pMAG to nMAG before MN is connected with nMAG contains identification of MN, LMA address of MN, multicast driving information of MN and so on. After nMAG obtains the context of MN, and if it is necessary, it updates multicast forwarding state as well as MLD Proxy Membership Database in advance. Multicast communication is delivered to nMAG in pMAG in the same way as

FPMIPv6. By doing so, as soon as MN is connected to the new network, MN is able to receive the multicast communication directly from nMAG [6].

3 Inter-domain Multicasting-Supported Mobility Management

In the case of PMIPv6 multicast and FPMIPv6 multicast handover, the mobile multicast approach is only for the case in which MN in LMA moves to nMAG in pMAG. However, network size is becoming larger and usage scope of network is expanding. Thus, this paper proposes a better technique through the performance analysis of the aforementioned two techniques by proposing the two handover techniques for the case in which MN between LMAs moves by expanding it.

FPMIPv6 multicast handover procedure between LMAs through the proposed MAG tunneling is established basically based on FPMIPv6. FPMIPv6 consists of the following two methods: PredictiveMode and ReactiveMode. In PredictiveMode, bidirectional tunnel is established between pMAG and nMAG before MN accesses nMAG, as shown in Fig. 1. As for ReactiveMode, bidirectional tunnel is established after MN accesses nMAG. MN transmits nMAG ID to pMAG through MN, which is expected to access with MN ID when handover is imminent. It notifies the imminence of MN handover by transmitting MN ID and nMAG ID. Herein, MN informs network information of nMAG to pMAG through L2 report. That is, MN prepares for handover from pMAG to nMAG when L2 trigger is transmitted to pMAG. Using L2 trigger, MN obtains network access information of nMAG such as network identification. Thus, MN provides network identification information as well as its own identification information to pMAG. Moreover, pMAG provides service to MN through sending L2 report message. MLS of the proposed multicast handover procedure begins with handover Initiate (HI) message including MN identification information, HNP of MN, LMA address of MN and multicast support option (MSO). Multicast subscription information of MN included in MSO is transmitted from pMAG to nMAG. Also, it is used as a parameter for MLS. When nMAG acquires HI message, the message is confirmed when the state of nMAG allows for providing service to MLS for MN. nMAG sends pre-PBU + MSO message to LMA2 before sending HAck message to pMAG. Then, LMA2 conducts authentication and set connection to domains by utilizing the information thereof. LMA2 conducts proxy binding procedure in advance by sending pre-PBA + MSO message when it is updated. nMAG resends HAck message including acceptance or rejection value to pMAG. After then, pMAG generates multicast communication tunneling and pMAG renews multicast transmission state as to LMA1 MN by sending DeReg.PBU message including identification information of MN and HNP and MSO of MN. As for the response, LMA1 resends DeReg.PBU message to pMAG. nMAG sends multicast data to MN, which was buffered to reduce the loss associated with L2 connection notification and multicasting communication for MN that entered domain. MN having received L2 connection notification conducts IP address allocation procedure (RS and RA procedure). If RA procedure is completed, LMA2 becomes means to conduct multicasting communication immediately because it has already conducted proxy binding procedure. Multicast communication loss is

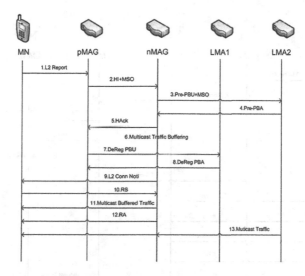

Fig. 1. Multicasting handover procedures between pMAG and nMAG.

reduced substantially during MN handover because buffer, pre-PBU and pre-PBA procedure are already implemented.

Basically, FPMIPv6 multicast handover procedure between LMAs through LMA tunneling is equivalent to the process of sending L2 report message in which MN network information from LMA2 to pMAG through initial-phase L2 report of As shown in Fig. 2, FPMIPv6 multicast handover procedure between LMAs through MAG tunneling. MLS of the proposed multicast handover procedure begins with HI message including identification information of MN, LMA address of HNP and MN of MN and MSO. In regard to multicast subscription information of MN included in MSO, pMAG transmits DeReg PBU message to LMA1. It is also used as a parameter for MLS. LMA1 transmits HI and MSO to LMA2, whereas LMA2 transmits HAck message including acceptance or rejection value to LMA1 and generates tunneling between LMA1 and LMA2. LMA1 sends DeReg PBA message to pMAG as a response. nMAG sends multicast communication to MN, which was buffered to reduce L2 connection notification and multicasting communication loss to MN having entered the domain. MN having received L2 connection notification conducts IP address allocation procedure (RS and RA procedure). It becomes able to conduct multicasting communication immediately when RA procedure is completed. The proposed multicast handover procedure reduces substantially multicast communication loss during MN handover by reducing pre-PBU and pre-PBA procedure of PMIPv6 multicast handover procedure between LMA domains by utilizing MAG.

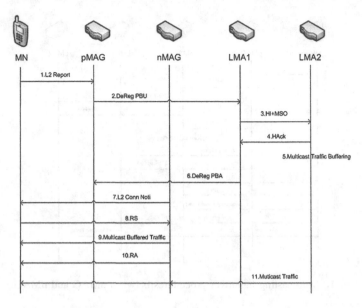

Fig. 2. Multicasting handover procedures between LMA1 and LMA2.

4 Performance Evaluation

In this section, by mathematical modeling of the proposed multicast handover procedure's retardation time and overall network overhead, we will perform a performance evaluation.

In the mathematical modeling of the handover retardation time, MN performs a handover procedure between LMA domains. The communication path between LMA and LMA, LMA and MAG is a wired connection, the communication path between MAG and MN is a wireless connection. Also, we assumed that the processing time of each component can be ignored, and a message is transmitted through wired/wireless link without the error. In the mathematical modeling of the entire network overhead, we assumed that Session Arrival Rate is same in each MN and average file size in Session is also same. In addition, all average numbers of LMA (in case of PMIPv6 network) or HA (in case of HMIPv6 network) are equal, and the standard IP switching cost is ignored. MN in the network is distributed uniformly, and finally, the location DB is searched by the binary search. Table 1 describes the definition of the parameters for the performance analysis.

Table 1. Parameters for defining the network overhead costs [7, 9, 10].

Parameters	Description	Value
N_m	The number of MN	10
N_c	The average number of CN per HN	1
N_h	The number of HA	10
β_c	The transmission costs of a query message per Hop	0.6
β_{dp}	The transmission costs of an average data packet per Hop	5.72
β_{da}	The transmission costs of data ACK (Acknowledgement) packet per Hop	0.6
β_{rr}	The transmission costs of RR (Return Routablitiy) message per Hop	0.6
β_{rc}	The transmission costs of RCoA (Regional Care of Address) accept/reject message per Hop	0.6
β_{lr}	The transmission costs of LCoA (on-Link Care of Address) accept/reject message per Hop	0.6
Φ_{hc}	Hop count between MAP (Mobility Anchor Point) and HA (Home Agent)	35
Φ_{mm}	Hop count between MN and MAP	35
Φ_{mh}	Hop count between HA and CN (Corresponding Node)	35
Φ_{mc}	Hop count between MN and CN	35
σ	Proportional constant of switching from the radio to a radio link	10
n	Linear coefficients of the look-up costs	0.3
T_r	Subnet duration	70
λ_s	Average session arrival rate of each MN	0.01
x, y	The number of AR (Access Router) in rows and columns	51, 34
k	The number of AR per MAP	12
m	The number of MAP at m = xy/k	144.5
κ	The maximum transmission unit	512
α	The average session size	10240
δ_{rc}	Each RCoA registration processing costs in MAP	5
δ_{lc}	Each LCoA registration processing costs in MAP	30
δ_h	LU (Location Update) processing costs in HA	30
X	Each data (ACK) average number of retransmissions	3
ς	IP routing table look-up linear coefficient	0.3
ξ	Encapsulation costs	0.5
N_{LMA}	The number of LMA	40000
$\Phi_{MAG-LMA}$	Hop count between MAG and LMA	35
Φ_{LMA-CN}	Hop count between LMA and CN	35
$\Phi_{LMA-LMA}$	Hop count between LMA and LMA	35
$\Phi_{MAG-MAG}$	Hop count between MAG and MAG	35
β_{pc}	The transmission costs of PC (Proxy Care Of Address) accept/reject message per Hop	0.6
$\beta_{m-query}$	Transmission costs of MLD membership query message	0.6
$\beta_{m-report}$	Transmission costs of MLD membership report message	0.6

(*continued*)

Table 1. (*continued*)

Parameters	Description	Value
β_{pc-mso}	The transmission costs of PC (Proxy Care Of Address) accept/reject message including MSO per Hop	0.6
δ_{pc}	PBU processing costs in the LMA	30
δ_{pc-mso}	PBU processing costs, including the MSO in LMA	30

4.1   The Entire Overhead Modeling in the Network

The entire overhead in the network can be defined as the sum of the query message, registration message and packet tunneling costs [7, 9, 10].

(1) PMIPv6 Network

The costs of query message in PMIPv6 network are similar to the costs of query message in HMIPv6 network. The costs of query message from the entire CN in the network are as follows:

$$\Lambda^{Query} = N_m N_c \lambda_s (2\beta_c \Phi_{LMA-CN} + \eta N_{LMA}(\log N_m - \log N_{LMA})) \tag{1}$$

It shows a large difference between the registration message and those of HMIPv6 network. In case of the registration message in HMIPv6 network, there are three kinds of registration messages. However, in case of the registration message in PMIPv6 network, it only occurs through PBU and PBA message between MAG and LMA. Therefore, the costs of the registration message are as follows:

$$\Lambda^{Registation} = N_m \frac{2\beta_{pc}(\Phi_{MAG-LMA} - 1 + \sigma) + \delta_{pc}}{MT_r} \tag{2}$$

The costs of packet tunneling in PMIPv6 network is similar to those of HMIPv6 network. The costs of packet tunneling are as follows:

$$\Lambda^{Packet\_T} = N_m N_c \lambda_s \left\lceil \frac{\alpha}{\kappa} \right\rceil \begin{pmatrix} (x+1)((\beta_{dp} + \beta_{da})(\Phi_{cnLMA-mnLMA}) + 2\xi \\ + (\beta_{dp} + \beta_{da})(\Phi_{mnMAG-mnLMA} - 1 + \sigma) + \\ 4\xi + n\log_2 \frac{N_m k}{xu} + \varsigma \log_2 k \end{pmatrix} \tag{3}$$

The entire overhead in the network is defined as the sum of the costs of query message, registration message and packet tunneling, then it is as follows:

$$\Lambda_{Network} = \Lambda^{Query} + \Lambda^{Registation} + \Lambda^{Packet\_T} \tag{4}$$

(2) PMIPv6 Multicast Network

The costs of query message in PMIPv6 multicast network are similar to the costs of query message in PMIPv6 network. The costs of query message from the entire CN in the network are as follows:

$$\Lambda^{Query} = N_m N_c \lambda_s (2\beta_c \Phi_{LMA-CN} + \eta N_{LMA} (\log N_m - \log N_{LMA})) \tag{5}$$

The registration message comes a parameter called $\beta_{m-query}$ and $\beta_{m-report}$. It is a parameter for processing MLD Membership Report when performing the message procedure of PBU and PBA. Therefore, the costs of the registration message are as follows:

$$\Lambda^{Registation} = \left(N_m \frac{2\beta_{pc}(\Phi_{MAG-LMA} - 1 + \sigma) + \delta_{pc}}{MT_r} + N_m \sigma(\beta_{m-report}) \atop + N_m \beta_{report} \Phi_{cnLMA-mnLMA} \right) \tag{6}$$

The costs of packet tunneling in PMIPv6 multicast network is similar to those of PMIPv6 network. The costs of packet tunneling are as follows:

$$\Lambda^{Packet\_T} = N_m N_c \lambda_s [\frac{\alpha}{\kappa}] \left(\begin{array}{l} (x+1)((\beta_{dp} + \beta_{da})(\Phi_{cnLMA-mnLMA}) + 2\xi \\ + (\beta_{dp} + \beta_{da})(\Phi_{mnMAG-mnLMA} - 1 + \sigma) + \\ 4\xi + n \log_2 \frac{N_m k}{xu} + \varsigma \log_2 k \end{array} \right) \tag{7}$$

The entire overhead in the network is defined as the sum of the costs of query message, registration messgae and packet tunneling, then it is as follows:

$$\Lambda_{Network} = \Lambda^{Query} + \Lambda^{Registration} + \Lambda^{Packet\_T} \tag{8}$$

(3) FPMIPv6 Multicast Network Between LMA Through MAG Tunneling

The costs of query message in proposed FMIPv6(MAG) multicast network are similar to the costs of query message in PMIPv6 network. The costs of query message from the entire CN in the network are as follows:

$$\Lambda^{Query} = N_m N_c \lambda_s (2\beta_c \Phi_{LMA-CN} + \eta N_{LMA} (\log N_m - \log N_{LMA})) \tag{9}$$

The registration message of proposed FPMIPv6(MAG) network does not need the performing procedure for MLD Membership Report of PMIPv6 multicast. Therefore, the costs of the registration message are as follows:

$$\Lambda^{Registration} = N_m \frac{2\beta_{pc}(\Phi_{MAG-LMA} - 1 + \sigma) + \delta_{pc-mso}}{MT_r} \tag{10}$$

The costs of multicast network tunneling of proposed FPMIPv6(MAG) are simpler than the costs of the multicast network of PMIPv6. Packet can be transmitted between MN and cnMAG, and that cost is $(\beta_{dp} + \beta_{da})\sigma$. Packet is transmitted between cnMAG and nmMAG through the encapsulation. That costs is $(\beta_{dp} + \beta_{da})\Phi_{cnMAG-mnMAG} + 2\xi$. Finally, the sum of the costs of packet transmission between mnMAG and mnLMA and the costs of packet transmission between MN and mnMAG are $(\beta_{dp} + \beta_{da})$ $(\Phi_{mnMag-mnMAG} + \sigma) + 2\xi$, which are the costs of the entire packet tunneling. Therefore, the costs of packet tunneling are as follows:

$$\Lambda^{Packet\_T} = N_m N_c \lambda_s \lceil \frac{\alpha}{\kappa} \rceil \left(\begin{array}{c} (x+1)((\beta_{dp} + \beta_{da})(\sigma + \Phi_{cnLMA-mnLMA}) + 2\xi \\ + (\beta_{dp} + \beta_{da})(\Phi_{mnMAG-mnLMA} + \sigma) + 2\xi \end{array} \right) \quad (11)$$

The entire overhead in the network is defined as the sum of the costs of query message, registration messgae and packet tunneling, then it is as follows:

$$\Lambda_{Network} = \Lambda^{Query} + \Lambda^{Registation} + \Lambda^{Packet\_T} \quad (12)$$

(4) FPMIPv6 Multicast Network between LMA through LMA Tunneling

The costs of query message in proposed FMIPv6(LMA) network are similar to the costs of query message in proposed FMIPv6(MAG) network. The costs of query message from the entire CN in the network are as follows:

$$\Lambda^{Query} = N_m N_c \lambda_s (2\beta_c \Phi_{LMA-CN} + \eta N_{LMA}(\log N_m - \log N_{LMA}) \quad (13)$$

The registration message of proposed FPMIPv6(LMA) network does not need the procedure for pre-PBU and pre-PBA of proposed FPMIPv6(MAG). Therefore, the costs of the registration message are as follows:

$$\Lambda^{Registation} = N_m \frac{(\sigma + \delta_{pc-mso})}{MT_r} \quad (14)$$

The costs of multicast network tunneling of proposed FPMIPv6(LMA) are as follows. Packet is transmitted between MN and cnMAG. Also, packet is transmitted between cnMAG and cnLMA. The sum of packet transmission costs between MN and cnMAG, cnMAG and cnLMA, cnLMA and mnLMA is $(\beta_{dp} + \beta_{da})(\Phi_{cnMag-cnMAG} + \sigma) + \Phi_{cnLMA-mnLMA} + 2\xi$. Also, the sum of the packet transmission costs between mnLMA and mnMAG, mnMAG and MN is as follows:

$$\Lambda^{Packet\_T} = N_m N_c \lambda_s \lceil \frac{\alpha}{\kappa} \rceil \left(\begin{array}{c} (x+1)((\beta_{dp} + \beta_{da})(\sigma + \Phi_{cnMAG-cnLMA} + \Phi_{cnLMA-mnLMA}) + 2\xi \\ + (\beta_{dp} + \beta_{da})\sigma \end{array} \right) \quad (15)$$

As described in the introduction, the entire overhead in the network is defined as the sum of the costs of query message, registration message and packet tunneling, then it is as follows:

$$\Lambda_{Network} = \Lambda^{Query} + \Lambda^{Registation} + \Lambda^{Packet\_T} \tag{16}$$

4.2 Analysis Result

We analyzed the multicast handover retardation time and the entire overhead by a mathematical model, and tried to evaluate the performance in two different ways. The handover retardation time is by reference to the parameter values of [6], the entire overhead is by reference to the parameter values of [7], it is the same as in Table 1.

4.3 The Entire Overhead Analysis

This section provides performance evaluation results according to the entire overhead costs. As explained in Sect. 4.2, the costs of the entire overhead is the sum of query message, registration costs, and costs of packet tunneling. The explanation and the value of the parameter which has been applied are by reference to [2]. A formula for calculating the network overhead costs of HMIPv6 [8] and PMIPv6 is a data for a mathematical modeling of each multicast network costs, and it is excluded from the performance evaluation.

Figure 3 is the overhead of entire network in accordance with an increase in MN per MAG. With the increase of the number of MN, both PMIPv6 multicast handover procedure and two proposed multicast handover procedure linearly increased. Although multicast network between LMA by second proposed LMA tunneling is lower than PMIPv6 multicast network proposed from IETF, we can find that the entire overhead of multicast network between LMA through first proposed MAG tunneling is lowest.

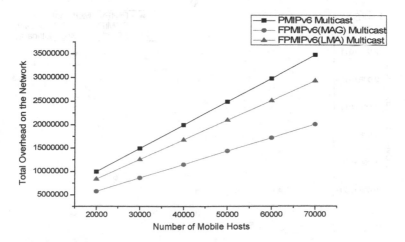

Fig. 3. The overhead of entire network in accordance with an increase in MN per MAG.

Figure 4 is the overhead of entire network in accordance with an increase in SMR. SMR is defined as $T_r \times \lambda_s$ and we fix λ_s as 0.01 and increase T_r to calculate SMR in Fig. 4. We can find that the overhead of entire network decreases according to increasing of SMR (Session to Mobility Ratio). Although multicast network between LMA by second proposed LMA tunneling is lower than PMIPv6 multicast network proposed from IETF, we can find that the entire overhead of multicast network between LMA through first proposed MAG tunneling is lowest.

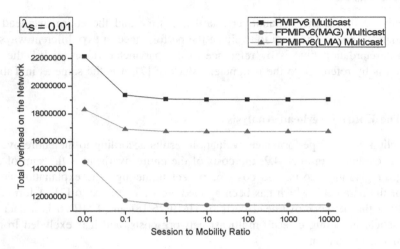

Fig. 4. The overhead of entire network in accordance with an increase in SMR. ($\lambda_s = 0.01$).

Figures 5 and 6 are also the overhead in accordance with SMR, and it differs from Fig. 4 because it presented the overhead of entire network according to fixing T_r and increasing λ_s. We can find that the overhead of entire network increases according to

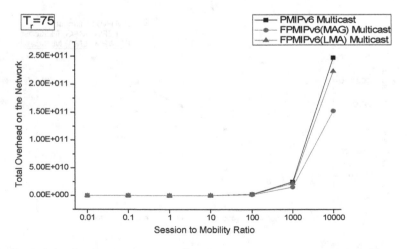

Fig. 5. Overhead of entire network in accordance with an increase in SMR. ($T_r = 75$).

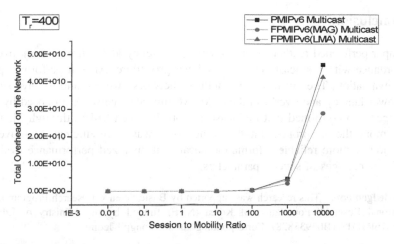

Fig. 6. Overhead of entire network in accordance with an increase in SMR. ($T_r = 400$).

fixing T_r and increasing λ_s, and although the fixed value of T_r increases, the overhead of entire network increases much more.

Figure 7 is the overhead in accordance with an increase in CN. As CN increases, the overhead of entire network increases linearly. Although multicast network between LMA by second proposed LMA tunneling is lower than PMIPv6 multicast network proposed from IETF, we can find that the entire overhead of multicast network between LMA through first proposed MAG tunneling is lowest.

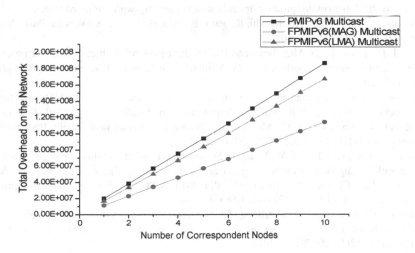

Fig. 7. The overhead of entire network in accordance with an increase in CN.

5   Conclusion

This paper performed mathematical modeling of latency and entire network overhead in accordance with multicast network handover procedure. Also, it performed performance evaluation, The our proposed multicast networks were found to have substantially lower latency and overhead than PMIPv6 multicast network proposed by IETF. This paper also confirmed that multicast network between LMAs through MAG tunneling among the our proposed multicast networks was more efficient. Moreover, this paper showed more reliable information because it analyzed performance evaluation through the changes of several parameters.

Acknowledgements. This research was supported by Basic Science Research Program through the National Research Foundation of Korea (NRF) funded by the Ministry of Education (NRF-2016R1D1A1B03933828). Corresponding author: Jongpil Jeong.

References

1. Romdhani, I., Kellil, M., Lach, H.-Y.: IP mobile multicast: challenges and solutions. IEEE Commun. Surv. Tutor. **6**(1), 18–41 (2004)
2. Gundavelli, S., Leung, K., Devarapalli, V., Chowdhury, K., Patil, B.: Proxy Mobile IPv6. IETF RFC 5213 (2008)
3. Li, Y., Su, H., Su, L., Jin, D., Zeng, L.: A comprehensive performance evaluation of PMIPv6 over IP-based cellular networks. In: Vehicular Technology Conference (VTC Spring), pp. 1–6 (2009)
4. IETF MultiMob working group. https://datatracker.ietf.org/wg/multimob/charter/
5. Yokota, H., Chowdhury, K., Koodli, R., Patil, B., Xia, F.: Fast Handovers for Proxy Mobile IPv6. IETF RFC 5949 (2010)
6. Lee, J.-H., Ernst, T., IMARA Team and INRIA: Fast PMIPv6 multicast handover procedure for mobility-unaware mobile nodes. In: Vehicular Technology Conference (VTC Spring), pp. 1–5 (2011)
7. Hossain, M.S., Atiquzzaman, M., Ivancic, W.: Cost analysis of mobility entities of hierarchical mobile IPv6. In: Military Communications Conference, pp. 2280–2285 (2011)
8. Soliman, H., Castelluccia, C., Malki, K.E., Bellier, L.: Hierarchical Mobile IPv6 mobility management (HMIPv6). IETF RFC 5380 (2008)
9. Jang, H., Song, B., Cheong, Y., Jeong, J.: Sensor-based global mobility management scheme with multicasting support for building IoT applications. In: Rocha, Á., Correia, A.M., Adeli, H., Reis, L.P., Costanzo, S. (eds.) WorldCIST 2017. AISC, vol. 570, pp. 289–299. Springer, Cham (2017). doi:10.1007/978-3-319-56538-5_30
10. Cho, C., Choi, Y.J., Jeong, J., Chung, T.M.: Performance analysis of inter-domain handoff scheme based on virtual layer in PMIPv6 networks for IP-based internet of things. PLoS ONE **12**(1), e0170566 (2017)

Software Techniques for Implementing Dynamic Network-Aware Energy-Efficient Download Managers

Louis Soleyn and Dwaine Clarke[(✉)]

University of the West Indies, Bridgetown, Barbados
louis.soleyn@mycavehill.uwi.edu, declarke@declarke.net

Abstract. We introduce novel software techniques to implement dynamic, network-aware, energy-efficient download managers that significantly reduce battery drain due to weak Wi-Fi signal strength. These techniques are designed to be used in download managers that are implemented as an option for data-intensive, delay-tolerant mobile applications to use to download data. The techniques include polling the network to determine when the Wi-Fi signal strength is above a user-configurable signal-strength threshold to start or continue downloading files, and polling the network during file downloads to determine if the signal strength falls below the signal-strength threshold to pause file downloads. When a file download is paused because the signal strength is below the signal-strength threshold, the user has the option of overriding this feature to continue the file download if the user needs the file immediately. We also introduce a novel dynamic, network-aware, energy-efficient download manager, the Lemur download manager, that implements these techniques. We present results that demonstrate that the Lemur download manager significantly reduces battery drain due to weak Wi-Fi signal strength.

Keywords: Battery drain · Dynamic · Energy efficiency · Software techniques · Wireless networks

1 Introduction

The rate at which smartphone ownership is increasing is remarkable. While there have been many advances in the capabilities and design of modern smartphones, one of the most problematic areas continues to be that of battery capabilities. Research has been conducted to highlight various elements that contribute to battery drain. These elements include the signal strength of the Wi-Fi network. Factors that can cause weak Wi-Fi signal strength to increase battery drain include increased frame transmission time, data link layer retransmissions, access point disassociations and reassociations, and decreased TCP throughput [5,7].

We introduce novel software techniques to implement dynamic, network-aware, energy-efficient download managers that significantly reduce battery

© Springer International Publishing AG 2017
M. Younas et al. (Eds.): MobiWIS 2017, LNCS 10486, pp. 237–249, 2017.
DOI: 10.1007/978-3-319-65515-4_20

drain due to weak Wi-Fi signal strength. The techniques include polling the network to determine when the Wi-Fi signal strength is above a user-configurable signal-strength threshold to start or continue downloading files, and polling the network during file downloads to determine if the signal strength falls below the signal-strength threshold to pause file downloads. When the file download is paused because the signal strength is below the signal-strength threshold, the user has the option of overriding this feature to continue the file download if the user needs the file immediately. We also introduce a novel dynamic, network-aware, energy-efficient download manager, the Lemur download manager, that implements these techniques to reduce battery drain due to weak Wi-Fi signal strength.

The techniques we introduce in this paper are designed to be used in download managers that are implemented as an option for data-intensive, delay-tolerant mobile applications to use to download data. Many mobile applications can download data in the background without affecting user experience [17]. Examples of data-intensive, delay-tolerant mobile applications include a video tutorial mobile application that allows a user to download videos onto a smartphone in the background for the user to view at a later time and a digital media management application that allows a user to upload photos and videos onto a server in the background for the user to use at a later time.

An example of a scenario where these techniques can be useful is a student who experiences his smartphone battery typically draining faster when he is at the university he attends than when he is at home. The student observes that the Wi-Fi signal strength is generally weak at the university whereas the Wi-Fi signal strength is generally strong at home. The student may opt to use the Lemur download manager for data-intensive, delay-tolerant mobile applications to dynamically conserve battery power when he experiences weak Wi-Fi signal strength.

The main contributions of this paper include:

- the introduction of novel software techniques to implement dynamic, network-aware, energy-efficient download managers that significantly reduce battery drain due to weak Wi-Fi signal strength.
- the introduction of a novel dynamic, network-aware, energy-efficient download manager, the Lemur download manager, that implements the software techniques we introduce in this paper. We implement the Lemur download manager as an option for data-intensive, delay-tolerant mobile applications to use to download data to reduce battery drain due to weak Wi-Fi signal strength.
- the establishment of bases for recommended values for the polling intervals.
- results demonstrating that the Lemur download manager significantly reduces battery drain due to weak Wi-Fi signal strength. Our experiments use files from a web site that is designed for a mobile application. We present results using a hardware power monitor.

2 Design

2.1 Algorithm

Figure 1 presents the algorithm that presents the software techniques we introduce in this paper. The download manager has a user-configurable setting for a Wi-Fi signal strength threshold, the signal strength threshold (SST). When the Wi-Fi signal strength is above the SST, the Wi-Fi signal strength is considered to be strong. When the Wi-Fi signal strength is below the SST, the Wi-Fi signal strength is considered to be weak. When the download manager has a file to download, it first queues the file then checks the Wi-Fi signal strength. If the Wi-Fi signal strength is weak, the download manager pauses the file download and polls the network to determine when the Wi-Fi signal strength is above

```
If there is a file to download
    Queue the file to download.
    Check Wi-Fi signal strength.
    If Wi-Fi signal strength < SST
        BelowThresholdMethod()
    Else
        AboveThresholdMethod()


BelowThresholdMethod()
    After below threshold seconds, check Wi-Fi signal strength.
    If Wi-Fi signal strength > SST
        AboveThresholdMethod()
    Else
        BelowThresholdMethod()


AboveThresholdMethod()
    If there is a file to download in the queue
        Download the next above threshold bytes of the file.
        Check Wi-Fi signal strength.
        If Wi-Fi signal strength < SST
            BelowThresholdMethod()
        Else
            AboveThresholdMethod()


If the user opts to download a paused file download
    Download the file.


If the user opts to cancel a paused or active file download
    Cancel the file download.
```

Fig. 1. Algorithm.

the SST. We denote the interval at which the download manager is below the SST and polls the network to determine when the Wi-Fi signal strength is above the SST to start or continue downloading files as below threshold seconds. The below threshold seconds interval is measured in seconds, i.e., every below threshold seconds, the download manager re-checks the network to determine if the Wi-Fi signal strength is strong. When the Wi-Fi signal strength is above the SST, the download manager starts to download the file and polls the network to determine if the Wi-Fi signal strength falls below the SST. We denote the interval at which the download manager is above the SST and polls the network during file downloads to determine if the Wi-Fi signal strength falls below the SST to pause file downloads as above threshold bytes. The above threshold bytes interval is measured in bytes, i.e., every above threshold bytes of the file that the download manager has downloaded, the download manager re-checks the network to determine if the Wi-Fi signal strength is weak. If the Wi-Fi signal strength falls below the SST, the download manager pauses the file download until the Wi-Fi signal strength is above the SST again. Similar to the SST, below threshold seconds and above threshold bytes are also settings that a user can configure in the download manager.

When the download manager pauses a file download because the Wi-Fi signal strength is weak, the user has the option of overriding this feature to continue the file download if the user needs the file immediately. The user also has the option of setting the SST to zero, effectively disabling the SST, to override all of the paused file downloads to continue all of the file downloads if the user needs all of the files immediately.

The user also has the option of canceling a paused file download or canceling a file download that is active. If the user chooses to cancel a file download, the download manager cancels the file download.

The techniques we introduce in this paper are designed to be used in download managers that are implemented as an option for data-intensive, delay-tolerant mobile applications (cf. Sect. 1) to use to download data. An example of a scenario where these techniques can be useful is a student who experiences his smartphone battery typically draining faster when he is at the university he attends than when he is at home. The student observes that the Wi-Fi signal strength is generally weak at the university whereas the Wi-Fi signal strength is generally strong at home. The student may opt to use the Lemur download manager for data-intensive, delay-tolerant mobile applications to dynamically conserve battery power when he experiences weak Wi-Fi signal strength.

2.2   Dynamic, Network-Aware, Energy-Efficient Download Manager

We also introduce a novel dynamic, network-aware, energy-efficient download manager, the Lemur download manager, that implements the software techniques we introduce in Sect. 2.1. The Android download manager [8] does not take into consideration Wi-Fi signal strength when transferring data. We implement the Lemur download manager as an option for data-intensive, delay-tolerant mobile applications (cf. Sect. 1) to use to download data. Continuing with our example in Sect. 2.1 of the student who observes that the Wi-Fi signal strength is generally weak at the university he attends, an example of a mobile application for which the student may want to use the Lemur download manager instead of the Android download manager to dynamically conserve battery power when he experiences weak Wi-Fi signal strength is the edX mobile application [9]. The edX mobile application, similar to other video tutorial mobile applications, allows a user to download a course's lectures' videos onto the user's smartphone in the background for the user to view at a later time. The edX mobile application is popular, with over one million downloads on the Google Play digital distribution service [10].

When a mobile application requests that the Lemur download manager download a file onto the user's smartphone, the Lemur download manager downloads the file in the background using the software techniques we introduce in Sect. 2.1 to transfer data during periods of strong Wi-Fi signal strength to reduce battery drain. When the Lemur download manager pauses a file download because the Wi-Fi signal strength is weak, the user has the option of overriding this feature to continue the file download if the user needs the file immediately. If the user chooses this option, the Lemur download manager advises the user that the Wi-Fi signal strength is weak and downloading the file can significantly increase the user's smartphone's battery drain, and asks the user to confirm the user's decision before the Lemur download manager continues the file download in the background. The user also has the option of setting the SST to zero, effectively disabling the SST, to override all of the paused file downloads to continue all of the file downloads if the user needs all of the files immediately. If the user chooses to set the SST to zero, the Lemur download manager advises the user that downloading files when the Wi-Fi signal strength is weak can significantly increase the user's smartphone's battery drain, and asks the user to confirm the user's decision before setting the SST to zero. The user also has the option of canceling a paused file download or canceling a file download that is active. If the user chooses to cancel a file download, the Lemur download manager cancels the file download.

3   Implementation

We chose to develop the Lemur download manager using the Android mobile operating system [3] because of the operating system's popularity. The Lemur download manager provides a menu in which a user can configure the SST, below threshold seconds and above threshold bytes. We provide recommended values for below threshold seconds and above threshold bytes based on our results in Sect. 4.

Three of the main Java classes in our implementation of the Lemur download manager are the InformationReceiver Java class, the DownloadService Java class and the UserInterface Java class. When a mobile application requests that the Lemur download manager download a file, the Lemur download manager's InformationReceiver class receives the file's information from the mobile application.

The Lemur download manager uses its DownloadService class, which extends the IntentService class [11], to download files in the background. We implement and use the Lemur download manager's DownloadService class instead of using the Android download manager because the Android download manager does not allow for pausing of a download based on a condition such as the strength of the Wi-Fi signal. The Lemur download manager's DownloadService class performs downloads on a background thread, which helps to conserve energy. The Lemur download manager's UserInterface class informs the mobile application's user about the status of a file download, i.e., no connection, paused, complete, etc. The Lemur download manager's UserInterface class also provides a user interface that allows a user to view the statuses of file downloads, override paused file downloads and cancel file downloads.

As described in Sect. 2.2, when a mobile application requests that the Lemur download manager download a file, the Lemur download manager downloads the file in the background using the software techniques we introduce in Sect. 2.1 to transfer data during periods of strong Wi-Fi signal strength to reduce battery drain. When a mobile application requests that the Lemur download manager download a file, the InformationReceiver class receives the file's information, including the file's title and the file's Uniform Resource Locator (URL), from the mobile application. The InformationReceiver class first queues the file then calls the DownloadService class to check the Wi-Fi signal strength. If the Wi-Fi signal strength is weak, the DownloadService class notifies the InformationReceiver class that the file download is paused. The InformationReceiver class then creates an instance of the AlarmManager class [2] to run the DownloadService class to re-check the Wi-Fi signal strength after below threshold seconds. The choice of using the AlarmManager was important since the AlarmManager is a system service that can run in the background and run the DownloadService class at specific intervals even if the Lemur download manager is not currently running. It is also important to note that the AlarmManager's alarms can be batched by the OS to conserve energy when multiple alarms fire simultaneously.

The InformationReceiver class uses the AlarmManager to repeatedly run the DownloadService class to re-check Wi-Fi signal strength after below threshold seconds until the Wi-Fi signal strength is above the SST. When the Wi-Fi signal strength is strong, the DownloadService class opens an HTTP connection to the server then starts to download the file or resumes the file download if it was previously downloading then paused. After the DownloadService class downloads above threshold bytes of the file, the DownloadService class re-checks the Wi-Fi signal strength to determine if it is still above the SST. If the Wi-Fi signal strength is still strong, the DownloadService class continues the file download, repeatedly checking the Wi-Fi signal strength each time above threshold bytes of the file is transferred. If the Wi-Fi signal strength is determined to be weak at any of these checks, the DownloadService class pauses the file download, closes the HTTP connection to conserve energy, and notifies the InformationReceiver class as previously described. When the DownloadService class completes the file download, it notifies the InformationReceiver class that the file download is complete.

When the DownloadService class notifies the InformationReceiver class about a file download, it also notifies the UserInterface class about the file download as well. The UserInterface class informs the mobile application's user about the status of a file download, i.e., no connection, paused, complete, etc. The UserInterface class also provides a user interface that allows a user to view the statuses of file downloads. This user interface also allows a user to override paused file downloads if the user needs the files immediately. This user interface also allows a user to cancel file downloads.

4   Results

We use hardware-based energy measurement [19] using the Monsoon Power Monitor [14] for accurate energy measurement. The Monsoon Power Monitor has an output sampling rate of 5000 Hz. We use a factory default settings Samsung Galaxy S4 Android smartphone for our experiments. A Samsung Galaxy S4 smartphone has a battery that can be detached from the smartphone, allowing the smartphone to be connected to and powered by the Monsoon Power Monitor.

For our experiments, we downloaded MP4 videos from a course provided by edX [9]. The edX mobile application, similar to other video tutorial mobile applications, allows a user to download a course's lectures' videos onto the user's smartphone in the background for the user to view at a later time. For our hardware-based energy measurement experiments, we use a set of MP4 videos from one of the lectures of one of the courses provided by edX. The total size of the lecture's set of video files is 105.9 MB. An Apache 2.4 HTTP server running on a Linux machine with 32 GB of RAM and 3.40 GHz processor hosts the 105.9 MB set of video files.

We use two routers: one router is located within the same room as the smartphone and generates the maximum Wi-Fi signal strength; the second router is located on a different floor from the smartphone and typically generates a signal 27% to 35% of the maximum Wi-Fi signal strength. We set the SST to 50% of the maximum Wi-Fi signal strength. Thus, when the smartphone is connected to the network generated by the router in the same room as the smartphone, it is connected to a network with strong Wi-Fi signal strength and when the smartphone is connected to the network generated by the router on a different floor from the smartphone, it is connected to a network with weak Wi-Fi signal strength. Each router is connected to the same wired network.

We conducted experiments to establish a basis for a recommended value for below threshold seconds. For each setting of below threshold seconds, we repeated the experiment 20 times and present the average result. Table 1 presents the energy consumption after the Lemur download manager runs for 10 min when the smartphone is connected to the network with weak Wi-Fi signal strength for different values of below threshold seconds. The Lemur download manager polls the network without transferring data. Based on the results presented in Table 1, we recommend and use 60 s (1 min) as our value for below threshold seconds in the Lemur download manager as the reduction in the energy consumption tapered off at 60 s.

Table 1. Energy consumption after the Lemur download manager runs for 10 min on the weak network for different values of below threshold seconds.

Below threshold seconds (s)	Energy consumption (μAh)
5	8581.7
30	2850.148
60	2248.9825
120	2183.762

Table 2. Time and energy consumption for the Lemur download manager to download the 105.9 MB set of video files from the server on the strong network for different values of above threshold bytes.

Above threshold bytes (MB)	Time (s)	Energy consumption (μAh)
0.1	392.7955	14932.05
0.5	381.305	14291.54
1	346.02	12770.52
2	343.8625	12827.72

We conducted experiments to establish a basis for a recommended value for above threshold bytes. For each setting of above threshold bytes, we repeated the experiment 20 times and present the average result. Table 2 presents the time and energy consumption for the Lemur download manager to download the 105.9 MB set of video files from the server on the strong network for different values of above threshold bytes. Based on the results presented in Table 2, we recommend and use 1MB as our value for above threshold bytes in the Lemur download manager as the reduction in the energy consumption tapered off at 1 MB.

Table 3. Time and energy consumption of basic dm on weak network, Lemur dm on weak network then strong network, Lemur dm on strong network and basic dm on strong network.

	Time (s)	Energy consumption (μAh)
Basic dm on weak network	609.2935	22511.99
Lemur dm on weak network then strong network	669.1985	14270.3185
Lemur dm on strong network	352.2025	12849.41
Basic dm on strong network	342.6165	12443.26

We also implemented a basic download manager that does not implement the software techniques we introduce in this paper. The basic download manager downloads files from a server but does not check the Wi-Fi signal strength.

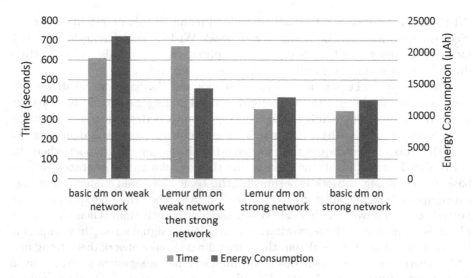

Fig. 2. Comparison of the time and the energy consumption of basic dm on weak network, Lemur dm on weak network then strong network, Lemur dm on strong network and basic dm on strong network.

We implemented a video tutorial application and configure it to use either the Lemur download manager or the basic download manager. We use this video tutorial application for our experiments to evaluate the performances of the Lemur download manager and the basic download manager. For each of the following experiments, we repeated the experiment 20 times and present the average result. Table 3 presents the time and energy consumption of the basic download manager when the basic download manager downloads the 105.9 MB set of video files from the server when the smartphone is connected to the network with weak Wi-Fi signal strength (basic dm on weak network), the Lemur download manager when the smartphone is connected to the network with weak Wi-Fi signal strength for approximately 5 min then the smartphone is switched to the network with strong Wi-Fi signal strength and the Lemur download manager downloads the 105.9 MB set of video files from the server (Lemur dm on weak network then strong network), the Lemur download manager when the Lemur download manager downloads the 105.9 MB set of video files from the server when the smartphone is connected to the network with strong Wi-Fi signal strength (Lemur dm on strong network), and the basic download manager when the basic download manager downloads the 105.9 MB set of video files from the server when the smartphone is connected to the network with strong Wi-Fi signal strength (basic dm on strong network). Figure 2 compares the time and the energy consumption of the four experiments using the results in Table 3. In the Lemur dm on weak network then strong network experiment, the time of 5 minutes was chosen because, as presented in Table 3, the Lemur download manager takes 352.2025 s to complete the download on the network with strong

Wi-Fi signal strength and the basic download manager takes 609.2935 s to complete the download on the network with weak Wi-Fi signal strength. This is a measure to control for factors in the smartphone that could also affect battery drain during the duration that the experiments are run.

Comparing the Lemur dm on strong network and the basic dm on strong network experiments, even with the Lemur download manager's added functionality, which results in polling while the file is being downloaded, the increase in energy consumption $(406.15\mu Ah)$ is minimal. This is significant because it demonstrates that the software techniques that we introduce have minimal impact when the Wi-Fi signal strength is strong. Comparing the basic dm on weak network and the basic dm on strong network experiments, the basic download manager's energy consumption is significantly greater $(10,068.73\mu Ah)$ when the smartphone is connected to the network with weak Wi-Fi signal strength than when the smartphone is connected to the network with strong Wi-Fi signal strength. Comparing the basic dm on weak network and the Lemur dm on weak network then strong network experiments, the Lemur download manager has a significant reduction in energy consumption $(8,241.6715\mu Ah)$ when compared with the basic download manager. Table 3 and Fig. 2 show that, even with the Lemur download manager's added functionality which results in polling the network, the Lemur download manager significantly reduces battery drain when the Wi-Fi signal strength is weak and the Lemur download manager's energy consumption in both of its experiments are similar to the basic download manager's energy consumption on the strong network.

5 Related Work

Ding et al. [7] examined the factors that can cause weak Wi-Fi signal strength to increase battery drain. The authors also conducted studies that revealed that, on average, smartphone users experience weak Wi-Fi signal strength roughly 25% of the time. The authors present a power model that incorporates Wi-Fi signal strength. In this paper, we introduce novel software techniques to implement dynamic, network-aware, energy-efficient download managers that significantly reduce battery drain due to weak Wi-Fi signal strength. We also introduce a novel dynamic, network-aware, energy-efficient download manager, the Lemur download manager, that implements these techniques to reduce battery drain due to weak Wi-Fi signal strength.

Aqil et al. [4] present a system that allows a user to select a lower resolution video to download onto the user's smartphone to reduce battery drain. Though a lower resolution video has a smaller file size, it also has a lower quality. Thus, this approach lessens the quality of the user experience, which is particularly not good for instructional and tutorial videos.

Li and Chen [13] present a mobile application implementing an algorithm that runs the sleep function in between Wi-Fi signal strength checks, even when there is strong Wi-Fi signal strength that allows file downloads. As described in Sect. 2, in the algorithm we introduce in this paper, there are different methods for when there is strong Wi-Fi signal strength and for when there is weak Wi-Fi signal strength. Furthermore, when there is strong Wi-Fi signal strength, our algorithm checks the Wi-Fi signal strength after each above threshold bytes of a file download. Also, in our algorithm, when the download manager pauses a file download because the Wi-Fi signal strength is weak, the user has the option of overriding this feature to continue the file download if the user needs the file immediately. The user also has the option of canceling a paused file download or canceling a file download that is active. In this paper, we introduce the Lemur download manager, a novel dynamic, network-aware, energy-efficient download manager. We implement the Lemur download manager as an option for data-intensive, delay-tolerant mobile applications to use to download data to reduce battery drain due to weak Wi-Fi signal strength. As described in Sect. 3, when there is weak Wi-Fi signal strength, our implementation of the Lemur download manager uses the AlarmManager to run the DownloadService class at specific intervals because of the advantages the AlarmManager provides.

Nicholson and Noble [15] present a system that tracks the movement of a device's owner to forecast when he will be in time intervals of strong Wi-Fi signal strength. However, if the device's owner changes his habits, a mobile application that uses this system can download data when the Wi-Fi signal strength is weak. The Lemur download manager dynamically determines when there is strong Wi-Fi signal strength to download files.

Krashinsky and Balakrishnan [12] present an alternative to the IEEE 802.11 power-saving mode (PSM) that dynamically adapts to network activity to reduce battery drain. Rozner et al. [18] reduced the energy consumed by PSM implementations to reduce battery drain. Cui et al. [6] introduce PerEs, an adaptive online scheduling algorithm that uses information about task deadlines, application profiles and user preferences to reduce the energy consumption of mobile devices in cellular networks. Ra et al. [17] examine the energy-delay trade-off in mobile applications and present the SALSA algorithm, designed using the Lyapunov optimization framework, to automatically determine whether and when to send data over Wi-Fi or 3G/EDGE networks. Zhang et al. [20] introduce PowerBooter, an automated power model construction technique, and PowerTutor, a power monitor mobile application that utilizes the model generated by PowerBooter for online power estimation. Pering et al. [16] introduce CoolSpots, a system in which a mobile device automatically switches between Wi-Fi and Bluetooth to reduce the mobile device's energy consumption during wireless communication. Agarwal et al. [1] modify the VoIP architecture to reduce battery drain for VoIP on smartphones. Zhang and Shin [21] present a mechanism to reduce the clock rate of the radio when a device is idly listening to reduce energy consumption in Wi-Fi networks.

6   Future Work

The Android download manager [8] is a system service that downloads files in the background. The Lemur download manager's DownloadService class extends the

IntentService class [11] and also downloads files in the background. An area of future work is implementing the software techniques we introduce in this paper in the Android download manager to develop an implementation of the Android download manager that significantly reduces battery drain due to weak Wi-Fi signal strength. Future work also includes introducing other algorithms, such as an exponential-increase/additive-increase algorithm, to implement dynamic, network-aware, energy-efficient download managers.

7   Conclusion

We have introduced novel software techniques to implement dynamic, network-aware, energy-efficient download managers that significantly reduce battery drain due to weak Wi-Fi signal strength. These techniques are designed to be used in download managers that are implemented as an option for data-intensive, delay-tolerant mobile applications to use to download data. We also introduced a novel dynamic, network-aware, energy-efficient download manager, the Lemur download manager, that implements these techniques. We presented results that demonstrate that the Lemur download manager significantly reduces battery drain due to weak Wi-Fi signal strength.

References

1. Agarwal, Y., Chandra, R., Wolman, A., Bahl, P., Chin, K., Gupta, R.K.: Wireless wakeups revisited: energy management for VoIP over Wi-Fi smartphones. In: 5th International Conference on Mobile Systems, Applications and Services (MobiSys 2007), pp. 179–191. ACM, June 2007
2. AlarmManager.   https://developer.android.com/reference/android/app/Alarm Manager.html
3. Android. https://www.android.com/
4. Aqil, A., Atya, A.O.F., Krishnamurthy, S.V., Papageorgiou, G.: Streaming lower quality video over LTE: how much energy can you save? In: 23rd IEEE International Conference on Network Protocols (ICNP 2015), pp. 156–167. IEEE Computer Society, November 2015
5. Chen, X., Ding, N., Jindal, A., Hu, Y.C., Gupta, M., Vannithamby, R.: Smartphone energy drain in the wild: analysis and implications. In: 2015 ACM SIGMETRICS International Conference on Measurement and Modeling of Computer Systems (SIGMETRICS 2015), pp. 151–164. ACM, June 2015
6. Cui, Y., Xiao, S., Wang, X., Li, M., Wang, H., Lai, Z.: Performance-aware energy optimization on mobile devices in cellular network. In: 2014 IEEE Conference on Computer Communications (INFOCOM 2014), pp. 1123–1131. IEEE, April 2014
7. Ding, N., Wagner, D., Chen, X., Pathak, A., Hu, Y.C., Rice, A.: Characterizing and modeling the impact of wireless signal strength on smartphone battery drain. In: 2013 ACM SIGMETRICS International Conference on Measurement and Modeling of Computer Systems (SIGMETRICS 2013), pp. 29–40. ACM, June 2013
8. DownloadManager. https://developer.android.com/reference/android/app/Down loadManager.html
9. edX. https://www.edx.org/

10. Google Play: edX. https://play.google.com/store/apps/details?id=org.edx.mobile
11. IntentService.   https://developer.android.com/reference/android/app/Intent Service.html
12. Krashinsky, R., Balakrishnan, H.: Minimizing energy for wireless web access with bounded slowdown. In: 8th Annual International Conference on Mobile Computing and Networking (MobiCom 2002), pp. 119–130. ACM, September 2002
13. Li, H., Chen, L.: RSSI-aware energy saving for large file downloading on smartphones. IEEE Embed. Syst. Lett. **7**(2), 63–66 (2015)
14. Monsoon Solutions Inc. Power Monitor. https://www.msoon.com/LabEquipment/ PowerMonitor/
15. Nicholson, A.J., Noble, B.D.: BreadCrumbs: forecasting mobile connectivity. In: 14th Annual International Conference on Mobile Computing and Networking (MobiCom 2008), pp. 46–57. ACM, September 2008
16. Pering, T., Agarwal, Y., Gupta, R.K., Want, R.: CoolSpots: reducing the power consumption of wireless mobile devices with multiple radio interfaces. In: 4th International Conference on Mobile Systems, Applications and Services (MobiSys 2006), pp. 220–232. ACM, June 2006
17. Ra, M.-R., Paek, J., Sharma, A.B., Govindan, R., Krieger, M.H., Neely, M.J.: Energy-delay tradeoffs in smartphone applications. In: 8th International Conference on Mobile Systems, Applications and Services (MobiSys 2010), pp. 255–270. ACM, June 2010
18. Rozner, E., Navda, V., Ramjee, R., Rayanchu, S.K.: NAPman: network-assisted power management for WiFi devices. In: 8th International Conference on Mobile Systems, Applications and Services (MobiSys 2010), pp. 91–106. ACM, June 2010
19. Tarkoma, S., Siekkinen, M., Laagerspetz, E., Xiao, Y.: Smartphone Energy Consumption: Modeling and Optimization. Cambridge University Press, New York (2014)
20. Zhang, L., Tiwana, B., Qian, Z., Wang, Z., Dick, R.P., Mao, Z.M., Yang, L.: Accurate online power estimation and automatic battery behavior based power model generation for smartphones. In: 8th International Conference on Hardware/Software Codesign and System Synthesis (CODES+ISSS 2010), pp. 105–114. ACM, October 2010
21. Zhang, X., Shin, K.G.: E-MiLi: energy-minimizing idle listening in wireless networks. In: 17th Annual International Conference on Mobile Computing and Networking (MobiCom 2011), pp. 205–216. ACM, September 2011

New Formulations for an Optimal Connectivity Approach for Mobile Ad-hoc Networks

Pablo Adasme$^{(\boxtimes)}$, Ismael Soto, and Fabian Seguel

Departamento de Ingeniería Eléctrica, Universidad de Santiago de Chile,
Avenida Ecuador 3519, Santiago, Chile
{pablo.adasme,ismael.soto,fabian.seguelg}@usach.cl

Abstract. In this paper, we propose new formulations for the optimal connectivity of a tree backbone topology for mobile ad-hoc networks (MANETs). Applications of MANETs include military communications, emergency and disaster recovery, and e-commerce to name a few. Formally, given a graph $G = (V \cup K, E)$ with set of wireless sensor nodes V, a set of connection links E, and a set of K users, the problem is to find a backbone spanning tree network topology with as many leaves as possible in order to maximize capacity at the lowest power costs for the users which are connected to the leaf nodes of the backbone network. For this purpose, we model a MANET by means of disk graphs where each disk represents the Euclidean distance transmission range of a node $v \in V$. We propose an exponential and a compact polynomial formulation for the problem. The exponential model is characterized with constraints from the classical maximum leaf spanning tree polytope [18] whilst the compact formulation is characterized with constraints adapted from the classical minimum dominating tree problem [2]. The latter formulation is further strengthened with selected valid inequalities referred to as generalized sub-tour elimination constraints [9]. Our preliminary numerical results indicate that the compact model with additional valid inequalities allows to solve instances to optimality in significantly short CPU time for transmission distances ranging from 100 to 150 ms.

1 Introduction

Mobile ad-hoc networks (Manets) has become a hot topic research field within last decades [12,14–17,19,22]. Mainly, due to the innumerable real-life applications in engineering and wireless network design problem domains. Applications of MANETs include: military communications, emergency and disaster recovery, e-commerce, medicine, transportation, agriculture, industrial process control, environmental and health monitoring systems, smart buildings and cities, among many others [3,4,22].

In particular, concerning backbone network configurations for MANETs, the literature is diverse and problem dependant [5,11,13,20,21,23,24]. For instance in [24], the authors consider the problem of constructing an energy-efficient virtual network backbone for broadcasting applications using directional antennas.

© Springer International Publishing AG 2017
M. Younas et al. (Eds.): MobiWIS 2017, LNCS 10486, pp. 250–262, 2017.
DOI: 10.1007/978-3-319-65515-4_21

Whereas in [13], the authors propose distributed solutions based on reducing the density of the networks in order to minimize the energy consumption. In [20], the authors propose a multicast routing scheme using multiple reliable rings as a backbone network configuration. In this paper, we propose new formulations for the optimal connectivity of a tree backbone topology. Formally, given a graph $G = (V \cup K, E)$ with set of wireless sensor nodes V, a set of connection links E, and a set of K users, the problem is to find a backbone spanning tree network topology with as many leaves as possible in order to maximize capacity at the lowest power costs for the users which are connected to the leaf nodes of the backbone network. For this purpose, we model a MANET by means of disk graphs where each disk represents the Euclidean distance transmission range of a node $v \in V$. We propose an exponential and a compact polynomial formulation for the problem. The exponential model is characterized with constraints from the classical maximum leaf spanning tree polytope [18] whilst the compact formulation is characterized with constraints adapted from the classical minimum dominating tree problem [2]. The latter formulation is further strengthened with selected valid inequalities referred to as generalized sub-tour elimination constraints [9].

It is well known that there exists a direct equivalence between the classical maximum leaf spanning tree and minimum dominating tree problems [10,18]. Given a graph $G - (V, E)$ with set of nodes V and links E, a subset $S \in V$ is called dominating if every vertex of $V \setminus S$ shares an edge of G with a vertex of S. The dominating subset S is said to be connected when the subgraph $G_S = (S, E(S))$, where the set $E(S)$ denotes the set of links with both endpoints in S, is connected or else contains a single vertex. Consequently, the minimum connected dominating tree problem consists in finding a connected dominating tree of G with minimum vertex cardinality. As a consequence, given a connected dominating tree S of G, one can enlarge such a tree into a spanning tree T of G where all the vertices in $V \setminus S$ are leaves. Conversely, given a maximum leaf spanning tree T of G, a minimum connected dominating tree with subset S can be straightforwardly obtained. As a result, we have that given an optimal solution to one problem, an optimal solution to the other can be efficiently obtained. Finally, we mention that both, the maximum leaf spanning tree and minimum dominating tree problems are NP-hard [8]. As far as we know, new modeling approaches based on these classical NP-Hard problems have not been considered yet in the literature for optimal user connectivity on MANETs.

The remaining of the paper is organized as follows. In Sect. 2, we present a brief system description of the problem and state both the exponential and compact formulations of the problem with and without generalized sub-tour elimination constraints. Subsequently, in Sect. 3, we present an explain an exact iterative procedure which allows to obtain optimal solutions using the exponential model. This procedure is straightforwardly adapted from [1]. Then, in Sect. 4 we conduct preliminary numerical results in order to compare all the proposed models. Finally, in Sect. 5 we give the main conclusions of the paper.

2 System Description and Problem Formulation

In this section, we present a brief system description of the problem and formulate both the exponential and compact formulations of the problem with and without generalized sub-tour elimination constraints.

2.1 System Description

We represent a MANET by means of a disk graph as depicted in Fig. 1. As it can be observed, Fig. 1 represents a feasible solution where the black and circular nodes represent wireless nodes which are connected under a tree network configuration according the their radial transmission ranges. These nodes conform the backbone. This solution has only 3 leaves. Notice that there are 8 users connected only to the leaf nodes of the backbone. This is a reasonable assumption since the dominating nodes manage all the traffic between them. It is clear that there might be a huge number of tree topologies forming the backbone and a huge number of possibilities for the users to be connected to the leaf nodes of the backbone. Furthermore, it is evident that the number of solutions depend on the radial transmission ranges of each node in the network. Notice that the latter also affects directly the density of the disk graphs. The shorter the radial transmission range, the higher the sparsity of the graph. On the opposite, the larger the radial transmission range, the higher the density of the graph. The adaptability of the radial transmission range is a crucial aspect in MANETs as

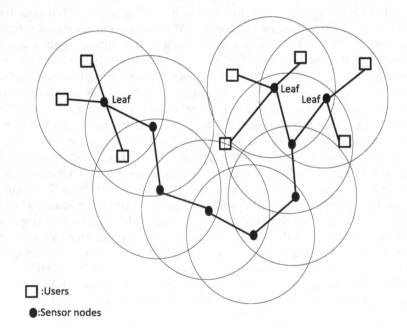

☐ :Users

● :Sensor nodes

Fig. 1. A feasible tree topology network solution.

it allows to control the power consumption of the whole network. This can be explained by the fact that the power consumption increase with the distance between nodes. Thus, we seek for a tree network topology with as many leaves as possible in order to maximize the capacity at the lowest power consumption of all the users to be connected to the leaf nodes of the backbone.

2.2 An Exponential Formulation

In this subsection, we present and explain an exponential formulation for the problem presented in Subsect. 2.1. In particular, we use an exponential number of sub-tour elimination constraints (SECs) to avoid cycles in the resulting backbone network configuration [18]. Let $C_{ku} \in \mathbb{R}_+$ and $P_{ku} \in \mathbb{R}_+$ denote the achievable capacity and power consumption of user $k \in K$ when connected to node $u \in V$, respectively. Let $\alpha \in [0,1]$ be defined as a weighting factor used to handle the two conflicting objectives of capacity and power consumption. We define the binary variables x_e, y_{ku} and z_u, for all $e \in E$, $k \in K$ and $u \in V$ as follows. The variable x_e equals one if the edge e is in the network solution, and equals zero otherwise. Variable y_{ku} equals one if user k is connected to node u, and equals zero otherwise. Similarly, the variable z_u equals one if and only if node u is a leaf node, and equals zero otherwise. Consequently, the exponential model we propose can be formulated as follows

$$P_0: \quad \max_{\{x,y,z\}} \quad \alpha \left\{ \sum_{k\in K} \sum_{u\in V} C_{ku} y_{ku} \right\} - (1-\alpha) \left\{ \sum_{k\in K} \sum_{u\in V} P_{ku} y_{ku} \right\} \tag{1}$$

$$\text{s.t.} \quad \sum_{e\in E} x_e = |V| - 1 \tag{2}$$

$$\sum_{e\in E(S)} x_e \leq |S| - 1, S \subseteq V, |S| \geq 3 \tag{3}$$

$$\sum_{e\in N_{(u)}} x_e + (|N_{(u)}| - 1)z_u \leq |N_{(u)}|, u \in V \tag{4}$$

$$\sum_{e\in N_{(u)}} x_e + z_u \geq 2, u \in V \tag{5}$$

$$y_{ku} \leq z_u, u \in V, k \in K \tag{6}$$

$$\sum_{u\in V} y_{ku} \leq 1, k \in K \tag{7}$$

$$x \in \{0,1\}^{|E|}, z \in \{0,1\}^{|V|} \tag{8}$$

$$y \in \{0,1\}^{|K|\times|V|} \tag{9}$$

Notice that when $\alpha = 1$, the objective function in P_0 only maximizes the capacity of the network. On the opposite, when $\alpha = 0$, the objective function in P_0 only minimizes the capacity of the network. For all the values of $0 < \alpha < 1$, we have the two conflicting objectives in the objective function. In P_0, constraint (2) ensures that the number of edges in the backbone network equals $|V| - 1$.

Whilst the constraints (3) avoid cycles for any subset of nodes $S \subseteq V$ with cardinality $|S| \geq 3$. As mentioned above, this is an exponential number of constraints. Constraints (4)–(5) ensure that if a node $u \in V$ is a leaf node, then its degree should be equal to one. Otherwise, its degree should be between 2 and the maximum number of neighbors the node u has which is equal to $|N_{(u)}|$. The set $N_{(u)}$ is defined as $N_{(u)} = \{v \in V | (u, v) \in E\}$. Constraints (6) ensure that the users can only be connected to leaf nodes whereas the constraints (7) guaranty that each user can be connected to at most one leaf node. Finally, constraints (8)–(9) are domain constraints for the decision variables.

2.3 A Compact Polynomial Formulation

In order to propose an equivalent compact polynomial formulation for P_0, we consider the directed disk graph $H = (V \cup K, A)$ instead of $G = (V \cup K, E)$, where the set of arcs A is obtained from E by replacing each edge $(u, v) \in E$ by the two arcs (u, v) and $(v, u) \in A$. Next, we denote by T the dominating nodes forming a tree backbone and define the binary variables $w_{uv} = 1$ if arc (u, v) belongs to T and $w_{uv} = 0$, otherwise. Additionally, we define the sets $N_{(v)}^{-} = \{u | (u, v) \in A\}$, $N_{(v)}^{+} = \{u | (v, u) \in A\}$, $N_{(v)} = N_{(v)}^{-} \cup N_{(v)}^{+}$, and $N_{[v]} = N_{(v)} \cup \{v\}$. Finally, we associate with each node $v \in V$ a non-negative continuous variable π_v and let $|N_{(v)}|$ represent the degree of node v in the undirected graph G. Thus, an equivalent compact formulation for P_0 can be written by means of the following proposition.

Proposition 1. *The following compact formulation is equivalent to P_0*

$$P_1: \max_{\{w,y,z,\pi\}} \alpha \left\{ \sum_{k \in K} \sum_{u \in V} C_{ku} y_{ku} \right\} - (1 - \alpha) \left\{ \sum_{k \in K} \sum_{u \in V} P_{ku} y_{ku} \right\} \quad (10)$$

$$\sum_{(u,v) \in A} w_{uv} = |V| - 1 - \sum_{u \in V} z_u,$$

$$\pi_v - \pi_u + |V|(1 - w_{uv}) \geq 1, \quad \forall (u, v) \in A, \quad (11)$$

$$\pi_v - \pi_u - |V|(1 - w_{uv}) \leq 1, \quad \forall (u, v) \in A, \quad (12)$$

$$\sum_{u \in N_{(v)}^{+}} w_{vu} + \sum_{u \in N_{(v)}^{-}} w_{uv} + z_v \geq 1, \quad \forall v \in V, \quad (13)$$

$$\sum_{u \in N_{(v)}^{+}} w_{vu} + \sum_{u \in N_{(v)}^{-}} w_{uv} + |N_{(v)}| z_v \leq |N_{(v)}|, \quad \forall v \in V, \quad (14)$$

$$\sum_{u \in N_{(v)}} z_u \leq |N_{(v)}| - 1, \quad \forall v \in V, \quad (15)$$

$$\sum_{u \in N_{(v)}^{-}} w_{uv} \leq 1, \quad \forall v \in V, \quad (16)$$

$$1 \leq \pi_v \leq |V| - 2, \quad \forall v \in V, \tag{17}$$

$$y_{ku} \leq z_u, u \in V, k \in K$$

$$\sum_{u \in V} y_{ku} \leq 1, k \in K$$

$$w \in \{0,1\}^{|A|}, z \in \{0,1\}^{|V|}$$

$$y \in \{0,1\}^{|K| \times |V|}$$

Proof. It is straightforward to prove the correctness of this formulation. First, let us define the complementarity binary variable $\bar{z}_u = 1 - z_u$ to be equal to one if node $u \in V$ is a dominating node in T, and $\bar{z}_u = 0$ otherwise. Then, obviously if its complementarity variable $z_u = 1$, it means that node $u \in V$ is not a dominating vertex in T, which is equivalent to say that it is a leaf node. Subsequently, in [2] (Theorem 1) the authors proved that all possible connected dominating trees can be characterized by the following set of constraints

$$\sum_{(u,v) \in A} w_{uv} = \sum_{u \in V} \bar{z}_u - 1$$

$$\pi_v - \pi_u + |V|(1 - w_{uv}) \geq 1, \quad \forall (u,v) \in A$$

$$\pi_v - \pi_u - |V|(1 - w_{uv}) \leq 1, \quad \forall (u,v) \in A$$

$$\sum_{u \in N^+_{(v)}} w_{vu} + \sum_{u \in N^-_{(v)}} w_{uv} \geq \bar{z}_v, \quad \forall v \in V$$

$$\sum_{u \in N^+_{(v)}} w_{vu} + \sum_{u \in N^-_{(v)}} w_{uv} \leq |N_{(v)}| \bar{z}_v, \quad \forall v \in V$$

$$\sum_{u \in N_{(v)}} \bar{z}_u \geq 1, \quad \forall v \in V$$

$$\sum_{u \in N^-_{(v)}} w_{uv} \leq 1, \quad \forall v \in V$$

$$1 \leq \pi_v \leq |V| - 2, \quad \forall v \in V$$

$$w \in \{0,1\}^{|A|}, \bar{z} \in \{0,1\}^{|V|}$$

from where the proof follows by using the mapping $\bar{z}_u = 1 - z_u$. $\square$

In P_1, the objective function is the same as in P_0. Constraint (10) ensures that T has $\sum_{v \in V} \bar{z}_v - 1$ arcs. Constraints (11)–(12) ensure that if an arc (u,v) belongs to T, then $\pi_v - \pi_u = 1$, otherwise these constraints become redundant. Constraints (11)–(12) together with (16) avoid cycles in any feasible solution. Constraints (16) limit the number of arcs arriving at a node $v \in V$ to at most one. Constraints (13) ensure that if node v is a dominating vertex, then at least one arc is adjacent to v. Constraints (14) indicate that if node v is not a dominating vertex, then no arc is adjacent to v; otherwise, at most $|N_{(v)}|$ arcs can be adjacent to this node. Constraints (15) are domination constraints and ensure that any node v in V has a neighbor in T. Constraints (17) are bound constraints limiting the possible values for the variables π. These constraints are required as any directed path in T spans at most $|V| - 2$ nodes.

We note that P_1 can be further strengthened with selected valid inequalities in the form of generalized sub-tour eliminations constraints which are valid for the classical minimum connected dominating tree problem [9]. For this purpose we replace the constraints (14) with the following set of constraints

$$w_{uv} + z_u \leq 1, \quad \forall (u, v) \in A$$

$$w_{uv} + z_v \leq 1, \quad \forall (u, v) \in A$$

$$\sum_{(u,v) \in A(N_{[i]})} w_{uv} \leq \sum_{j \in N_{[i]}} (1 - z_j) - 1, \quad \forall i \in V$$

and constraints (16) with the following ones

$$\sum_{u \in N_{(v)}^-} w_{uv} + z_v \leq 1, \quad \forall v \in V$$

Hereafter, we denote this resulting model by P_2. Finally, we denote the corresponding linear programming (LP) relaxations of P_1 and P_2 by LP_1 and LP_2, respectively. In the next section, we briefly present and explain an iterative procedure that we adapt from [1] to obtain optimal solutions for P_0.

3   Iterative Procedure to Obtain Optimal Solutions for P_0

In order to compute optimal solutions for P_0, we adapt the exact iterative Algorithm 2 proposed in [1]. The reader is referred to Algorithms 1 and 2 in [1] for a deeper comprehension. For sake of simplicity, the main procedure can be summarized as follows. First, we solve P_0 without constraints (3). By doing so, we obtain a graph $\tilde{G}$ that may contain one or more cycles with at least three nodes. These cycles can be detected by using a depth-first search procedure [6]. If $\tilde{G}$ contains a cycle with 3 or up to $|V|$ nodes, then Algorithm 1 adapted from [1] detects it. A subset of nodes inducing a cycle defines a new constraint (3)

Algorithm 1. Iterative procedure to compute optimal solutions for P_0

Data: A problem instance of P_0.
Result: An optimal solution (x, y, z) for P_0 with objective function value f.
Step 0: Set $t = 0$ and $StopCondition = false$;
Step 1: **while** $not(StopCondition)$ **do**
  | $StopCondition = true$;
  | Solve problem P_{0_t} and let (x^t, y^t, z^t) be its optimal solution of value f^t at iteration t;
  | Construct the graph $\tilde{G} = (V, \tilde{E})$ with the solution (x^t, y^t, z^t) ;
  | $\mathcal{C} = searchCycles(\tilde{G}, V)$;
  | **foreach** $cycle \in \mathcal{C}$ **do**
  | | Add the corresponding constraint (3) to P_{0_t};
  | | $StopCondition = false$;
  | Set $t = t + 1$;
return the optimal solution (f^t, x^t, y^t, z^t);

which cuts off this cycle from the solution space. Problem P_0 is re-optimized iteratively while including the new found constraints. Finally, this iterative process continues until the underlying current optimal solution of P_0 has no more cycles. The whole procedure is presented in Algorithm 1. The *searchCycles()* procedure corresponds to Algorithm 1 in [1]. Notice that the number of cycles is finite, then so is the number of constraints (3) in P_0. The number of constraints (3) is at most $\mathcal{O}(2^{|V|})$. Consequently, Algorithm 1 which is adapted to solve P_0, converges to the optimal solution of the problem in at most $\mathcal{O}(2^{|V|})$ outer iterations. The proof can be deduced from Theorem 2 in [1].

4   Preliminary Numerical Results

In this section, we present preliminary numerical results. A Matlab program is developed using CPLEX 12.6 to solve P_0, P_1, P_2 and the LP relaxations. The numerical experiments have been carried out on an Intel(R) 64 bits core (TM) with 2.6 Ghz and 8G of RAM. CPLEX solver is used with default options. Each entry in matrices $C = C(k, u)$ and $P = P(k, u)$ for all $k \in K$, $u \in V$ corresponds to an integer number of bits and a rational number randomly and uniformly distributed in the intervals $[1; 16]$ and $[0; 1]$, respectively. The parameter α is set to $\alpha = 0.5$ for the numerical results presented in Tables 1 and 2. Connected disk graphs, for each instance, are generated randomly for radial transmission distances of 100, 125 and 150 ms, respectively.

In Table 1, we solve P_0 with Algorithm 1. Column 1 shows the instance number. Columns 2–3 present the instance dimensions and column 4 presents the density of each graph. These density values are calculated by dividing the number of edges of the graph over the total number of possible edges. Next, in columns 5–9 we present the optimal solution of each instance obtained with CPLEX [7], the number of branch and bound nodes, the CPU time in seconds, and the number of cycles and iterations required by Algorithm 1, respectively. For the instances in Table 1, we limit CPLEX to 2 hours of CPU time in order to solve the linear models.

The legend in Table 2 is as follows. Column 1 shows the instance number. Columns 2–6 and 7–11 present the optimal solution of P_1 and P_2, the number of branch and bound nodes used by CPLEX, the CPU time in seconds to solve the mixed integer linear programs and their corresponding LP relaxations together with their CPU time in seconds, respectively. Finally, in columns 12–13, we present gaps that we compute by $\left[\frac{LP-Opt}{Opt}\right] * 100$ for P_1 and P_2, respectively. We mention that each row in Tables 1 and 2 corresponds to the same instance.

From Table 1, first we observe that the density values decrease when the distances get smaller. Regarding the optimal solutions, we observe similar objective function values for the instances 1–12 and 13–24, respectively. In general, we see that the number of branch and bound nodes increase rapidly with the size of the instances and in particular when the radial transmission distances are small. Similar trends can be observed for the CPU times. For the second set of instances 13–24, these values are significantly larger. This shows that the instances are

Table 1. Numerical results obtained with Algorithm 1 for P_0.

#	Inst. Dim.		d_G	P_0				
	$|V|$	$|K|$		Opt.	B&B	Time (s)	#Cycles	#Iter
150 m								
1	10	50	35.56	352.01	78	0.18	0	1
2	20	50	24.74	373.59	7273	17.84	52	48
3	30	50	17.47	385.66	3707	8.18	27	18
4	50	50	19.18	392.06	2	28.03	85	69
125 m								
5	10	50	28.89	333.98	47	0.91	4	3
6	20	50	16.32	361.56	4056	4.78	30	16
7	30	50	12.18	375.93	23328	43.25	48	14
8	50	50	14.69	390.96	73670	58.61	114	44
100 m								
9	10	50	22.22	310.16	0	0.25	1	2
10	20	50	14.74	366.17	493	2.17	8	5
11	30	50	12.87	376.15	86021	165.99	82	36
12	50	50	10.20	389.44	99206	131.50	115	41
150 m								
13	10	100	22.22	637.60	0	0.29	1	2
14	20	100	17.89	742.67	639	1.32	4	3
15	30	100	22.53	771.52	209066	506.63	181	65
16	50	100	21.80	785.69	119093	202.21	122	66
125 m								
17	10	100	37.78	689.02	361	2.26	7	8
18	20	100	20.00	735.88	22823	63.40	39	17
19	30	100	15.63	768.57	73380	193.85	71	43
20	50	100	13.71	784.63	2476323	5338.11	448	233
100 m								
21	10	100	22.22	636.69	0	0.30	1	2
22	20	100	12.11	703.07	26	1.14	4	4
23	30	100	10.80	744.16	19633	77.34	38	16
24	50	100	10.29	-	-	-	-	-

-: No solution found with CPLEX in 2 h.

harder to be solved with CPLEX when the number of users to be connected to the backbone network increase. We note that the instance #20 requires almost two hours of CPU time to be solved whereas the instance #24 cannot be solved with CPLEX in two hours. Finally, we observe similar trends for the number of cycles and iterations required by Algorithm 1. We see that these values are

Table 2. Numerical results obtained with CPLEX for P_1 and P_2.

#	P_1					P_2					Gaps	
	Opt	B&Bn	Time (s)	LP	Time (s)	Opt	B&Bn	Time (s)	LP	Time (s)	Gap_1 %	Gap_2 %
150 m												
1	352.01	0	0.13	352.45	0.11	352.01	0	0.13	352.01	0.10	0.13	0
2	373.59	10933	4.71	375.79	0.14	373.59	29	0.53	374.74	0.12	0.59	0.31
3	385.66	106001	46.20	386.39	0.16	385.66	0	0.21	385.66	0.16	0.19	0
4	392.06	1465965	278.25	392.08	0.23	392.06	2104	0.98	392.08	0.23	0.01	0.01
125 m												
5	333.98	238	0.32	351.03	0.10	333.98	0	0.14	333.98	0.12	5.10	0
6	361.56	9920	5.42	373.79	0.15	361.56	0	0.19	361.56	0.14	3.38	0
7	375.92	5462572	3600	381.98	0.16	375.93	64	0.98	377.88	0.21	1.61	0.52
8	390.96	5204406	2487.82	391.09	0.21	390.96	481	0.80	391.01	0.23	0.03	0.01
100 m												
9	310.16	20	0.23	347.97	0.10	310.16	0	0.13	310.16	0.11	12.19	0
10	366.17	5828	6.03	377.92	0.14	366.17	0	0.19	366.17	0.18	3.21	0
11	376.15	2746053	2032.90	385.93	0.16	376.15	1630	2.51	380.12	0.15	2.60	1.06
12	389.44	2867786	3600	390.00	0.19	389.44	950	3.03	389.71	0.23	0.14	0.07
150 m												
13	637.60	13	0.18	646.69	0.13	637.60	0	0.15	637.60	0.13	1.43	0
14	742.67	556	0.93	746.33	0.15	742.67	0	0.20	742.67	0.14	0.49	0
15	771.52	39222	49.75	773.75	0.21	771.52	4	1.80	771.98	0.19	0.29	0.06
16	785.69	9067	10.73	786.01	0.33	785.69	0	1.03	785.72	0.44	0.04	0
125 m												
17	689.02	0	0.17	689.02	0.16	689.02	0	0.16	689.02	0.11	0	0
18	735.88	5365	9.99	747.15	0.15	735.88	0	0.44	737.11	0.15	1.53	0.17
19	768.57	2690	4.19	770.05	0.21	768.57	4	0.89	769.33	0.26	0.19	0.10
20	784.63	277896	375.38	785.39	0.33	784.63	1694	3.49	784.91	0.45	0.10	0.04
100 m												
21	636.69	13	0.64	674.43	0.12	636.69	0	0.14	636.69	0.11	5.93	0
22	703.07	580	1.24	735.84	0.13	703.07	0	0.20	703.07	0.13	4.66	0
23	744.16	827785	947.93	765.68	0.23	744.16	1608	3.29	751.80	0.24	2.89	1.03
24	780.72	566688	854.07	782.93	0.30	780.72	3250	8.00	781.50	0.39	0.28	0.10

very small which evidences the effectiveness of Algorithm 1. This implies that the large CPU times obtained with Algorithm 1, for some of the instances, can be explained due to the high CPU time required to solve each mixed integer linear program within each iteration of the algorithm.

From Table 2, we observe that the optimal objective function values are exactly the same as those obtained with P_0 for all the instances with the exception of instance #24 that could not be solved to optimality. Concerning the number of branch and bound nodes, we see that they are significantly low for P_2. This evidences the effectiveness achieved with the selected valid inequalities used in P_2. The CPU times confirm this achievement too. Notice that in particular for the instances #7 and #12 CPLEX cannot certificate that it finds the optimal solution in one hour using P_1. On the opposite, these two instances are solved to optimality in less than 4 seconds of CPU time with P_2. In general, we observe that the LP optimal objective function values are very tight when compared to the optimal solutions for all the instances. In fact, for P_2 these values are lower than 1% whilst for P_1, they are lower than 1% for 13 instances out of 24. The worst value, in this case, is 12.19% which is a large value. This also confirms that P_2 outperforms significantly the other formulations.

In order to give more insight with respect to the optimal objective function values and CPU times obtained with P_2 when varying the parameter $\alpha \in (0,1]$, in Fig. 2 we plot for the instance #24 of Table 1 these results. Notice that for $\alpha = 0$, the solution is trivial. From Fig. 2, we mainly observe that the optimal objective values increase directly with the increase of α. We also see that these curves overlap each other which shows that the radial transmission ranges do not affect significantly these values. With respect to the CPU times, we see that P_2 can solve this instance in less than ten seconds for all the values of α. However, in this case we also see that for the values of $0.7 \leq \alpha \leq 1$ the CPU times are large when the transmission distance equals 150 ms.

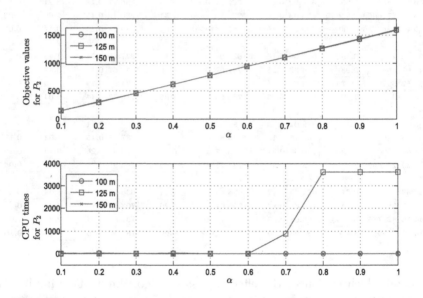

Fig. 2. Objective values and CPU times obtained with CPLEX for P_2.

5   Conclusions

In this paper, we proposed new formulations for the optimal connectivity of a tree backbone topology for MANETs. More precisely, we proposed an exponential and a compact polynomial formulation for the problem. The exponential model is characterized with constraints from the classical maximum leaf spanning tree polytope [18] whilst the compact formulation is characterized with constraints adapted from the classical minimum dominating tree problem [2]. The latter formulation is further strengthened with selected valid inequalities referred to as generalized sub-tour elimination constraints [9]. Formally, the problem is described as follows. Given a graph $G = (V \cup K, E)$ with set of wireless sensor nodes V, a set of connection links E, and a set of K users, the problem is to find a backbone spanning tree network topology with as many leaves as possible in order to maximize capacity at the lowest power costs for the users which are connected to the leaf nodes of the backbone network. We considered disk graphs instances, as it is the case for real wireless networks, where each disk represents the Euclidean distance transmission range of a node $v \in V$.

Our main conclusions can be summarized as follows. First, the density of the graphs decreases significantly with the radial transmission distances. Second, by adding valid cuts in the form of generalized sub-tour elimination constraints to the compact model, we can solve instances to optimality in significantly less CPU time and also reduce the branch and bound tree considerably for transmission distances ranging from 100 to 150 ms. Finally, the transmission ranges do not seem to affect significantly the optimal solutions of the problem.

As future research, we plan to develop new approximation algorithms and stochastic modeling approaches for this problem.

Acknowledgments. The authors acknowledge the financial support of Proyectos Dicyt Códigos 061413SG, 061513VC_DAS, 061713AS and CORFO 14IDL2-29919, and Vicerrectoría de Investigación, Desarrollo e Innovación.

References

1. Adasme, P., Andrade, R., Letournel, M., Lisser, A.: Stochastic maximum weight forest problem. Networks **65**(4), 289–305 (2015)
2. Adasme, P., Andrade, R., Lisser, A.: Minimum cost dominating tree sensor networks under probabilistic constraints. Comput. Netw. **112**, 208–222 (2017)
3. Balasundaram, B., Butenko, S.: Graph domination, coloring and cliques in telecommunications. In: Resende, M.G.C., Pardalos, P.M. (eds.) Handbook of Optimization in Telecommunications, pp. 865–890. Springer, New York (2006)
4. Butenko, S., Cheng, X., Du, D.Z., Pardalos, P.M.: On the construction of virtual backbone for ad-hoc wireless networks. In: Butenko, S., Murphey, R., Pardalos, P.M. (eds.) Cooperative Control: Models, Applications and Algorithms, vol. 1, Dordrecht edn, pp. 43–54. Kluwer, Dordrecht (2002)
5. Cheng, B., Coyle, A., McGarry, S., Pedan, I., Veytser, L., Wheeler, J.: Characterizing routing with radio-to-router information in a heterogeneous airborne network. IEEE Trans. Wirel. Commun. **12**(8), 4183–4195 (2013)
6. Cormen, T.H., Leiserson, C.E., Rivest, R.L., Stein, C.: Introduction to Algorithms. MIT Press and McGraw-Hill, Cumberland (2009)
7. Ibm, ILOG, CPLEX High-performance mathematical programming engine .http:// www.ibm.com/software/integration/optimization/cplex/
8. Garey, M.R., Johnson, D.S.: Computers and Intractability: A Guide to the Theory of NP-Completeness. W.H. Freeman, New York (1979)
9. Gendron, B., Lucena, A., de Cunha, A., Simonetti, L.: Benders decomposition, branch-and-cut, and hybrid algorithms for the minimum connected dominating set problem. Inform. J. Comput. **26**(4), 645–657 (2014)
10. Guha, S., Khuller, S.: Approximation algorithms for connected dominating sets. Algorithmica **20**(4), 374–387 (1998)

11. Ibrahim, H.M., Omar, N.M., William, E.K.: A secure technique for construction and maintenance of a trusted mobile backbone network in MANET. In: IEEE 12th International Conference on Networking, Sensing and Control, pp. 116–121 (2015)

12. Jia, R., Yang, F., Yao, S., Tian, X., Wang, X., Zhang, W., Xu, J.: Optimal CapacityDelayTradeoff in MANETs with correlation of node mobility. IEEE Trans. Veh. Technol 66(2), 1772–1785 (2017)

13. Jie, W., Fai, D.: Virtual backbone construction in MANETs using adjustable transmission ranges. IEEE Trans. Mob. Comput. 5(9), 1188–1200 (2006)

14. Keller, T., Hanzo, L.: Adaptive multicarrier modulation: a convenient framework for time frequency processing in wireless communications. Proc. IEEE 88, 611–640 (2000)

15. Kim, I., Lee, H.L., Kim, B., Lee, Y.H.: On the use of linear programming for dynamic subchannel and bit allocation in multiuser OFDM. In: IEEE GLOBECOM 2001, vol. 6, pp. 3648–3652 (2001)

16. Liu, J., Sheng, M., Xu, Y., Li, J., Jiang, X.: End-to-End delay modeling in buffer-limited MANETs: a general theoretical framework. IEEE Trans. Wirel. Commun. 15(1), 498–511 (2016)

17. Luo, Z., Gan, X., Wang, X., Luo, H.: Optimal ThroughputDelay tradeoff in MANETs with supportive infrastructure using random linear coding. IEEE Trans. Veh. Technol. 65(9), 7543–7558 (2016)

18. Lucena, A., Maculan, N., Simonetti, L.: Reformulations and solution algorithms for the maximum leaf spanning tree problem. Comput. Manag. Sci. 7, 289–311 (2010)

19. Selvi, P.F.A., Manikandan, M.S.K.: Ant based multipath backbone routing for load balancing in MANET. IET Commun. 11(1), 136–141 (2017)

20. Rajashekhar, B., Sunilkumar, M.: Multicast routing in MANET using multiple reliable rings backbone. In: 3rd International Conference on Advances in Recent Technologies in Communication and Computing (ARTCom 2011), pp. 56–61 (2011)

21. Sheikhan, M., Hemmati, E.: High reliable disjoint path set selection in mobile ad-hoc network using hopfield neural network. IET Commun. 5(11), 1566–1576 (2011)

22. Stankovic, J.: When sensor and actuator networks cover the world. ETRI J. 30, 627–633 (2008)

23. Vodnala, D., Aluvala, S., Phani, Kumar, S.: A backbone based multicast routing protocol for route recovery in MANETs. In: 2nd International Conference on Electronics and Communication Systems (ICECS), pp. 237–241 (2015)

24. Yang, S., Wu, J., Dai, F.: Efficient directional network backbone construction in mobile ad hoc networks. IEEE Trans. Parallel Distrib. Syst. 19(12), 1601–1613 (2008)

On Cost-Effective Inter-LMA Domain Handover Scheme in NEMO-PMIPv6 Networks

Shinyeol Park, Changyong Um, and Jongpil Jeong[(✉)]

Department of Smart Factory Convergence, Sungkyunkwan University, Suwon,
Gyeonggi-do 16419, Republic of Korea
parkshinyeol@gmail.com, e7217@naver.com, jpjeong@skku.edu

Abstract. Recently, there are many MNs (Mobile Nodes) are efficient and stable when they move to operate with variety schemes have emerged. Recently, there is a growing interest about PMIPv6 (Proxy Mobile IPv6) and, this paper is the based on the way to mobility support system will stand on the basis from PMIPv6 network to NEMO (NEtwork MObility). PMIPv6 is mobility support system from single domain, it actual network is composed with nested in a multiple domain structural system. The proposed scheme in the domain of two or more, the LMA (Local Mobility Anchor) communication between LMA and MAG (Mobile Access Gateway) of movable domain can increase performance in terms of handover delay and signaling.

Keywords: PMIPv6 · NEMO · LMA · Inter-domain handover

1 Introduction

The current mobile network wants the internet connection which is not disconnected even when it is moved to a new region. The MIPv6 [1] is the protocol which represents IP layer at the IPv6 network. But it is limited to apply it in practice, because the amount of usage increases in wireless section due to the signaling between mobile terminals and AR (Access Router), and because complicated standardized specification must be realized at the terminals. As these problems emerge, the NETLMM working group of IETF was newly established, and then the standardization of the network-based mobility protocol is in process.

The network-based mobility protocol contains typically the NBS (NEMO Basic Support) protocol [2]. The MR (Mobile Router) of the NBS carries out the AR role. If the MN is in the home network, it will gain the IP address which is called HoA (Home Address) by the HA (Home Agent). This IP maintains the same address even when it moves out of the same domain to a new region. If the MR moves to a new region, the MR receives a new network prefix, on whose base a new address called as CoA (Care-of Address) is generated. Then the BU (Binding Update) message which contains the CoA is sent to the HA, so that the connection with the HA is maintained. The HA sends BA (Binding Acknowledgement) message to the MR as the response which means it receives the BU

© Springer International Publishing AG 2017
M. Younas et al. (Eds.): MobiWIS 2017, LNCS 10486, pp. 263–275, 2017.
DOI: 10.1007/978-3-319-65515-4_22

message. The MNN (Mobile Network Node) in the region of the MR doesn't pass through any procedure because the MR carries out the signaling. But, the NBS also is the host-based mobility management protocol like the MIPv6. In the case of the host-based management protocol, when the MR moves, the MNN adjacent to it carries out the signaling, and consequently the performance delay is caused. Thus, recently network-based protocol is being paid attention. The typical protocol of it is the PMIPv6 (Proxy Mobile IPv6) [3–5].

This paper uses the scheme which applies the NEMO to the PMIPv6 domain [6]. The MN of the existing PMIPv6 first passes through the MAG(Mobile Access Gateway) and communicates with external nodes, and here the MR is placed in the middle. One MAG has a lot of MNs (Mobile Nodes). Here the MR regroups again a lot of MNs, and carries out vicariously the unnecessary signaling between the MN and the MAG. But, the current PMIPv6 doesn't support the whole area mobility of the host. If the MR moves to other domain, the subsequent handover delay occurs.

This paper, to compare the performances of domains, compared and analyzed the NBS, Light-NEMO (PMIPv6 which supports the NEMO), and proposed scheme. This paper first presents signaling cost in domain, packet tunneling cost, and handover delay, and analyzed the performances in terms of signaling cost between domains, packet tunneling cost, and handover delay. As the result of the analysis, in terms of signaling cost, handover delay, and 'in domain' and 'between domains,' the proposed scheme generates less cost than the NBS and the Light-NEMO. In terms of packet tunneling cost, the proposed scheme is same as the Light-NEMO, but less than the NBS.

This paper describes the protocol related to the Sect. 2. And Sect. 3 describes the proposed scheme, Sect. 4 analyzes the performance of the proposed scheme. Finally, Sect. 5 draw conclusions.

2   Related Work

NEMO (NEtwork MObility) is a technology that can provide a seamless service on the network connected to the MNNs (Mobile Network Nodes). NEMO is performed as to each of the terminals belonging to the operation associated with the mobility in MNNs, the router that is dedicated to the MNNs as a representative to the MR. Signaling that the existing terminals perform direct MR can use the network because they do instead is more efficient [2–7].

PMIPv6 of the mobile node from the mobility management domain is managed by a PMIPv6. In the terminal domain are subject to the control of the LMA(Local Mobility Anchor) and MAG. LMA performs the role of the home agent to the mobile node. This is placed in position within the domain gateway, the home network prefix allocated to it and also plays a role to send to the mobile node. MAG is responsible for the connectivity and routing for the network of the mobile node. When the mobile node is connected to the access router, rather than by using the information of the mobile node to the LMA and the authentication and connection [8].

NEMO is the support PMIPv6 domain, LMA has a binding list, including the HNP and MNP of the MR. Therefore, LMA is able to delete the record in the other MAG to move the address relocation and an existing area of the MR. When MR move to a new MAG in the existing area MAG zone, the new MAG is sent to the LMA through PBU message. LMA is the binding update list by using the existing registered information such as HNP and MNP. MAG is newly created through a PBA message transmitted to the LMA, and updates the list information on the MR. Because HNP is a permanent address, MR is continued to use the existing information even if the move to the new MAG.

3   Cost-Effective Inter-LMA Domain Handover Scheme in NEMO-PMIPv6 with NEMO Supporting

This paper purposes that the proposed scheme improves the performance regarding handover delay due to movement of the MR in more than two domains. The LMA of the PMIPv6 manages one domain. If the number of domains is two, the domains, which have their own LMA different from each other, cannot communicate with each other because their network bandwidths are different each other.

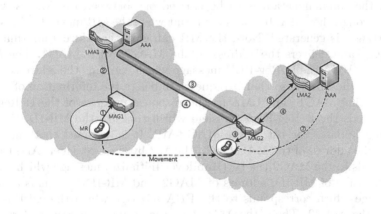

Fig. 1. Handover based on proposal scheme.

As in Fig. 1, if the MR moves to a new domain, the LMA gains the information of the MR, and carries out the binding list update to it. After that, the MAG of corresponding area can recognize the MR. This paper proposes the improvement of performance for handover delay by reducing the communication process, when the MR moves out of the PMIPv6 domain which is different from each other to a new PMIPv6. It is assumed that when the MR is about to move to the MAG3 of other PMIPv6, the MAG2 recognizes the information of it as the L2 trigger which contains addresses of the MAG3 and the LMA when the MR moves to a new domain. The MAG1 transmits the DeReg-PBU message to the LMA1, and then the LMA1 in this process knows of the PMIPv6 domain which the MR will move to and the IP address of the MAG3. If the MR moves to a new domain, it must exchange the information with the LMA. But by the scheme proposed by this paper, because the LMA1 knows the address of the MAG3, it doesn't pass through the LMA2, and then immediately exchanges the information of the MR. the LMA1 and the MAG3 take over the communication process between the LMA1 and the LMA2. Figure 2 shows the structure of a data packet tunnel between LMA1 and MAG3.

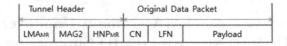

Fig. 2. Tunneled data packet from LMA to MAG2.

If the MR in the PMIPv6 domain which supports the NEMO moves to the new MAG2, the MAG2 gains the information of the MR (MR-ID, HNP, MNP) through the LMA which is responsible for the basic data communication. This paper proposes that before the proposed scheme, if the MR moves in one PMIPv6 domain, the communication is to be carried out between the MAGs without passing through the LMA. It is assumed that when the MR moves to the MAG2, the L2 trigger is generated. Now, the MR can gain the address information of the MAG2, and delivers the address of the MAG2 to the MAG1. The MAG1 sends to the LMA the DeReg-PBU message which contains the addresses of the MR-ID and the MAG2, so that it requests to delete the information of the MR in the existing MAG1. The LMA as the response message of the DeReg-PBU message sends the DeReg-PBA message which contains the MR-ID, HNP and MNP, and updates the list of the MAG2-MR. It is assumed that the MAG1 knows of the address of the MAG2 from the MR by the L2 trigger. And then the MAG1 sends to the MAG2 the HI (Handover Initialize) message which contains the information of MR-ID, address of MAG2, and MR-HNP. This is as similar as the stage which corresponds to the PBA message which the existing LMA sends to the MAG2. Then, the MAG2 as the response message of reception transmits the HAck (Handover Ack) message. In the process, the MAG2 knows of the information about the MR. The MAG2 has the buffering process. Till the MR is connected to a new domain through the buffering, the MAG2 stores the information of the HI message, and sends to the LMA2 the Pre-PBU message which beforehand has the information of the MR. The LMA2 as the response to it responds with the Pre-PBA message. Not long after the MR is linked down to the existing MAG1, it is linked up at the MAG2. And the two-way tunnel between the MAG1 and the MAG2 is formed. After the certification procedure through the certification server, the MR transmits the RS message to the MAG2, and the MAG2 transmits to the MR the RA message which contains the HNP and the MNP. The MR forms addresses by using the HNP, and advertises the MNP to the mobile nodes by the broadcasting method.

This paper proposes the scheme that the method by which the communication is operated between the MAGs in one PMIPv6 domain is improved and developed to the method by which the communication is operated in two domains without passing through the LMA, as shown in Fig. 3. It is assumed that when the MR in the MAG2 of the LMA1 moves to the MAG2 of the LMA2, the L2 trigger is generated in the MR. The MAG2 acquires the information of the MR-ID and the LMA2 through this L2 event. The MAG1 transmits to the LMA1 the DeReg-PBU message which contains the LMA2 address which is transmitted from the MR, the MAG2 address and the MR-ID. The LMA1, as the response to receive the DeReg-PBU message, transmits to the MAG1 the DeReg-PBA message, and deletes the information of the MR from the binding list. The LMA1 knows about the address of the MAG2. And the LMA1 sends to the MAG2 the HI which contains the MR-ID and the HNP. The MAG2, as the response to receive the HI, sends the HAck message. The MAG2 transmits to the LMA2 the Pre-PBU message which contains the MR-ID, and registers the information of the LMA2-MR in the binding list. The LMA2, as the response to the PBU message, sends so the MAG2 the Pre-PBA which contains the MR-ID, the HNP and the MNP. Then it is linked up to the MR, and passes through the certification procedure by the certification server in the domain. After the certification, the MR transmits the RS message to the MAG2, and the MAG3 sends to the

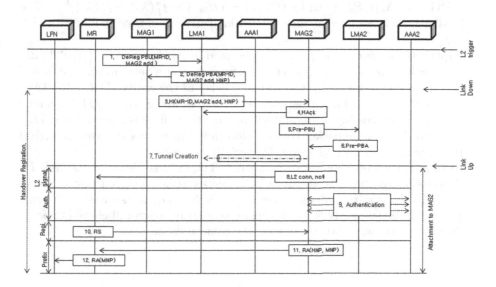

Fig. 3. Handover procedure from a PMIPv6 domain to another domain.

MR the RA message which contains the HNP and the MNP. The MR forms the address by using the HNP, and advertises the MNP to the mobile nodes by the broadcasting method.

4   Performance Analysis

In this section, the NBS, Light-NEMO and our scheme will be compared and analyzed. Signaling, packet tunneling cost, handover delay in respect will present numerical results.

In relation to authentication and access of the MR in this experiment had will assume the same value. In this paper, we'll learn why the handover latency values IP layer traffic value. The following notation is used in the proposed performance analysis.

- A session connection for the MR is estimated utilizing a Poisson distribution. Therefore, the continuous time of the session connection MR is used for the λ_s an exponential distribution.
- $E(S)$ refers to the length of the session MR and it's determined by the number of the fixed packet size.
- $1/\mu_L$ is used, which means the density distribution of time to be connected to MR. The density function is using the $f_{L(t)}$. $f_{L(s)}$ means a Laplace transform of the $f_{L(t)} \cdot f_{L(s)}^* = \int_{t=0}^{\infty} e^{-st} f_L(t) dt$.
- N_n is the number for the link to move the MR. $P_r[N_L = K] = a(K)$ is the probability for the moves to be MR, the session is maintained for K links. S_σ refers to the SMR containing λ_s/μ_L. The session is $a(0) = 1 - (1 - f_L^*(\lambda_s))/S_\sigma$, given by $(k \geq 1) = 1/S_\sigma(1 - f_L^*(\lambda_s))^2(f_L^*(\lambda_s))^{k-1}$. The holding time is assumed as the exponential distribution time to link with MR, $1/\mu_L$.
- Laplace transform of the $f_{L(t)}$ is represented as $f_L^*(\lambda_s) = e^{-st} \prod \mu_L e^{-\mu_L t} dt$.
- D_P which means a service packet delay, packet service delay means the sum of the processing delay and a transmission delay of the entity (MR, AR/MAG, HA_{MR}/LMA_{MR}). Packet services will delay applying the M/M/1 queuing model. The processing procedure will assume that there is a packet loss. $1/\mu_p$ refers to the average packet transmission time, λ_P means the average arrival rate. D_P is given by $1/(1 - p)u$. (Especially, $p = p/\mu_p$)
- Enlarge delay also should be considered. The enlarge delay of the link D_a depends on the physical distance by an entity d and a wired link ψ speed. D_a is given by d/ψ. Enlarge delay for a wireless D_B is assumed to be $1us$. Wired link is not nearly failed during message transmission, believed to occur during the message transmission on the radio link fails.

Table 1 describes The notations for the performance analysis.

Table 1. the notations for the performance analysis.

H_{X-Y}	Average of hops between the X and Y
S_{bu}	BU message size used in the NBS
S_{ba}	BA message size used in the NBS
S_{pbu}	PBU message size used in the proposed technical
S_{pba}	PBA message size used in the proposed technical
S_{hd}	cIPv6 header size required by the bi-directional tunnel
τ	By weight of the tunnel
n_f	Message transmission failures in the wireless link
P_f	Radio link failure probability
n_t	The total number of the LFNs belonging to the area of the MR
n_n	The total number of active LFNs belonging to the area of the MR
T_{L2}	Handover delays for the 2-layer
T_{AU}	Certification delay
$T_{W\,RS}$	RS message random delay by the MR to MAG
T_W	Signaling in the radio link
T_{RS}	Arrival delay of RS message toward the MAG from MR
T_{RA}	Arrival delay of RA message toward the MAG from MR
T_{DAD}	Delay is required in the course of the DAD process
$T_{LU}^{(NBS)}$	Delay in the handover process of registration NBS
$T_P^{(NBS)}$	Delay is the first packet of the HAMR from up to MR
$T_{LU}^{(PRO)}$	Delay in the registration process of the handover in the proposed technology
$T_P^{(PRO)}$	Delay is the first packet from the LMA$_{MR}$ to MR

4.1 Cost Analysis

Signaling cost is given by the signaling occurring in the handover for the mobile registration process. On the other hand, the packet is sent from CN to MR, the tunneling cost, is determined by the data packet [9–26].

$C_{LU}^{(PRO)}$ is the time of signaling cost for our proposed scheme.

– If within a domain

$$
\begin{aligned}
C_{LU}^{(PRO)} &= [i \sum_{i=0}^{\infty} a(i) \times LU^{(PRO)} \\
&= [\sum_{i=1}^{\infty} \frac{i}{S\sigma}(1 - f_L^*(\lambda_s))^2 (f_L^*(\lambda_s))^{i-1}] \times LU^{(PRO)} \\
&= T_w
\end{aligned}
\tag{1}
$$

– If between domains

$$C_{LU}^{(PRO)} = [i \sum_{i=0}^{\infty} a(i) \times LU^{(LM)} + H_{LMA1-MAG2}(Q_{req} + Q_{res}) \tag{2}$$
$$= T_w + H_{LMA1-MAG2}(Q_{req} + Q_{res})$$

$LU^{(PRO)}$ is the cost of location updates from the proposed scheme. In the proposed scheme, since $LU^{(PRO)}$ to update the location of the MR in advance, HI/HAck message transmission process include only T_w.

$$LU^{(PRO)} = T_w \tag{3}$$

$C_{PT}^{(PRO)}$ is the cost per packet tunneling in the proposed scheme. It is calculated as follows:

$$C_{PT}^{(PRO)} = n_n H_{LMA1-MAG2} S_{hd} E(S) \tag{4}$$

4.2 Handover Delay Analysis

In Fig. 4, Light-NEMO in the Intra Domain handover procedure, shows the time required in each stage of the diagram. $L_{(HO)}^{(LM)}$ is one of the Light-NEMO handover delay. This analysis is similar with the formula in NBS. The result shows the following:

– If within a domain

$$L_{HO}^{(LM)} = T_{L2} + T_{AU} + T_{WRS} + T_{RS} + T_{LU}^{(LM)} + T_P^{(LM)} \tag{5}$$

T_{RS} shows the following:

$$T_{RS} = \frac{P_f H_{MR-MAG}(D_P + D_E)}{1 - P_f} \tag{6}$$

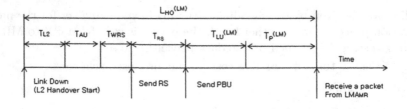

Fig. 4. Handover timing diagram for the Light-NEMO handover procedure.

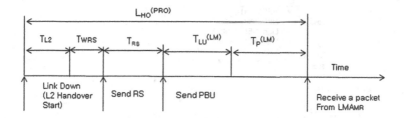

Fig. 5. Handover timing diagram for the proposed handover procedure.

In the proposed handover procedure, MAG sends the PBU for the handover messages on behalf of the registered MR. LMA_{MR} sends a MR with the PBA message and the data packets. $T_{LU}^{(LM)} + T_P^{(LM)}$ represents the following:

$$T_{LU}^{(LM)} + T_P^{(LM)} = H_{MAG-LMA_{MR}}(D_P + D_a) + max(T_{PBA}, T_P^{(LM)}) \quad (7)$$

T_{PBA} is the arrival delay of the PBA message directed to the MR in LMA_{MR}. T_{PBA} and $T_P^{(LM)}$ is calculated as follows:

$$T_{PBA} = H_{MAG-LMA_{MR}}(D_P + D_a) \quad (8)$$
$$T_P^{(LM)} = \frac{P_f H_{MR-MAG}(D_P + D_B)}{1 - P_f} + \tau[H_{AR-HA_{MR}}(D_P + D_a)]$$

τ affects only tunnel between the proposed technology MAG and LMA_{MR}.

– If within a domain

$$L_{HO}^{(LM)} = T_{L2} + T_{AU_{LMA1-LMA2}} + T_{WRS} + T_{LU}^{(LM)} + T_P^{(LM)} \quad (9)$$

The handover timing diagram for the proposed scheme is shown in Fig. 5.

$$L_{HO}^{(PRO)} = T_{L2} + T_{WRS} + T_{RS} + T_P^{(PRO)} \quad (10)$$

Finally, the equation of inter domain handover is equal to that of intra domain.

4.3 Numerical Results

The signaling costs are given in Fig. 6. Value of N_L, P_f is 0.1 or 0.5 when, we will assume one kinds from eight kinds. The proposed scheme is numerically when viewed as a result of rising costs because of location update signaling is likely twice two times higher than the NBS.

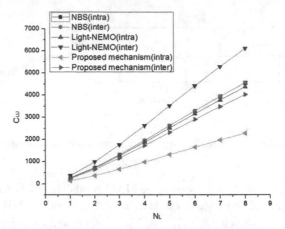

Fig. 6. Signaling cost *versus* N_L.

Figure 7 shows the packet tunneling costs for three schemes. Packet tunneling cost is proportional to $E(S)$. NBS only affected by the P_f. The proposed scheme is less than the NBS in terms of the packet tunneling cost.

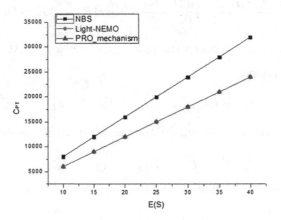

Fig. 7. Packet tunneling cost *versus* $E(S)$.

Figure 8 was compared to handover performance in comparison to the proposed method and the comparative protocol. From the graph, it shows the high packet loss ratio, such as the retransmission of the MR from the NBS.

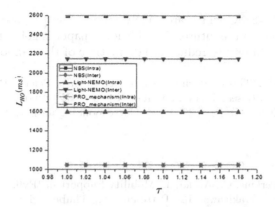

Fig. 8. Network layer handover latency *versus* τ.

Table 2 summarizes parameters used for the mathematical evaluations [9–26].

Table 2. Parameters and values.

Parameters	Values	Parameters	Values
τ	1.0, 1.5	P_f	0.1, 0.5
$E(S)$	10	S_σ	0.01, 10
n_t	5	ρ	0.1
S_{bu}	72 $bytes$	S_{ba}	52 $bytes$
$S_{pbu} = S_{pba}$	76 $bytes$	S_{hd}	40 $bytes$
$Q_{req} = Q_{res}$	38 $bytes$	λ_P	50 $packet/s$
T_{AU}	550 ms	$T_{AU_{LMA1-LMA2}}$	110 ms
d	1000 m	ϑ	$2 \times 10^8 m/s$
$MAX\_RTR\_SOLICITATION\_DELAY = RetransTimer$			1000 ms
$H_{MR-AR} = H_{MR-MAG}$			1
$H_{AR-HA_{MR}} = H_{MAG-MLA_{MR}}$			3
$H_{LMA1-LMA2}$			5

5   Conclusion

This paper proposed the scheme that when the MR moves between two domains which support the NEMO, not the communication between the LMAs but the communication between the LMA and the MAG is to be operated. While the existing studies have intensively dealt with the handover in one domain, it is the key of this paper to enable the performance improvement from the perspective of the delay and signaling in a case of handover between domains. Consequently, it has been demonstrated that in comparison with the PMIPv6 which supports the NBS and the NEMO which are widely known, the proposed scheme shows better performance. In the future, the additional paper is going to be conducted to propose the possibility to reduce the delay time of the handover.

Acknowledgments. This research was supported by Basic Science Research Program through the National Research Foundation of Korea (NRF) funded by the Ministry of Education (NRF-2016R1D1A1B03933828). Corresponding author: Jongpil Jeong.

References

1. Johnson, D., Perkins, C., Arkko, J.: Mobility Support in IPv6. RFC 3775 (2004)
2. Devarapalli, V., Wakikawa, R., Petrescu, A., Thubert, P.: Network Mobility: NEMO, Basic Support Protocol. RFC 3963 (2005)
3. Lee, J.H., Han, Y.H., Gundavelli, S., Chung, T.-M.: A comparative performance analysis on hierarchical mobile IPv6 and proxy mobile IPv6. Telecommun. Syst. **41**(4), 279–292 (2009)
4. Lee, J.H., Ernst, T., Chung, T.-M.: Cost analysis of IP mobility management protocols for consumer mobile devices. IEEE Trans. Consum. Electron. **56**(2), 1010–1017 (2010)
5. Gundavelli, S., Leung, K., Devarapalli, V., Chowdhury, K., Patil, B.: Proxy Mobile IPv6. RFC 5213 (2008)
6. Lim, H.-J., Kim, M., Lee, J.H., Chung, T.-M.: Route optimization in nested NEMO: Classification, evaluation and analysis from NEMO fringe stub perspective. IEEE Trans. Mobile Comput. **8**(11), 1544–1572 (2009)
7. Muhanna, A., Khalil, M., Gundavelli, S., Chowdhury, K., Yegani, P.: Binding Revocation for IPv6 Mobility. RFC 5846 (2010)
8. Choi, J.Y., Cho, Y., Lee, T., Cho, J.D., Jeong, J., Roh, S.S., Kim, H.T.: Cost analysis of integrated HIP-PMIPv6 handoff scheme in multicasting-based mobile networks. Adv. Sci. Lett. **21**(3), 321–327 (2015)
9. Jang, H., Song, B., Cheong, Y., Jeong, J.: Sensor-based global mobility management scheme with multicasting support for building IoT applications. Adv. Intell. Syst. Comput. **570**(5), 289–299 (2017)
10. Cho, C., Choi, J.Y., Jeong, J., Chung, T.M.: Performance analysis of inter-domain handoff scheme based on virtual layer in PMIPv6 networks for IP-based internet of things. PLoS ONE **12**(1), e0170566 (2017)
11. Im, I., Jeong, J.: Cost-effective and fast handoff scheme in proxy mobile IPv6 networks with multicasting support. Mobile Inf. Syst. **10**(3), 287–305 (2014)
12. Jeong, J., Cho, C., Kang, J.J.: Hashing based lookup service in mobile ad-hoc networks with multi-hop stretchable clustering. Int. J. Sens. Netw. **15**(3), 183–197 (2014)
13. Cho, C., Kang, J.J., Jeong, J.: Design and performance analysis of a dynamic-paging AAA mobility management scheme for PMIPv6based wireless networks. Int. J. Sensor Netw. **15**(4), 214–222 (2014)
14. Cho, C., Choi, J.Y., Cho, J.D., Jeong, J.: Design and performance analysis of a cost-effective proxy-LMA mobility management scheme in IP-based mobile networks with global mobility support. Int. J. Ad Hoc Ubiquitous Comput. **21**(4), 273–289 (2016)
15. Song, B., Shin, J., Kwon, Y., Jeong, J., Kim, Y.: On bandwidth-efficient handoff scheme for PMIPv6 networks. Procedia Comput. Sci. **94**, 152–159 (2016)

16. Song, B., Kwon, Y., Jang, H., Jeong, J., Cho, J.-D.: On efficient SC-based soft handoff scheme in proxy mobile IPv6 networks. In: Gervasi, O., Murgante, B., Misra, S., Rocha, A.M.A.C., Torre, C., Taniar, D., Apduhan, B.O., Stankova, E., Wang, S. (eds.) ICCSA 2016. LNCS, vol. 9787, pp. 251–262. Springer, Cham (2016). doi:10.1007/978-3-319-42108-7_19

17. Jeong, J., Cho, J.-D., Choi, Y., Kwon, Y., Song, B.: On multicasting-based fast inter-domain handover scheme in proxy mobile IPv6 networks. In: Huang, D.-S., Han, K., Hussain, A. (eds.) ICIC 2016. LNCS, vol. 9773, pp. 494–505. Springer, Cham (2016). doi:10.1007/978-3-319-42297-8_46

18. Song, B., Shin, J., Jang, H., Lee, Y., Jeong, J., Cho, J.-D.: On cross-layer based handoff scheme in heterogeneous mobile networks. In: Huang, D.-S., Han, K., Hussain, A. (eds.) ICIC 2016. LNCS, vol. 9773, pp. 482–493. Springer, Cham (2016). doi:10.1007/978-3-319-42297-8_45

19. Choi, J.Y., Jeong, J.: Design and performance analysis of cost-optimized handoff scheme based on fuzzy logic for building smart car IoT applications. Information (Japan) **18**(10), 4339–4345 (2015)

20. Jang, S., Jeong, J.: Cost-effective approach inter-LMA domain management and distributed mobility control scheme in proxy mobile IPv6 networks. Inf. Syst. **48**, 248–261 (2015)

21. Song, M., Cho, J.D., Jeong, J.: Optimization of authentication cost based on key caching for Inter-MME handover support. Information (Japan) **18**(3), 1095–1100 (2015)

22. Song, B., Shin, J., Kim, S., Jeong, J.: On PMIPv6-based mobility support for hierarchical P2P-SIP architecture in intelligent transportation system. In: Proceedings of the Annual Hawaii International Conference on System Sciences, pp. 5446–5452 (2015)

23. Song, M., Cho, J.D., Jeong, J.: Multicasting service for Inter-Domain mobility management scheme in sensor-based PMIPv6. Information (Japan) **18**(3), 1073–1078 (2015)

24. Choi, J.Y., Yang, S., Jeong, J.: On QoS provisioning based on user mobility patterns for Proxy mobile IPv6 networks. In: Park, J., Stojmenovic, I., Jeong, H., Yi, G. (eds.) Computer Science and its Applications. Lecture Notes in Electrical Engineering, vol. 330, pp. 983–989. Springer, Heidelberg (2015)

25. Cho, C., Kang, J.J., Jeong, J.: Performance analysis of DNS-assisted global mobility management scheme in cost-optimized proxy mobile IPv6 Networks. Inf. Syst. **48**, 226–235 (2015)

26. Song, M., Cho, J.D., Jeong, J.: Global mobility management scheme for seamless mobile multicasting service support in PMIPv6 networks. KSII Trans. Internet Inf. Syst. (TIIS) **9**(2), 637–658 (2015)

Web, Cloud and Distributed Systems

Adopting SOA in Public Service Provision

Gebremariam Mesfin[1], Tor-Morten Grønli[2(✉)], Gheorghita Ghinea[2,3],
and Muhammad Younas[4]

[1] Addis Ababa University, Addis Ababa, Ethiopia
mesfin.assres@gmail.com
[2] Westerdals Oslo ACT, Oslo, Norway
tmg@westerdals.no
[3] Brunel University, Brunel, Uxbridge, UK
george.ghinea@brunel.ac.uk
[4] Oxford Brookes University, Oxford, UK
m.younas@brookes.ac.uk

Abstract. Ensuring accessibility of utility and social services is one of the public obligations of governments. Today, nations make use of the notion of e-government to expose such services to citizens. In line with this, many public organizations in Ethiopia are automating their workflows, and the Ministry of Communication and Information Technology (MCIT) is attempting to unify certain services as part of its e-government initiative. However, the architectural patterns in use generally lack the required flexibility, and scalability for future expansion needs and business models with respect to the option that latest technologies such as SOA can offer. Literature shows that the loosely-coupled nature of SOA addresses the above-mentioned limitations and many e-government initiatives are exploiting its potential. Thus, it is apparent that SOA can address the e-government needs in Ethiopia too. In this paper, we conducted an SOA e-readiness assessment against the available e-readiness frameworks and found out that the infrastructural, legal, government, customer, and human resource requirements are met. Thus, we recommend that SOA be applied to incrementally and loosely integrate the existing (and upcoming) systems and realize "ubiquitous" public service provision.

Keywords: E-Readiness · SOA · e-government · Ubiquity · Incremental · Software integration

1 Introduction

Literature shows that ICT plays important role to socio economic wellbeing of nations [4, 5]. Thus, the Federal Democratic Republic of Ethiopian (FDRE) launched ambitious initiatives by establishing national ICT Development Agency in 2003 with proclamation no. 360/2003 which was later upgraded into a ministry level, namely, MCIT in the year 2010 with proclamation no.691/2010. Hence, the use of Service-Oriented Architecture (SOA) for "ubiquitous" public service provision could be dealt as part of such initiatives.

© Springer International Publishing AG 2017
M. Younas et al. (Eds.): MobiWIS 2017, LNCS 10486, pp. 279–289, 2017.
DOI: 10.1007/978-3-319-65515-4_23

The SOA is an emerging computing paradigm since the past few years. Research such as in [1–3] witnesses that there is a rapid progress in SOA adoption which represents a paradigm shift following the mainstream object-oriented approach.

According to [1], this paradigm shift is changing the way we develop and use software and hardware; and the central themes of conferences, journals, books, research, experimentation, tools, and products. Principles such as the SOA, service-oriented enterprise, and web services and the associated protocols and standards have emerged and solid foundation of SOA is grounded.

Khanbabaei *et al.* [2] describes SOA as an evolutionary distributed computing paradigm based on request/response for synchronous and asynchronous applications (see Fig. 1). This implies that SOA can be applied in situations where legacy systems require upgrading with more functionality and/or when different chunks of legacy systems require integrating with each other.

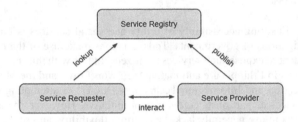

Fig. 1. SOA components and interactions

IT managers, business managers, designers and implementers of systems have different perspectives on SOA. As discussed by Michael Bell [3], IT managers perceive SOA as a style of architecture that includes patterns and rules which culminate in the development of characteristics like modularity, loose coupling, and reuse; business managers perceive it as a set of services that organizations wish to provide for their clients or partners; and developers perceive it as a style of programming which uses unanimously agreed and technology-independent standards and supports the intractability between software elements regardless of their platform and implementation technology.

SOA is a set of software engineering principles and methodologies used for the development of well-defined business functionalities called services that are interoperable. These set of software engineering principles include reliability, standardized service contract, loose coupling, hiding of internal implementation, service composeability, service autonomy/statelessness, discoverability and possessing virtual framework [2] which is a huge promise to facilitate seamless integration between stakeholder systems.

Governments and the public sector organizations around the world, on the other hand, are facing challenges to reform their public service organizations and deliver more efficient and cost effective services, as well as to provide better information and knowledge to their stakeholders. To this end, many governments [4–6] are attempting to exploit the potential of e-governance. For example, the AgriNet, WoredaNet, SchoolNet,

RevenueNet, and EthERNet are among the ICT initiatives launched in Ethiopia [6] aiming at implementing the e-government.

E-Governance is defined as the support for digital interrelationships between government and the stakeholders - citizens, businesses, employees, and other governments [7]. It is the use of ICT such as the Internet, local area networks, wide area networks, mobiles, etc., by governments to improve effectiveness, efficiency, and service delivery to citizens and promote transparency through seamless interaction of the stakeholders. E-Governance is thus at the heart of the interoperability characteristic of SOA.

Literature such as [7] indicates that SOA is being implemented to foster the interoperability requirements of e-government initiatives by creating automated and seamlessly integrated systems. However, there is no evidence that the existing hardware infrastructure in Ethiopia [6] is being utilized enough to deploy automated software systems and content, nor is on the utilization of SOA for "ubiquitous" public service provision such as payment of utility bills, taxes, and contributions; social security; and health insurance.

In addition, citizen-centric organizations like the "kebelle", microfinance centers, *etc.* lack to provide "one-stop" or "no-stop" collective public services except that some utility service providing organizations just started a unified billing for telecom, electric, and water supply bills to be paid in certain payment centers; and the Ethiopian radio and television agency has attempted to (manually) delegate microfinance centers to collect payments of bills for television broadcasting services.

However, the issue of public service provision is critical when we consider the large number of service categories, and the possibility of involving private customer service centers as part of the notion of public-private partnership. For example, with payment alone, we can see categories such as pension tax, sales tax, value added tax, land use tax, water bill, electric bill, telecom bill, television bill, and government house rent bill and linking all these to the banking system. On the other hand, a service provider may need to outsource or delegate some of its services to two or more independent customer service centers which in turn work for multiple service providing organizations with certain service-level agreements (SLA). Such e-government integration needs require high level system's flexibility (join or leave centers as needed) and scalability that SOA implementation can easily address [2].

In this research work, we investigate the e-readiness level in Ethiopia for the implementation of SOA principles and practices to integrate software systems of government agencies and corporations thereby enabling "ubiquitous" public service provision. We also put forward a set of recommendations in this regard.

This paper is organized as follows. In the next section, the research methodology used is discussed. The subsequent section discusses related work on the application of SOA principles for E-Governance and is followed by a discussion section on SOA based E-Governance readiness. The last section concludes the paper by recommending SOA principles, methodologies and web service technologies to be applied to incrementally integrate the existing (and upcoming) systems thereby realizing "ubiquitous" public service provision.

2 Research Methodology

As mentioned in the introductory section, the objective of this research work is to investigate the e-readiness for the application of SOA principles and technologies to implement "ubiquitous" public service provision in Ethiopia. Thus, we adopt the methodology
proposed by Dzhusupova *et al.* [19] which directly maps into our research context, and
the current status in Ethiopia is analyzed against this framework.

Based on the framework [19], we conducted a review of related work focusing on
the implementation of SOA based e-government systems and analyzed government
policy documents, strategic documents, regulations, annual reports, and experts' views
on issues related to the deployment of IT and telecom infrastructure, citizens' grievances
on governments' service provision, and government's commitment. In addition, IT and
telecom experts in the MCIT were consulted to reflect on the issue.

The current state of affairs of the IT and telecom infrastructure is explored by
assessing the different islands of automated systems owned by the different government
owned service providers in the Ethiopian governance system; the servers and local area
networks of the respective owners; the extent of connectivity into the Internet and or
national communication backbone; and the level of automation of the business processes
in the citizen-centric organizations.

3 Related Work

The aim of e-government is to allow seamless interaction between governments and
citizens (G2C), governments and business enterprises (G2B), and inter-agency relationships (G2G). Through e-government these interaction scenarios can be made friend-
lier, convenient, more transparent, and less expensive with the goals of providing better
services to citizens, leverage transparency and accountability, empower people through
information, improve efficiency within governments, and improve the interface with
businesses and industry [21]. Figure 2 depicts the components of the e-government
framework and their interaction.

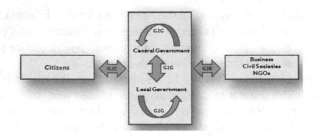

Fig. 2. e-government project framework

Researchers in [9] indicate that successful implementation of e-government has actually improved the efficiency, accountability and transparency of government processes, and achieved better public service delivery, accountability, and cost reduction thereby better empowerment of citizens.

An e-government implementation project life cycle requires core activities such as survey, training, development of services and infrastructure, dissemination (or deployment), and continued support based on research [20]. Figure 3 describes the constituents and interactions of these core activities.

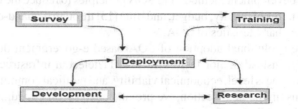

Fig. 3. e-government project framework

The success of an e-government implementation is measured according to a phased model of adoption. Gartner [12] describes these phases as providing information, interaction, transaction, and transformation services to citizens. Each successive stage represents an increased capability to provide information and services (added value) and the cost and public demand forces the government to move from the previous step to next.

At earlier stages of the e-government adoption, citizens can have access only to government information through one way communication but at later stages they can have two way communications with government bodies thereby leading to integrated services provision [11]. These stages are not dependent on each other nor need one phase be completed before another can begin [11]. Instead one can simply jump into a desired stage by deploying the necessary resource to do so. Literature [13] shows that e-government initiatives are being challenged by multi-dimensionality and complexity issues. Some of the main challenges are related to IT and telecom infrastructure, computer literacy, legislation support, education and training level of users, change management, partnership, strategic thinking, and leadership support.

The problem of providing "ubiquitous" public service provision fits somewhere between the transaction and transformation phases in which complete transactions can be done without going to an office and citizens can get services at one counter using integrated information systems respectively [12]. Although developing countries in general are supposed to be at the early stages of e-government development [14], Ethiopia has aggressively launched considerable e-government development initiatives over the past few years [6]. However, to the best of the knowledge of the authors, there is no work like this, in Ethiopia, that attempts to explore the possibility of implementing SOA based "ubiquitous" public service provision.

In addition, many e-government initiatives in developing countries are reported to fail mainly because of the diving of project leaders into such risky business of introducing "big thing" from scratch where there is no sufficient understanding of the socio cultural setting of the deployment environment [16]. Moreover, today's business requirement is changing dynamically. To this end, some e-government models [11] incorporate additional phases to move from access to integrated services into dynamically adopting demand driven services across enterprises.

Behara *et al.* [18] explain that SOA enables different government units to reuse existing assets, reduce the dependency of the backend applications, and promote collaboration of citizens and government departments irrespective of delivery models. Accordingly, the implementation of "ubiquitous" public service provision can adopt the evolutionary software development methods and SOA principles to reduce the risk of software project failure in terms of quality, budget, and time [15] through demand-driven, scalable and interoperable characteristics of SOA.

However, the evolutional adoption of SOA based e-government does not happen straightforwardly. Instead, major factors such as IT/telecom infrastructure readiness, stakeholders' awareness level, economical viability, and political commitment [14] must be explored. Thus, in the next section, we provide analysis on e-readiness in Ethiopia with respect to the attributes of e-readiness framework [19].

4   Readiness

This research utilizes government policy documents, strategic documents, regulations, and annual reports gathered from the utility service providing organizations and government authorities as primary sources of information. These documents are analyzed as per the requirements of the e-government readiness framework [19] and with a focus on the enabling environments, e-government demand, e-government capabilities, stakeholders' technology possession, and perceptions and challenges pillars.

Thus, the infrastructural, trained manpower, government, and customer attributes (see Table 1 below) are considered and interpreted in terms of the affinity of government organizations and citizens towards "ubiquitous" public service provision and the availability of the necessary IT infrastructure.

All the organizations that are affiliated with the provision of utility and social services are government owned and they provide services such as telecom, water, electric, services related to immigration and nationality; and collection of taxes, and collection of contributions.

In addition, government authorities that are responsible to the IT infrastructure expansion and quality citizen-services (good governance) are included. Thus, the government, citizen, infrastructural and human e-readiness [19] in Ethiopia for the realization of SOA based public service system is described as below.

Table 1. Categorizing primary data sources per the e-readiness criteria [19]

E-readiness criteria	Category	Organization	Remark on the content of organization's plan (or report) with respect to the e-readiness criteria
Government			
	Strategic plan 2010–2015	MCIT	Ambitious IT/telecom infrastructure expansion plan, and backed by legal support.
	Strategic plan 2010–2015	Ethiopian Water & Sewerage	Goals, indicators, and initiatives are set for enhancing customer satisfaction
	Strategic plan 2010–2015	Ethiopian Electric Power Authority	Enhancing customer satisfaction on services delivery
	Strategic plan 2010–2015	Immigration & Nationality Authority	Extending immigration services to localities
	Strategic plan 2010–2015	Revenue & Customs	Enhancing customer satisfaction on tax collection
Citizens			
	Annual report 2011/12	Ethiopian Electric Power Authority	All reports of these organizations illustrate that accessibility of their services (including payment) is one of their organizational weaknesses and they pledge to capitalize on their resources to address the issue.
	Annual report 2011/12	Ethiopian Water & Sewerage	
	Annual report 2011/12	Immigration & Nationality	
	Annual report 2011/12	Ethio Telecom	
	Annual report 2011/12	Revenue & Customs	
Infrastructure			
	Annual report 2011/12	Ethio Telecom	Internet penetration index getting enhanced
	Annual report 2011/12	MCIT	Describes an ever increasing infrastructure and e-government expansion activities and outputs
Human resource			
	Annual report 2011/12	Ministry of Education	Statistical data on the availability of trained manpower in the area of IT.

4.1 Infrastructural Readiness

The reports from the MCIT, and Ethio Telecom (see Table 1) indicated that the Internet penetration index in Ethiopia is improving. Thus, many public and private organizations, and individuals are able to subscribe wired as well as wireless broadband Internet connection; and infrastructural development initiatives such as the AgriNet, SchoolNet, WeredaNet, RevenueNet and EthERNet has contributed to the overall accessibility.

The development of national computer network expansion master plan has also leveraged 19 FDRE offices to be hooked into the national network backbone in the first round. According to the reports, step by step, all FDRE offices will be part of the network. In addition, government authorities and government owned service providing organizations like the Ethiopian Electric Power Authority (EEPCO), Addis Ababa Water and Sewerage Authority (EWSA), Ethiopian Immigration and Nationality Affairs, Ethiopian Revenues and Customs Authority (ERCA) and Ethio Telecom have deployed their own automated systems and all have access to the broadband Internet.

Thus, it can be generalized that the availability of IT/telecom infrastructure with respect to the expectation of SOA based implementation of "ubiquitous" public service provision systems is met.

4.2 Government's Readiness

The readiness of the FDRE government for the implementation of SOA based system for "ubiquitous" public service provision is twofold. On the one hand, MCIT took the initiative to launch an automation project for the provision of unified billing service in one window [10]; on the other hand, government owned service providing organizations have implemented customer service improvement initiatives and also planned to further enhancing customer satisfaction.

In addition, the government is deploying the necessary financial resource for the implementation of e-government projects. For example, thus far government has financed the unified billing system project to establish 41 such technologically equipped and interconnected service centers each having 3–11 service windows.

Moreover, MCIT has the plan to scaled-up to all areas by adding more services including registration for student matriculation, and placement of students in universities. The report indicates that there is a plan to establish "government cloud".

Thus, it is possible to assert that the government's readiness for the implementation of SOA based "ubiquitous" public service provision systems is achieved.

4.3 Citizens' Readiness

We attempt to portray the citizens' readiness using the customer grievances that the government owned service providing organizations came across. Accordingly, Ethiopian Electric Power Authority, Ethiopian Water & Sewerage, Immigration & Nationality Affairs, Ethio Telecom, and Revenue & Customs Authority in their annual reports (see Table 1) indicated that they have acute limitations on accessibility as compared to the demand of customers. Thus, we can clearly see that the citizens' readiness attribute for the implementation of SOA based "ubiquitous" public service provision systems is met.

4.4   Human Resource Readiness

In the academic year 2010/11, over 7000 students were enrolled in the areas of ICT such as Computer Science, and Information Technology in government owned universities alone in Ethiopia. Moreover, the trend continued with improvement [17]. Adding the number of enrollments in (and graduations from) graduate schools, and private colleges; it seems to outweigh the demand. Thus, the e-readiness from human resource requirements perspective is met.

In general, the current status in Ethiopia according to the four e-readiness criteria (as used in this study) are found to be that the government's readiness is at a level of strategic concern, citizens have acute demand, and the minimal required human resource and infrastructure is sufficiently available (see Table 2).

Table 2.   Summary of conformity with the required e-readiness criteria [19]

Readiness criteria	What is required?	What is available?	Remark
Government			
	Government's readiness (commitment) to satisfy citizens	Strategic level concern	Eg. Strategy is set, finance & manpower deployed, etc. for e-government expansion
Citizens			
	Citizens' aspiration for ubiquitous public service systems	Acute demand	Eg. Customers appreciate small service improvements, express aspirations, etc.
Infrastructure			
	Islands of automated systems, and Internet connectivity possibilities	The required minimum is available	Eg. Wired and wireless broadband Internet subscription, corporate databases, etc.
Human resource			
	Trained manpower to deploy, maintain & use	Sufficiently available	Eg. Many graduates in IT related fields, end-users working on legacy systems, etc.

In addition, once the legacy systems of the above listed organizations are integrated, new automated systems (possibly SOA based) can be incrementally integrated using the SOA techniques with flexibility and scalability thereby minimizing project risks.

5   Conclusion

In this research, our review of literature indicated that the minimal e-readiness criteria for the implementation of SOA based "ubiquitous" e-government systems for public service provision is determined by the commitment of the government and citizens, and availability of IT infrastructure and trained manpower. We applied these e-readiness framework attributes as pillars in our e-readiness evaluation criteria for the implementation of SOA based "ubiquitous" public service provision system.

The current e-readiness status in Ethiopia for the selected service providing organizations demonstrates that citizens are in acute need of "ubiquitous" public services and this is a strategic level of the government as well. In addition, the minimal required legal support, trained manpower, and infrastructure are available and the SOA technologies will leverage the flexibility and scaling to seamlessly incorporate more service providers into such a system.

Considering the above mentioned findings, we put forward the following conclusion. The SOA principles, methodologies, and Web service technologies can be successfully implemented in Ethiopia. The existing (and upcoming) software systems of the government service providers would loosely and incrementally integrate their services thereby realizing an integrated automated system for "ubiquitous" public service provision.

Our future work will be on the economic feasibility of addressing detailed functional and non-functional requirements of domain specific SOA based applications. We will focus on specific service providers and with respect to certain software development methodologies and technologies; and the legacy systems.

References

1. Tsai, W.T.: Service-oriented system engineering: a new paradigm. In: Proceedings of IEEE International Workshop on Service-Oriented System Engineering (2005)
2. Khanbabaei, M., Asadi, M.: Principles of service-oriented architecture and web services application in order to implement service-oriented architecture in software engineering. Australian J. Basic Appl. Sci. (2011)
3. Bell, M.: Service-Oriented Modeling: Service Analysis, Design, and Architecture. Wiley, Hoboken (2008)
4. Heeks, R.: e-government in Africa: Promise and Practice, Institute for Development Policy and Management University of Manchester (2002)
5. Groenendijk, N.S., Reussing, G.H., Meesters BA, M., Zuurmond, A.: e-government trends within the European Union (2006)
6. Belachew, M.: e-government Initiatives in Ethiopia. ACM (2010)
7. Behara, G.K., Varre, V.V., Rao, M.: Service Oriented Architecture for E-Governance, Behera (2009). Communications of the Association for Information Systems (2004)
8. Asogwa, B.E.: The state of e-government readiness in Africa: a comparative web assessment of selected African countries. J. Internet Inf. Syst. (2011)
9. Palvia, S.C.J., Sharma, S.S.: e-government and E-Governance: definitions, Domain Framework and Status around the World (2008)
10. The F.D.R.E Ministry of Communication and Information Technology. Annual Journal 2011/12

11. Al-Hashmi, A., Darem, A.B.: Understanding phases of e-government project, New Delhi (2006)
12. Backus, M.: E-Governance in Developing Countries, IICD Research Brief (2001)
13. Ndou, V.: e-government for developing countries: opportunities and challenges. Electr. J. Inf. Syst. Developing Countries (2004)
14. Karokola, G., Yngström, L.: Discussing e-government maturity models for developing world-security view. In: Proceedings of the Information Security South Africa Conference (2009)
15. Pressman, R.S.: Software Engineering: A Practitioner's Approach, 5 edn. (2014)
16. Dada, D.: The failure of e-government in developing countries: a literature review. EJISDC (2006)
17. Ethiopian Education Statistics Annual Abstract 2010/11
18. Behara, G.K., Varre, V.V., Rao, M.: Service oriented architecture for E-Governance, BPTrends, October 2009
19. Dzhusupova, Z., Shareef, M., Ojo, A., Janowski, T.: Methodology for e-government readiness assessment-models, instruments, implementation. In: Proceedings of the International Conference on Society and Information Technologies (ICSIT 2010), April 2010
20. Janowski, T., Estevez, E., Ojo, A.: A project framework for e-government, United Nations University (2007)
21. E-Governance Project Lifecycle, National Institute for Smart Government, India. www.nisg.org

Linux Server Monitoring and Self-healing System Using Nagios

Tanapat Anusas-amornkul$^{(\boxtimes)}$ and Sirasit Sangrat

King Mongkut's University of Technology North Bangkok, Bangkok, Thailand
tanapat.a@sci.kmutnb.ac.th

Abstract. In an administrator perspective, a system repair is a tedious work because a server can be down any time, even at night. In addition, it takes some time to repair and bring the server back online. Therefore, a self-healing server is needed to decrease workload of an administrator. Nagios is open source monitoring tools and is normally used for monitoring networks, servers or applications. In this work, a self-healing function in Nagios is proposed in order to automatically solve Linux server problems. Nagios is used for both monitoring and solving problems in Apache web servers and Oracle database servers, which were analyzed using a root cause analysis. Two scenarios, a practical scenario and a simulated problem scenario, are tested with number of corrections and time to solve problems as performance metrics. The experimental results showed that the time to solve problems using self-healing approach for Apache web servers was improved 31.42% and that for Oracle database servers was improved 40.40% comparing with manual solving approach.

Keywords: Nagios · Self-healing · Root cause analysis

1 Introduction

With the advancement of the Internet today, computers are inter-connected and utilized for academics, e-commerce, entertainments, and e-governments. Typical application architecture for the Internet is a client-server architecture. In a business perspective, computer servers are important for a business to run applications to support customers in e-commerce. Sometimes, a server is not working and it has to be solved as soon as possible. However, a system administrator does not work 24/7 and a problem can occur anytime, even at night. The administrator may need to remotely log-in to a server or come to an office and solve the problem physically in order to conform to a service level agreement (SLA).

A system administrator needs some tools to monitor computers and Nagios application is normally used to support the administrator. Nagios is an open source software that monitors computer systems, networks and infrastructure [1]. It was designed to have a monitoring function only. However, it can add some plug-ins in order to enhance its function. When a server has problems, Nagios can be used to find problems but it cannot solve the problems. The objective of this work is to add a self-healing function to Nagios such that some problems in Linux servers can be solved automatically without human intervention or called self-healing. Apache web servers

© Springer International Publishing AG 2017
M. Younas et al. (Eds.): MobiWIS 2017, LNCS 10486, pp. 290–302, 2017.
DOI: 10.1007/978-3-319-65515-4_24

and Oracle database server are used to test our work. Before solving problems, root causes of both Apache web servers and Oracle database server problems were analyzed for understanding the causes of server problems.

The organization of this paper is as follows. Next section is a related work which reviews some researches that related to this work using self-healing concepts. In Sect. 3, the proposed work was described in details about a root cause analysis and self- healing system for both web and database servers. Next section is the experimental result discussion and the paper summary is concluded at the end.

2 Related Work

Ghosh surveyed research in self healing systems and proposed a strategy of synthesis and classification [2]. The authors provided the definition of self-healing system:

"Self-healing systems attempt to "heal" themselves in the sense of recovering from faults and regaining normative performance levels independently. The concept derives from the manner in which a biological system heals a wound."

Naccache proposed a self-healing framework for web service-based application. The framework was analyzed using a theoretical Queuing Network model [3]. However, this is a software-based self-healing framework. System Architecture of an Autonomic Element was proposed to design architecture to solve a problem automatically using 4 components, i.e. monitor, analyze, plan and execute [4]. Each component was connected with a mechanism to control the data flow such that the deadlock was prevented. Each component was based on some computer languages to develop for specific usages.

Pervila [5] proposed to use Nagios to monitor faults in a self-healing environment. The author explained the interconnection between Nagios and other applications for a fault recovery after service failures. However, no implementation and experiment were tested to verify the proposed idea.

Automatic Software Self-healing Using REscue points (ASSURE) was proposed to protect from software failures in server applications [6]. By using rescue points, a Linux prototype system with ASSURE could provide faster recovery time than human-driven patch deployment methods.

Psaier surveyed a research on self-healing systems and described a self-healing principles in details [7]. In addition, the analysis of self-healing approaches was summarized with different research areas.

A self-healing model was proposed to solve software problems in Windows Operating Systems automatically [8]. Four activities, i.e. monitoring, error detection and diagnosis, analysis and selection of a repair operation, and execute repair and operation, were proposed using a hash function to help detecting a fault or error. This model was able to recover a deleted file and delete a malicious file.

A Self-Healing Framework for Web-based Applications (SHoWA) was proposed to monitor, analyze, pinpoint, and recover from performance anomalies automatically in web-based applications [9]. The performance analysis showed that SHoWA gave a response time delay with less than 2 ms and a throughput impact was less than 1%.

Automated Repair Management (ARM) method [10] was proposed for IT system repairs for a helpdesk using PERL language. It gained the efficiency from 43% to 88%.

From the literature, a self-healing concept was proposed for resolving software problems or restoring back to the point before failure. In addition, the concept was not used specifically for each type of servers or devices.

3   Proposed Work

The self-healing concept is defined for software architecture but not for a specific type of servers. In production environment, a self healing capability is needed for servers to be functioned 24/7. In a system administrator perspective, a system repair is a tedious work because a server can be down any time, or even at night. In addition, it takes some time to repair and bring a server back online.

In this work, a self-healing plug-in was proposed and developed in Nagios for adding a new function as shown in Fig. 1. Therefore, Nagios is able to monitor servers and also solve problems in web and database servers automatically.

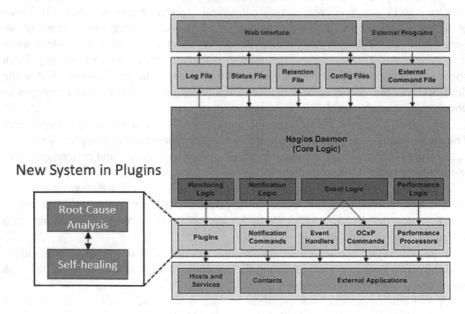

Fig. 1. A proposed model

In a real world, a server can be down with different reasons. Some problems can be solved with scripts. Normally, hardware problems cannot be solved with scripts. However, in order to solve problem correctly, root causes of problems in the specific servers must be identified and analyzed in details.

In this section, Apache web server and Oracle database server problems are analyzed using a root cause analysis. Then, a self-healing system for the web and database servers is explained. The last part is to describe performance metrics to measure the potential improvement of self-healing approach over a manual solving approach.

3.1 Root Cause Analysis

Apache Web server

Root causes of a Apache web server problems are analyzed as shown in Fig. 2. There are 5 main causes, i.e. harddisk problems, memory overload, software bugs, process problems, and configuration problems. From Fig. 2, green texts are problems that can be solved using scripts. However, red texts are problems that need attentions from an administrator. When problems are analyzed, some problems can be avoided by using protection scripts but some problems are not avoidable. Here are the causes of Apache web server problems.

- *Harddisk problem.* A server normally has a limited storage space which may be full causing from a lot of log files, or inode problem, which happens when lots of temporary files were created such that the inode number was full. Problems with hardware or file access right cannot be solved with scripts.
- *Memory overload.* A service is hanged or has problems such that system memory is used up. The problem may be caused from a hanged PERL script, a hanged HTTP service, a hanged Listener or a problem in Oracle database. However, if a problem causes from hardware failures, the problem cannot be solved with scripts.
- *Software Bugs.* Internal software bugs cannot be solved using scripts.
- *Process problem.* If an Apache server is not working or there are plenty of zombie processes in the server, apache process may cause the problem.
- *Configuration problem.* Apache server has to be configured in order to work properly. If a configuration file is not configured correctly or the domain name is unreachable, a problem occurs. However, if the SSL is misconfigured, this problem cannot be solved with a script.

Oracle Database server

Root causes of Oracle database server problems are analyzed in Fig. 3. There are 6 main causes, i.e. software bugs, harddisk problems, memory overload, table space problems, listener problems, and date problems. Green texts are problems that can be solved using scripts. In contrast, red texts are problems that need attentions from an administrator.

- *Software bugs.* Internal software bugs can't be solved using scripts.
- *Harddisk problems.* If log files or trace files are generated such that the storage or inode is full, this problem can be solved. If problems are from hardware failures or access right problem, a script can't be run to solve them.
- *Memory overload.* This problem is similar to a problem with Apache server.
- *Table space problems.* 4 main tables, i.e. Table Space SYSTEM, Table Space SYSAUX, Table Space User, and Table Space UNDOTBS, in Oracle database may be full, but this problem can be solved with scripts.

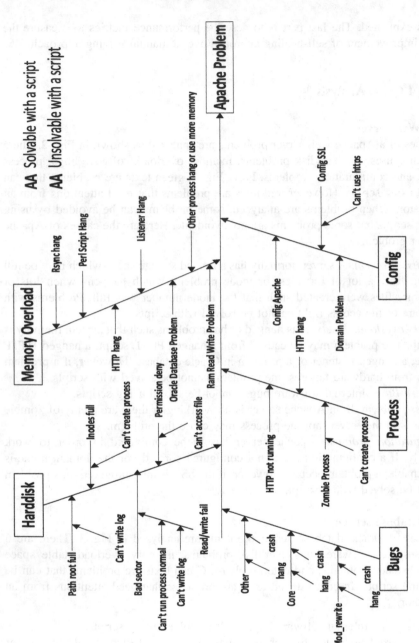

Fig. 2. Root cause analysis for an Apache web server (Color figure online)

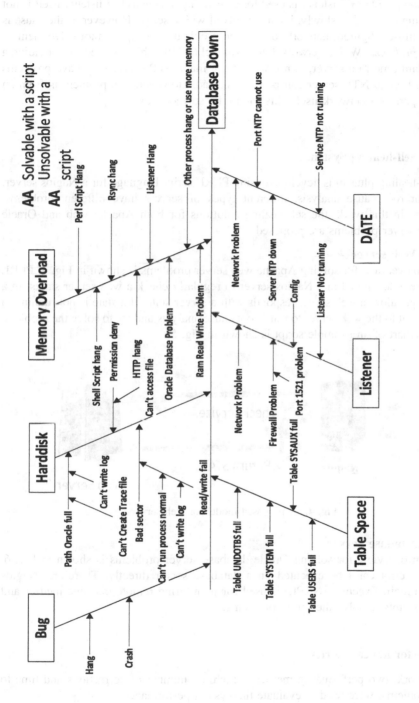

Fig. 3. Root cause analysis for an Oracle database server (Color figure online)

- *Listener problems.* Listener is used for connecting a database. If listener itself is not working or working slowly, it can be solved with a script. However, if the cause is from mis-configured, network, or firewall problems, a script cannot solve them.
- *Date problems.* When Network Time Protocol (NTP), which is used for providing a standard time to a server, is not working, a main NTP server may have problems and a backup NTP server can be used instead. However, if a problem is from an NTP port or a network itself, this cannot be solved with a script.

3.2   A Self-healing System

The self-healing plug-in is developed using PERL script language for a Nagios server. From our root cause analysis, different types of servers have different problems. Therefore, in this work, the self-healing solutions for both Apache web and Oracle database server problems are proposed.

Apache Web server
A system overview for solving Apache web server problems is shown in Fig. 4. PERL scripts were developed in a Nagios server to regularly check a web server status. In a normal operation, a web server responds with a server state. If a state is not running, a script is sent to the web server to run a root cause analysis and try to solve the problem. The flowchart of an example script is shown in Fig. 5.

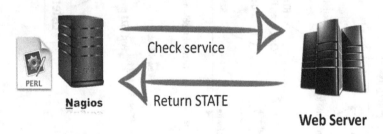

Fig. 4. A proposed model for web servers

Oracle Database Server
A system overview for solving Oracle database server problems is shown in Fig. 6. A PERL script can't be executed on a database server directly. Therefore, Nagios Remote Plugin Executor (NRPE) is used for monitoring remote machine metrics and running scripts to solve the server problems.

3.3   Performance Metrics

In this work, two performance metrics, which are number of corrections and time to solve problems, were used to evaluate the system performance.

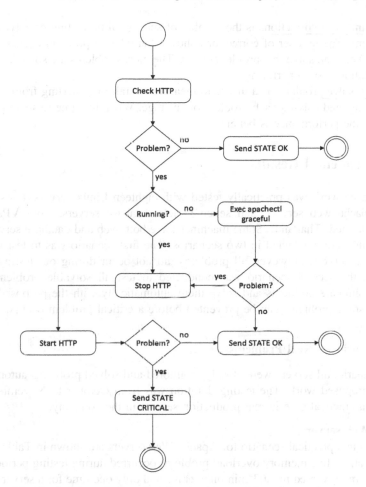

Fig. 5. An example flowchart for checking problems in a web server

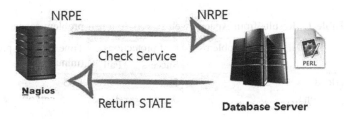

Fig. 6. A proposed model for database servers

- The number of corrections is the number of successful protecting or solving server problems. The number of corrections shows that when a problem occurs, the proposed work can solve that problem or not. The more problems are solved, the better self-healing system performs.
- Time to solve problems is a metric to measure overall time starting from detecting, analyzing, and solving each problem on average. When the time to solve problems is less, the performance is better.

4   Experimental Results

The proposed work was practically tested with eighteen Linux servers, consisting of fifteen Apache web servers, and seven Oracle database servers, from VPAdvance company limited (Thailand). Some machines have both web and database servers. The experiments were conducted in two scenarios. The first scenario was to test with real problems in servers. However, all problems did not occur during our testing period. Therefore, the second scenario was conducted to test all solvable problems using scripts to simulate problems and solve them automatically with the proposed scripts. Note that some problems can be prevented before a critical problem occurs.

4.1   Scenario 1 - Real Problems

In this scenario, all servers were closely monitored and solved problems automatically with the proposed work. The testing duration was from October to November 2015. This was a practical case in real production servers in the company.

Apache Web servers
The results in a practical scenario for Apache Web servers are shown in Table 1. From the observation, five memory overload problems occurred during testing period and all of them were prevented in 1.03 min on average and only one time for a server to be no service was solved in 0.34 min.

Table 1. Results from Apache web servers in a real problem scenario

Problems	# of problems	# of protections		Time to solve problems (minutes)
		Success	Fail	
Memory overload	5	5	0	1.03
HTTP configuration problem	0	0	0	–
Storage space	0	0	0	–
Zombie process	0	0	0	–
Problems	# of problems	# of corrections		Time to solve problems (minutes)
		Success	Fail	
No web service	1	1	0	0.34

Oracle Database servers

For Oracle database servers, sixteen problems occurred and they were categorized into nine memory overload, three Oracle Table Space, three full inode and one no service problems. Most of problems were prevented from hanged (no service) database servers.

Time to solve problems was varied depending on problems. For the full inode problem, the cause of this problem was bugs in a source code on a webpage and time to solve (protection) this problem was 25 min on average. After that the bugs was manually solved because it was a software bug. Only one no service problem occurred and it was solved in 2.49 min as shown in Table 2.

Table 2. Results from Oracle database servers in a real problem scenario

Problems	# of problems	# of protections		Time to solve problems (minutes)
		Success	Fail	
Memory overload	9	9	0	0.58
Oracle Table Space	3	3	0	4.42
Oracle Listener	0	0	0	–
Storage space	0	0	0	–
Full inode	3	3	0	25.0
NTP Date	0	0	0	–
Problems	# of problems	# of corrections		Time to solve problems (minutes)
		Success	Fail	
No service	1	1	0	2.49

4.2   Scenario 2 - Simulated Problems

In this scenario, several problems were simulated using PERL scripts. Each script was developed to simulate a problem. For this scenario, the time to solve was compared between manual solving and self-healing approaches. Each problem was simulated 10 times and calculated average time to solve problems. For manual solving approach, an administrator was at the servers and solved problems manually by using command lines. For a self-healing approach, PERL scripts were running periodically and tried to solve problems automatically. The self-healing scripts checked servers every 1 min. It means that at most 1 min was delayed for detecting server problems in the self-healing approach. For a manual solving approach in practice, problems may occur at night and this could add even more time to solve problems in terms of hours.

Apache Web servers

There were six scripts to simulate problems in web servers. Table 3 shows the results from this experiment. All problems were solved for both manual solving and self-healing approaches. However, time to solve problems of self-healing approach was faster than that of manual solving approach. The average improvement was over 30 percents on average for self-healing approach.

Table 3. Results from Apache web servers in a simulated problem scenario

Problems	# of tests	Time to solve problems (minutes)		% improvement
		Manual solving	Self-healing	
No service	10	1.50	1.02	32.00
Memory overload	10	1.57	1.07	31.84
HTTP configuration problem	10	1.58	1.05	33.54
Storage space	10	1.41	1.02	27.65
Zombie process	10	1.59	1.01	35.84
Domain unreachable	10	1.41	1.02	27.65

Table 4. Results from Oracle database servers in a simulated problem scenario

Problems	# of tests	Time to solve problems (minutes)		% improvement
		Manual solving	Self-healing	
No service	10	3.30	1.31	60.30
Memory overload	10	1.59	1.08	32.07
Oracle Table Space	10	3.26	1.30	60.12
Oracle Listener	10	2.05	1.10	46.34
Storage space	10	1.43	1.05	26.57
Full inode	10	2.09	1.39	33.49
NTP Date	10	1.34	1.02	23.88

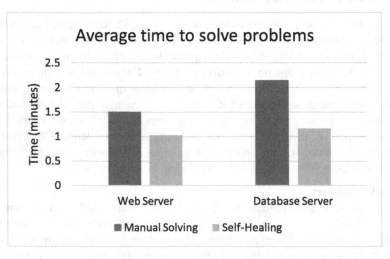

Fig. 7. Comparison chart for average time to solve problems

Oracle Database servers

For Oracle database servers, eight scripts were developed to simulate problems. Table 4 shows the results from the experiment. The results were similar to the results from Apache Web servers. Time to solve problems for self-healing approach was faster than that for manual solving approach. The self-healing approach was able to improve the time to solve problems significantly for Oracle database servers.

Figure 7 compares average time to solve problems for both manual solving and self-healing approaches in Scenario 2. The average time to solve problems for self-healing approach is faster than that for manual solving such that the self-healing approach can improve the performance drastically over 40% on average.

5   Conclusion and Future Work

In this work, a root cause analysis of Linux server problems was proposed for both Apache web, and Oracle database servers. From the root cause analysis, the problems can be classified to be preventive, solvable and non-solvable problems. For the preventive problems, the self-healing scripts tried to solve them before a critical problem occurred. However, after critical problems occurred, a self-healing approach solved some solvable problems automatically. This proposed work did not solve all Linux server problems but solvable problems were solved using proposed PERL scripts with a Nagios server. The results showed that all specific problems can be solved with the proposed work. The time to solve problems for Apache web servers was improved 31.42% when using a self-healing approach. In addition, the time to solve problems for Oracle database servers was significantly improved 40.40%. For our future work, an e-mail server is a server that has been used widely on the Internet today, similar to web and database servers. Therefore, problems in e-mail servers should be analyzed and solved with our self-healing approach.

References

1. Nagios Homepage. https://www.nagios.com/. Accessed 1 Apr 2017
2. Ghosh, D., Sharman, R., Rao, H., Upadhyaya, S.: Self-healing systems — survey and synthesis. Decis. Support Syst. **42**(4), 2164–2185 (2007)
3. Naccache, H., Gannod, G.C.: A self-healing framework for web services. In: Proceedings of the IEEE International Conference on Web Services, Salt Lake City, UT, 2007, pp. 398–345 (2007)
4. Fuad, M.M., Oudshoorn, M.J.: System architecture of an autonomic element. In: Proceedings of the Fourth IEEE International Workshop on Engineering of Autonomic and Autonomous Systems (EASe 2007) (2007)
5. Pervila, M.: Using Nagios to monitor faults in a self-healing environment. In: Spring seminar on Self-healing Systems, pp. 1–6. University of Helsinki (2007). http://www.cs.helsinki.fi/u/niklande/opetus/SemK07/paper/pervila.pdf. Accessed 1 Apr 2017

6. Sidiroglou, S., Laadan, O., Perez, C., Viennot, N., Nieh, J., Keromytis, A.: ASSURE: automatic software self-healing using rescue points. In: Proceedings of the 14th International Conference on Architectural Support for Programming Languages and Operating Systems (ASPLOS XIV), pp. 37–48. ACM, New York (2009)
7. Psaier, H., Dustdar, S.: A survey on self-healing systems: approaches and systems. Computing **91**, 43–73 (2011)
8. Kumar, K.P., Naik, N.S.: Self-healing model for software application. In: Proceedings of the IEEE International Conference on Recent Advances and Innovations in Engineering (2014)
9. Magalhães, J.P., Silva, L.M.: SHõWA: a self-healing framework for web-based applications. ACM Trans. Auton. Adapt. Syst. **10**(1), 28 (2015). ACM. Article 4. doi:10.1145/2700325
10. Gorski, J., Kaminski, M.: Towards automation of IT systems repairs. Soft. Quality J. 1–30 (2016). ISSN = 1573-1367

Performance Analysis of Cloud Computing Infrastructure

Ales Komarek, Jakub Pavlik, and Vladimir Sobeslav[✉]

Faculty of Informatics and Management, University of Hradec Kralove,
Rokitanskeho 62, Hradec Kralove, Czech Republic
{ales.komarek,jakub.pavlik.7,vladimir.sobeslav}@uhk.cz

Abstract. This paper explains how to work with performance measurement tools to be able to make qualified decision during the election of the right cloud platform. The popularity of the cloud computing is increasing rapidly and there is a variety of cloud platforms from Open-source world as well as from the vendors. Choosing the right solution, either public cloud from large number of providers or private cloud, can significantly differ in cost and performance. This brings a lot of challenges to find suitable solution one for end user workload.

Keywords: Cloud · Performance testing · Virtualization · Network performance · Storage performance · Computing performance

1 Introduction

It has been a while since clouds appeared in IT world and during the time clouds became more spread all over the world. Nowadays there are plenty of cloud platforms which differ in many significant ways. It can be eigher perspective of openness, complexity or performance etc. While openness and complexity are often easy see on the first sight, it is much harder to differentiate based on performance. First difficulty comes with variety of domains that need to be involved like storage, network and computing performance. It becomes even more complex to suit exact application based on its needs - some needs more networking performance, other needs more storage IOPS etc. There are more and more things that need to be taken care of [5].

One of the issues of the companies is, that the finding of suitable cloud platform is not systematic process as it should be. It usually end up taking first option that is discovered. The process of making a right decision should always differ based on exact application. However there are some basic question that should be answered.

1. How to identify suitable virtual machine from different cloud providers?
2. Which type of virtual machine can serve the most demands for the lowest cost?

This thesis focuses on methodology of testing a variety of cloud platforms.

© Springer International Publishing AG 2017
M. Younas et al. (Eds.): MobiWIS 2017, LNCS 10486, pp. 303–313, 2017.
DOI: 10.1007/978-3-319-65515-4_25

2   The Performance of Cloud Services

This section covers quantification of basic characteristics that should be measured during performance analysis of cloud platform. The smallest unit of qualitative characteristic is metric which provides basic information about some attribute. Each metric has a definition about what it represents and it also has given values based on empiric testing. The different metrics serve different purposes, for example response time affects speed of service and ratio of served to discarded requests affects quality of service [4] (Fig. 1).

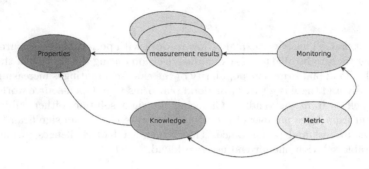

Fig. 1. The relationship between metric and property [11]

The figure describes relationship between metric and its property. Each cloud platform has its properties which represents this platform. It is important to understand these properties properly. This can be done through metrics. Metrics help cloud providers to represent their cloud solution by given values that helps customer to pick the proper solution that suits their demands (Fig. 2).

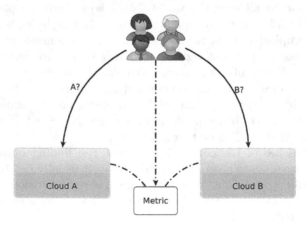

Fig. 2. Choice of cloud platform from custer point of view [12]

Metrics are the basic component of decision making process. Customer should be able to choose and measure specific metrics, that should help him to decide for the right solution.

3   Areas of Performance Measurement

This section describes the important metrics that need to be considered for performance analysis of cloud platform. There are three main areas of focus from given figure (Fig. 3).

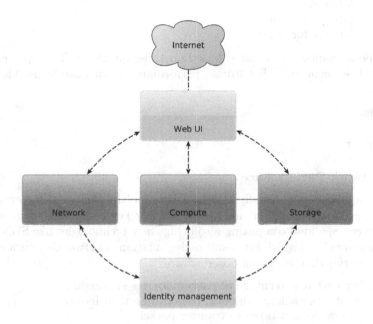

Fig. 3. Common architecture of cloud platform

The areas are:

1. Computing performance
2. Storage performance
3. Network performance

3.1   Computing Performance

Computing performance tells how many operations can be done per second - Floating-point Operations performance Second (FLOPS). It is basically telling how powerful the hypervisor is [3].

There are several testing tools that can be used for benchmarking of computing performance:

1. CoreMark
2. CloudCmp
3. SciMark 2.0
4. Tachyon benchmark
5. SPEC CPU2006

3.2   Storage Performance

The other area is performance of storage. Cloud environments usually provide different types and speeds of storage for Virtual machines. The basic metrics are:

1. Average latency.
2. Average latency for read.
3. Average latency for write.

The performance is calculated based on these metrics and it represented in IOPS (I/O per second). [1] For storage performance testing can be used following tools:

1. IOZone
2. Fio
3. Bonnie++

3.3   Network Performance

Since the application is usually spread across multiple physical hypervisors or needs to have access from outside world, another key component is networking performance. [8] Cloud computing also brings new technologies like SDN, which brings some overhead which can result in degradation of networking performance. The key metrics that are being observed are:

1. Reliability - what percentage of packets arrives successfully.
2. Throughput - the amount of data, that can be transferred.
3. Latency - how long it takes to transfer packet.

The network performance testing tools include:

1. Ping
2. Iperf
3. Netperf
4. Socketperf

4   Architecture

Due to large number of cloud platforms and cloud providers, it is hard task to implement universal solution, that would cover all these platforms or different use cases. The cloud environment can also significantly differ during time or even space. The large cloud platforms spread across multiple datacenters and the testing results in one datacenter can be different from those which were done in other datacenter. The current number of users that are sharing single hardware is also changing. [6] Because of this, the testing solution should do repeatable and reproducible to get the right statistical empiric data. The testing solution can be divided into three modules:

1. Collecting data
2. Data analysis
3. Data visualization

4.1   Collecting Data

Data collection is the most important and complex component of whole solution. It can be divided into for steps:

1. Creation/preparation of the testing environment.
2. Run of tests.
3. Send the test results.
4. Cleanup of testing environment.

The first thing that needs to be decided is the scenario, which will define which tests need to be run. Based on the scenario and Cloud platform specific orchestration tool the testing environment can be created. This will usually include step which will perform post install tasks for environment preparation. After the preparation the tests can run. The results of the tests need to be passed to data analysis module. It is also needed to clean whole environment as soon as the tests are done, because all resources are payed.

The proposed architecture uses Jenkins Continuous integration tool which has been here for a while and it is powerfull and open-source. Jenkins also has many modules that simplifies the creation of particular scenarios that are called jobs. The jobs are created by Job builder which is tool for management of large number jobs.

Listing 1.1. Scenario - environment preparation

```
- job-template:
  name: prepare-environment-{cloud}
  concurrent: false
  builders:
  - shell:
     !include-raw-escape scripts/prepare-environment.sh
  parameters:
    - string:
      name: ENGINE
    - string:
      name: CLOUD
    - string:
      name: TEST
```

Listing 1.2. Group of scenarios for run of tests

```
- job-group:
  name: {engine}-tests
  engine: perfkit
  test: ping, netperf, iperf, coremark, fio
  jobs:
    - prepare-environment-{cloud}
    - run-tests-{cloud}
    - publish-results-{cloud}
    - cleanup-environment-{cloud}
```

4.2   Data Analysis

Data analysis module contains several tools which work with data that are collected prior phase. This architecture model is using InfluxDB as time series database which supports storing data in Metrics 2.0 format.

Listing 1.3. Sample of Metrics 2.0 format

```
{
    host:  host1
    what:  diskspace
    mountpoint:  srv/node/host1
    unit:  B
    type:  used
    metric_type:  gauge
}
    meta:  {
    agent:  diamond,
    processed_by:  statsd2
}
```

4.3   Data Visualization

The last module is data visualization. This module should be able to get data and show them appropriate graph. The architecture contains tool Grafana which can be used for more advanced visualization and Matplotlib for box plots.

5   Test of Selected Cloud Platforms

This chapter focuses on demonstrating testing architecture on real cloud platforms - OpenStack, GCP, AWS and Azure. The picked flavors are summarized in following table (Table 1):

Table 1. Instance flavors

Provider	Type	vCPU	RAM (GB)
Openstack	m1.xlarge	8	16
GCP	n1-standard-4	4	15
AWS	m4.xlarge	4	16
Azure	A-4	8	14

The results of all performed tests on all these instances is visualized in the table below (Table 2):

Table 2. Testing results

Ping - latency	ms	0.41	0.44	0.47	0.53
Iperf - throughput	Mbits/sec	6750.6	6202.64	5668.73	4655.07
Netperf - CRR transaction	ops	2285.55	2099.5	1946.31	1556.49
Netperf - throughput	Mbits/sec	6966.34	6437.93	5874.48	4809.22
Cloudsuite-web-serving - latency	ms	113.41	121.7	130.42	147.14
Cloudsuite-in-memory-analytics - time of execution	s	32.79	35.28	37.45	42.72
Cloudsuite-web-search	ops	23.09	21.23	19.63	15.8
Cassandra-stress	ops	5422.5	5009.79	4558.45	3764.03
Cassandra-stress - latency	ms	27.44	29.46	31.33	35.59
Coremark - score	-	43922.35	40397.94	36698.11	30705.02
Scimark2 - score	Mflops	1251.66	1152.37	1053.01	871.06
Hpcc - throughput of stream	Mbits/sec	11.77	10.98	9.94	8.09
Hpcc - throughput of random access	Mbits/sec	0.03	0.03	0.03	0.02
Unixbench - throughput of pipe	Mbits/sec	4826547.44	4478302.66	4088074.45	3336586.21
Unixbench - score	-	3364.94	3111.18	2858.41	2300.71
Fio - number of I/O operations	Read IOPS	111.16	103.03	94.01	76.09
Fio - number of I/O operations	Write IOPS	1481.43	1373.52	1249.42	1001.98
Fio - latency	Write ms	648.39	696.95	743.62	839.45
Fio - latency	Read ms	8888.12	9543.13	10251.84	11584.95
Bonnie++ - speed of random deletion	Kb/sec	121897.74	111633.99	103315.63	84342.62
Bonnie++ - speed of file creation	Kb/sec	2811.1	2587.73	2369.85	1969.39
Bonnie++ - speed of file rewrite	Kb/sec	59144.9	54423.94	49351.44	41375.03

All these values were handled by analytics module which was described in previous chapter. In next subsection will be introduced examples of vizualization of compute, network and storage metrics from above table.

5.1 Compute Testing Results

The test of computing power shows that the best performance was on GCP on both Coremark (higher value is better) and Scimark (higher value is also better). The worst results were on Azure platform which is powered by Hyper-V virtualization (Figs. 4 and 5).

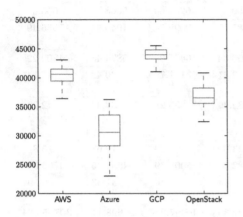

Fig. 4. Coremark score   **Fig. 5.** Scimark score

5.2 Network Testing Results

There are many tests and metrics that can be observed with network testing. Here will be shown only latency and throughput for demonstration. The throughput (higher value is better) and latency (lower value is better) results winner and loser is the same as in compute testing (Figs. 6 and 7).

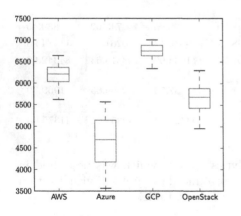
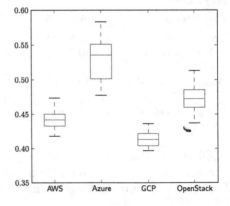

Fig. 6. Iperf throughput   **Fig. 7.** Ping latency

5.3   Storage Testing Results

The storage I/O results for both read and write (higher value is better) were on the other hand the best on AWS and Azure is the last here as well (Figs. 8 and 9).

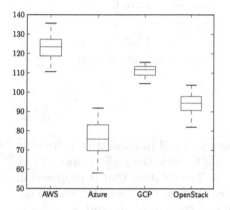

Fig. 8. Fio random read   **Fig. 9.** Fio random write

5.4   Price Comparison

One of the key question that was mentioned at the beginning is 'Which type of virtual machine can serve the most demands for the lowest cost?'. The amount of requests per second can be taken from previous testing and apply price for one request. The flavor of the virtual machine can be optimized based on this information which can save a lot of financial resources. The 30,436875 is average value of days in month. The function below is an example how to calculate a month price:

Listing 1.4. Function for price calculation

```
def get_price_per_request(price_per_month, requests_per_second):
    """Returns price per request
    """
    requests_per_month = requests_per_second * 60 * 60 * 24 * 30.4368
    return price_per_month / requests_per_month
```

Based on price for month, the best results are on GCE (Table 3).

Table 3. Table of price results

Provider	Price/month	Requests/s	Price of request $
GCE	105 $	23	1.735 996 039 373 644 106
OpenStack	150 $	20	2.851 993 493 256 700 5 106
AWS	190 $	21	3.440 500 087 103 322 106
Azure	280 $	15	7.098 294 916 550 011 106

6 Conclusion

This paper introduced one of the issues that goes hand to hand with increasing cloud computing popularity - how to be able to pick the right cloud service provider based on best price and performance. The solution that is proposed in this paper assumes that there is a need for continuous testing to be able to get empiric statistical data based on which can end user make an erudite decision. To manage such a solution effectively, there is a need for some modular solution.

The testing model was divided into three parts. First module, that is responsible for data collection should be able to perform various tests among multiple cloud providers and hand the data to analytics module. This module is than responsible for storing data and make differents statistics on these data. The last module should represent data in human readable form - visualization. It should be able to create different type of graphs.

The last part demonstrated testing of particular cloud platforms which included statistical summary and also visualization.

Acknowledgement. This work and the contribution were also supported by project of specific science, Faculty of Informatics and Management, University of Hradec Kralove, Czech Republic.

References

1. Gregg, B.: Systems Performance: Enterprise and the Cloud, 1st edn. Prentice Hall, New Jersey (2014)
2. Jackson, K., Bunch, C., Sigler, E.: OpenStack Cloud Computing Cookbook- Third Edition, 1st edn. Packt Publishing, Birmingham (2015)
3. Kratzke, N., Quint, P.-C.: About Automatic Benchmarking of IaaS Cloud Service Providers for a World of Container Clusters (2015). http://paper.uscip.us/jccr/JCCR.2015.1002.pdf. Accessed 28 Mar 2016
4. Anon: (2017). http://nvlpubs.nist.gov/nistpubs/Legacy/SP/nistspecialpublication 800-145.pdf. Accessed 25 Jan 2017
5. Gillam, L., Li, B., O'Loughlin, J.: Benchmarking cloud performance for service level agreement parameters. Int. J. Cloud Comput. 3(1), 3 (2014)

6. Li, C., Zhang, X.: Performance evaluation on open source cloud platform for high performance computing. J. Comput. Appl. **33**(12), 3580–3585 (2013)
7. Suakanto, S.: Performance measurement of cloud computing services. Int. J. Cloud Comput. Serv. Architect. **2**(2), 9–20 (2012)
8. Chadalpaka, M.B.: System and Method for Storage Virtualization Computer and Network Technology (ICCNT), U. S. patent 6, 845, 403B2, 01 18 (2005)
9. Newman, S.: Building Microservices: Designing Fine-Grained Systems. OReilly (2015)
10. Sahoo, J., Mohapatra, S., Lath, R.: Virtualization: A survey on concepts, taxonomy and associated security issues. In: Second International Conference Computer and Network Technology (ICCNT), pp. 222–226 (2010)
11. NIST: Cloud Computing Service Metrics Description NIST Cloud Computing Reference Architecture and Taxonomy Working Group NIST Cloud Computing Program Information Technology Laboratory (2015)
12. Siegel, J., Perdue, J.: Cloud services measures for global use: the service measurement index (SMI). In: Service Research Innovation Institute (SRII) Global Conference, pp. 24–27. IEEE (2012)

Analysis and Solution Model of Distributed Computing in Scientific Calculations

Josef Horalek and Vladimír Soběslav[(⊠)]

Faculty of Informatics and Management, University of Hradec Kralove,
Hradec Kralove, Czech Republic
{josef.horalek,vladimir.sobeslav}@uhk.cz

Abstract. Processing huge amounts of data is currently of concern in various fields of science and commercial data processing, such as pharmaceutical drug development, astronomical probe data processing, security analysis of large amounts of communication data, etc. Generally, centrally administered methods are used, but their employment and operation are very expensive. The aim of this paper is to present a model of high-capacity data processing that is based on the technology of Apache Hadoop with emphasis on use of volunteer host devices with the service distribution via the Internet.

Keywords: Hadoop · Cluster · HDFS · Apache hadoop · Distributed computing

1 Introduction

The most frequent approach to processing high-capacity data is the use of one cluster containing hundreds or thousands of nodes that process all the user requests. If the nodes are used to their limit, additional nodes can be added to the cluster. Figure 1 depicts traditional access of one user to the cluster [3]. Any computing performed in the cluster is conducted by the manager responsible for their administration, running, and terminating. Once the program is terminated, the output data is stored to Hadoop distributed file system (HDFS) and the client is informed about the computation being completed. However, given cluster is not accessed by a single user, but by tens, hundreds, thousands, or millions of them at the same time, depending on the given cluster use. Therefore, with higher numbers of users, time required to process all the tasks elongates. Moreover, in this case it is necessary for the client to provide not only data to be processed, but also a program written in the supported language. Many users using the performance of distributed computing centres are scientific workers that care mostly about the correct final result and primarily are not concerned about the optimisation of the code used or additional scripts. All these imperfections lead to prolonging the time needed to execute the tasks, but it can also be the cause of incorrect calculations, or it can lead to a crash of the whole cluster.

M. Younas et al. (Eds.): MobiWIS 2017, LNCS 10486, pp. 314–324, 2017.
DOI: 10.1007/978-3-319-65515-4_26

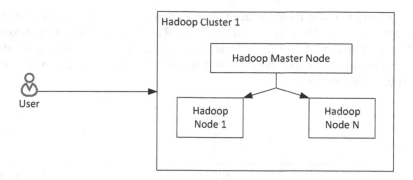

Fig. 1. Standard user access to a hadoop cluster

The aim of this article is to present an innovative approach to high-capacity data processing, including the application draft. The purpose of the application is to improve the work of the users using automation and simplifying the communication between the used and Hadoop Clusters. Therefore, the application allows for higher computing performance and redistributing the data processing between multiple clusters. Rules for the user interface are also defined, as well as basic functionality and methods required to process the data [1, 2].

2 Principal Solution Draft

The suggested approach of processing high-capacity data [4, 5] lies in interconnecting distributed computing technologies with volunteer computing through Apache Hadoop. In volunteer computing, users are engaged as computing nodes that provide processing power necessary for complicated calculations. The node is defined as any device capable of performing required calculations, along with hardware allowing for being integrated into the cluster and with being compatible with Apache Hadoop, i.e. device with any supported OS (Linux, Windows, BSD, Mac OS/X, or OpenSolaris) [6]. All these nodes log in a larger unit that represents one Hadoop cluster. Logging into the cluster is performed via client application installed on the device. Every Hadoop cluster then handles its nodes and makes use of their computing power. Additional nodes can be added to the cluster dynamically, without the need of restarting or shutting it down, as referenced in [6]. This ability allows for adding nodes into the cluster when the devices are not being used, and can, therefore, process the data only in time intervals when the user does not use them actively. All the Hadoop clusters are then logged in the designed application. The application serves as a link between the users and the Hadoop clusters, as a means of adding nodes into the clusters, and as a way of managing the Hadoop clusters logged in [7]. The placement of the application, Hadoop clusters, and nodes, is depicted in Fig. 2. Before the detailed presentation of the application draft, it is essential to present real life situations where our approach to high-capacity data processing using distributed computing can be used. As an example we can use the campus of the university, which has 11 buildings at disposal, where each building can serve as one Hadoop cluster. In every building there are many devices that are connected to each other via the computer network. These devices are never used at 100 percent capacity, neverthe-less, they are running 24/5 or 24/7. Especially during the evening hours, no one is working on those devices and, therefore, it is possible to use them as computing nodes as a part of a Hadoop cluster.

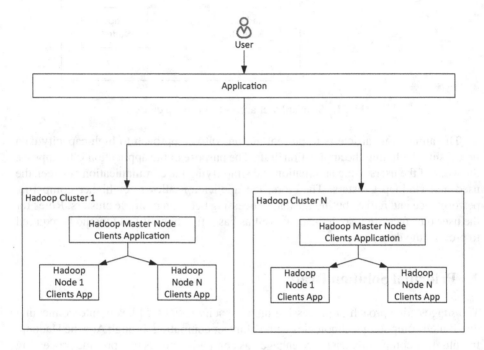

Fig. 2. Extended data processing access scheme

All the university building/clusters are connected to the server where this application of ours is running and handling the cluster management. This computing power can be used for time-demanding and complicated computations. A great advantage lies in low initial financial requirements as the Hadoop cluster master node is already owned by the university as it is the university's standard IT equipment [8, 9].

3   Application and Basic Functions

From the scheme of our approach to high-capacity data processing above it is apparent that two main applications are being used. The main server application is designated for the users that have registered into it, and after that it allows them to download the respective client application, which is designated for the nodes that are to be connected to the Hadoop cluster maintained by the server application. Figure 3 depicts the basic scheme of communication between the server application, the client application, and the Hadoop clusters (Hadoop Master Node or Hadoop Data Node). The server application is built on two foundations: Web interface and App Core. As can be seen in Fig. 3, the user communicated only with the server application via web interface, which provides them with all the requisite information. The user's main concern is whether the processed tasks have been computed or if an error has occurred during the calculation, which tasks have been executed, how long has their computation taken etc. All the user's communication with the Hadoop cluster is managed by the App Core, which substitutes tasks that formerly had to be performed by the user, such as data upload, task execution, or gathering information about the running tasks.

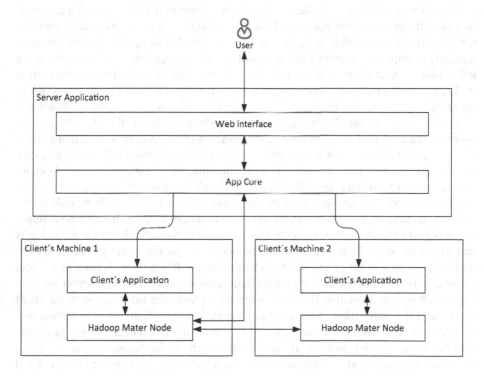

Fig. 3. Application and client station communication scheme

App Core also secures directing the tasks to the clusters for the optimal performance usage of the particular nodes. Another advantage of the users' access to the clusters using the application is that the users do not overload the Hadoop cluster with their task execution queries as they are executed exclusively by the server application. As Hadoop Master Node is designated for common hardware, it cannot be guaranteed that all of the queries will be successfully processed should many of them occur at the same time. The server application also communicates with the client device via the client application or directly with the Hadoop cluster (Hadoop Master Node), which provides the requisite information about the tasks being processed. Should a failure of the Hadoop Master Node occur and should there be a Hadoop Secondary Master Node available, the server application would start to communicate with the latter as if it were the Master Node. App Core communicates with Hadoop and the client application via XML/JSON object exchange, which is procured via the Internet network using HTTP/HTTPS, which is commonly used for the Internet communication.

3.1 Client Application

The purpose of the client device application is to maintain the connection of the given device to the cluster. After being installed, the client checks whether Hadoop is installed on the device and then prompts the user to set up configuration settings using a graphical interface. If the user does not have Hadoop installed, the application automatically prompts the user to install it. If the user chooses to install Hadoop, the application automatically prompts the user whether to download all the requisite files from the server and guides the user through the installation. After validating or during the installation of Hadoop, Hadoop cluster configuration settings pop up. The user can choose to select the preferred Hadoop cluster to which their device will connect, to connect automatically, or to act as a NameNode, i.e. become a Hadoop cluster. If the user chooses the option of the preferred Hadoop cluster, the device will always connect to that cluster. During the first use, the user is prompted with a list of available Hadoop clusters they can connect to. Once the user confirms their selection, the client application takes care of the connection. When repeatedly logging in the chosen cluster, it is not necessary to contact the server application again as the connection of the given DataNode to the cluster is secured by the client application. Should an error occur during connecting – e.g. maximum number of nodes in the cluster reached, NameNode offline etc. – log is sent to the server and the user is informed about the problem and prompted by the application with the list of available Hadoop clusters. If the user chooses to connect automatically, whenever they log in, the client application contacts the server application, which selects a suitable Hadoop cluster, then passes the information to the client and secures the connection of the computing node in a way similar to connecting to a manually chosen cluster. The advantage of the automatic cluster selection is primarily an ability to balance the cluster workload. Another factor is the distance of the connected node from the NameNode, which communicates with the newly connected node in fixed intervals, and files to be processed are interchanged between them. The last option is to become the NameNode to which other DataNodes will connect, which creates another Hadoop cluster. The user can specify the maximum usage of memory, CPU, and data storage. This information is stored into Hadoop configuration of the given node.

3.2 Server Application

The purpose of the server counterpart of the application is to balance workload, manage Hadoop clusters, and handle addition of new clusters, DataNodes (computing nodes), to the existing clusters. The App Core is the core of the server application and its purpose is to handle users' requests and users' task termination notifications, manage Hadoop clusters, balance workload, and handle errors that occur throughout the whole system. Using web interface, it is possible to log into the application with one of the two basic account types (User type or Admin type). User type allows the user to manage the programs installed and to display the statistics of the running tasks. Before being able to use this account, the user has to register using the application web interface (if this option is allowed by the application admin) or has an account created by the admin. After the account is created, the user receives an email with the required information. After logging in, the user can access a portal, where they can view an **Overview** with the statistics of the running tasks and the finished tasks, including their successful or failed completion. Another option can be found in **My programs**, where the user can obtain a list of MapReduce programs that have been uploaded by the user. The last option is thorough **Program upload wizard** for uploading a new program. The other account type is Admin, which allows to configure the application settings and to handle errors that occur in the applications. Using the web portal, Admin can also manage Hadoop clusters and tasks running on those clusters, and receive information about all the clusters' workload.

Application server part methods

The App Core on the server side offers several essential methods for the implementation of our model. The main method is **Task routing**, i.e. choosing the cluster to execute the given task. **Secure communication with Hadoop clusters** support is required as well as it, upon choosing which cluster to use to execute the task, secures the connection and uploads the required data to the cluster. **Uploading and file processing** method serves for uploading source codes and data to be processed through the web interface. Should any error occur while executing the calculations, the information is logged on the given cluster, which is secured by **Logging and error handling** method, which also serves for gathering the data about the error from the cluster and informing the user with the description of the error that had occurred. **Create cluster** method serves to add required entries to the database while creating a cluster for the cluster to be usable for calculations. **Delete cluster** method serves to terminate all the running tasks on the given cluster. If there are any pending tasks, they are moved to the active clusters. If there is a running task, its state is set to error, and after set time, the task is started in another active cluster. The method also secures removal (permanently deleting information) or deactivation (temporary removing) of the cluster. Another significant method is **Add computing node**, which performs the requisite configuration in the database and sets the required configuration to the Hadoop cluster main node. Selection of the Hadoop cluster can be fixed or automatic. In case of automatic selection, **Select Hadoop cluster** method, which selects the cluster to connect to, is called. **Remove node** method removes the node from the NameNode configuration and secures the adjustments to the database. Selection of a suitable cluster for a new computing node to connect to is secured by **Select Hadoop cluster** method, and to gather information about cluster workload, a method of the same name, which gathers information from Resource Manager API for the given cluster, is used.

Databases

In the application, databases (DB) are used to store data. For the model application, it is possible to use either of the two lead types, i.e. SQL and NoSQL. In terms of databases, the principal requirements for the application are good scalability, data loading/saving speed, high-capacity data handling, and their diversity. With similar qualities, an application is designed in NoSQL database as those have more independent structure than relation databases, which offers better scalability and performance capabilities of the database [10, 11]. The application model is going to store the required data in the database and as it will manipulate with large amounts of data, document storage type has been chosen. The choice of NoSQL is supported by the fact that the communication between the application and the Hadoop clusters is performed via exchange of XML or JSON objects, which can be stored in the database without any extensive modifications [12, 13]. As for technical solution, MongoDB open source solution has been chosen. For the purposes of the model, a basic collection that will be used to store the data in the application has been defined. In particular, Users collection stores basic information about users that log into the system. Clusters collection serves to store requisite information about the clusters (cluster address, total number of nodes, number of active nodes) from Resource Manager REST API. ClusterScheduler collection contains information about tasks running on a cluster, which is used by the forwarding algorithm. This information is being refreshed periodically and during typical events (finishing a calculation on the cluster). Program collection contains information about programs that have been uploaded and contains information who uploaded it, description of the program, name of the program, whether the program is private or public, how many times it has been run, and average time required to process 1 MB by the program per cluster.

4   Forwarding Algorithms and Workload Balancing

The main aim of our application is chiefly work with higher number of clusters and it is, therefore, to ensure proper forwarding of the tasks to free Hadoop clusters, where the calculations will be performed. Forwarding of the tasks to the clusters is determined by the following rules:

- Information about the number of available nodes within Hadoop clusters and their available memory is gathered from Resource Manager API, if no available node exists or all available memory of the cluster is used, the given cluster is removed from executing further calculations.
- Basic calculation for a suitable Hadoop cluster, where the task is to be run, is time required to process the amount of data uploaded by the user and this information is gathered by repeatedly running the given tasks on the cluster:

$$V \cdot \left(\frac{1}{v_{avg_n}} + t_{avg_n} \right)$$

V – amount of data being processed in MB, **n** – chosen Hadoop cluster, v_{avg_n} – total average speed (MB/s) of data transfer between the server application and the Hadoop cluster (n) in distance of **z** is calculated by:

$$v_{avg_n} = \frac{v_1 + v_2 + \cdots + v_{z-1} + v_z}{z}$$

z – number of connection between the application and the Hadoop cluster, v_l – average speed of data transfer between **z-1** and **z** nodes, speed is calculated when the node is logging into the application in MB/s. t_{avg_n} – average time required to process 1 MB on the chosen cluster for the chosen task:

$$t_{avg_n} = \frac{\dfrac{t_1 + 2 + \cdots + t_{j-1} + t_j}{j}}{V_1 + V_2 + \cdots + V_{j-1} + V_j}$$

If the program has not yet been run on the given cluster, t_{avg_n} is set to average value of performance of other clusters, and if the program has not yet been run on any Hadoop cluster, t_{avg_n} is set to a value that had been recorded during functionality testing after user's uploading of the program. This configuration is used to prevent eliminating or discriminating clusters where the given program had not been run yet as the average time would be 0, which would significantly influence the cluster's position in the list. t_j – time required to execute the task on the cluster. This time is acquired as the difference of ending from beginning of the execution of the task from API Hadoop Cluster for the tasks that have been successfully executed (state set to "SUCCEEDED"). j - number of tasks run in the past.

The outcome of the formula above is a list of potential clusters where the calculation can be performed. The list is ordered from the lowest value to the highest. From this list, the first cluster in order is picked and then the required operations for data transfer and task execution are performed on the given cluster. To ensure the shortest distances between the clusters and the application's server, we will use one of the common algorithms for calculating the shortest path, such as Dijkstra's or Floyd–Warshall algorithm. The required information about the cluster and its nodes is obtained using Resource Manager Api, which provides the requisite functions. The gathered information is saved to the database and subsequently used by the application. One method of adding data nodes to the clusters is automatic addition. For this method, two criteria are evaluated. One is the number of nodes in the cluster, where the value is compared to an average number of nodes. If the cluster contains below-average number of nodes, it is put into a list of candidates for addition of a node. The other is distance/data penetration between the data node and the cluster to which the given node is to be connected. After evaluating the criteria, a list of potential clusters DataNode can be connected to is assembled and then the first cluster from the list is picked.

5   Data Error Rate and Validation

Another significant merit of the application is error handling and data validation. Data validation can be divided into two groups: data to be processed by the chosen program and user entries. Data validation/cleansing during processing by the given program is reserved solely to the programmer of that program. For such situations, the application contains a method that displays the necessary information about an occurring validation error to the user and logs information about the error to a text file reserved for this purpose

[14, 15]. Entry validation, which the user fills in a web browser, is handled in two ways: client validations and server validations.

Client validation is for mandatory fields, correct value types in the forms, i.e. validation of the form field for number, correct date format, email, etc. Secondary validation is performed at the server, where more complicated validations are used. Should an error occur during the validation process, the user is informed via information in the web browser. We distinguish between data transfer errors and errors that occur during processing within Hadoop clusters. Data transfer errors can occur during the data transfer from the user to the application servers, as well as during the file transfer from the application to the clusters where they are to be processed. As already existing protocols, such as http/https or ftp/ftps, are used for data storing, basic error codes returned by these protocols are used. The application responds to the errors by notification and logging relevant information into a special error log. Handling errors of the second type is reserved to Hadoop, which handles them based upon its model. Hadoop then differentiates errors [2] into several categories. One category is **Task errors**, whose errors are most frequently thrown during program runtime. Next category is **Application Master Failure**, where similarly to the tasks run by MapReduce procedures, the main application is provided with multiple attempts for successfully executing the program. **Resource Manager Failure** error is essentially an error within the resource manager, which is a grave error as without resource manager no programs are run nor task containers assigned. The last category is **HDFS Failure**. This error can be handled by using replication, but it is necessary to keep in mind that NameNode is still the weakest component as the requisite configurations are stored locally and if this node fails, it results in the inability to perform any tasks or communicate with the cluster or the user.

6   Conclusion

The realization of the application itself takes requirements and logics of the model itself into account. For that very reason, an implementation using Spring framework, which is designed for development of Java-based enterprise application, has been used for the app core. As for the web interface, whose primary purpose is communication between the user and the server application and viewing statistics, a language that can be provided with the requisite data by the app core and displayed by the language of the web interface. For the web interface implementation, Angular 2 framework or React library can be used. The client application is required to be multi-platform and able to use GUI. For its implementation, we can use any language that matches the requirements above. For instance, it is possible to use already mentioned languages or their Java, .Net, or Scala frameworks.

We have already mentioned several times that Apache Hadoop is very popular and that it is used in many large institutions for work with high-capacity data. Especially for its good functionality and data processing speed, standard user access to Hadoop clusters is usually used in companies. This way of access is used by other companies, such as Cloudera, which offers modified Hadoop distribution as a company tool. There are several new approaches and differences of our model from the standard one. First, we group multiple Hadoop clusters in order to reach higher performance. Second, our model is built upon using computing devices that are already present in given institutions and, therefore, it is not necessary to spend large amounts of money on cluster establishment. The model is also focused on facilitating the users' work for the application to be an asset for them, both in data processing effectiveness and in terms of presenting results. If people do not use some of the Hadoop modifications, presentation of the result data will cost them more time to process the data further. As the application achieves higher computing performance by grouping Hadoop clusters, it can be utilized by wider communities of people, who can mutually share their MapReduce programs and thus it is not necessary to devise the same program several times. One of the last differences is that the model has been built as Open Source. Releasing the code to the public brings along possibilities of improvement of algorithms or the application model.

To conclude, it should be stated that the presented model allows for expanding the model which is currently discussed. The expansion is focused on the model of assembling MapReduce programs by the user directly from the web interface. That could be achieved chiefly by creating templates after which a MapReduce program code would be generated and templates for interpretation of outcome data. Therefore, the user does not have to understand the language of the code in which the given program is implemented, and only specifies the method of the program behaviour. This functionality would greatly speed up the process of program implementation and facilitate the users' work. Additionally, we would gain an opportunity to create templates regardless of the interpreted language that is supported by Hadoop.

Acknowledgment. This article has been produced in cooperation with Petr Volf, a graduate at FIM of UHK, to whom we hereby give our thanks for extraordinary assistance with proposing the solution using Hadoop in effective distributed computing. We would also like to thank to Ondrej Horning and Ladislav Balik, doctoral students who were helping with the simulation tests in laboratories. This work and the contribution were also supported by project of specific science, Faculty of informatics and Management, University of Hradec Kralove, Czech Republic.

References

1. Lu, Q., Li, S., Zhang, W., Zhang, L.: A genetic algorithm-based job scheduling model for big data analytics. EURASIP J. Wireless Commun. Netw. **2016**(1), 152 (2016)
2. Hashem, I.A.T., Anuar, N.B., Gani, A., Yaqoob, I., Xia, F., Khan, S.U.: MapReduce: review and open challenges. Scientometrics **109**(1), 389–422 (2016)
3. Kobayashi, K., Kaito, K.: Big data-based deterioration prediction models and infrastructure management: towards assetmetrics. Struct. Infrastruct. Eng. **13**(1), 84–93 (2017)
4. Govindarajan, K., Somasundaram, T.S., Boulanger, D., Kumar, V.S.: Kinshuk: A framework for scheduling and managing big data applications in a distributed infrastructure. In: ICoAC 2015 - 7th International Conference on Advanced Computing, art. no. 7562784 (2016)
5. Alekseev, A.A., Osipova, V.V., Ivanov, M.A., Klimentov, A., Grigorieva, N.V., Nalamwar, H.S.: Efficient data management tools for the heterogeneous big data warehouse. Phys. Part. Nucl. Lett. **13**(5), 689–692 (2016)
6. Hadoop wiki - faq. http://wiki.apache.org/hadoop/faq

7. Kranjc, J., Orač, R., Podpečan, V., Lavrač, N., Robnik-Šikonja, M.: ClowdFlows: Online workflows for distributed big data mining. Future Gener. Comput. Syst. **68**, 38–58 (2017)
8. Sobeslav, V., Maresova, P., Krejcar, O., Franca, T.C.C., Kuca, K.: Use of cloud computing in biomedicine. J. Biomol. Struct. Dyn. **34**(12), 1–10 (2016). Article in Press
9. Sobeslav, V., Komarek, A.: Opensource automation in cloud computing. In: Wong, W.E. (ed.) Proceedings of the 4th International Conference on Computer Engineering and Networks, pp. 805–812. Springer, Cham (2015). doi:10.1007/978-3-319-11104-9_93
10. Bao, X., Xiao, N., Lu, Y., Chen, Z.: A configuration management study to fast massive writing for distributed NoSQL systém. In: IEICE Transactions on Information and Systems, vol. E99D (9), pp. 2269–2282 (2016)
11. Li, C.-S., Franke, H., Parris, C., Abali, B., Kesavan, M., Chang, V.: Composable architecture for rack scale big data computing. Future Gener. Comput. Syst. **67**, 180–193 (2017)
12. Kobayashi, K., Kaito, K.: Big data-based deterioration prediction models and infrastructure management: towards assetmetrics. Struct. Infrastruct. Eng. **13**(1), 84–93 (2017)
13. Tran, M.C., Nakamura, Y.: Classification of HTTP automated software communication behaviour using NoSql database. In: International Conference on Electronics, Information, and Communications, ICEIC 2016, art. no. 7562957 (2016)
14. Holik, F., Horalek, J., Neradova, S., Zitta, S., Novak, M.: Methods of deploying security standards in a business environment. In: Proceedings of 25th International Conference Radioelektronika, RADIOELEKTRONIKA 2015, art. no. 7128984, pp. 411–414 (2015)
15. Holik, F., Horalek, J., Neradova, S., Zitta, S., Marik, O.: The deployment of security information and event management in cloud infrastructure. In: Proceedings of 25th International Conference Radioelektronika, RADIOELEKTRONIKA 2015, art. no. 7128982, pp. 399–404 (2015)

Analysis and Dynamical Simulation of Heart Rate Influence upon Physical Load

Jan Kubicek[✉], Martin Augustynek, Marek Penhaker,
Martin Cerny, and Iveta Bryjova

FEECS, VSB–Technical University of Ostrava, K450 17. Listopadu 15,
708 33 Ostrava–Poruba, Czech Republic
{jan.kubicek,martin.augustynek,marek.penhaker,martin.cerny,
iveta.bryjova}@vsb.cz

Abstract. The paper deals with a mathematical simulation of the dynamic heart rate progress depending upon a physical load. The whole simulation process has been implemented into MATLAB. The proposed simulation system allows for the physical load modification which reflects real-life conditions. The model has been tested in the dependence on various artificial physical loads which represent real stimuluses. The important part of the analysis is the verification procedure which compares real measured conditions with the model's obtained results.

Keywords: Heart rate · R-wave detector · Physical load · MATLAB · Simulation

1 Introduction

During the organism physic load, oxygen demands of the working muscles are increasing as well as reducing waste metabolism products. Due to those demands the blood circulation has to adapt on it. An adaptation utilizes two main mechanisms:

- increasing the minute volume,
- redistribution of the blood flow.

A study of the heart frequency dynamical features, as response on increased physical load, has showed up that a reaction is composed from the two main parts:

- Fast part – this part is independent on the physical load intensity. It is supposed that this part is caused by decreasing activity of nerve system, and therefore its influence on the heartbeat.
- Slow part – it is increasing while the physical loading is increasing. It has complex character based on a decreased nerve activity. Besides it, there is also influence of thermoregulation, breathing centre and biochemical impact.

Based on the mentioned facts, a dynamical model of the heart rate influence upon physical load is analysed in our paper. This model relevantly represents the physiological facts, on the other hand the model has potential of determination of the physical condition [1, 2].

M. Younas et al. (Eds.): MobiWIS 2017, LNCS 10486, pp. 325–333, 2017.
DOI: 10.1007/978-3-319-65515-4_27

2   Clinical Function Examination

The main aim of the functional examination by various medical devices is acquiring bio signals characterizing and describing the organ functions. The tracking and evaluation organism changes in the physical load dependence can discover the pathological reactions accessing to determine a stage of some diseases or they contribute to assessing of the diagnosis. The physical load tests are commonly clinically used in the field of neurophysiology, occupational therapy, ORL, or ophthalmology [1–4].

2.1   Physical Process

The physical process can be perceived as an organised complex of the regulation systems with autonomous controlling centres and other sectional regulation subsystems. The autonomous nerve system with CNS controls the basic physical processes and functions as the blood composition, the blood circulation, the digestion and the breathing.

The blood circulation regulation is ensured by the following major components:

- The heart contraction size,
- The arterial pressure receptors,
- The stable circulating blood volume.

During physical load, there are stronger conditions upon oxygen intake to tissues. This process is ensured by the following factors:

- **The cardiac output rise** – it is given by a product of the heart rate volume and heart rate.
- **The cardiac output redistribution** – it causes increasing blood intake to the working muscles at the expense of less important organs.
- **The oxygen extraction rise** – this extraction causes the increasing of arterial-venous oxygen difference especially into muscles [5–8, 15, 16].

2.2   The Organism Function Within Load

It is commonly used examination on the ergometer. The tested person is exposed by a load. At the load beginning the muscle's oxygen is used and the oxygen transport is consecutively increased. During the load increasing, the oxygen deficit is bigger with lactic acid production. The organism is adjusted itself on the load during the balance state. This particular state carries out balance between delivery and energy consumption. The balance state can be described by stable numbers (The heart rate output and CO_2, the minute ventilation and oxygen consumption).

For the reason of the metabolic balance it is not possible to execute long-term increased power in real-life conditions. During a physical load the active muscles requirements are increased on oxygen delivery and other nutrients and also in the same time on the pollutant outlet. After achieving the balance, the oxygen consumption during the load reaches quintuple up to twenty basal consumption. Nearly entire energy of healthy organism is obtained by aerobic way during the load after performance. The inhale volume using is much different on trained and untrained person. The balance state occurs on trained person faster than on untrained person [9–12, 17].

3 Model Building

An organism reacts itself on a physical load by increasing oxygen supplementing into muscles and outlet by metabolic products. A blood circulation must adopt itself to this phenomenon on the base of two main metabolisms: blood volume increasing and blood flowing redistribution. The minute heart volume is created by multiplication of the heart volume and the heart rate. This heart rate can be very simply measured.

The increased physical load response is composed by two major parts: slow and fast. The fast part is not depended upon the physical load, and vagus inhibition is suppressed. The slower part increases itself during the load, and contains complex neurohumoral character. The direct fast branch is realized by the following transfer function:

$$\frac{K_1}{T_1.s + 1} \tag{1}$$

Where:

K_1 denotes the vagus part constant which represents the fast branch boosting (Hz), T_1 represents time constant of fast vagus branch (s).

The slow feedback branch contains constant K_{ref} which determines the heart rate contribution within the load increasing about 1 W. K_{ref} denotes fitness of individual person. This parameter is given by the following expression:

$$K_{ref} = \frac{K_1}{W_r} \tag{2}$$

Where K_1 is constant of the vagus part, it means the fast branch boosting (Hz). W_r represents loading which can be done by vagus suppressing (W).

$$\frac{1}{T_i.s} \tag{3}$$

T_i represents time constant (s) [13, 14, 17].

The model simulation has been performed in SW MATLAB. All simulations have been performed primarily on the reference group of tested persons. The group including people with average physical load who irregularly exercise and do common procedures. The acquired values have been consequently compared with two other groups: sportsmen and people suffering from ischemic heart disease. The measured parameters are concluded for simulation purposes are summarized into the following Table 1:

Table 1. The basic parameters of individual groups

The group	$K_i(Hz)$	$T_1(s)$	$K_{ref}(\frac{Hz}{W})$	$W_r(W)$	$T_i(s)$
The reference group	0.33	10.3	0.011	30.2	105
The Athletes	0.95	10.5	0.0006	158.3	35
The ischemic people	0.15	5.5	0.014	10.7	160

4 Simulation of Step Load

In this part of the analysis, we have designed the model which reflects situation of step loading. This model is depicted on the following Fig. 1:

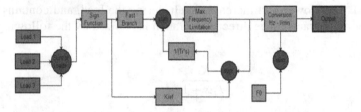

Fig. 1. The simulation model flow chart for the step load.

The Fig. 2 shows typical representation of the simulated step load. The simulated load in the time 0 s is equaled to 0 W. After taking 60 s, we can observe loading 50 W but on the base Sign function this change is given only by unit step.

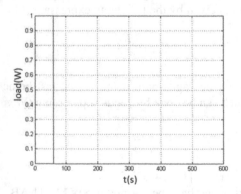

Fig. 2. Simulation of the step load.

In the resulting output, we can observe the heart rate change within the time, simultaneously it is visible that first 60 s the heart rate is kept on the reclined level 60 l/min and after load increasing this value is rapidly raised on the approximate level 75 l/min. After that, the heart beat returns itself to the stable level (Fig. 3).

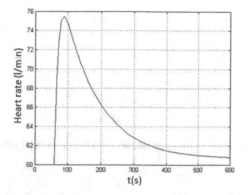

Fig. 3. The dynamical progress of heart rate after step load.

The Fig. 4 shows situation when step load is consequently changed within three steps. In the time of 60 s, there is the step rise on 50 W, after that in 120 s on 200 W and last step is carried out in the time 240 s on level 250 W.

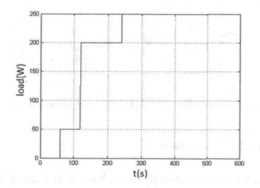

Fig. 4. The three phase step load.

Within the first load raising about 50 W the heart beat is increased approximately about 13 l/min, after that the heart rate goes down to the stable level. This decreasing part is interrupted in the time 120 s where the next step loading is performed. The heart beat increases again, this time up to value around 107 l/min. After taking this period it goes to the settling heart rate. Last increasing of the heart rate comes in the time 240 s, heart beat reaches on 91 l/min (Fig. 5).

The Fig. 6 points at the heart rate comparison of three analyzed groups. In the time 0 s the step load of 50 W was set. After taking 120 s it went to the increasing about 150 W.

In the case of the athletes group we can observe the rapid increasing of the heart rate, and also the rapid settle to quiescent value. In the case of the ischemic people the heart rate rise was the least significant, and return to the stable heart rate was the slowest.

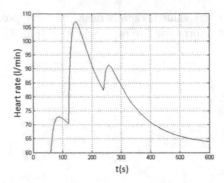

Fig. 5. The dynamical progress of the heart rate after taking three step loads – the reference group.

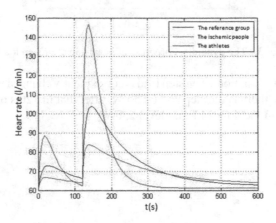

Fig. 6. The heart rate comparison for three analyzed groups of people – step load.

5   Simulation of Linear Load

In the second part of the simulation analysis we have tested the system response in the linear load dependence. The simulation flow chart is depicted on the Fig. 7.

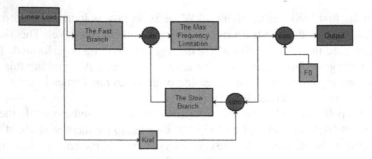

Fig. 7. The simulation model flow chart for the linear load.

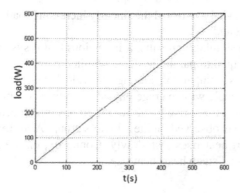

Fig. 8. Simulation of the linear load.

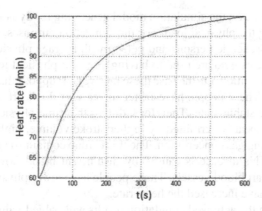

Fig. 9. The dynamical progress of the heart beat – the reference group.

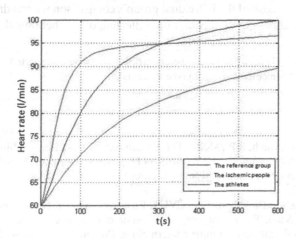

Fig. 10. The heart rate comparison for three analyzed groups of people – the linear load.

In the first attempt, we have tested the linearly increasing load with starting loading in the time 0 s (Figs. 8 and 9).

On the base of the simulation results, it is obvious that if system is linearly loaded, the heart rate will be equal to parabolic shape within the time.

The Fig. 10 brings comparison among individual analysed groups of athletes, ischemic people and people with average physical condition during the linear load. We can also observe the heart rate rise by all tested groups influenced by linear load. The steepest heart beat rise is observed on the athlete's group. After reaching of value 92 l/min the athlete's heart beat rises just slowly. Contrarily, on the ischemic people we cannot observe the initial steep heart beat rise.

6   Conclusion

The analysis is focused on the simulation model generating for dynamical simulation of the heart rate during the physical load. For the simulation purposes, the comparison of the athlete groups, ischemic persons and person with average physical condition have been used. The athletes who are used to having a regular physical load, and they have excellent physical condition. On the base these fact we can suppose that they cope greater physical load well. These people have faster increase of the heart rate, but contrarily smaller value in the stable state. Therefore, during the same physical load on trained persons lower heart beat is permitted by higher stroke volume, higher arterial-venous difference in breathing gas concertation. The third group contains people suffering from ischemic disease. This disease is caused by insufficient blood flow to the heart and narrowing of the heart blood vessels. Those people have lower physical condition, and consequently they have increased the heart rate.

After comparing the achieved simulation results with tabled values in literature we can state that the model's simulation closely reflect tabled values in the case testing of the step load. On the base of the individual group's comparison we can draw the conclusion, for example about physical condition, reflecting of the theoretical values.

Acknowledgment.   The work and the contributions were supported by the project SV4506631/2101 'Biomedicínské inženýrské systémy XII'.

References

1. van Wijk van Brievingh, R.P., Möller, D.P.F.: Biomedical Modeling and Simulation on a PC: A Workbench for Physiology and Biomedical Engineering. Springer, New York (1993)
2. Potůček, J.: Metodologie modelování biologických systémů. České vysoké učení technické, V Praze (2009)
3. Eck, V., Razím, M.: Biokybernetika. ČVUT, Elektrotechnická fakulta, Praha (1996)
4. Penhaker, M., Stula, T., Augustynek, M.: Long-term heart rate variability assessment. In: Proceedings of the 5th Kuala Lumpur International Conference on Biomedical Engineering, BIOMED 2011, pp. 532–535 (2011)

5. Augustynek, M., Penhaker, M., Semkovic, J., Penhakerova, P., Cerny, M: Measurement and diagnosis assessment of plethysmographycal record. In: Proceedings of the 5th Kuala Lumpur International Conference on Biomedical Engineering, BIOMED 2011, pp. 320–323 (2011)

6. Augustynek, M., Penhaker, M.: Finger plethysmography classification by orthogonal transformatios. In: 2010 Second International Conference on Computer Engineering and Applications, ICCEA, pp. 173–177. IEEE (2010)

7. Penhaker, M., Darebnikova, M., Cerny, M.: Sensor network for measurement and analysis on medical devices quality control. In: Yonazi, J.J., Sedoyeka, E., Ariwa, E., El-Qawasmeh, E. (eds.) e-Technologies and Networks for Development. CCIS, vol. 171, pp. 182–196. Springer, Heidelberg (2011). doi:10.1007/978-3-642-22729-5_16

8. Cerny, M., Pokorny, M.: Circadian rhythm evaluation using fuzzy logic. In: Nguyen, N., Trawiński, B., Katarzyniak, R., Jo, G.S. (eds.) Advanced Methods for Computational Collective Intelligence. Studies in Computational Intelligence, vol. 457, pp. 289–298. Springer, Heidelberg (2013). doi:10.1007/978-3-642-34300-1_28

9. Linhares, R.R.: Arrhythmia detection from heart rate variability by SDFA method. Int. J. Cardiol. **224**, 27–32 (2016)

10. Zaylaa, A.J., Saleh, S., Karameh, F.N., Nahas, Z., Bouakaz, A.: Cascade of nonlinear entropy and statistics to discriminate fetal heart rates. In: 2016 Proceedings of the 3rd International Conference on Advances in Computational Tools for Engineering Applications, ACTEA 2016, Article no. 7560130, pp. 152–157 (2016)

11. Pan, Q., Zhou, G., Wang, R., Yu, Y., Li, F., Fang, L., Yan, J., Ning, G.: The degree of heart rate asymmetry is crucial for the validity of the deceleration and acceleration capacity indices of heart rate: a model-based study. Comput. Biol. Med. **76**, 39–49 (2016)

12. Doost, S.N., Ghista, D., Su, B., Zhong, L., Morsi, Y.S. Heart blood flow simulation: a perspective review. BioMed. Eng. Online **15**(1), Article no. 101 (2016)

13. Cheng, H., Cheng, X.-F., Li, Y., Li, W.: A recognition method research based on the heart sound texture map. AIP Adv. **6**(6), Article no. 065003 (2016)

14. Perron, R.R.G., Iskander, M.F.: Dynamic 3D model of human thorax for the assessment of changes in lung fluid content and vital signs. In: 2016 IEEE/ACES International Conference on Wireless Information Technology, ICWITS 2016 and System and Applied Computational Electromagnetics, ACES 2016 - Proceedings, Article no. 7465380 (2016)

15. Arthurs, C.J., Lau, K.D., Asrress, K.N., Redwood, S.R., Alberto Figueroa, C.: A mathematical model of coronary blood flow control: Simulation of patientspecific three-dimensional hemodynamics during exercise. Am. J. Physiol. Heart Circ. Physiol. **310**(9), H1242–H1258 (2016)

16. Raphan, T., Cohen, B., Xiang, Y., Yakushin, S.B.: A model of blood pressure, heart rate, and vaso-vagal responses produced by vestibulo-sympathetic activation. Front. Neurosci. **10**, Article no. 96, March 2016

17. Khan, M.S.A., Yousuf, S.: A cardiac electrical activity model based on a cellular automata system in comparison with neural network model. Pak. J. Pharm. Sci. **29**(2), 579–584 (2016)

Author Index

Printed in the United States
By Bookmasters